MW01617954

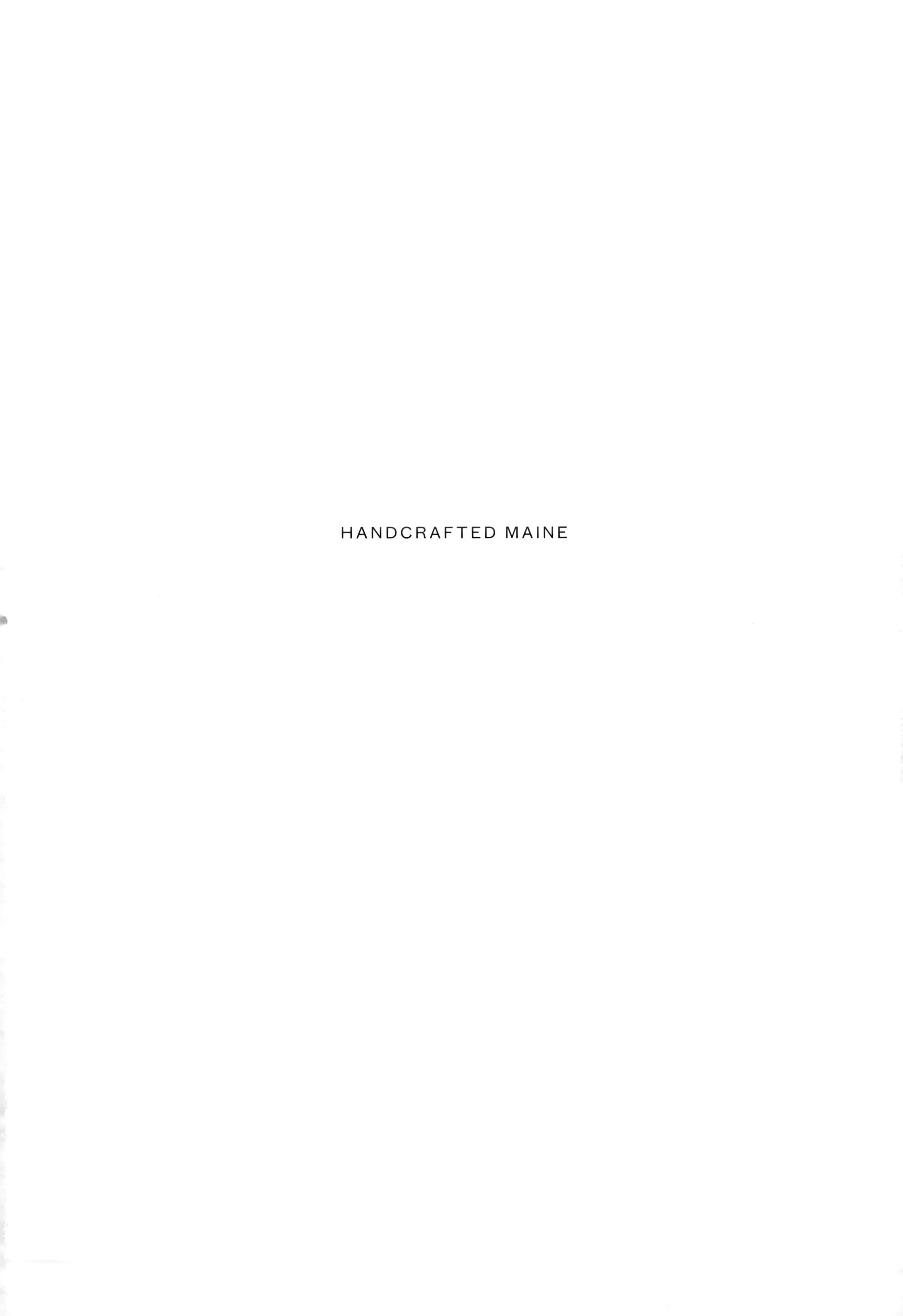

HANDCRAFTED MAINE

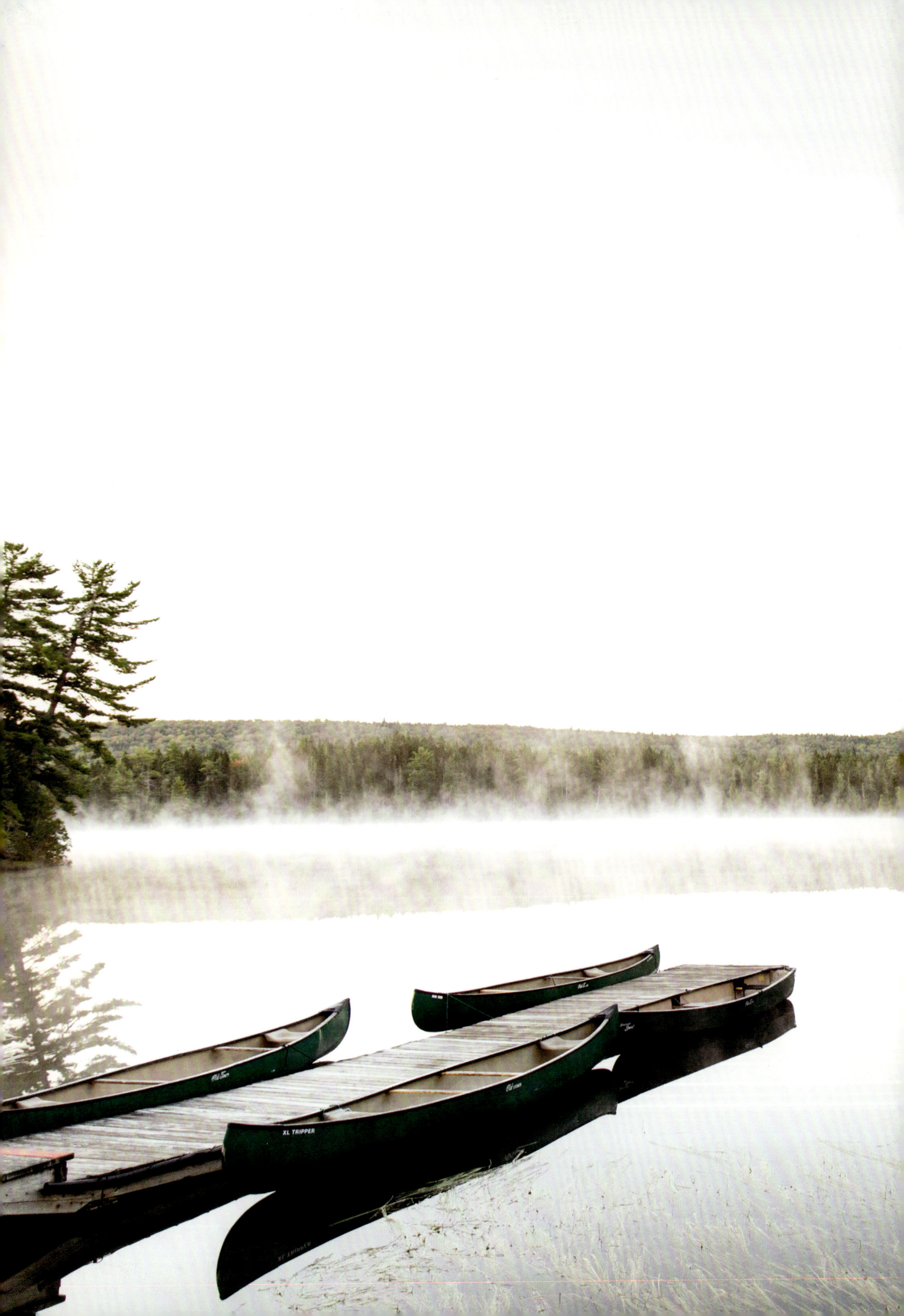
XL TRIPPER

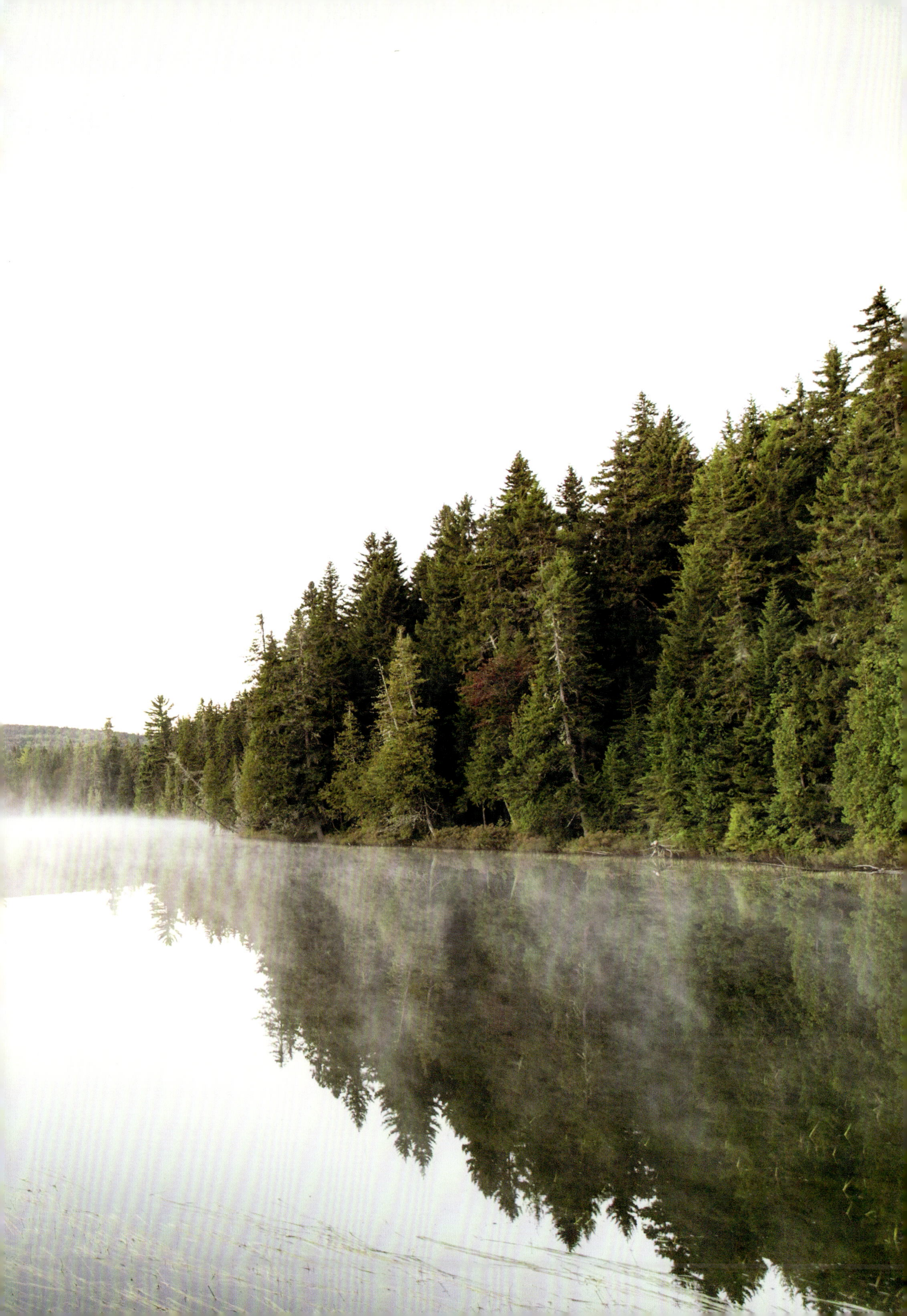

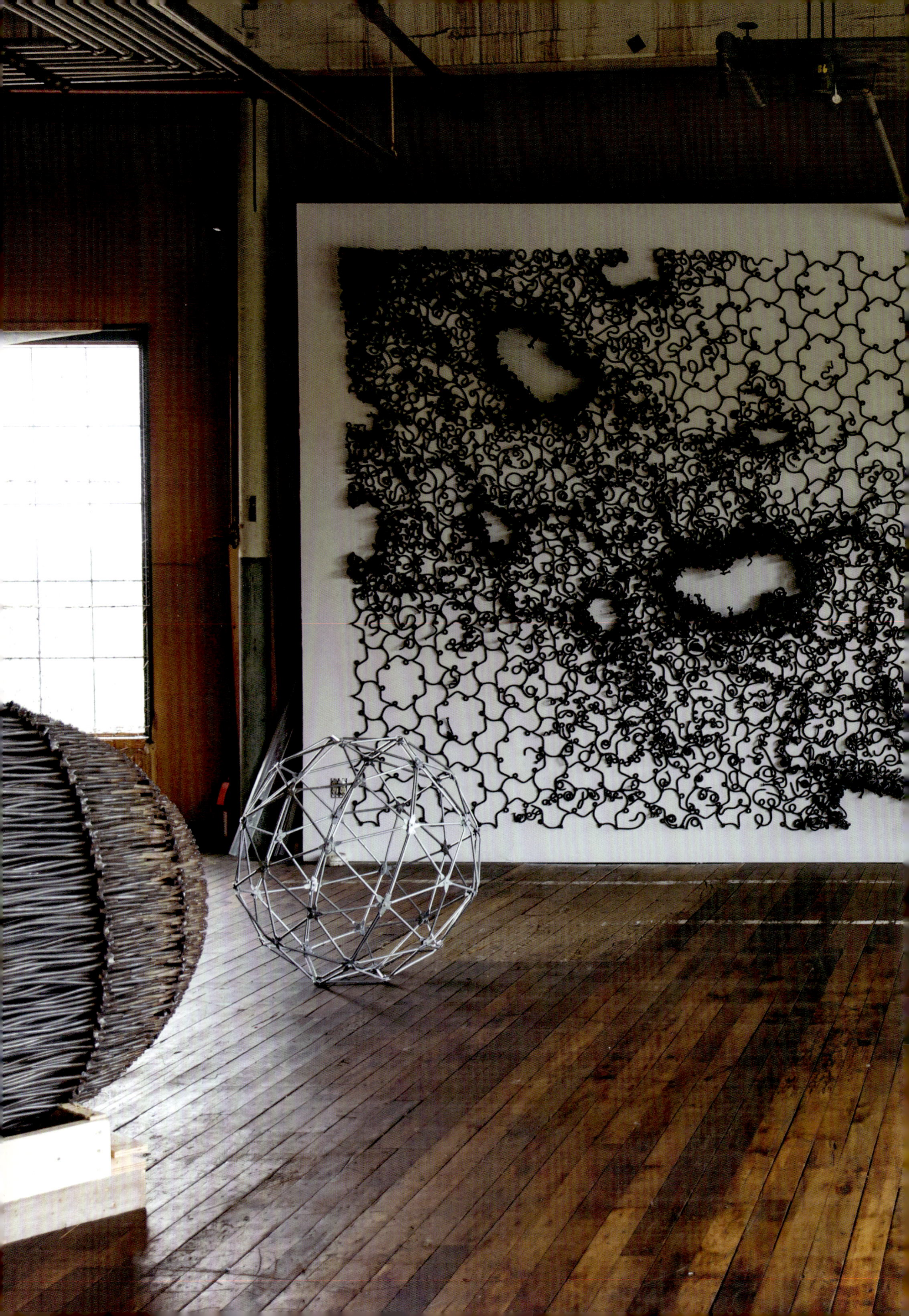

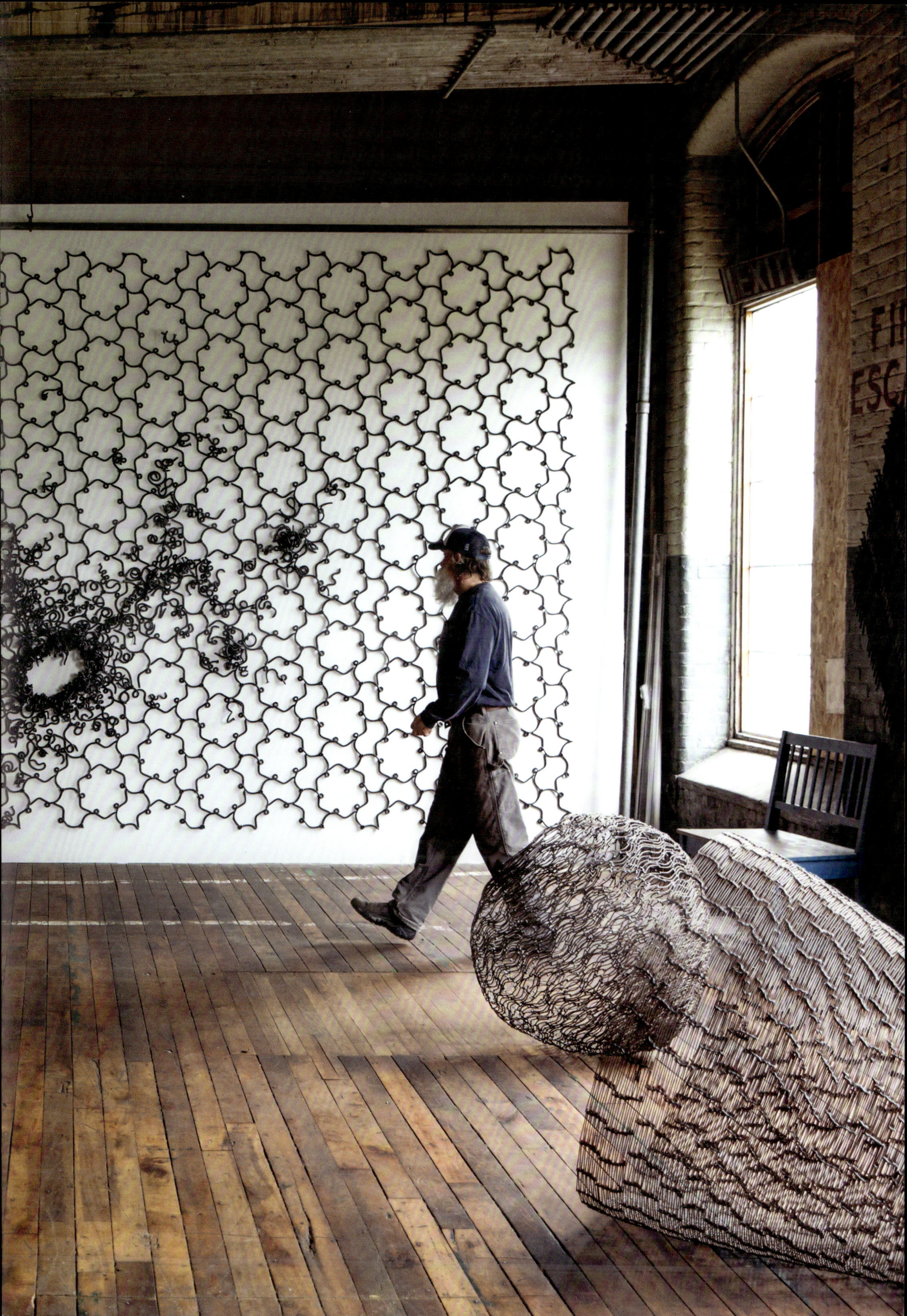

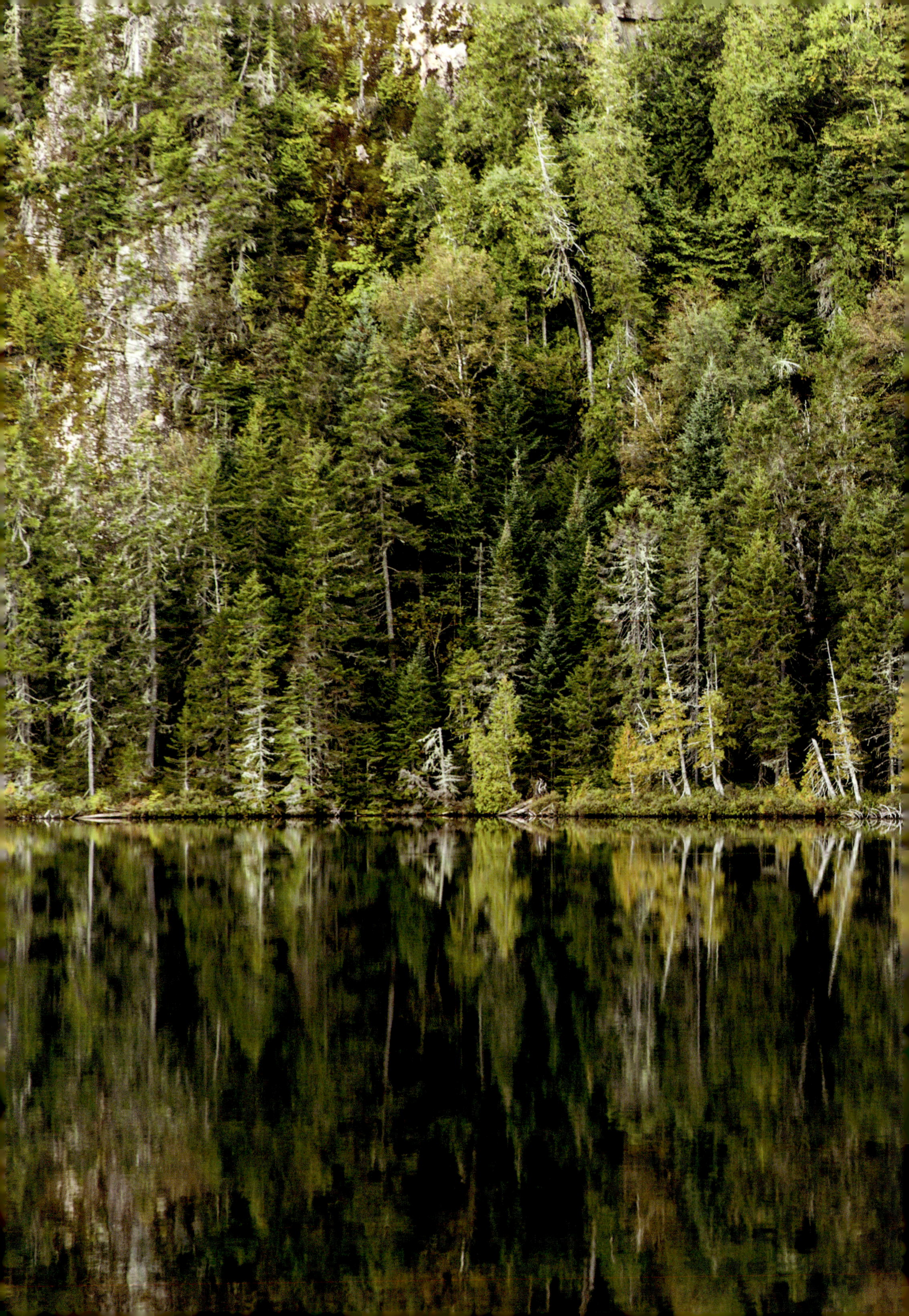

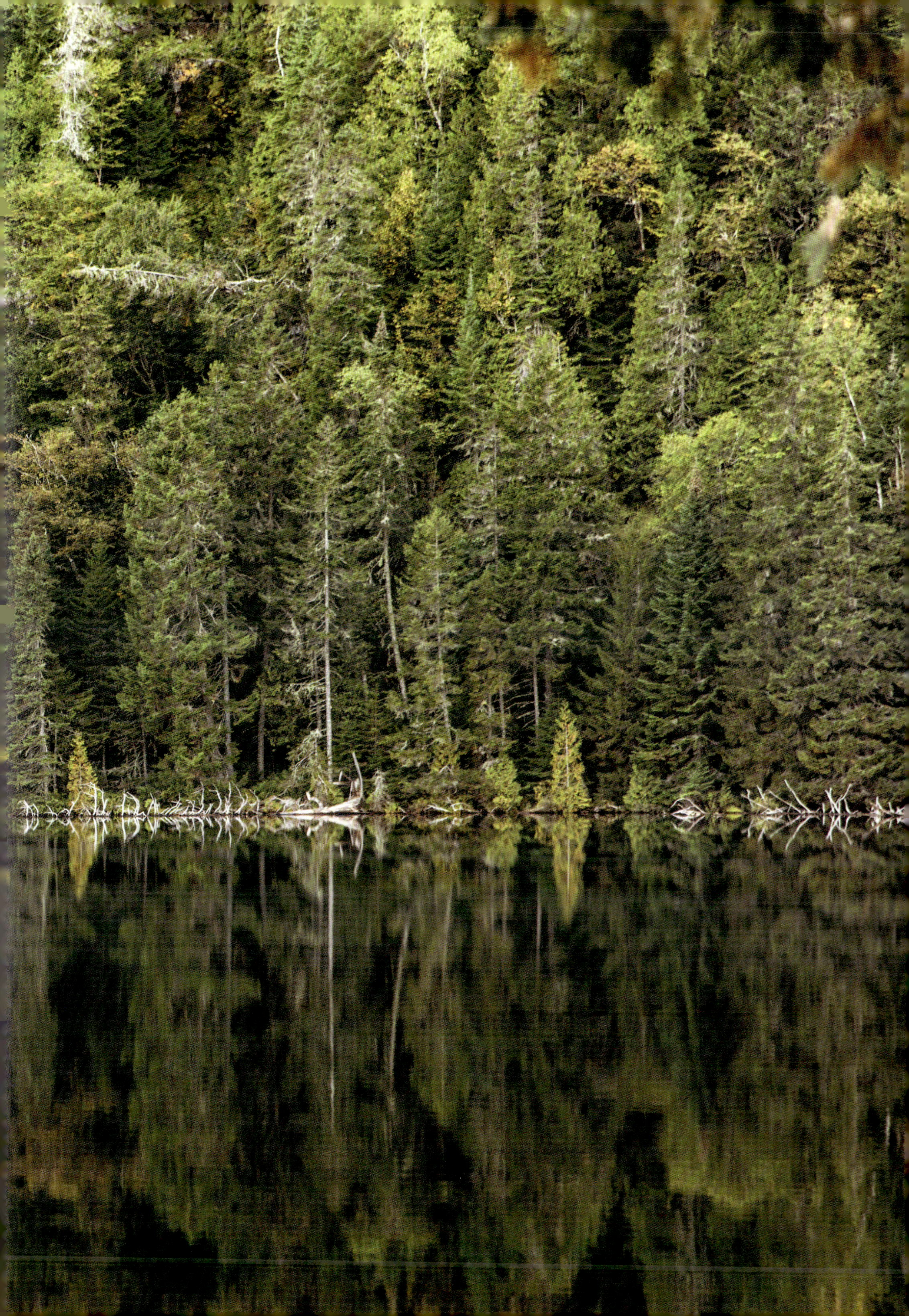

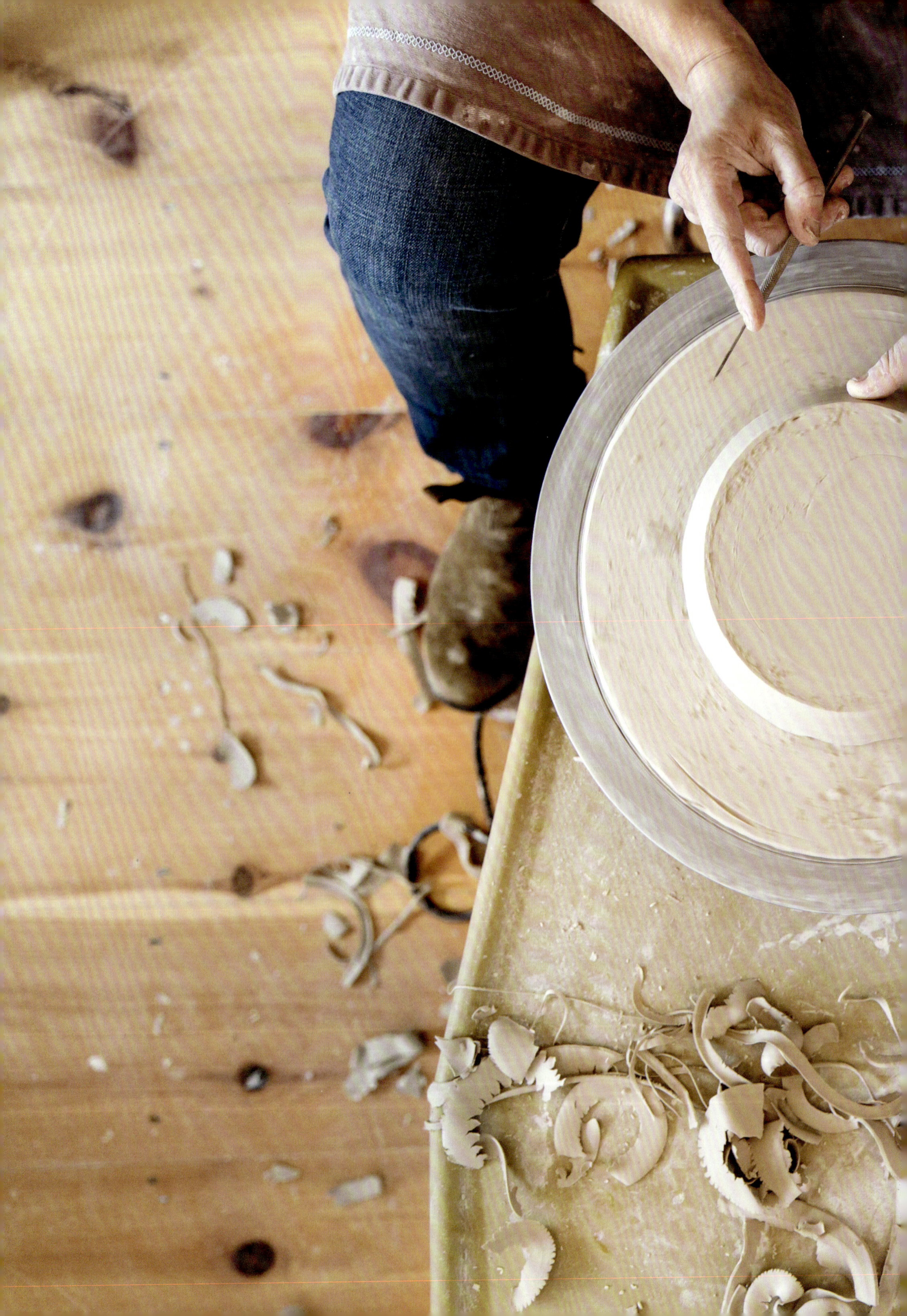

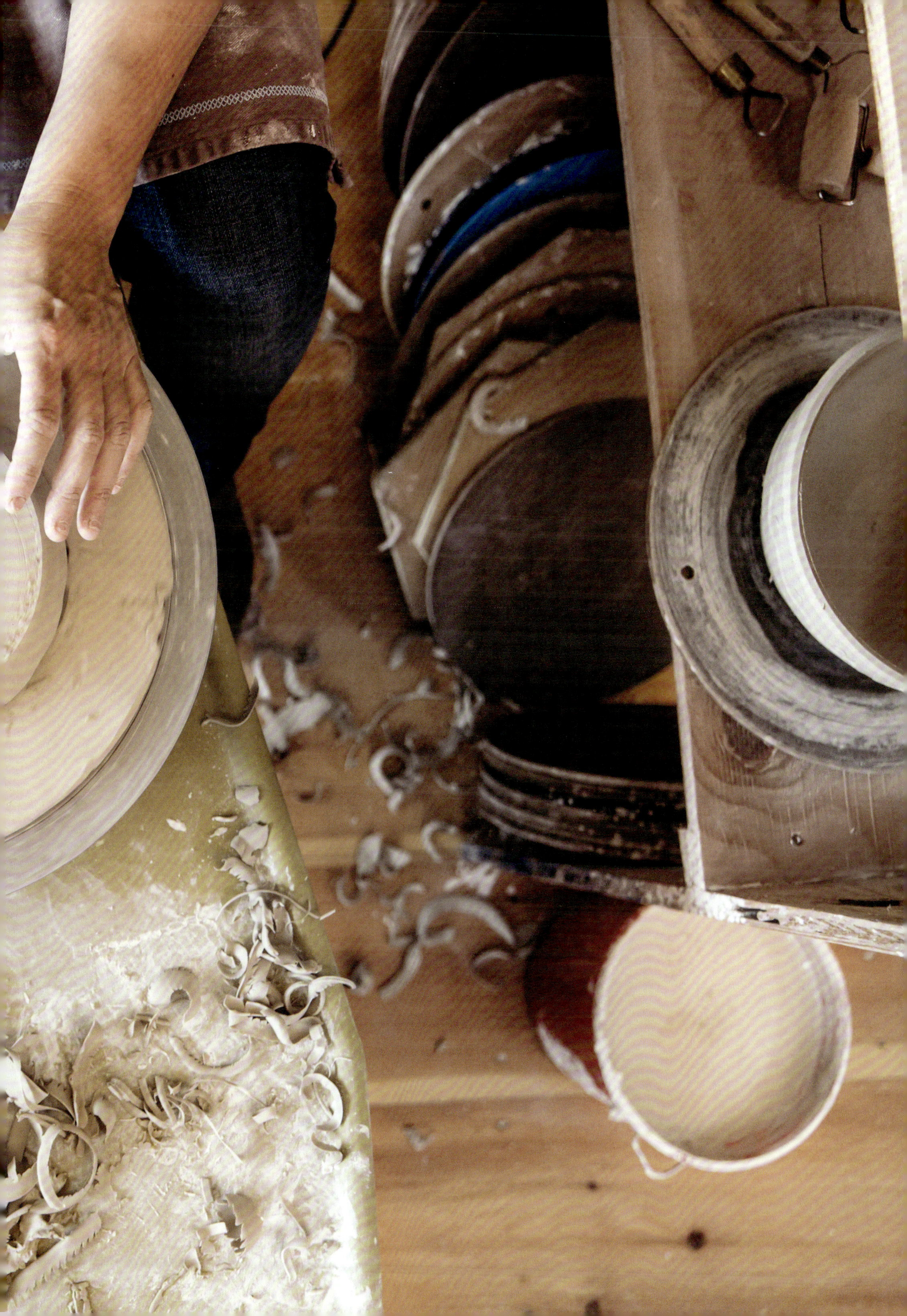

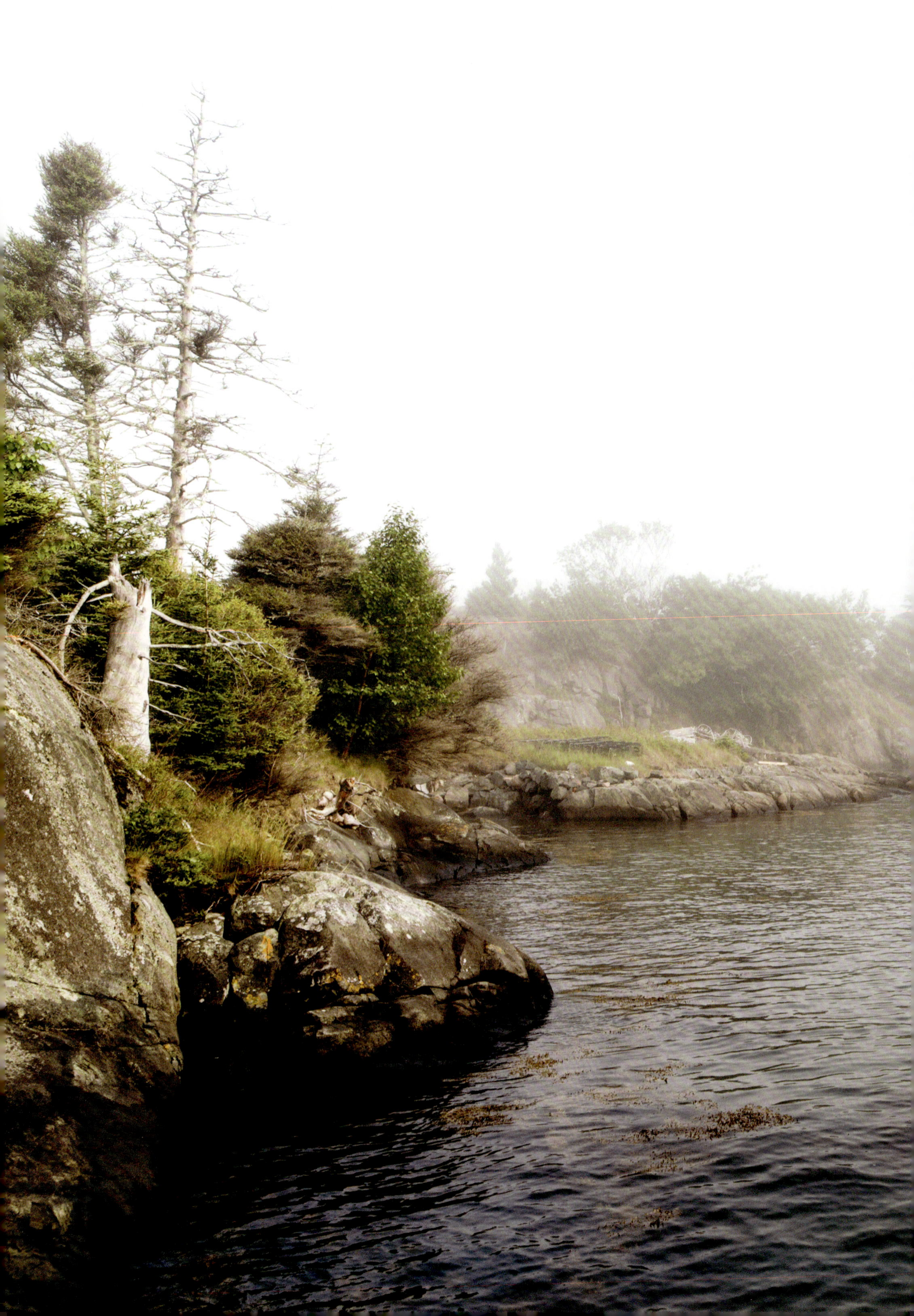

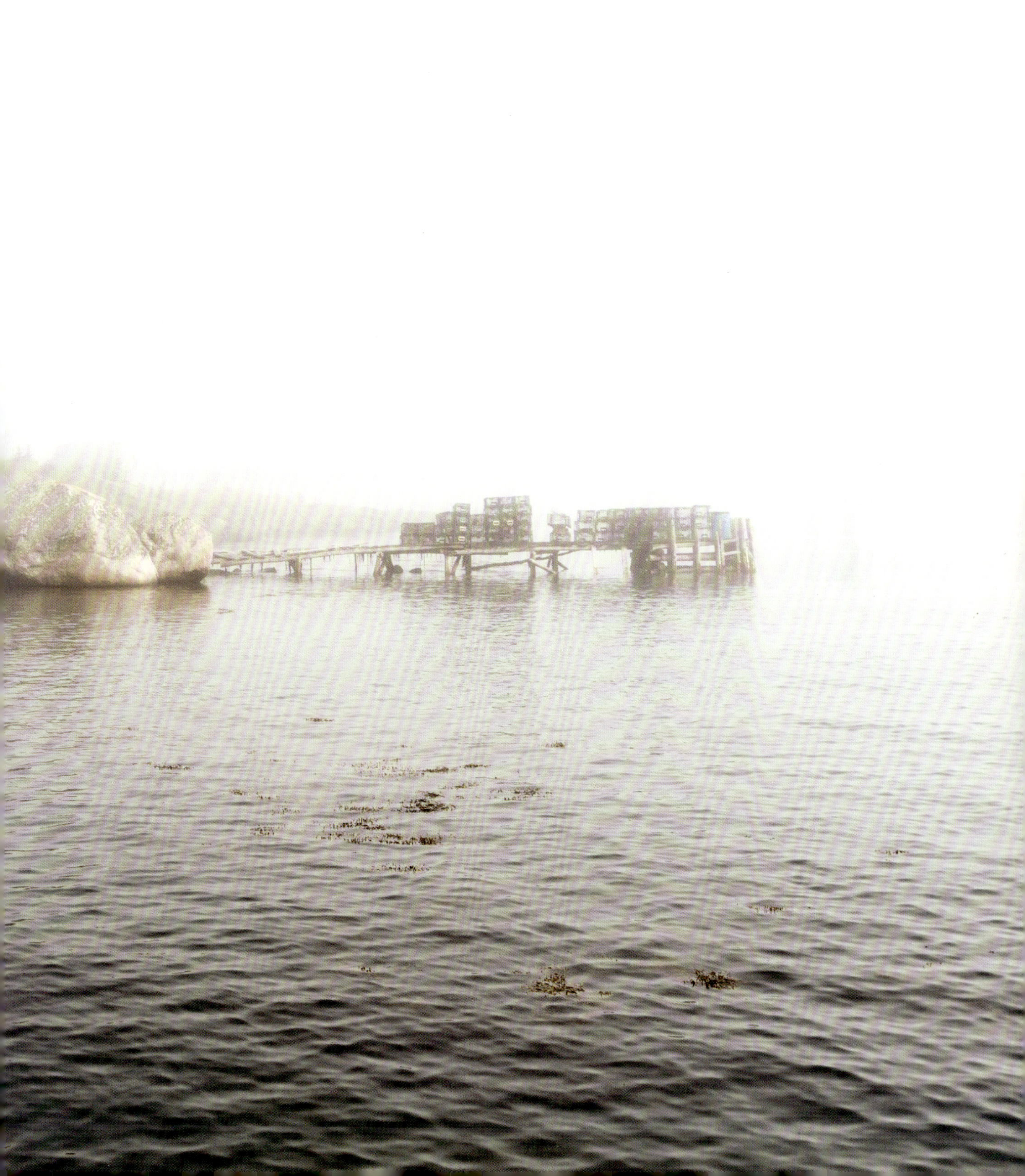

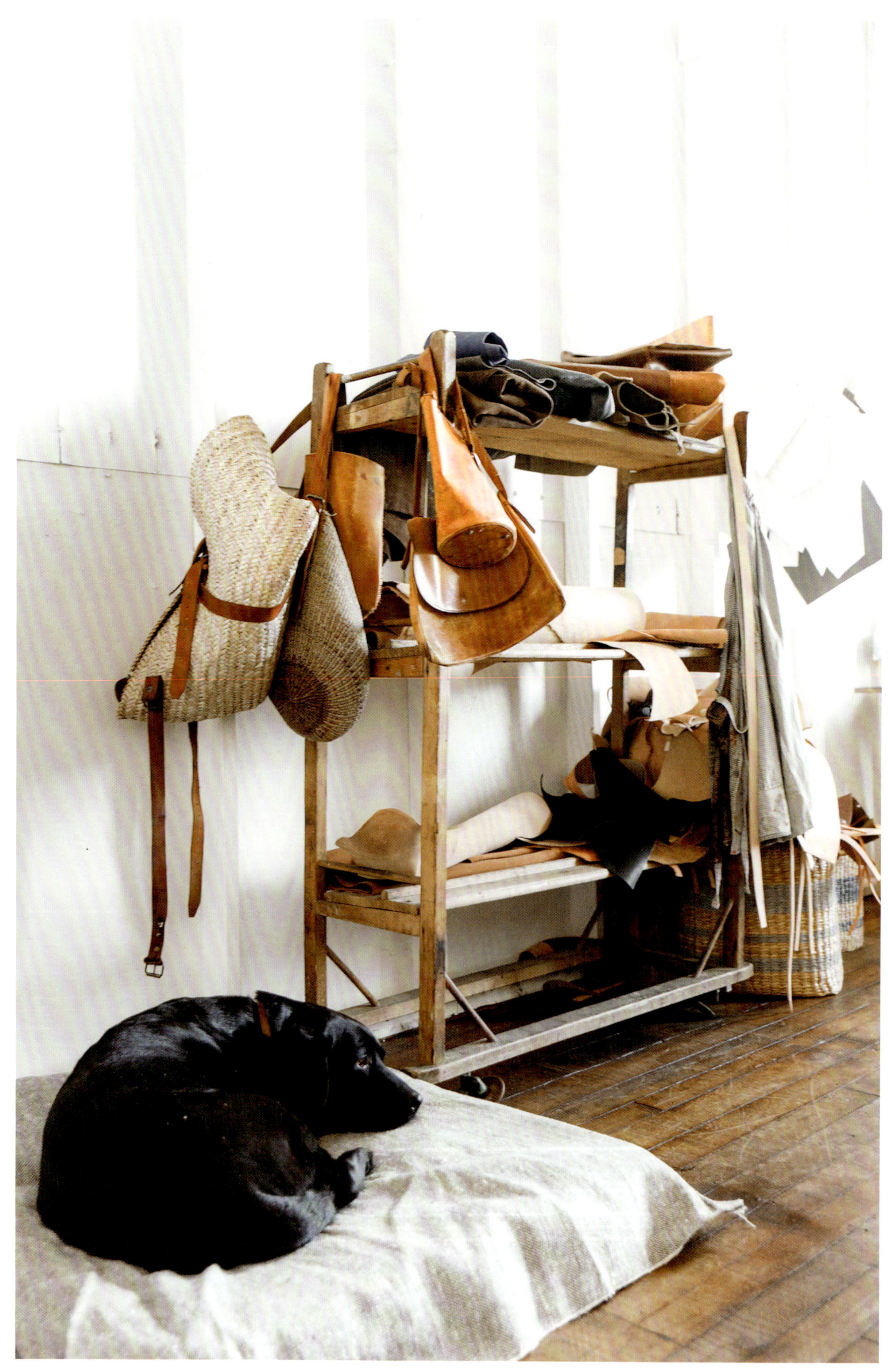

HANDCRAFTED
MAINE

Art, Life, Harvest & Home

TEXT BY

Katy Kelleher

PHOTOGRAPHS BY

Greta Rybus

PRINCETON ARCHITECTURAL PRESS · NEW YORK

Published by
Princeton Architectural Press
A McEvoy Group company
37 East Seventh Street, New York, NY 10003
202 Warren Street, Hudson, NY 12534
Visit our website at www.papress.com

Printed in China by C&C Offset Printing
20 19 18 17 4 3 2 1 First edition

Editors: Jan Cigliano Hartman, Jenny Florence
Designer: Paul Wagner

Special thanks to: Janet Behning, Nolan Boomer, Nicola Brower, Abby Bussel, Tom Cho, Barbara Darko, Benjamin English, Susan Hershberg, Lia Hunt, Mia Johnson, Valerie Kamen, Simone Kaplan-Senchak, Jennifer Lippert, Kristy Maier, Sara McKay, Eliana Miller, Wes Seeley, Rob Shaeffer, Sara Stemen, and Joseph Weston of Princeton Architectural Press
—Kevin C. Lippert, publisher

Library of Congress
Cataloging-in-Publication Data
Kelleher, Katy, author. | Rybus, Greta, photographer
Handcrafted Maine: Art, Life, Harvest, and Home
ISBN 978-1-61689-567-9
1. Occupations—Maine. 2. Artisans—Maine.
LCC GT5790 .K45 2017 | DDC 390/.2409741—dc23

THIS BOOK IS MADE POSSIBLE THROUGH
THE GENEROUS SUPPORT OF

The Robert P. & Arlene R. Kogod Family Foundation

TABLE OF CONTENTS

BUILDING & LIVING

FOOD & HARVEST

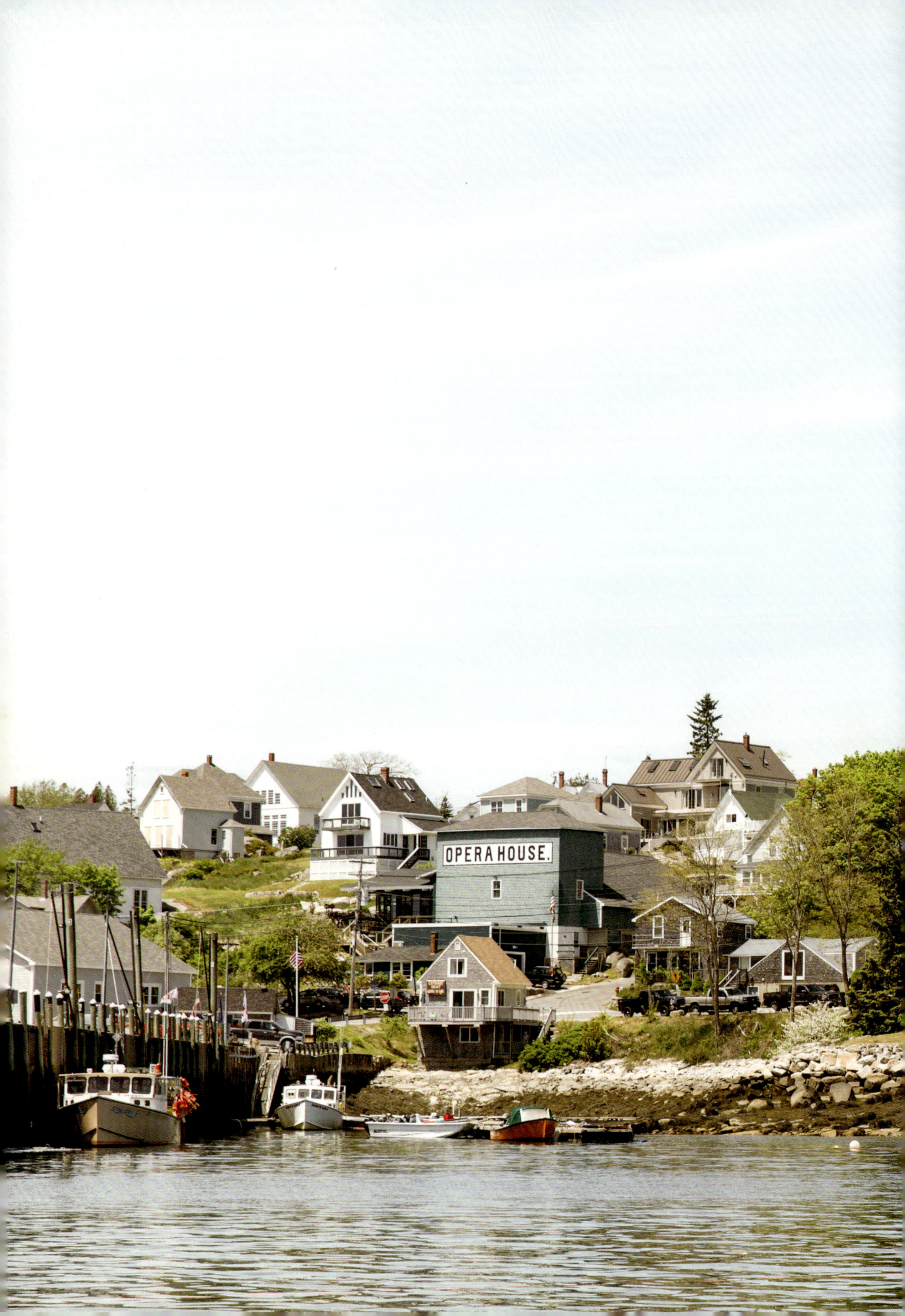
OPERA HOUSE.

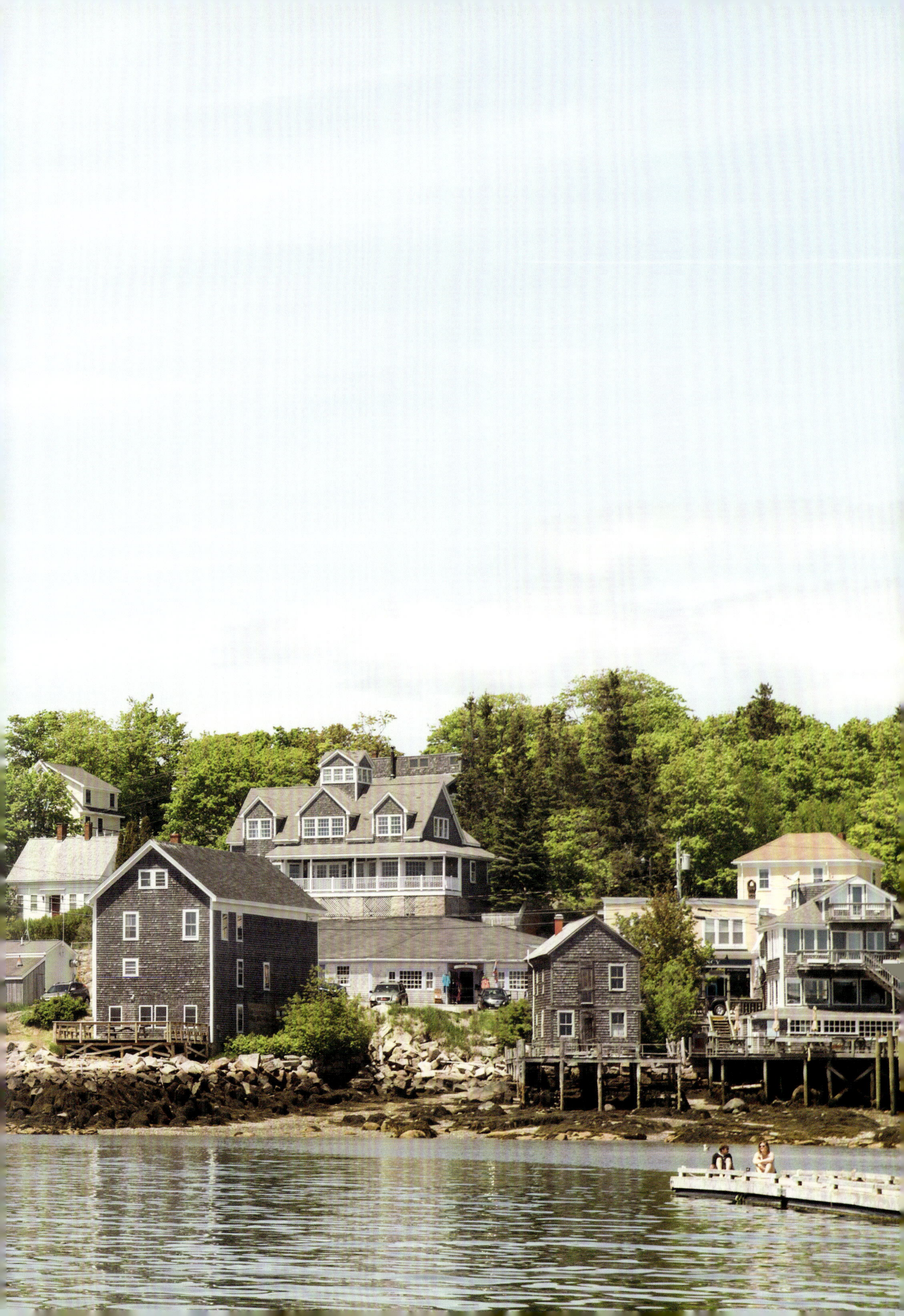

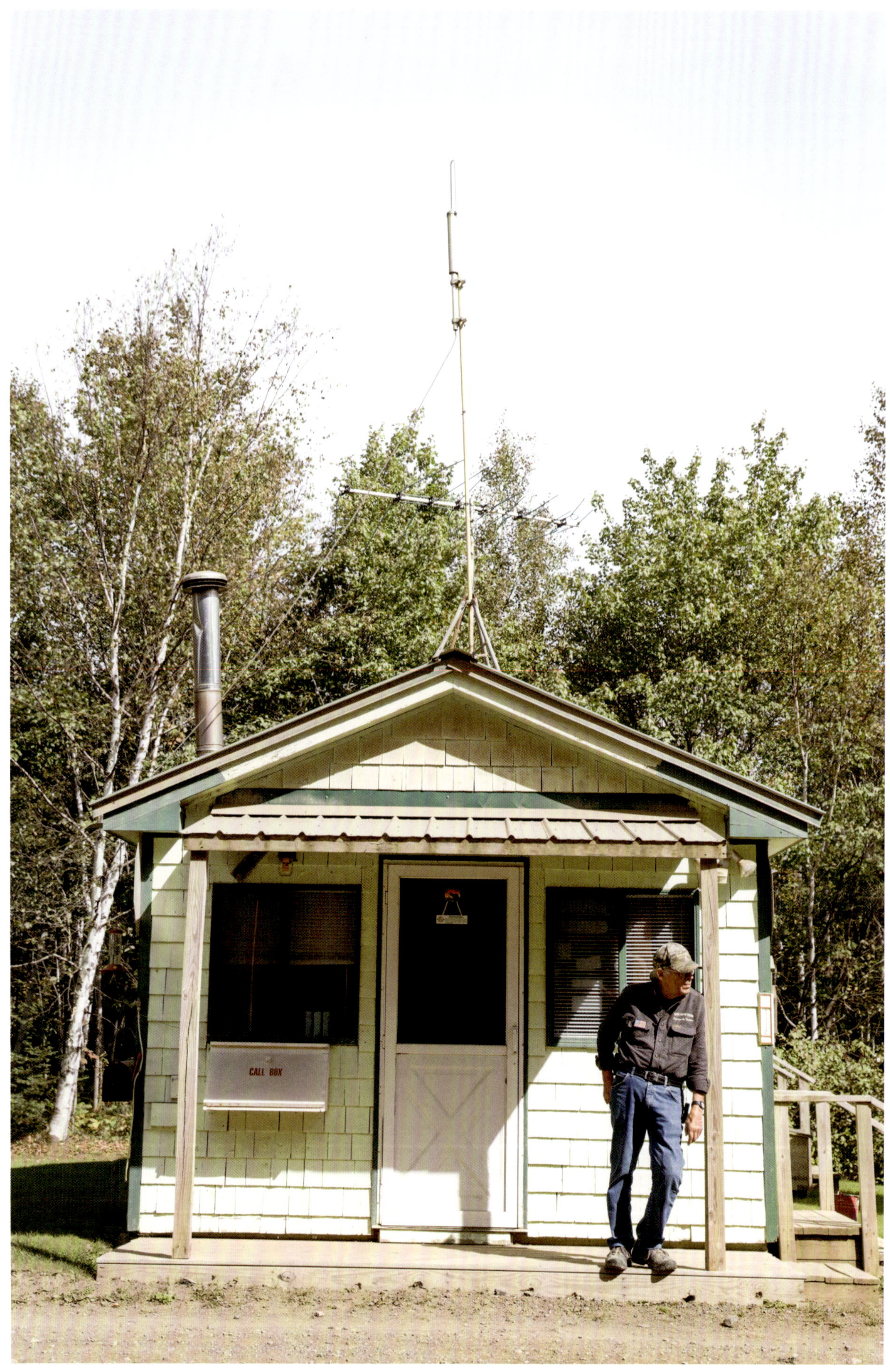
CALL BOX

Living the Handcrafted Life in Maine

When I moved to Portland, I noticed two hallmarks of local style. First, there were the Bean boots. Everyone, from doctors on their way to work at Maine Medical Center to teenage art students smoking in front of Space Gallery, wore a pair of L.L.Bean duck boots throughout the winter. The second thing I noticed were the Maine-shaped tattoos on the biceps and torsos of colleagues and acquaintances.

As soon as I tried on a pair of L.L.Bean boots, I understood the first phenomenon. Winter in Maine is terrible and they make it tolerable. The second trend was harder for me to puzzle out, but after a year of living in and traveling throughout Maine, I began to understand. People here are proud of their state—so proud that they're willing to get its outline permanently inked on their skin. Maine means something to people. This is true even for those who didn't grow up here, even for recent transplants like me. Maine signifies survival, hard work, and authenticity. Living in Maine means you're willing to suffer through harsh winters. It means you can make sacrifices. And—all too often—it means you're ready to deal with economic uncertainty, particularly if you're a member of the creative community. This can be said for artists and makers throughout the country, but it is particularly true in Maine: in order to make it as a creative, you must be willing to live with very little.

I know this because I am a member of Maine's creative community. At twenty-five I moved to Portland to take a job at a local magazine, but I stayed long after I had left that position to work as a freelancer. I stayed because, despite the hardships that come hand-in-hand with living in Maine, I was bowled over by the strength, passion, and ambition of its creatives. Not all young Mainers would make the same decision. Brain drain and youth exodus are very real issues for communities. Many college-bound Mainers leave the state and never return. Those who come from other states to study in Maine graduate and leave, reappearing only for reunions or vacations. In 2016, Maine had the oldest average population of any state in America. The previous year, it was ranked forty-eighth on *Forbes*'s annual list of "Best States For Business."

All this is beginning to change (Maine used to be forty-ninth on the *Forbes* list!) as more young creatives find in Maine an environment that nurtures their passions and feeds their ambitions. To understand the makers of Maine, you also have to understand the climate in which they operate. I read once that geniuses are made where hardship and oppression meet education and innovation. I think that Maine is such a place.

Maine is bordered by just one other state—New Hampshire. To leave Maine by car, you must drive through either New Hampshire or Canada. It's isolated geographically and the highway system is inconvenient unless your route takes you directly from north to south. (Proposals for an east-west highway have been introduced throughout the years, but at this time, it remains a fiction.) There's an old Maine saying—"You can't get there from here"—and while it's often used facetiously, there is some truth to the statement. Often, you can't get where you're going without journeying miles out of your way, chartering a boat, or maneuvering down dirt roads. This geographic isolation has bred a culture that can feel insular and uninviting. New Yorkers say that unless you were born in one of the five boroughs, you'll never be a true New Yorker. Mainers have a similar criterion, except ours (or I should say theirs) is more stringent. A fisherman once told me, "Unless you've been here for seven generations, you're not a real Mainer." We were sitting at a bar in Lubec. It was early spring, before tourist season had begun, and the room was empty save for me, him, and the bartender. He was friendly (as many Mainers are) but guarded in a sarcastic, teasing way (as many Mainers are). At first I thought he was pulling my leg—but then I asked around. The number of generations changed from response to response (some said three, some seven, some nine) but the sentiment remained: unless your forebears were born here, you are not a Mainer.

So why write a book glorifying a state that won't count me as one of its own? The answer is simple. I love Maine. I love the strangeness of its blood red late-summer sunsets, the muted calm of its winters, and the starkness of its granite mountains. I love the hardness of life here, the grit that it has already instilled in me. Like many of the makers profiled in this book, I have adopted Maine as my own. Also like many of these makers, I've had to earn my stripes.

In truth, I'm still earning them.

* * *

When I called up lobsterman John Williams and asked him to be in this book, one of the first things he said to me was, "I'm not sure how I'd fit in." "You practice a craft," I replied. "We want people who have skills rooted in tradition." We both agreed that lobstering is a craft, a trade that has been practiced in Maine for hundreds of years. But then he said, "I don't know if I'm really that creative."

He wasn't the only one who expressed this concern.

Every time I had the same reply: Creativity isn't just about painting or building or writing. For me, creativity is forging new pathways. It's coming at a problem from a new direction. It's building bridges where you see chasms.

A creative is someone who conceives of a new solution.

A maker is someone who turns that solution into a physical reality.

Creative people—people like John Williams and Tim Adams and Jeremy Frey—are continually encountering problems: John figures out where to set his lobster traps each season for the best haul. Tim blends wild-fermented aged beer to create one-of-a-kind beverages. Jeremy takes traditional forms of basket weaving and creates museum worthy art. Every person in this book practices creative thinking on a daily basis, whether they're baking bread or painting birds.

* * *

In the three years I spent researching and writing this book, I became aware of themes running through the lives of my subjects. While each maker possesses their own singular vision, many of them have faced similar hardships and experienced similar joys. I began to think of these ideas as the warp threads that hold the book together. There are many smaller commonalities among the makers, but there are five central themes that arise again and again: the influence of the natural world on the creation of a product, the importance of grit and sacrifice, the impact of a supportive creative community, the physical nature of this type of work and, finally, Maine's rich traditions. Each maker herein adds their own color to the tapestry, but these ideas are woven throughout.

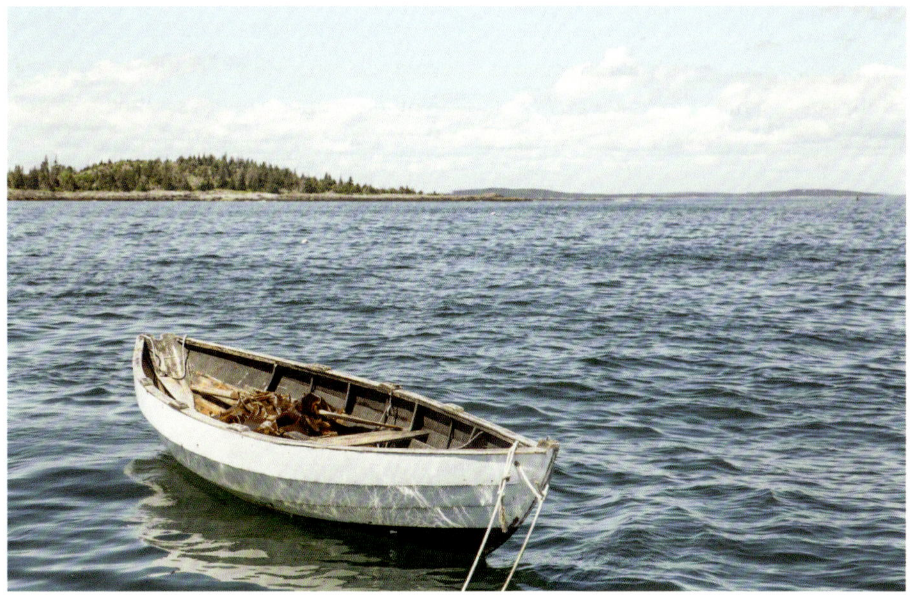

Respecting the Natural Landscape

For thousands of years, people have made their homes on the land we now call Maine. For over a century, people have been making the pilgrimage to "Vacationland" to see this wild place. Maine has rolling fields and verdant farmland. It has jagged mountains with razor-sharp peaks. It has hardwood forests and tiny islands covered in tall grasses. It is beautiful in a way that can feel foreboding. It is beautiful in a way that can feel restorative.

Every maker featured in this book has a direct connection to the place in which they live. Weaver Sara Hotchkiss has her wild garden with its many-hued blooms. She weaves the colors of the Atlantic into her rugs, as well as the bright red of poppies and the soft tones of lavender. Ayumi Horie takes clay from her property and mixes it into bricks, which she stamps with phrases and sets in the streets of Portland. Architect Will Winkelman designs buildings that speak with the landscape—homes with expansive windows and turf roofs, homes that disappear behind the tree line as you paddle by on the glassy waters of Sebago Lake.

Many of these creatives also make their living directly from the landscape, from Maine's natural resources. Micah Woodcock harvests seaweed, John Williams catches lobster, and Jeremy Frey weaves his baskets from ash and sweetgrass. Ray Murphy cuts trees from his lot to turn them into distinctive pieces of chainsaw art. And on a small Freeport farm, Masa Miyake raises pigs, which end up on small plates in his chic downtown Portland restaurant. These makers are all taking something from Maine, but they give back, too. They harvest responsibly. They design solar-efficient homes. They paint pictures depicting the glory of Maine's winters and the sublime starkness of its coastline. They make Maine better by their presence, and Maine makes their work better, too.

Resilience, Grit, and Perseverance

According to the Pew Research Center, in 2015 the richest 20 percent of American families owned 88.9 percent of the country's wealth. The income gap is larger than it has been since the Great Depression and the economic reality of living in America is grim. Choosing to make your living as an artist has always come with risks, but as more Americans have become aware of income disparity, it can seem amazing that anyone would decide to forgo a salaried position. Yet many people do. They sacrifice economic security in exchange for a different lifestyle. John Williams chose to take on significant debt in order to buy a lobster boat, hoping that his gamble would pay off (it did). When I interviewed Polly and Kevin of Mahoosuc Guide Service, which runs dogsledding trips, they were in the midst of a terrible Maine winter—one with no snow. But would they consider giving up guiding? "Not on your life," Kevin said. Tess and Anna at Beech

Hill Farm decided to pursue farm work, knowing full well that they could earn more elsewhere, doing something else.

It's not just money that people sacrifice. Several creatives confessed that they'd once wanted children, but gave up that dream to focus on their art. Others gave up time with their families to grow their businesses. Several makers recalled losing friendships, letting important relationships fall by the wayside because there were just never enough hours in the day.

Of course, everyone sacrifices something. And usually you gain something in return. Freedom, for instance. Integrity. Personal satisfaction. Critical acclaim. Artistic pride.

Community and Connection

Every time I visited sculptor John Bisbee's studio, there was someone new hanging around. Sometimes it was a fellow artist, like Emilie Stark-Menneg, a painter who creates brilliant pop art–infused portraits. Sometimes it was a student, a young man or woman ready to learn arc welding from a master. As Bisbee and I talked, people would drop by—I met a woodworker and a soda-maker, a college freshman, and a writer.

In Brunswick, Bisbee has built a creative community in his small welding shop, located at Fort Andross, a sprawling brick building filled with spaces to rent. In Brooksville, Tim Slater and Lydia Moffett have created a social hub for residents of the rural community in their farmhouse bakery. And in York, Mike Lavecchia and Brad Anderson have forged a connection between surfers and woodworkers, teaching wave-riders how to build wooden boards, and carpenters how to catch a wave.

In a place like Maine, where towns are spread across the map, community is incredibly important. Ideas aren't formed in a vacuum; collaboration is necessary for truly innovative work. Maine makers are willing to pool their knowledge, even with what others may view as their direct competition. Tim Adams of Oxbow Brewery has made beers in collaboration with the brewers at Shipyard, Lone Pine, Bunker, and Liquid Riot, and Micah Woodcock continues to turn to fellow seaweed harvester Larch Hanson for advice. I've observed that few makers seem afraid of competition. In fact, they relish it, seeing potential collaborators rather than immediate threats.

Perhaps Masa Miyake—another outsider in Maine—put it best: "Competition is always good. It makes you try new things. Where there is no competition, there is no growth."

Living with the Whole Body

When cheesemaker Rachel Bell was first starting her business, she spent hours leaning into the flank of a goat with a baby strapped to her back. She pulled rhythmically at the animal's teats, squirting milk into a pail, her own breasts heavy with the same substance she coaxed from the gentle Nubian. This ritual became a part of her daily life. Physicality plays a central role for nearly every maker represented within this book. These are people who craft pots with their hands, reach with their arms into the sea to harvest kelp, and run after pigs until their legs are sore and covered with muck. They are sunburnt in the summer and wind-chapped in the winter. They go to bed aching all over. They sleep the dreamless sleep of the truly exhausted. But they keep doing it. Unlike many Americans, for whom physical labor is a necessity thrust upon them by a dearth of opportunity, these people have chosen to pursue highly physical lifestyles. I do not wish to glorify physical labor, which can be grueling and dangerous—which can, quite literally, break you—but I do believe something happens when you invest your entire body in your work. In the words of Micah Woodcock, "You've got to have skin in the game."

Just as the locavore movement focuses on consuming based on proximity, the slow movement centers around the idea that we should respect the hours of attention and effort that go into each object we purchase, whether we're looking to buy a hand-stitched wallet or a loaf of bread. By taking into account the physical nature of work—and yes, by occasionally glorifying this work—we can better gauge the object's value. People—all people, not just makers or owners of small businesses—should be paid fairly for their labor. Perhaps the first step toward a more equitable system of compensation is recognizing the skin so many people have in this game.

For me, and for many creative people, sustained and spontaneous physical motion is necessary.

It staves off mental stagnation and unstops the blockages that make us want to tune out in front of the TV. Living with your whole body, from soil-covered, pine sap–sticky toes to snow-dusted, wind-tangled hair, is necessary for these modern makers. The things that feed the body also feed the soul.

Tradition and History

While this book celebrates contemporary makers and growers, none of this would be possible without Maine's rich cultural traditions. Every farmer I spoke with had learned their trade from another farmer, some as college students (such as Tess Faller at Beech Hill Farm), others in less formal settings, such as Rachel Bell, who simply walked down the street and asked her neighbors how they were handling their soil.

Maine's heritage extends far beyond farming and lobstering. In the mid-1800s, painters began sailing to Monhegan Island to work en plein air, a practice that continues to this day. People of the Penobscot Nation have been weaving baskets from sweetgrass for centuries, first for themselves, and later for nineteenth-century visitors to Bar Harbor. In 1857, Henry David Thoreau hired a Penobscot guide named Joe Polis to lead an expedition down the Allagash River, a journey that Thoreau immortalized in the classic naturalist book *The Maine Woods*. Mainers have been dogsledding, weaving blankets, building houses, and collecting seaweed far longer than I've been here. Far longer than any of us have been here.

If genius arises from hardship and education, then Maine's unique brand of creativity comes from its rough geography, its economic frailty, and its vibrant history. Many of the people in this book are self-educated. Some went to college. Others studied books. Still others learned from their elders. While they each brought something new to the table, none of them did it alone. They are part of a long tradition of makers, builders, farmers, and thinkers. They are part of Maine's great story.

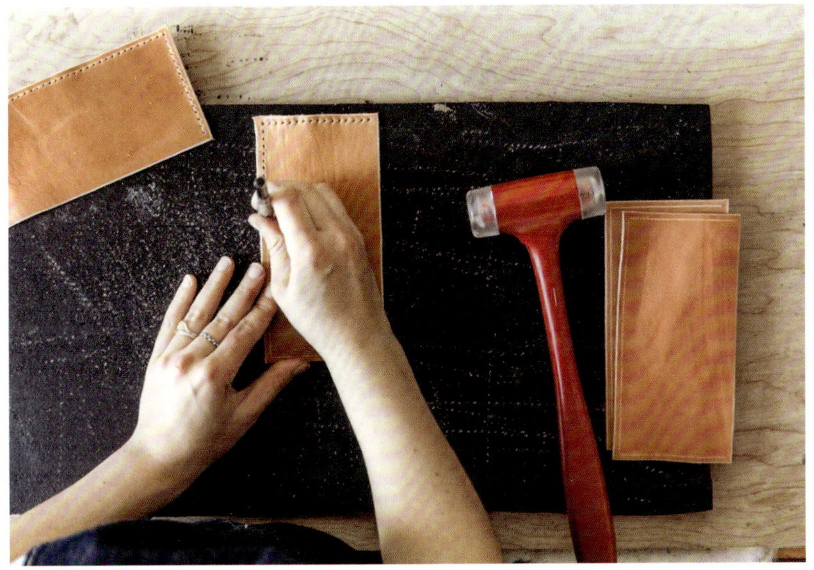

ART
&
CRAFT

Dozier Bell

Waldoboro

The light in Dozier Bell's studio has a slight blue tint to it. Even on a cold, overcast day, it pours in from several directions, indirect and refracted. Canvases line the walls and a table holds buckets of paint-brushes and a squirrel's foot fern. Two stools sit nearby, but other than these few furnishings, the room is bare. With the gray floors, white walls, and blue-tinged light, Bell could almost be inside one of her own paintings. She's even dressed the part in a soft palette of linens, blues and grays, and mauve-browns.

This palette, like much of Bell's inspiration, comes from Maine. Bell grew up in Bath, a small city dominated by a massive iron shipbuilding port, but she spent much of her time in the wilds of western Maine. "I've lived in many different places, but I always felt the need to return to Maine," she says with deliberation. After graduating from Smith College in Western Massachusetts, Bell received her master of fine arts degree from the University of Pennsylvania, which provided her with funding to attend the Skowhegan School of Painting and Sculpture after her first year of studies. She has received grants and scholarships to study in Germany and Italy and her paintings have hung in galleries and museums across North America and Europe. But while these places may have shaped her life, they haven't altered her work nearly as dramatically as might be expected. "The scenes and objects I paint are derived almost entirely from the first years of my life," Bell explains. "I think the first things you become conscious of have a real impact on how you see the world." The Maine winters and springs, seasons of browns and grays, have shaped her aesthetic tastes and, importantly, the way she understands herself.

Maine's remoteness plays a large role in her work. Her paintings have a softness to them, yet they are also stark, devoid of figures, populated mainly by birds. "There is something about the isolation of Maine, the ability to get away from people and the physical constructs of civilization, that allows me to tap into the environment and the landscape," she says. "Maine isn't like it was when I was a kid, but you can still access those quiet and untouched places." Bell frequently ventures outside her studio for inspiration. Sometimes she only goes as far as her own backyard, where she can observe her hive of honeybees and look above to the slow-moving

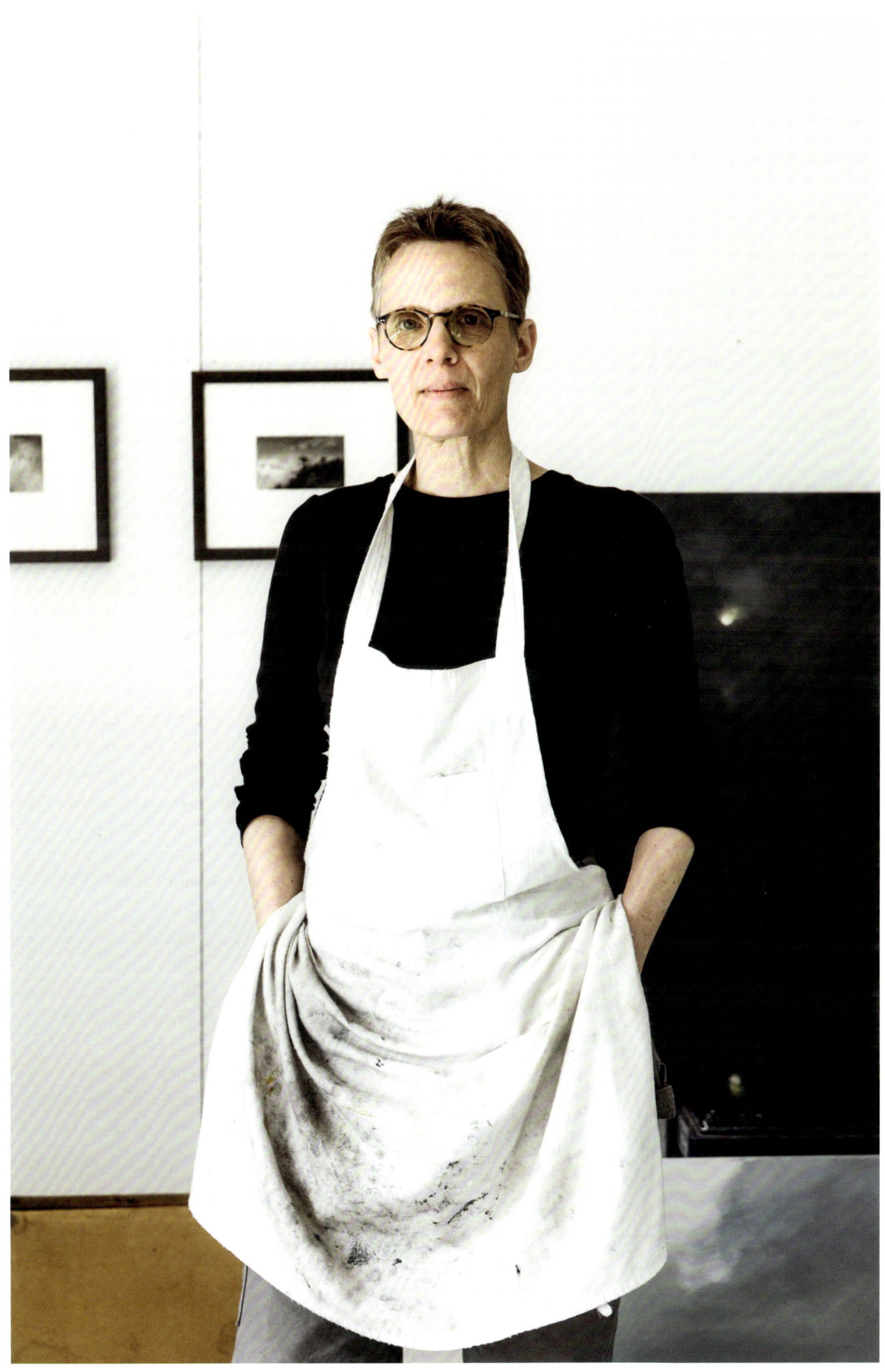

clouds and the patterns formed by migrating birds. Often she can be found walking along empty stretches of beach or hiking wooded trails to find the temporary waterfalls of spring's thaw. Although she lives with her husband, Ken Greenleaf, it's essential to Bell's creative process to spend time alone, which Greenleaf understands, being an artist himself.

While other artists paint directly from the landscape, Bell reproduces it from memory, drawing heavily on what she terms the "animal consciousness" or "environmental consciousness." By this she means a sense of place. Others might call this mindfulness and, indeed, some of her descriptions summon similar new age language ("It's the thing that fixes you in the universe and makes you aware," she says), but her paintings do more than document a moment. She filters her work through her deepest self. "My paintings are meant to communicate something to me, and fortunately for me, they also communicate to other people," she says. "I don't do things with someone else in mind." After some pressing, she admits, "But if I did, I would want the viewer to feel as though they had seen these seascapes before—somewhere far away, or in a dream."

Abstraction is one element Bell uses to create this dreamlike quality, as is her muted color palette. When seen together in a gallery (or in her studio), her paintings take on another meaning. Their consistency does not feel repetitive. Instead, it furthers a sense of déjà vu that's pleasantly disorienting. She also notes that her style has changed significantly over the past six years. "It is still clearly recognizable as my style, but I always added graphic elements in the past. I think they created a distance between the viewer and the scene, which I liked, but I wanted to make it possible to enter into the landscape without stopping to figure out the meaning of each mark," she says.

In conversation, Bell can be halting, a little slow to respond. Here is a woman who spends a lot of time alone or with her small brown dog, Leah. She thinks before she speaks and prefers to be around others who do so as well. You can almost see her turning inward before she responds to a question, searching for the right words. Bell is not a natural saleswoman, preferring that gallerists and dealers sell her work. She currently shows at Danese/Corey in New York. In the past, she has received grants from the Pollock-Krasner Foundation, the Adolph and Esther Gottlieb Foundation, and the National Endowment for the Arts. "I have made my living from my art almost my entire life," she says. "It's been difficult at times, but I've shaped my life around a certain income." This, she admits, has led to some difficult decisions, like the choice not to have children. Art, she explains, has shaped where she lives, where she travels, what she purchases, and how she survives—not the other way around.

Yet at the end of the day, when the light is waning in her studio and the shadows grow long, Bell is able to rest easily in her quiet home. "I've done what I wanted to do every single day of my life," she says. "And that has been wonderful."

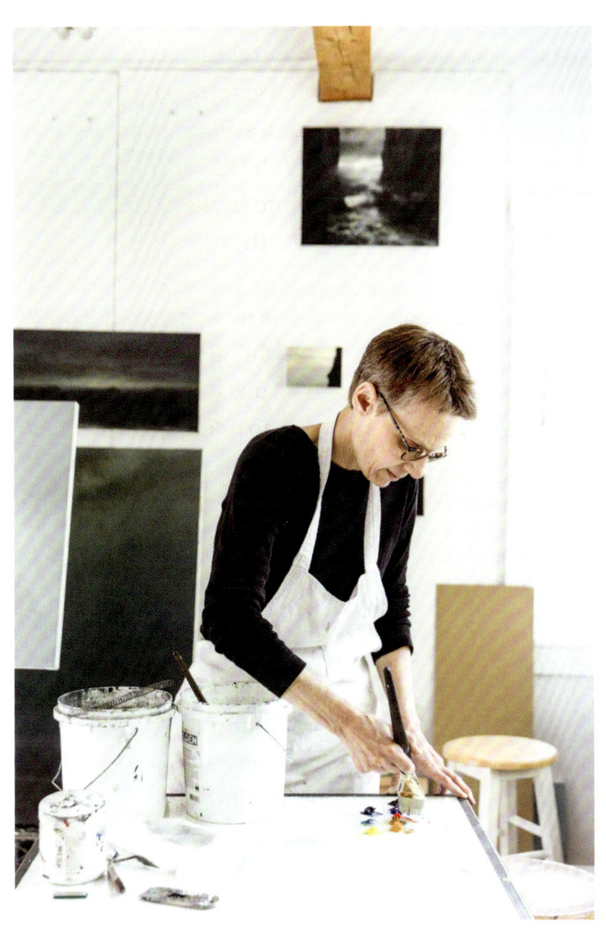

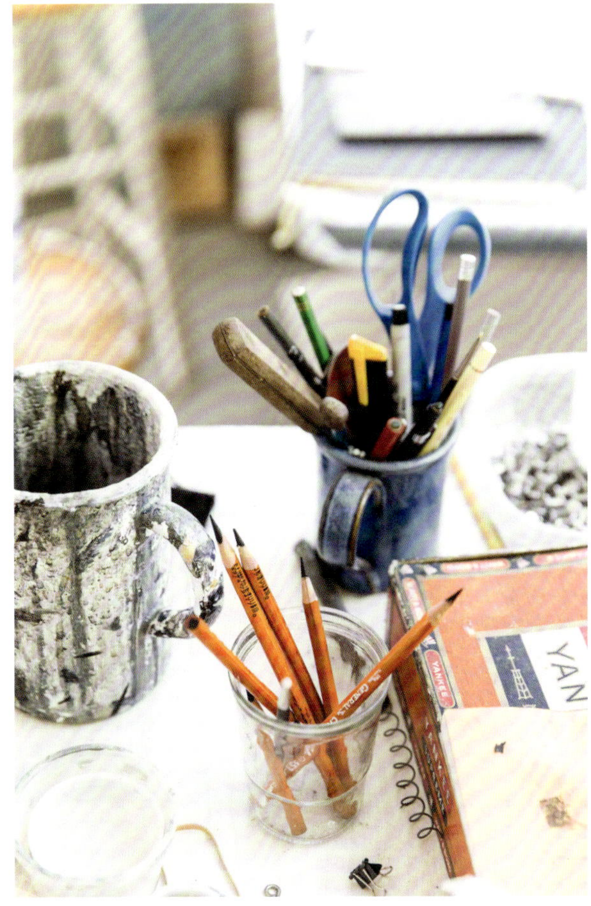
YAN

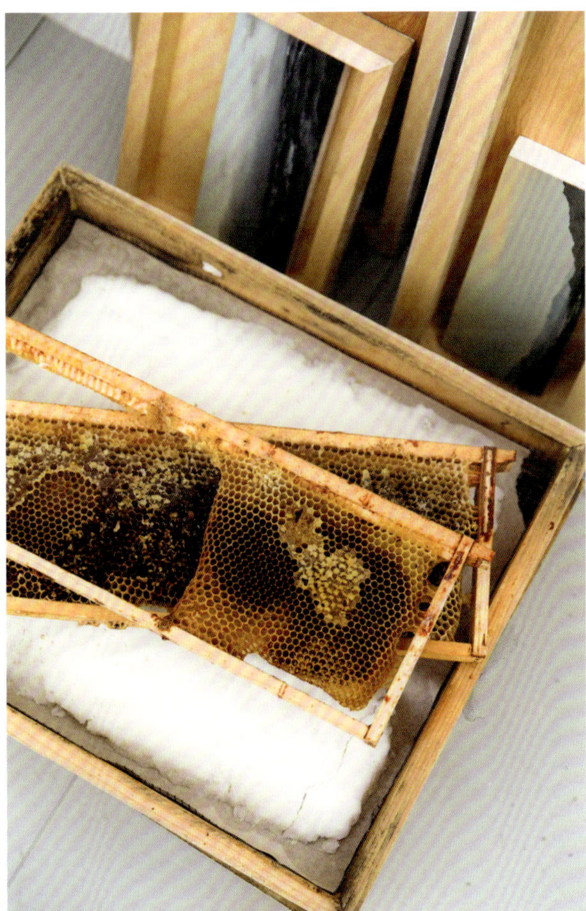

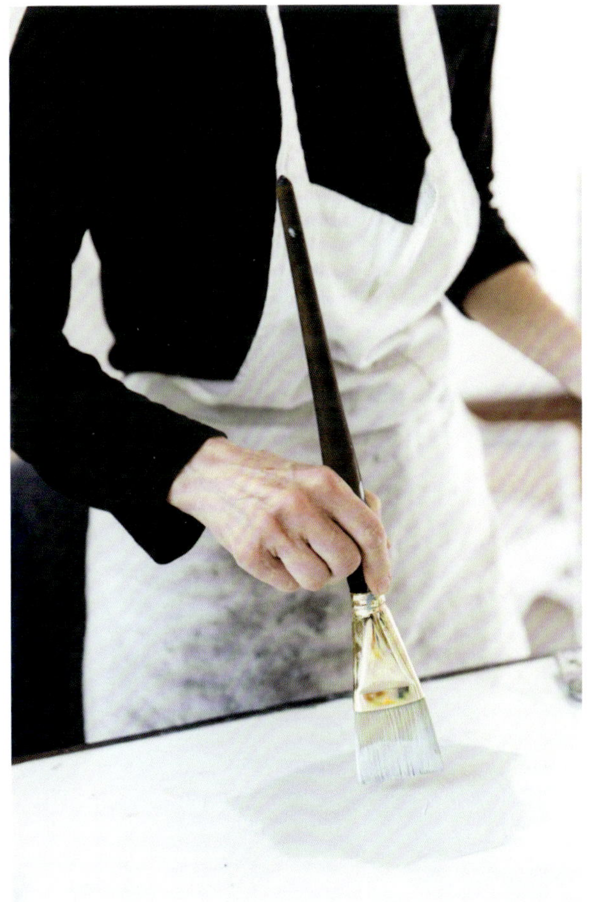

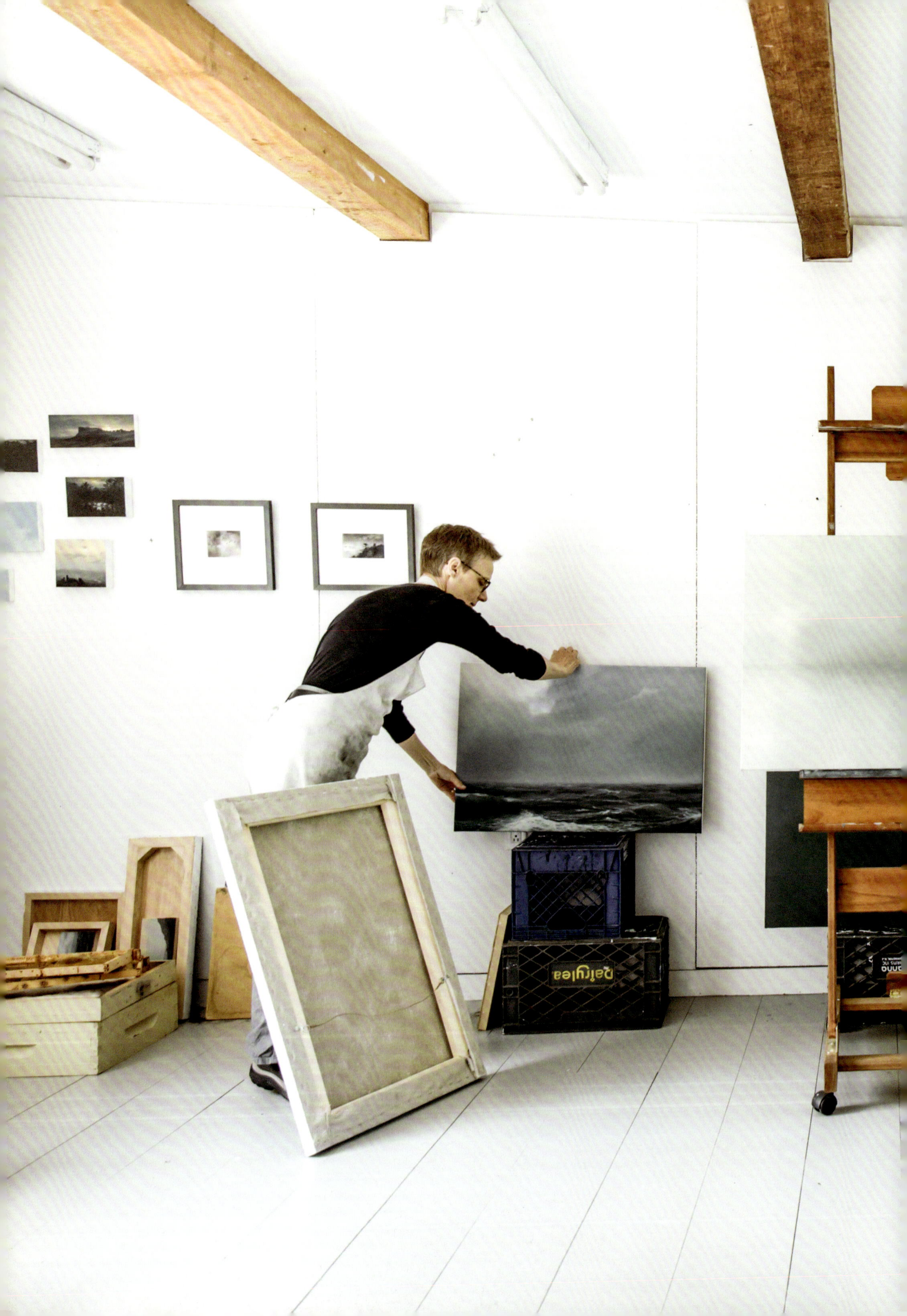
Dairylea

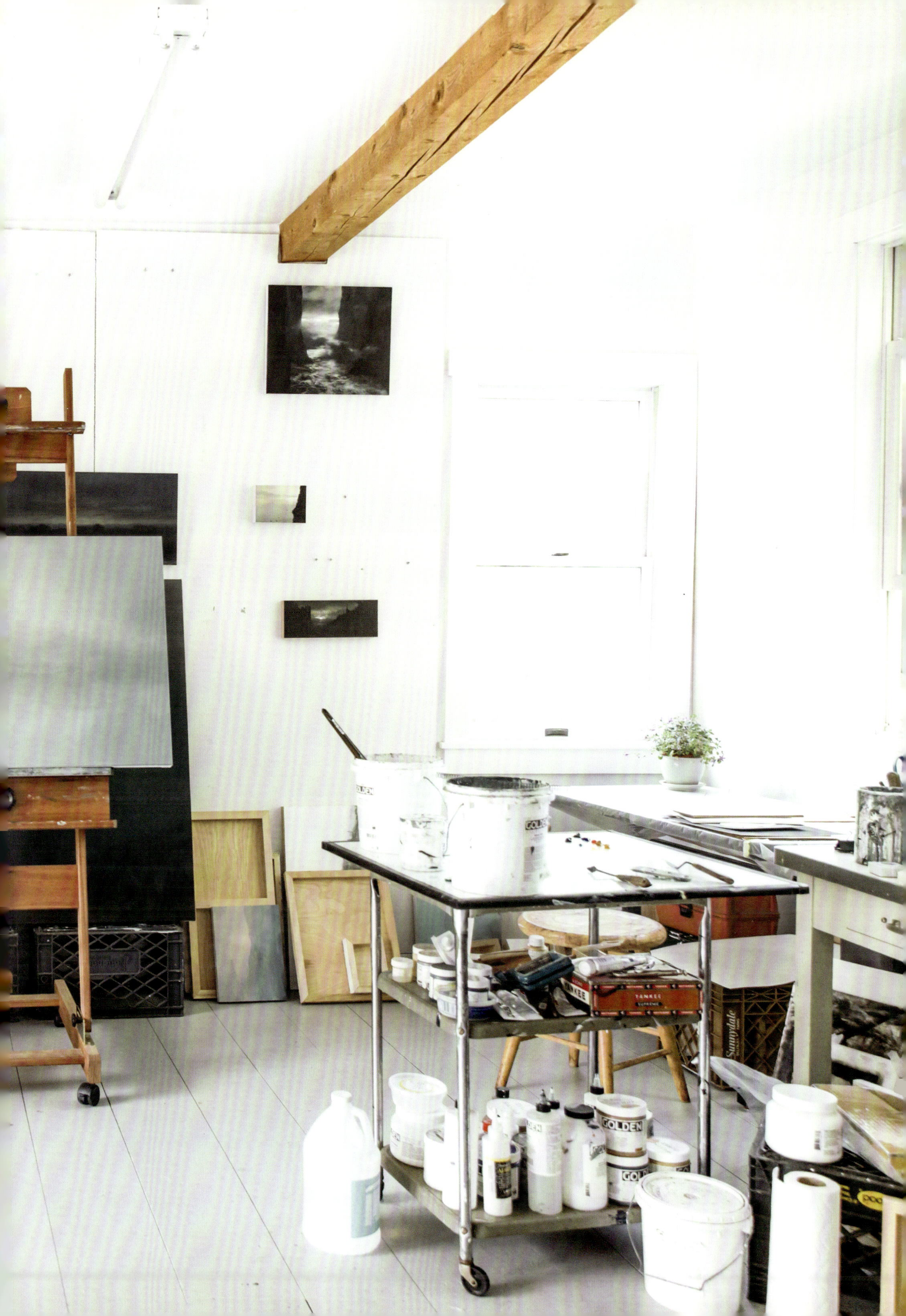
GOLDEN
YANKEE
Sunnydale

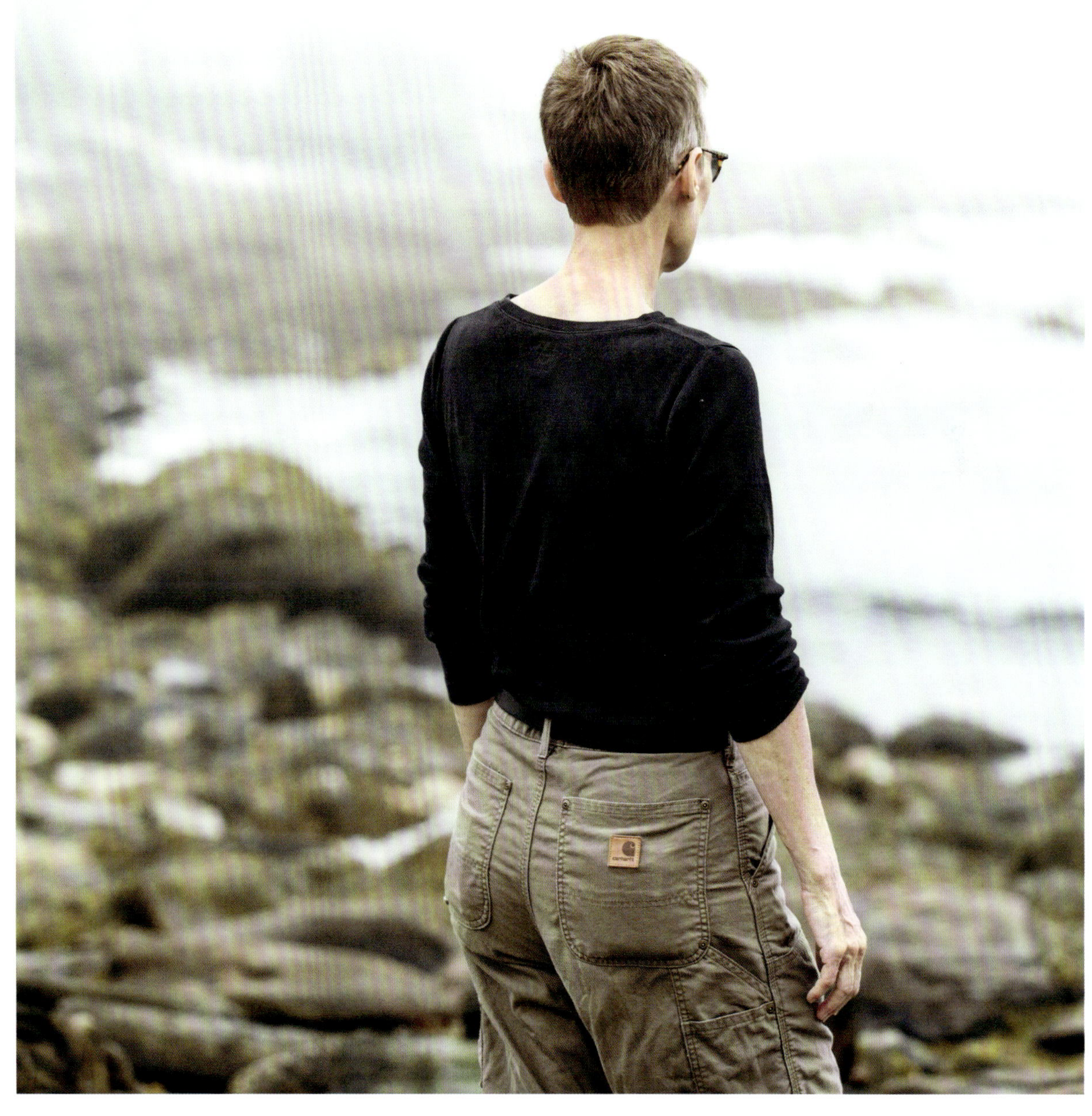

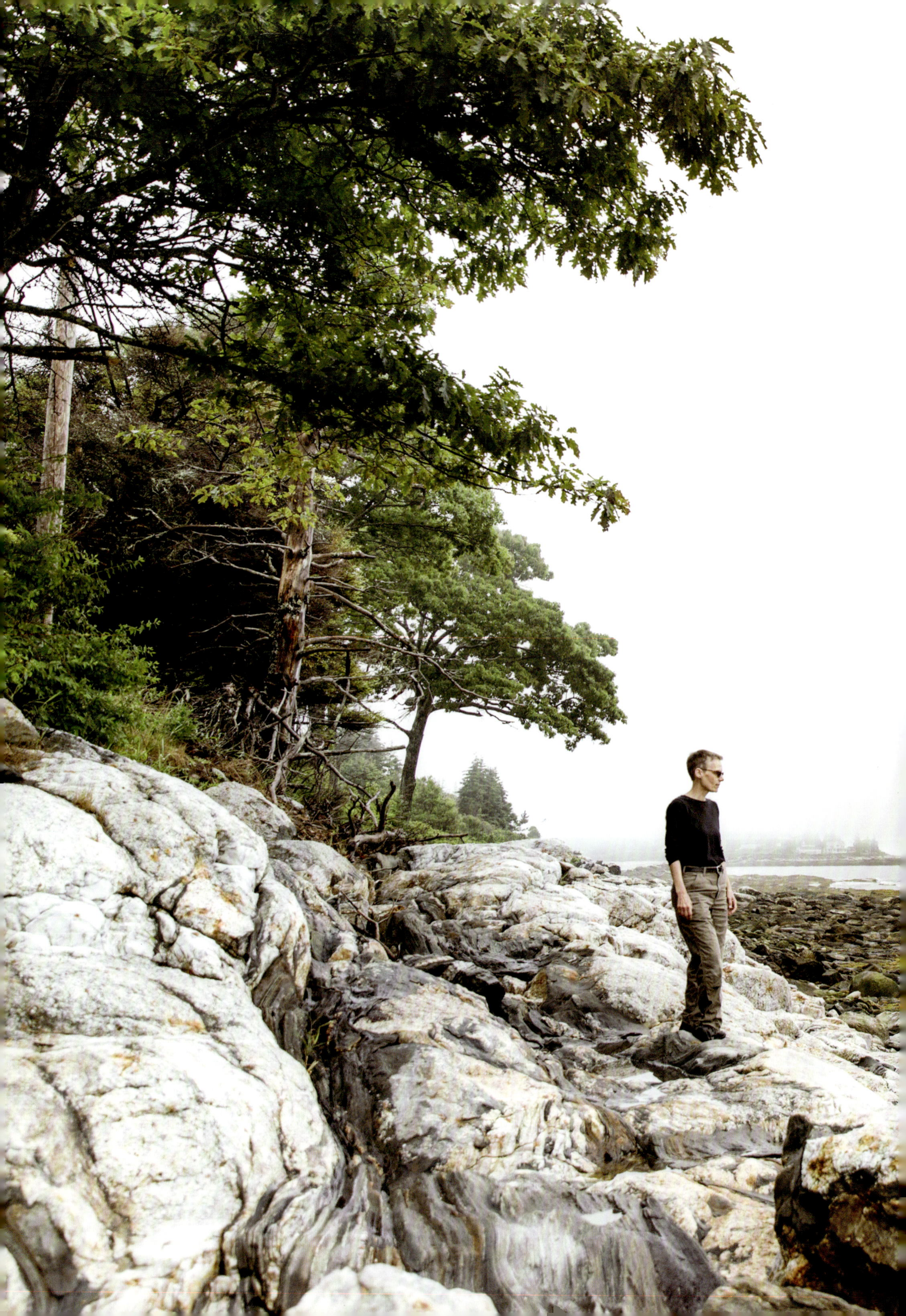

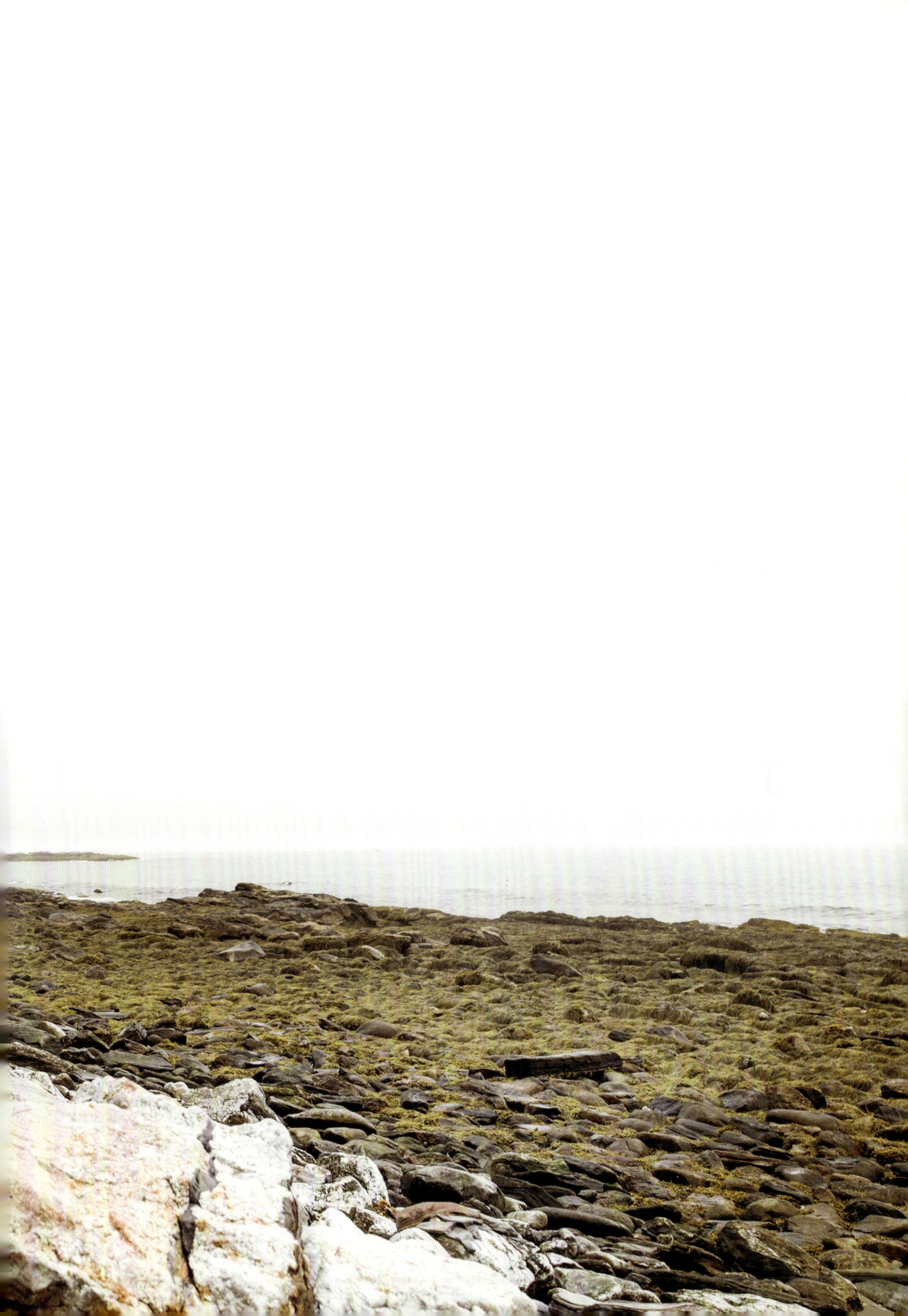

Jeremy Frey

Indian Island

"I always made art. Always," Jeremy Frey says. He grew up in Princeton, Maine, near the Pleasant Point Reservation. At a young age, his family moved to Indian Township, where he spent most of his teenage years. "I was an outsider on a small reservation in a small town," the artist recalls. "We were poor. Reservations are poor. The school wasn't great. But I had a good time."

By age twelve, Jeremy had explored the media available in the public school, from photography to pottery, and began teaching his art teacher about clay and paint. "Some people are great at math, others excel in science. Everyone has a strength," he says. "Making things has always been mine." Although he has had his mentors over the years, he considers himself largely self-taught. The one person who significantly shaped his career was Gal Frey, his mother. In his early twenties, following a year of "bad lifestyle choices and decisions" in Portland, Jeremy returned to Indian Township "to refresh myself and to get away." There he found his true medium. His mother had picked up a new hobby—basket weaving—having learned the craft from a reservation elder, Sylvia Gabriel. "I came home and there was ash all over the place, baskets on every surface, and I looked at it and said, 'Hey, why don't you teach me to weave baskets?'"

Basket weaving wasn't a foreign art to Jeremy—just one he hadn't fully explored. For the native people of Maine, particularly the Passamaquoddy tribe, basket weaving is an important tradition. One of the oldest forms of art in North America, it has been practiced by Jeremy's family for seven generations. "A lot of our history is completely erased," Jeremy says. "I don't even know the full history, but I know it's been in my family for generations and generations. My mother did it. My grandfather did it. His mother did it. She didn't speak English, but she made these baskets and sold them." Originally, the baskets were treated as functional pieces. "Fishermen used them as scale baskets and farmers used them for potatoes. For any industry that needed a lot of containers, we made containers."

These baskets were also treated as collectables by nineteenth-century summer visitors to Bar Harbor, who bought the native sweetgrass and ash baskets. While it's important to Jeremy to pay homage to his ancestors, he is also trying to shift the conversation.

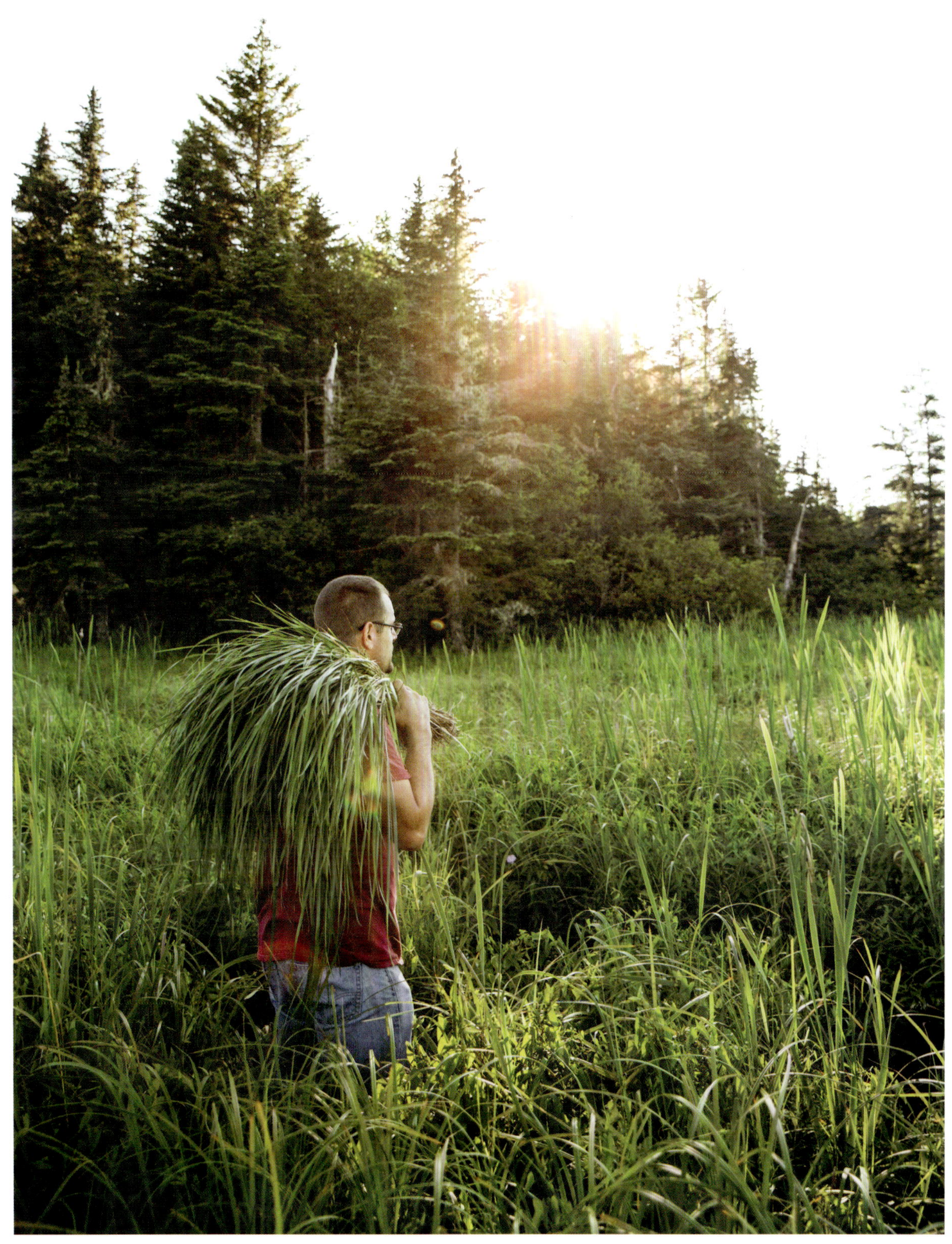

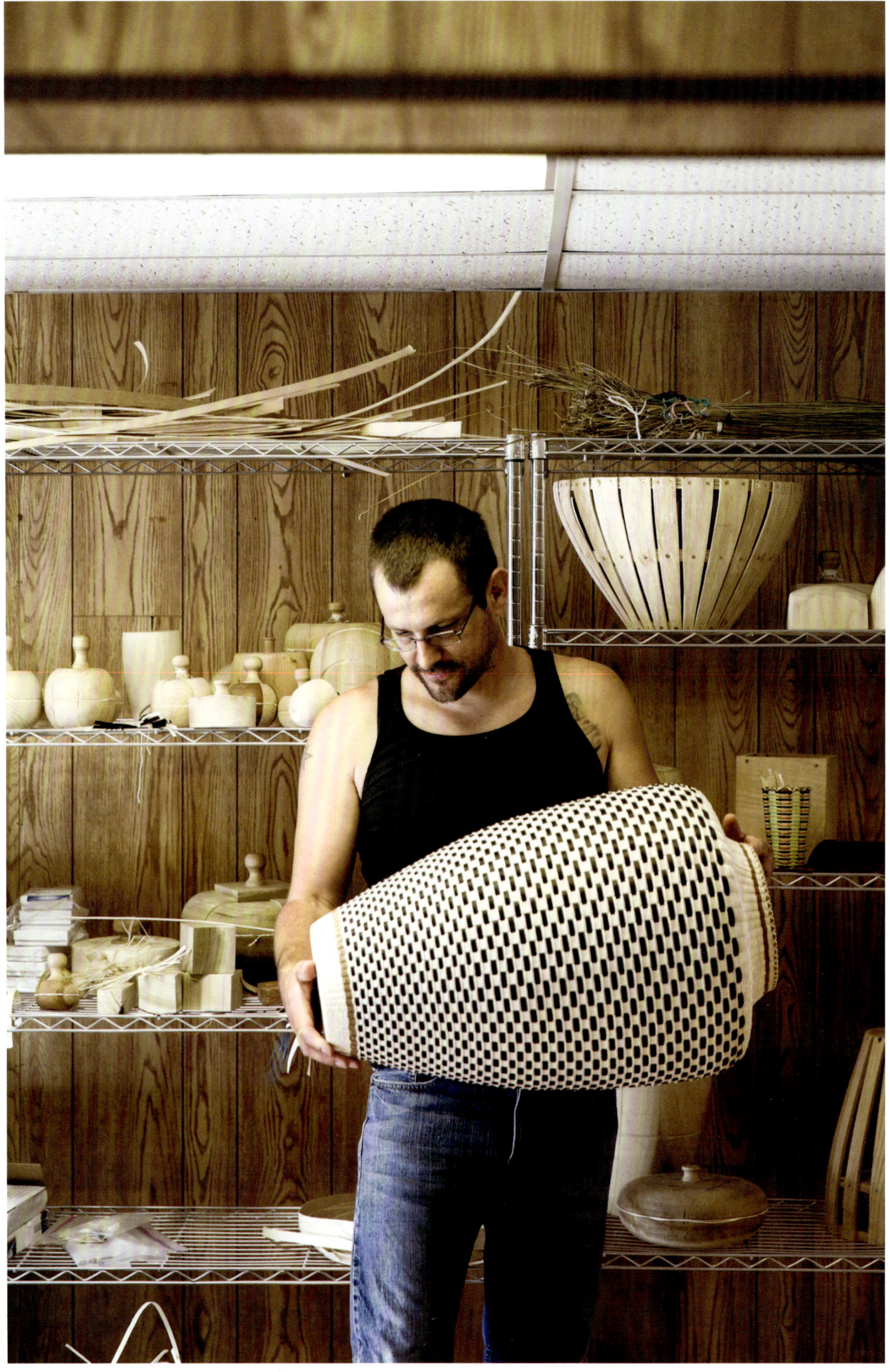

"If you think about the traditional native arts, they've never been taken seriously as fine art," Jeremy says. "People bought the baskets because they were 'native' art. They didn't see it as on par with something like oil painting." With each basket he creates, Jeremy challenges this way of thinking. "Art, I believe, can change the minds of the masses. It can inspire. Craft has always been considered functional. My goal is to take this craft to an artistic level, to elevate it," he says. "It is my dream to bridge the gap between native art circles and the larger art market. I want to take basket weaving to a level where people are buying 'a Jeremy Frey basket,' or better yet, just 'a Jeremy Frey'."

The art world has begun to recognize Jeremy, yet not without hesitation. In 2015, Jeremy's work was included in the Portland Museum of Art Biennial, alongside work by fellow Wabanaki basket weavers George Neptune, Theresa Secord, and Sarah Sockbeson. The press and critics praised the exhibition for the most part, but some took issue with curator Alison Ferris's inclusion of the Wabanaki baskets. Ferris supported Jeremy's work, pointing out that it has been recognized and exhibited nationally, appearing in the Smithsonian Institution's National Museum of the American Indian and the Mingei International Museum in San Diego. In 2011 Jeremy received a $50,000 fellowship grant from the United States Artists. But when it comes to Maine museums, Jeremy is placed in a "context that is not truly accurate," Ferris says. "Jeremy's work has been shown at the Maine Historical Society and the Abbe Museum, but no fine arts museum in Maine had ever exhibited or looked at his work, which I found really telling."

Jeremy, too, believes that Maine has fallen behind when it comes to understanding native culture and upholding native rights, but he doesn't like to dwell on this topic. Instead, he prefers to highlight his artistic innovations, such as the incorporation of braided ash. "No one had ever braided ash before." He thought differently about the hard wood. "I knew ash could be really flexible, and so I did it," he says. "I also work with braided cedar bark, and as far as I know, I'm the only one who does that."

Jeremy has distinguished himself—thrived, even—in the face of competition. He feeds off challenges, approaching each new task as something to be conquered, a challenge to overcome. "The best part of my work is coming up with brand-new concepts and showcasing them on baskets," he says, as his nimble fingers weave in and out, turning strands of pounded ash into a squat urchin-shaped vessel. In his hands, the wood moves as easily as string. Watching Jeremy weave is like watching a child play cat's cradle. There is no hesitation in his movements; he knows exactly where each switch of wood will go and how it will factor into the final piece. It can take him anywhere from two days to complete a very small vessel, to two months for something larger.

When asked what differentiates his work from traditional Wabanaki baskets, Jeremy brings up several key points, including the preparation of materials. "I prepare each element far beyond what you might do with a traditional basket. I explore form and function far beyond what traditional basket weavers did." While many basket weavers today buy their materials, Jeremy harvests and prepares every element himself. He identifies the ash trees, collects the wood, pounds it into thin, flexible strips, dyes it in his kitchen, and weaves in his living room. He even collects porcupine quills, which he frequently uses to adorn the tops of his baskets, from carcasses found on the side of the road.

In much of his work, Jeremy uses classical forms, elegant and elongated shapes that recall ancient Greek pottery. Sometimes he even plays with the very idea of a basket as a vessel, turning this craft into something else entirely. "One day I made a basket that had multiple tops woven together and that became smaller and smaller. You couldn't open the inside cover because it was trapped inside a smaller cover," he explains. That basket, he says, "was designed to be purely decorative. But it was also a loud statement. It said: I'm not a craft. I'm a piece of art."

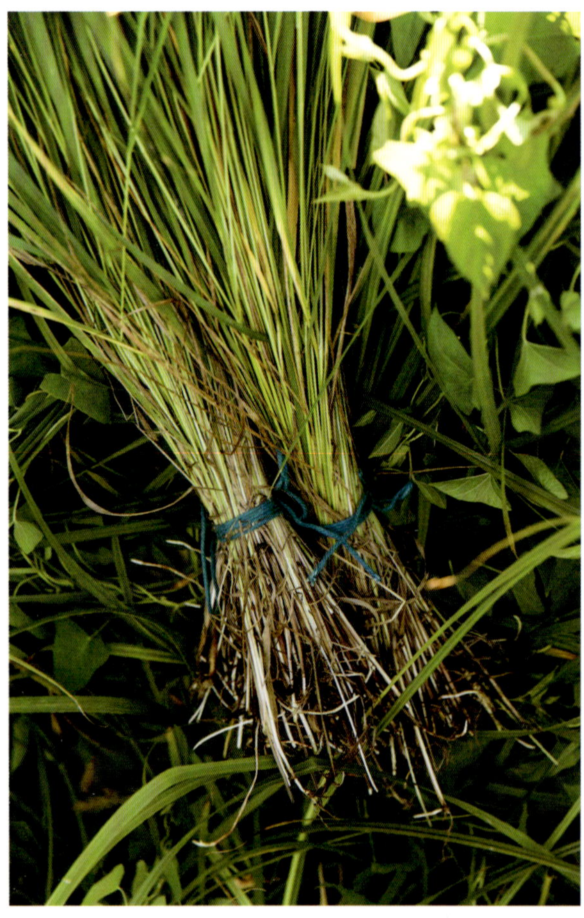

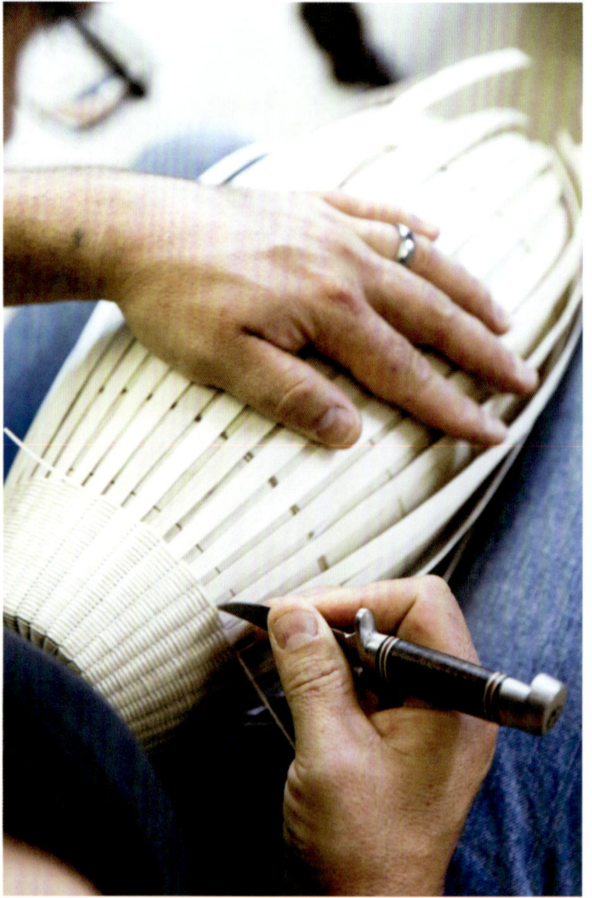

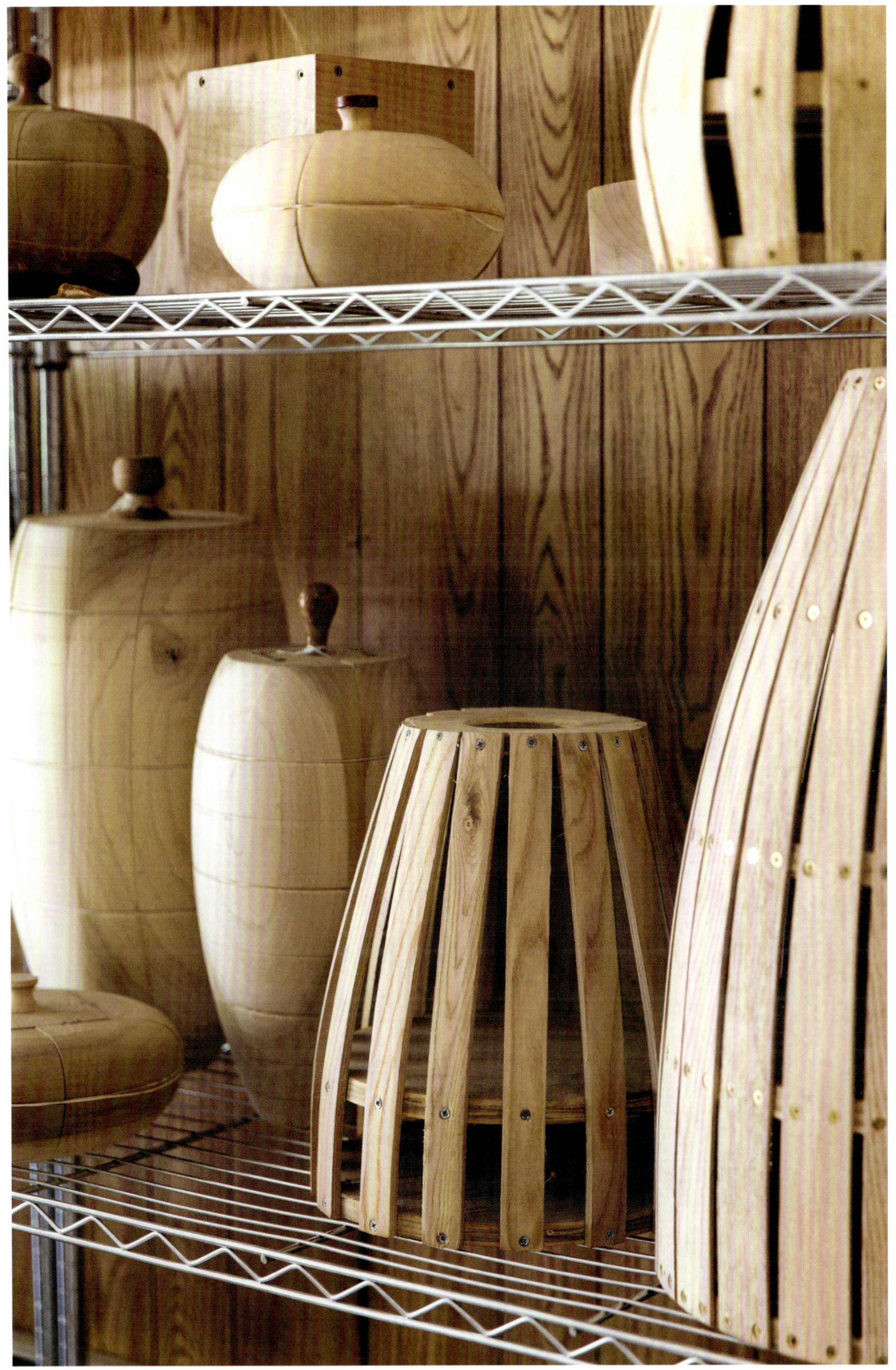

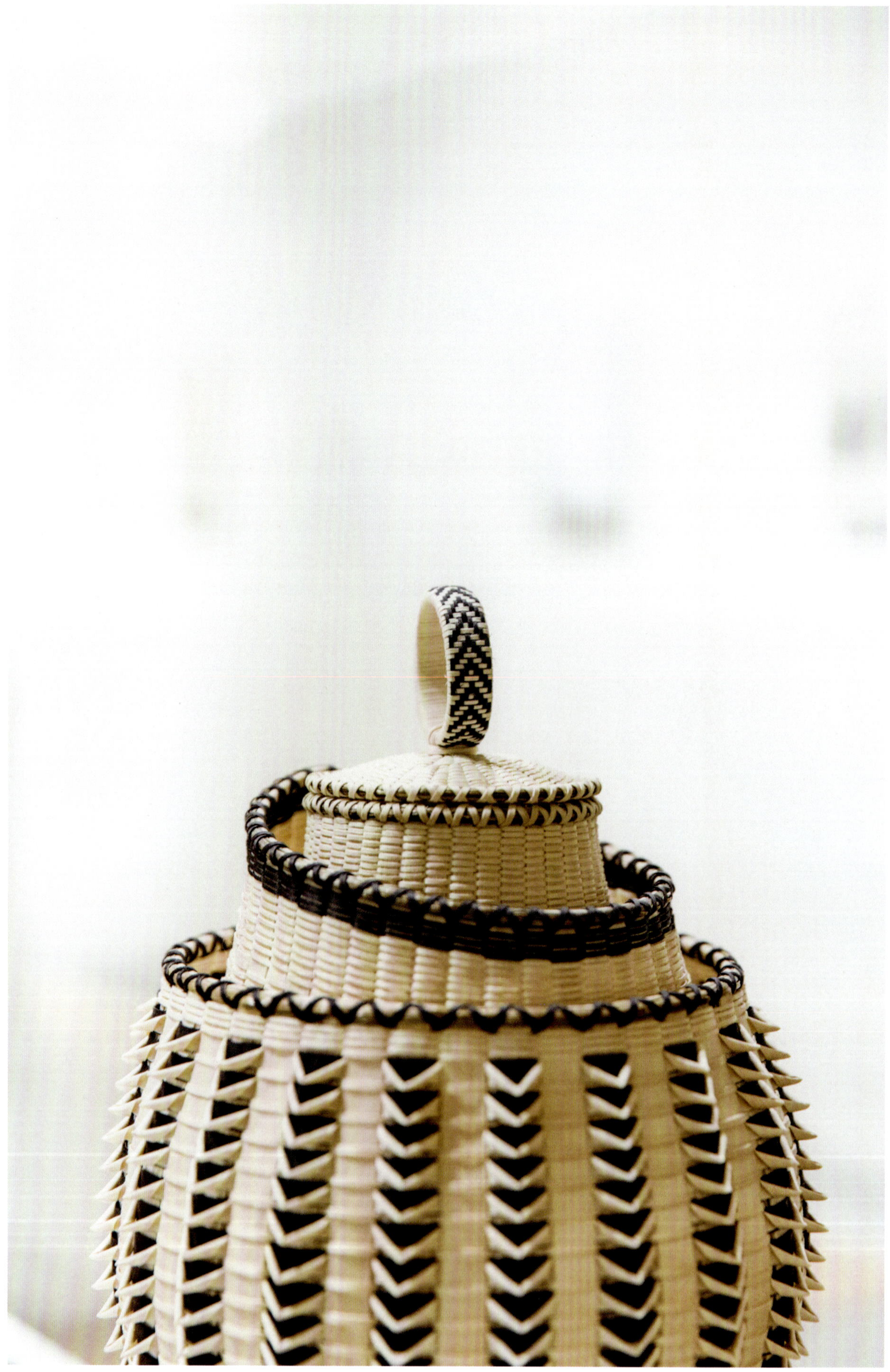

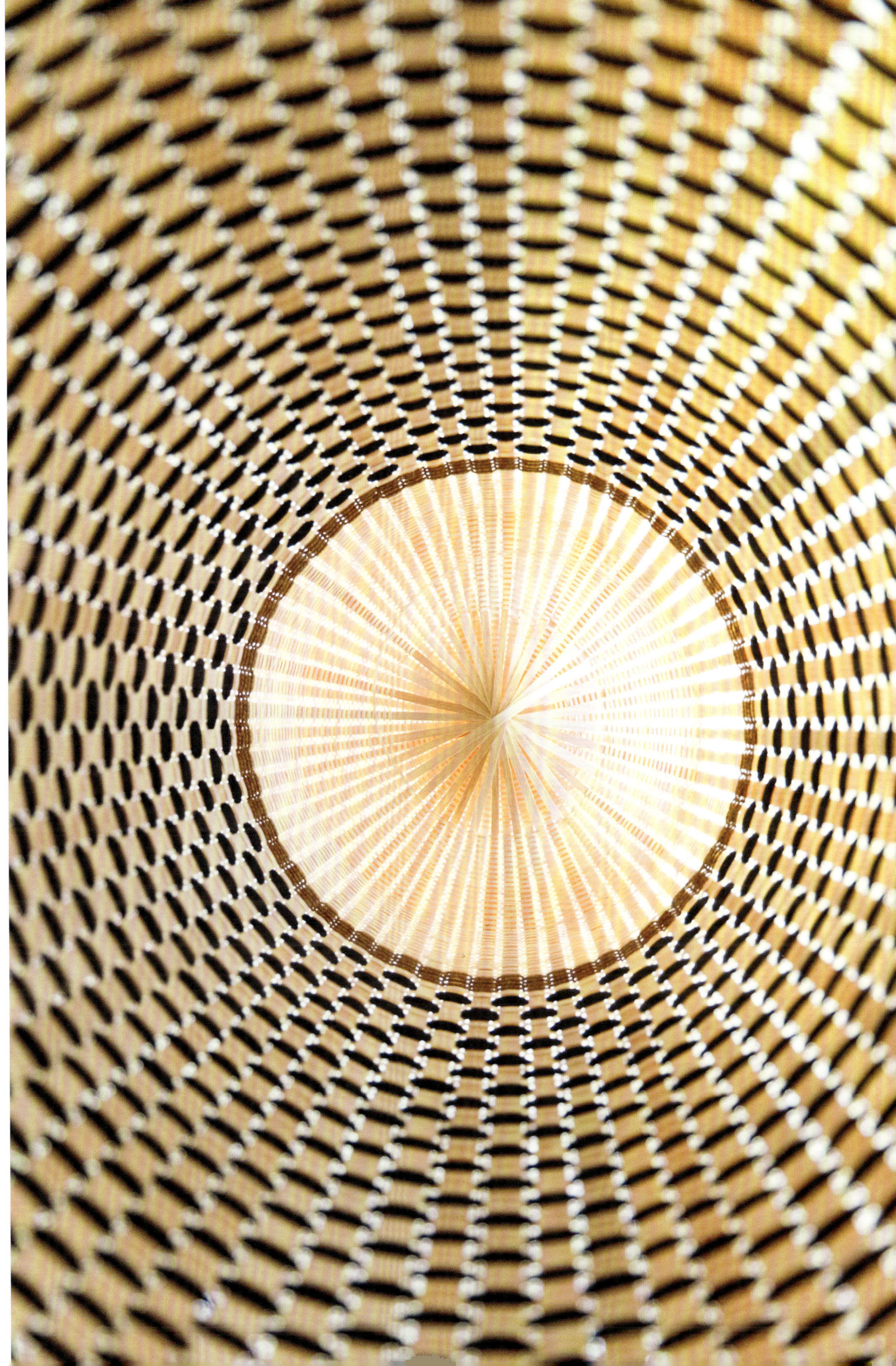

Ayumi Horie

Portland

Ayumi Horie believes that every dish should be selected with care. "There's always a moment when you're reaching into the cupboard for a mug and you think: Where am I going to drink this? Will it sit at the table with me or do I want to read on the sofa? Do I want to wrap my hands around it or set it down? You have to know where you'll be for the next half hour when you grab a mug. All these decisions are made in a split second—it's intuitive. But it drives Chloe a little crazy," she adds with a laugh. Chloe, her wife, looks up and smiles. She knows Ayumi's penchant for thinking ahead, her habit of anticipating every scenario as she selects dishes.

Ayumi creates art in her pottery, yet she doesn't like to call herself an artist. She prefers "potter" or "maker." In ceramics as in life, Ayumi is drawn to the practical and tactile. "My work exists primarily in the domestic sphere," she explains. "The bulk of my work is sold directly to individuals, who use my pieces in their homes." While she understands why some homeowners might choose standard inexpensive white plates from IKEA and other mass retailers, Ayumi dislikes this "toilet-bowl" look: "I have a real aversion to the minimalist aesthetic that seems to dominate these days." Every one of her pots, bowls, mugs, and plates bears the mark of their maker, whether in the form of her kawaii drawings or an intentionally placed thumbprint. "There is a natural softness to clay. When you press it, it leaves a mark, a little like the human body. I want to preserve that sensual nature and highlight it in my work," she explains. As she speaks, she runs her hands along her mug, which is full of green tea and decorated with a skull and crossbones and the name of the famous science educator Bill Nye. Unlike many of her pieces, which feature paintings, this drawing has been incised into the surface of the mug, leaving little cliffs of clay that rise with each letter, textured and imprecise. This considered coarseness runs through her work. "I am not a potter who makes fifty of the same mug or bowl. My process is much looser than that; I'm often surprised when something comes out of the kiln." Yet despite the spontaneity of her approach, Ayumi's work feels cohesive, tied together by her offbeat visual sense, which combines a range of influences. The maker draws widely for inspiration, looking to her personal history in Maine, her international travel, and her

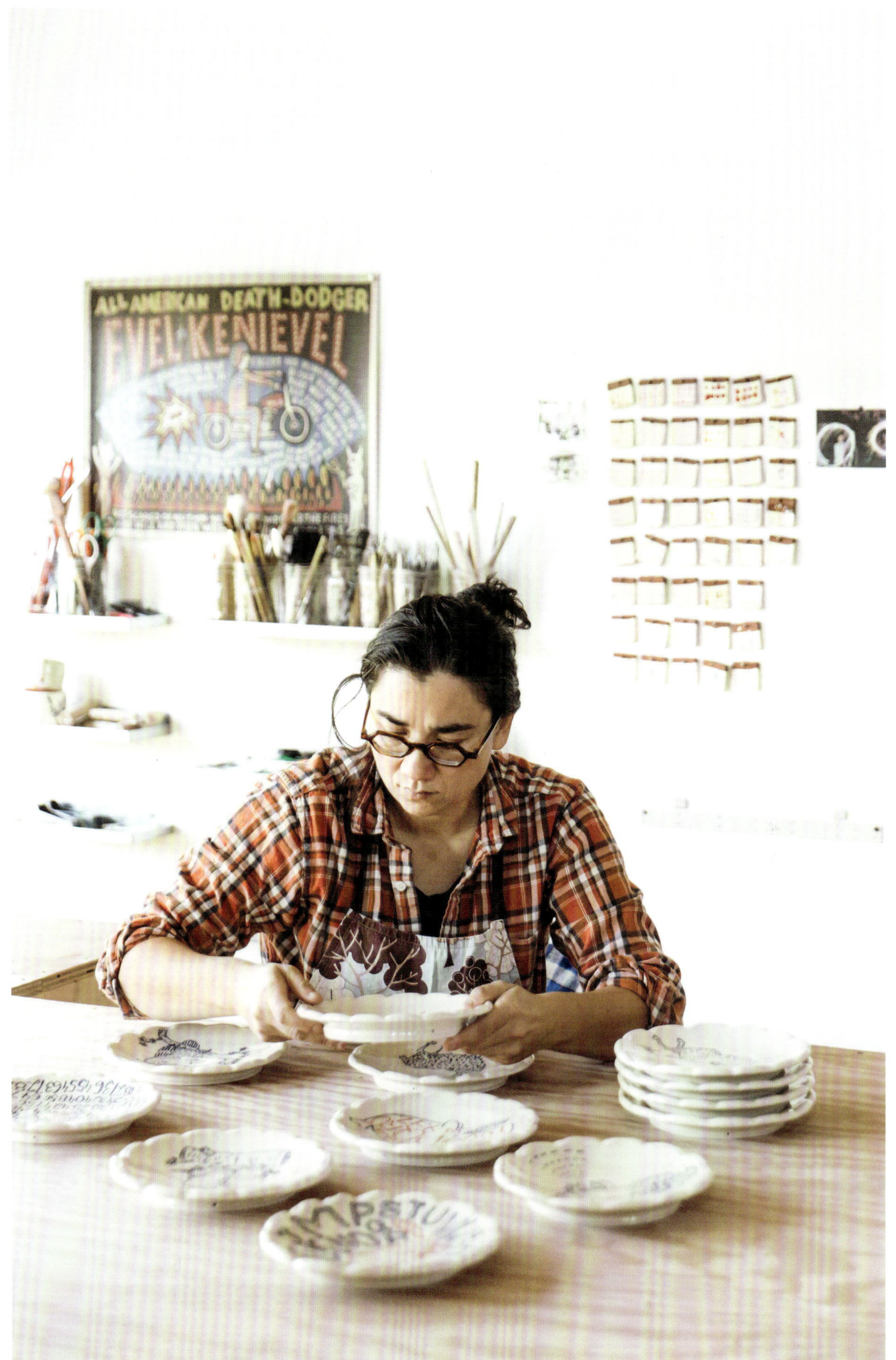
ALL AMERICAN DEATH-DODGER
EVEL KENIEVEL

bicultural heritage (her father is from Japan, and her mother from Maine).

Ayumi has been making pottery for over twenty years, a skill she learned at Alfred University (this is also where she pioneered her distinctive dry-throwing style). She has lived in Montana, upstate New York, Washington, and Maine. Raised in Lewiston-Auburn, Ayumi now lives in Portland in a historic brick-and-clapboard house that she painstakingly renovated and expanded for her studio and kiln. While she travels frequently, her decision to settle in Maine was an obvious one. "Even though I look globally for my inspiration, there is nowhere else in the world that I want to be my home base," she says. "I feel fed by Maine. There is a long craft tradition here, and a humbleness to its maker tradition. People in Maine have always made out of necessity." This, she says, "epitomizes the distinction between maker and artist. Makers do not look to glorify themselves. Their objects serve a need."

Aside from making objects intended for everyday use, Ayumi is also bringing pottery into the lives of Mainers through the Portland Brick Project, a public art installation that replaces bricks missing from Portland's streets with brand-new ones made in her kiln and stamped with wishes and memories shared by fellow locals. And in 2016, she became involved with the artistic activist initiative the Democratic Cup, a fundraiser designed to support progressive politics.

Ayumi is deeply curious about how others use her creations. A few years ago she started a campaign called Pots in Action (now an Instagram feed, @potsinaction) to "introduce a wider swath of the public to handmade pots." She is fascinated by how people choose their dishware, how they select mugs, how they use their ceramic pieces. She started the project by soliciting pictures of her work in use, but it has since expanded to involve potters from around the globe. "It became a way to close the loop between maker and user," Ayumi says. "We're trying to explore this topic from every angle. And Instagram has been the perfect venue. It generates energy in a way that no other social media platform does."

Ayumi is not just comfortable with social media, she's prolific. She has always had a robust online presence and online sales drive her business. "Selling my work online has allowed me to live and move wherever I want," she says. "When I got out of graduate school, the internet was on the rise. It seemed clear to me that that was the route I wanted to go. Up until that point, people were selling at galleries or craft shows, and neither of those felt very effective to me." In 2001, she launched her first website, and in 2005 she established an online shop. While she produces her work primarily in Maine, she sells it to fans around the globe. This wide reach allows her to make the kind of work she wants to see—not the kind the market demands.

In this way, Ayumi has created a life that is at once hands-on and digital, local and global. "Because I sell online, I only need to find one person who wants a really quirky rabbit cup. I don't need five hundred people to buy one quirky rabbit cup. Because the internet is so geared toward niche markets, it works for a maker with a particularly handmade aesthetic," she explains. "When I think about the maker revolution, I think about how technology has become a part of the definition as well." There is no longer a strict line between handmade items and pieces that are made using technology, or between fine art and craft. These definitions no longer describe the work that is being created today, work that crosses borders, plays with technology, and bridges the divide between the domestic and the public spheres. Or as Ayumi says, "The boundaries have completely broken down." And for many makers, that is a very good thing thing.

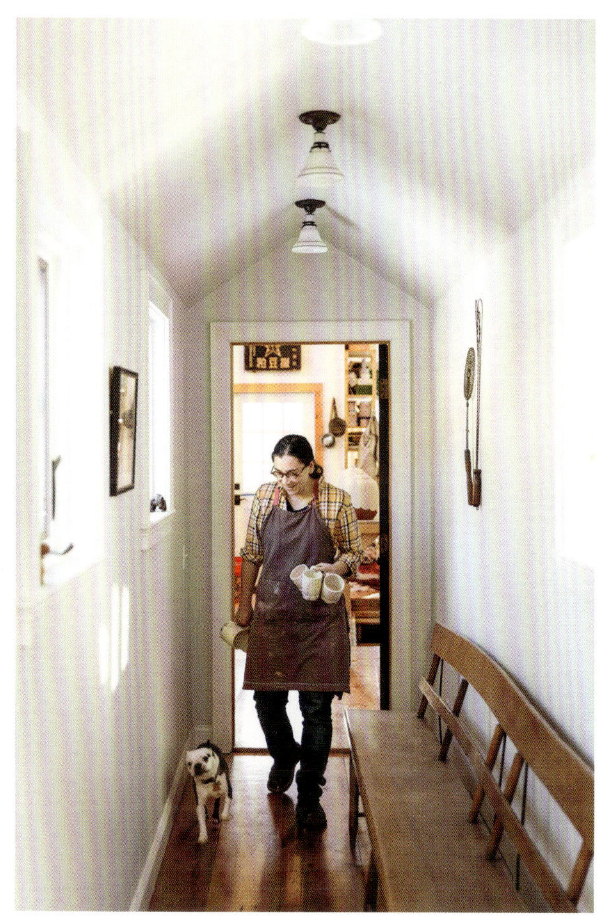

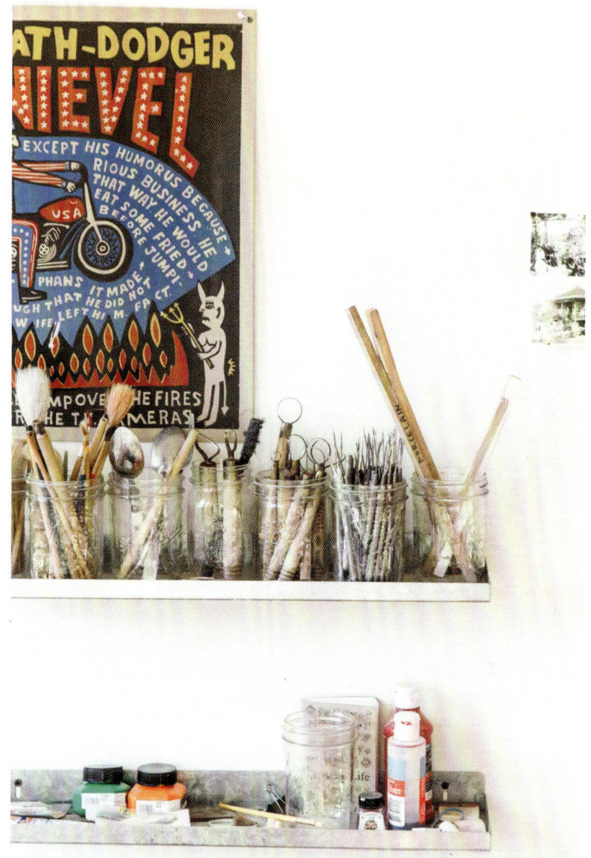
ATH-DODGER
NIEVEL
EXCEPT HIS HUMORUS BECAUSE
RIOUS BUSINESS HE
THAT WAY HE WOULD
EAT SOME FRIED
BEFORE JUMPI-
USA
PHANS IT MADE
UGH THAT HE DID NOT
W IFE LEFT HI M. FACT.
MPOVE HE FIRES
R HE T.V. MERAS

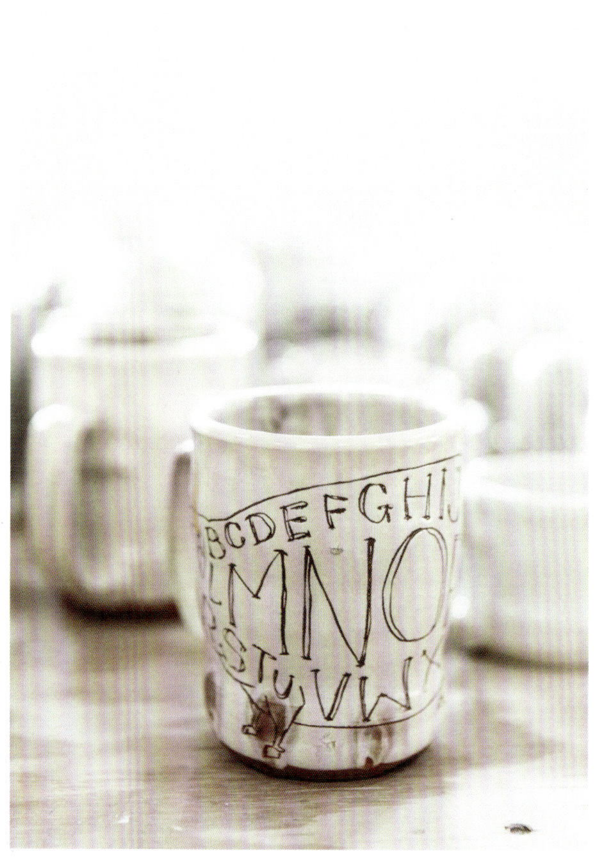

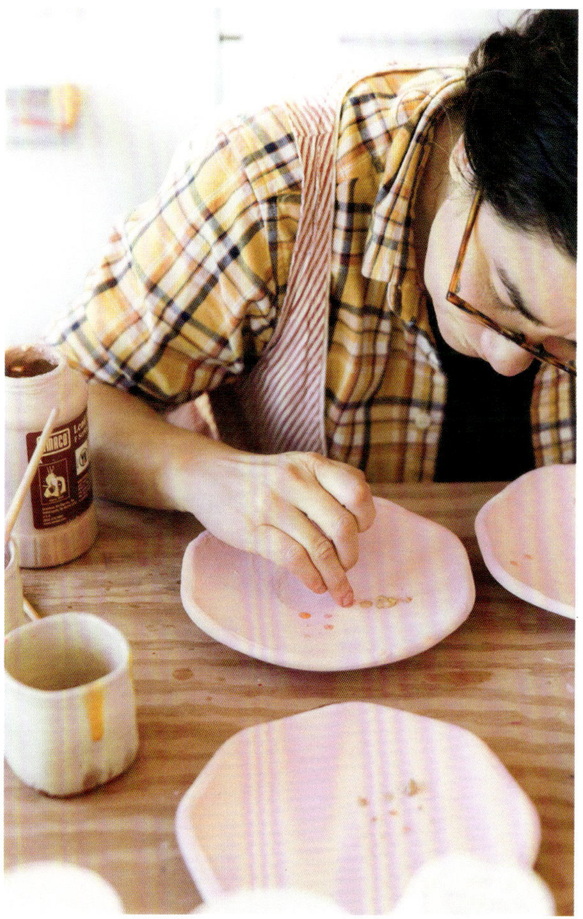

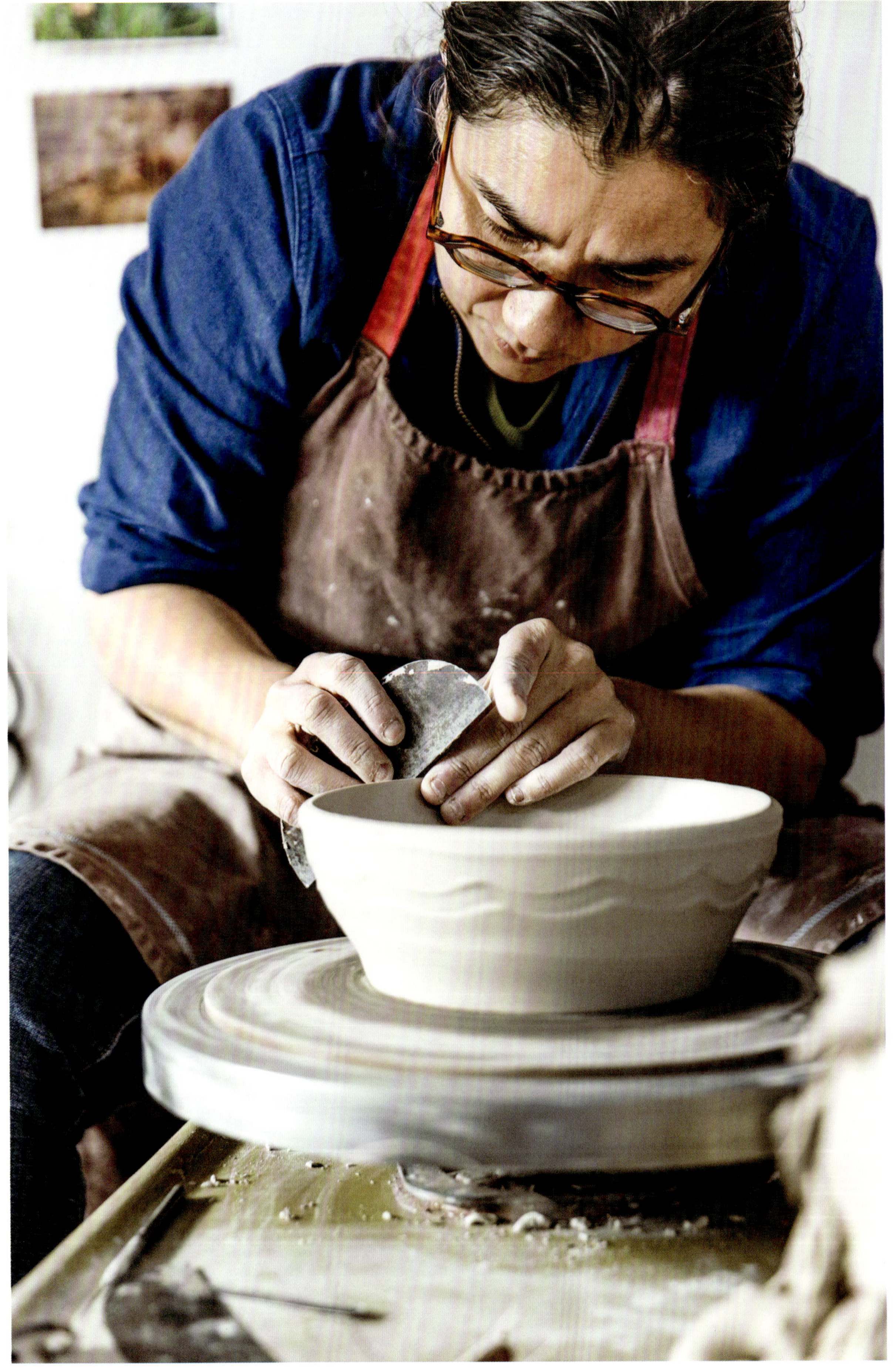

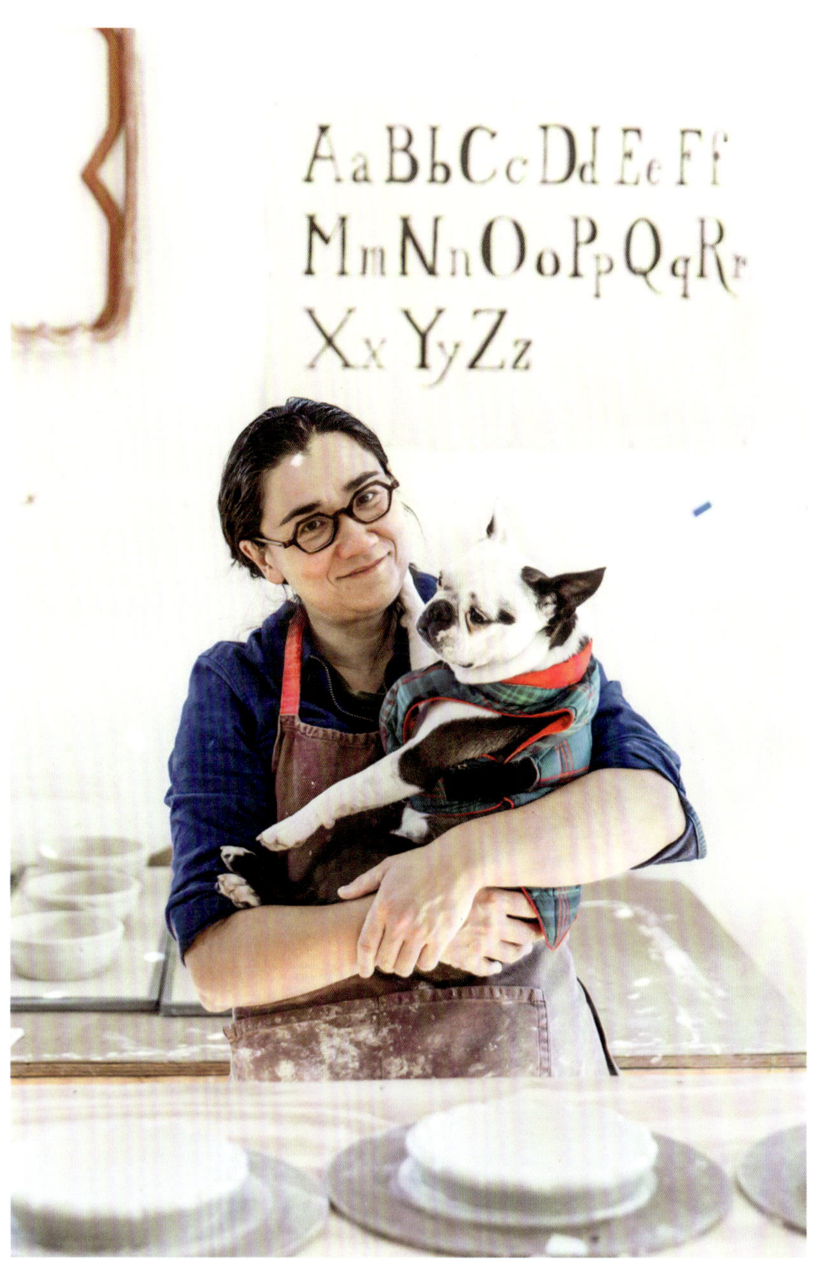
Aa Bb Cc Dd Ee Ff
Mm Nn Oo Pp Qq Rr
Xx Yy Zz

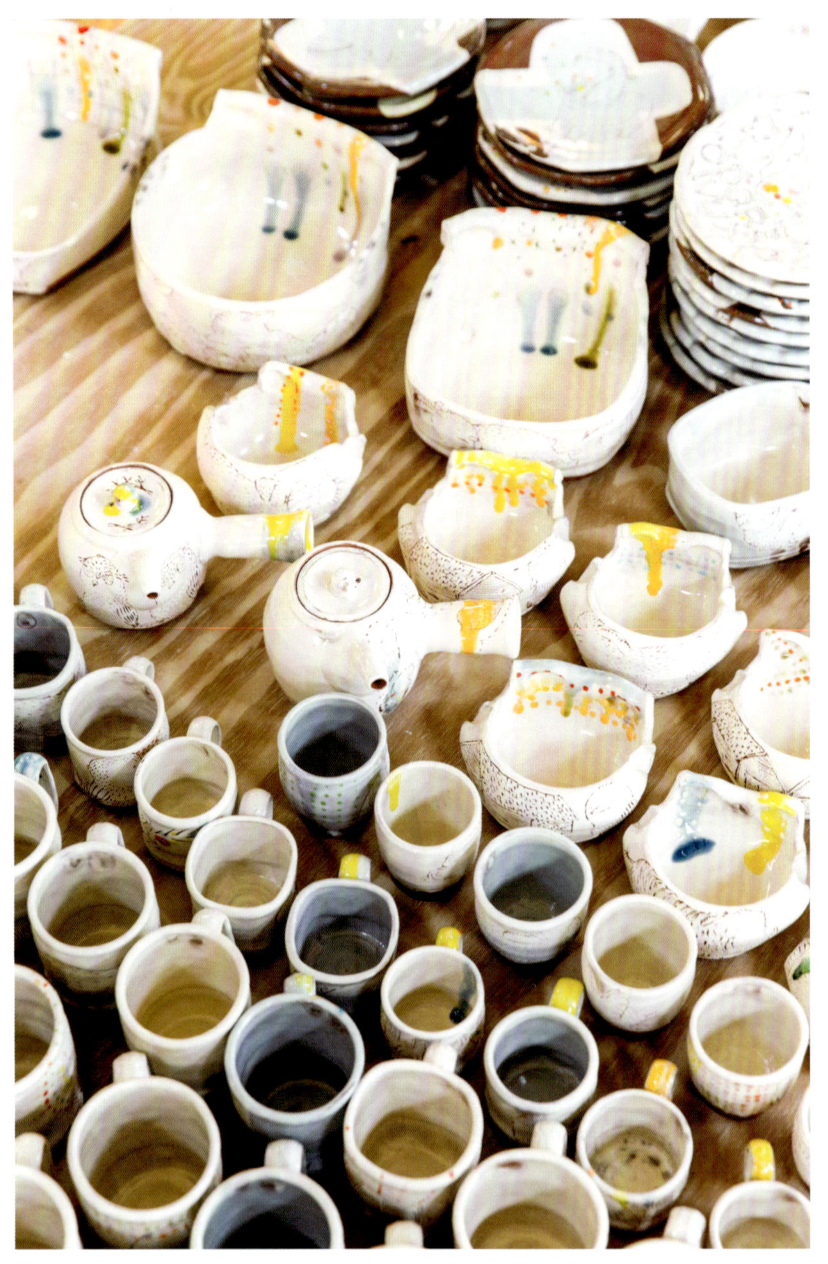

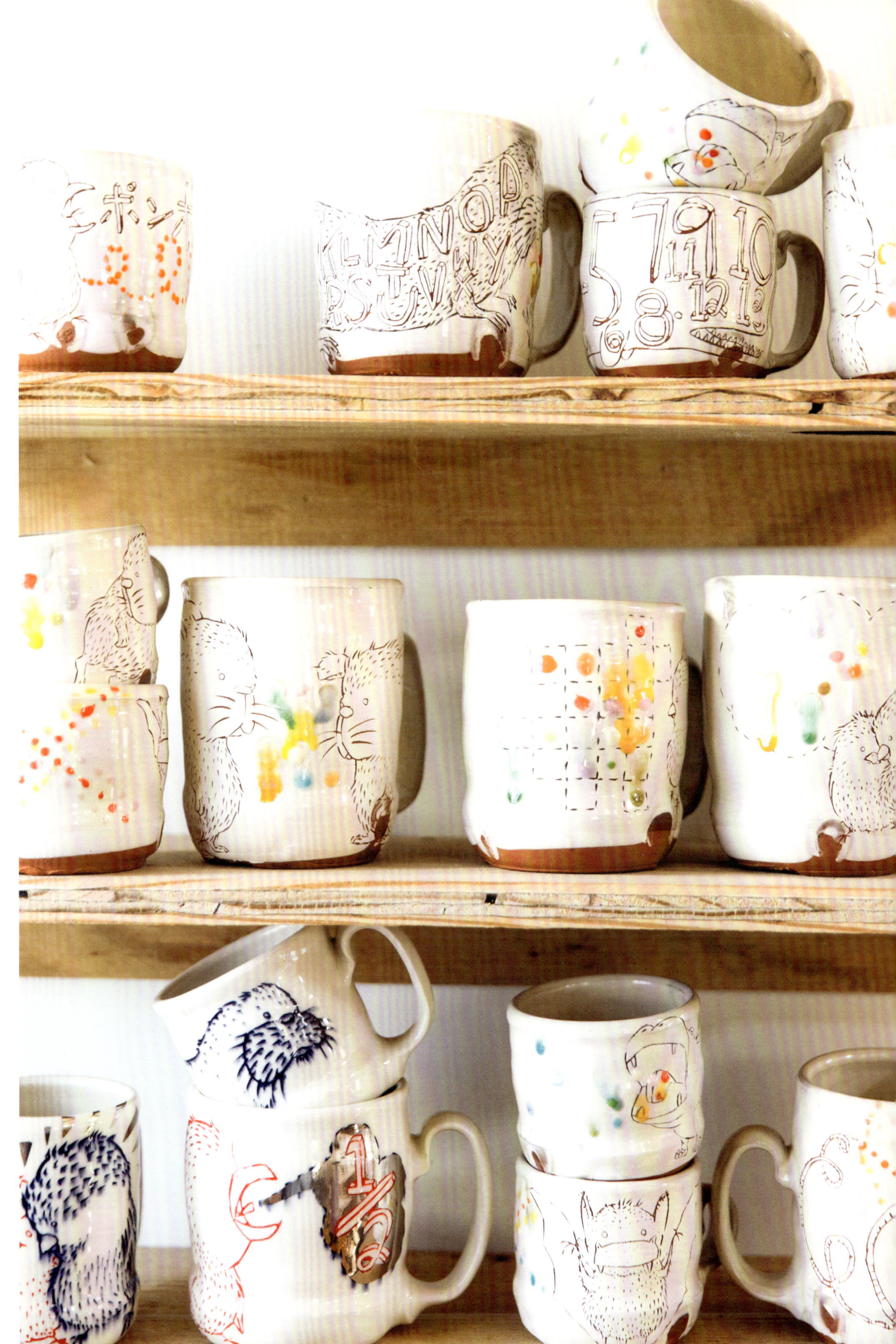

Sara Hotchkiss

Waldoboro

Sara Hotchkiss lives in a white clapboard house on a dirt road in the rural village of Waldoboro. Instead of a mowed expanse of green, her front yard is a patchwork of color. From the pink cosmos to the bright red poppies and the stalks of soft purple lavender, this yard is a gardener's dream—it's wild and lush in a purposefully messy way that results from hours of enjoyable labor.

The colors inside the artist's studio echo those found in her garden. Sara makes her inspired rugs and textiles in an airy room filled with looms so large they were once operated by teams of two. "I've been told they weigh as much as a small car," she says as she sits down to a loom, which she laughingly refers to as a "dinosaur machine." Twelve feet long, it's strung with colorful warp threads, and as she weaves, rows of sea-glass green fabric are tightly compressed until they blend harmoniously with rows of misty gray and dark, steely blue. This rug, she says, is inspired by the ocean and the dance of light and color that goes on below the waves. "For me, color is an intuitive thing. I can usually tell what colors people will be drawn to, what colors are theirs," Sara explains. "And I've never had a rug returned," she adds with a note of pride. Many of Sara's rugs are created for specific clients, which allows her to work closely with each individual to determine what will appeal to their aesthetic sense—and what will fit in the design scheme of their home. But it's not as simple as matching reds with reds or blues with blues. The process, as Sara describes it, sounds almost mystical. She asks clients what they read and what they collect. "I like to understand people," she says. "And knowing what they enjoy—what authors, painters, and objects—helps me to understand how serious they are, or how playful."

Sara has been weaving for over forty years and in that time she has become a master of her craft. In addition to being shown in exhibitions and galleries throughout New England, her work has also appeared in the American Craft Museum (now the Museum of Arts and Design) in New York City, San Francisco International Airport, and the Worcester Center for Crafts in Massachusetts. Her work has been published in regional and national magazines, including *Country Living*, *Better Homes and Gardens*, *Maine Home + Design*, and *Architectural Digest*. When asked when she started weaving, she replies simply,

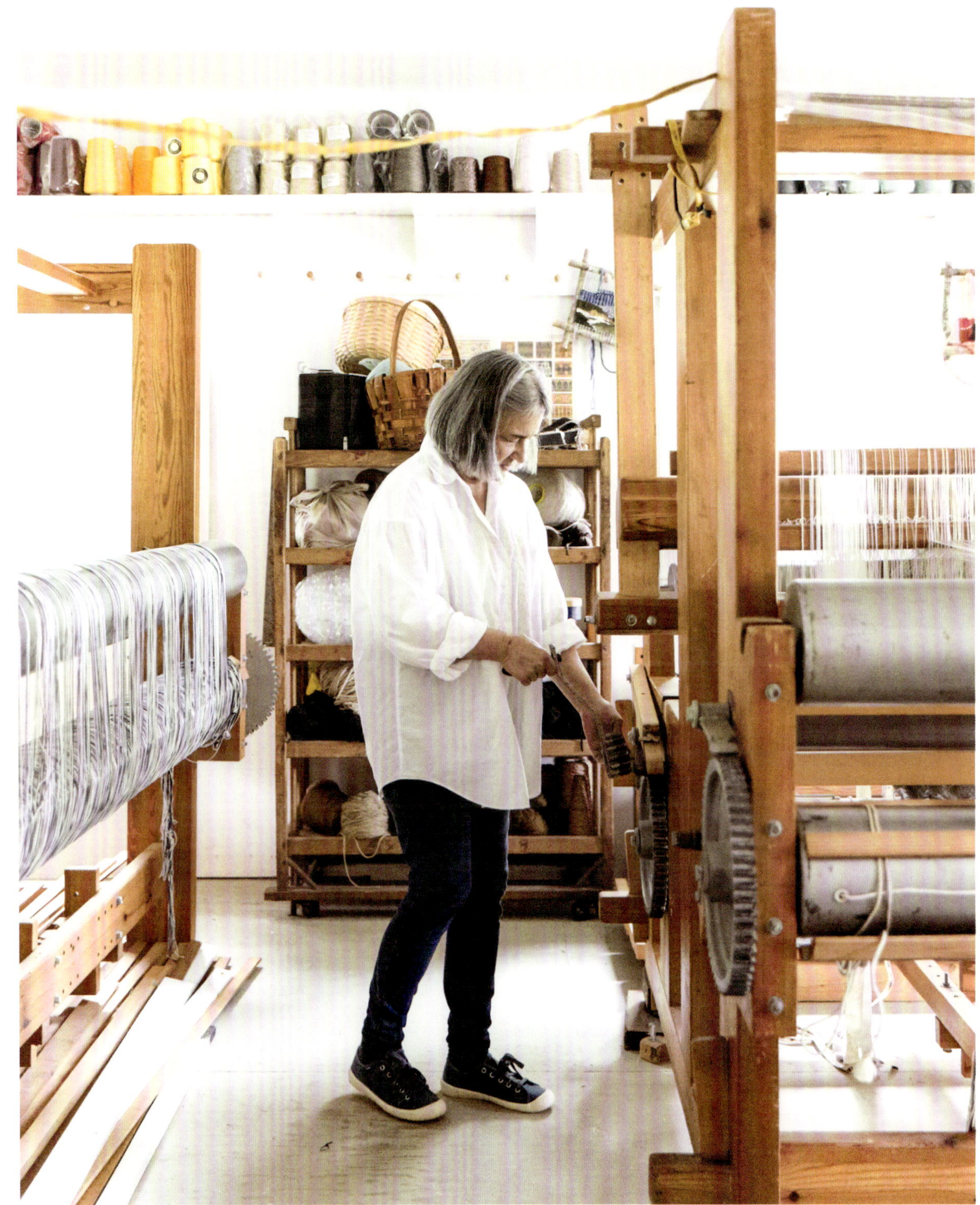

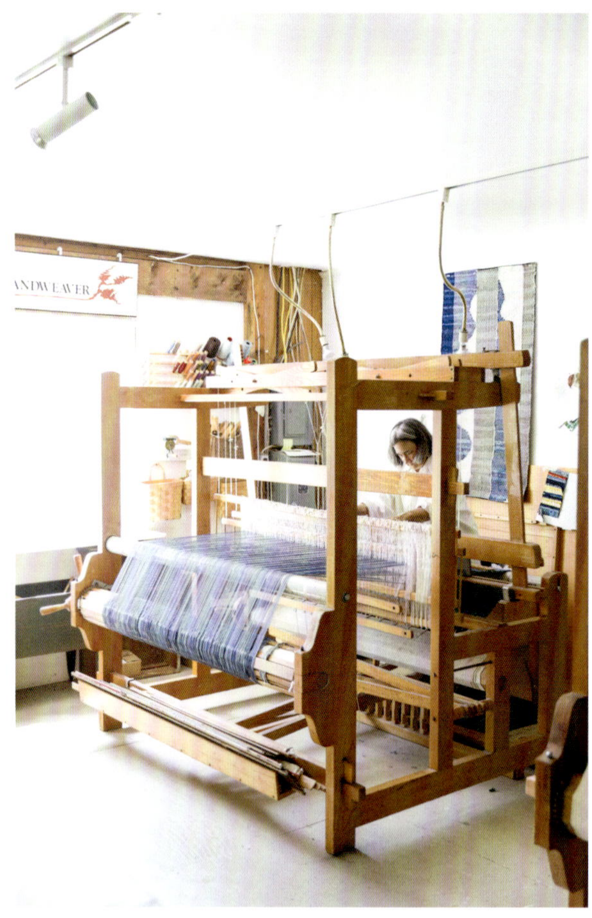

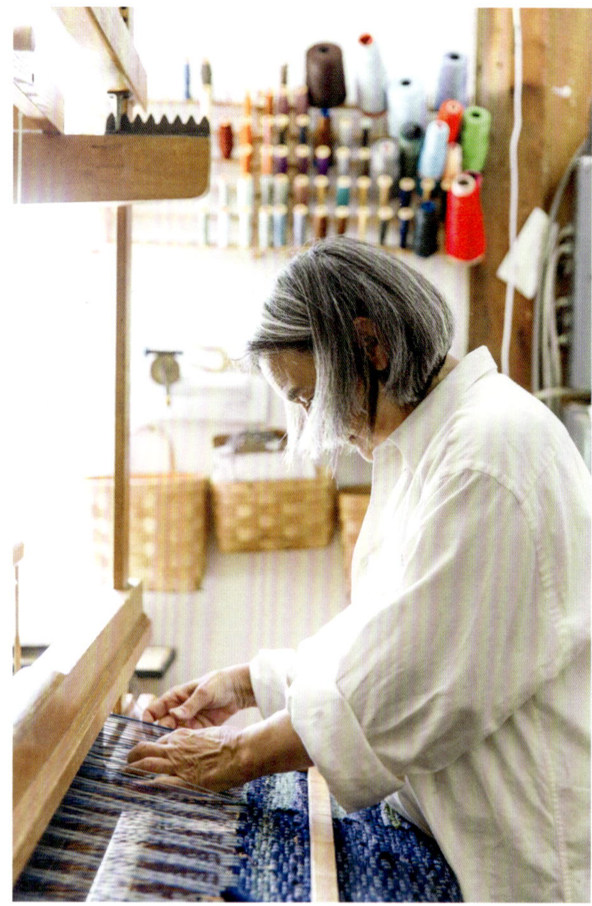

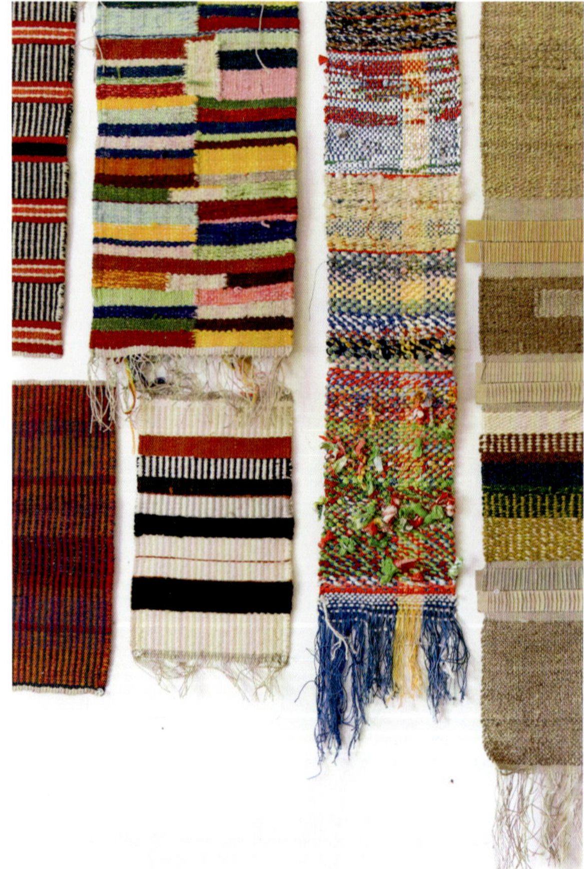

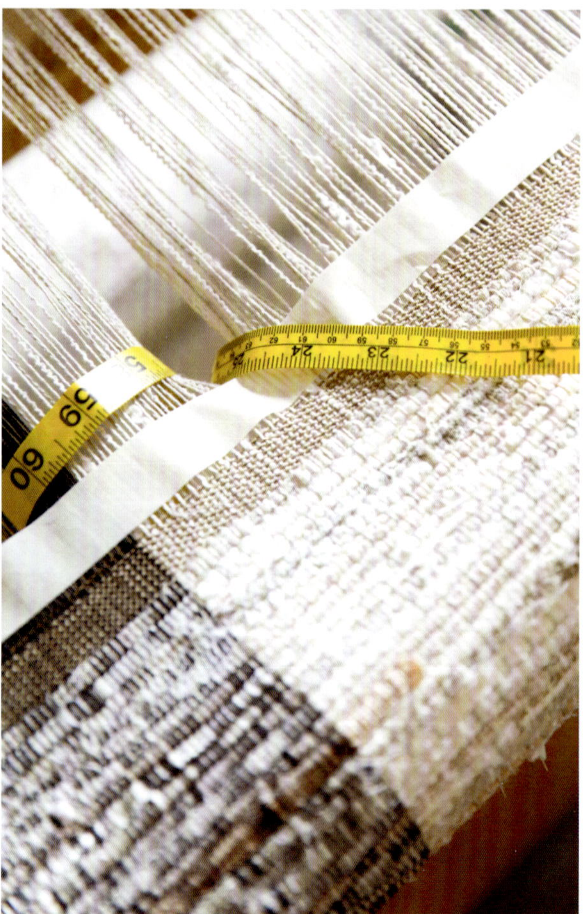

"When I was born." The real answer is slightly more complicated, but not by much. Like many young girls, she loved her dolls and looked up to her mother, who spent much of her time sewing and weaving. "I had dolls, and dolls needed clothes," she explains. "By the time I was in kindergarten, I was knitting them funky little sweaters." By third grade, she was sewing her own clothes by hand. As a young woman growing up in the 1960s, these domestic art forms were a practical and socially acceptable way to express her natural creativity.

As she grew older, Sara found herself experimenting more and more with color and technique. While her rugs are inspired by traditional tapestry weaving, they deviate from the ancient art form in several key ways. First, Sara uses swatches of fabric rather than yarn, which creates weavings with a very textural surface. Because of the thickness of the fabric, the warp threads are visible in the finished product. "In traditional tapestry weaving, everything is very smooth," she says. "But I like the bumps. They tell a story of the process." While they may be reminiscent of rag rugs, her pieces tend to be much larger and feature more intricate patterns, which Sara designs on graph paper. "I'm a bit of a Luddite," she admits. In her showroom, she has rugs with star patterns and flowers, geometric shapes and subtle ombré fades. The only kind of rug she truly doesn't like, she says, is a boring one.

Sara also frequently experiments with other fiber arts, creating pieces that are intended less for daily use and more for display. "This is the land of unfinished projects," she says with a smile, gesturing toward a picture frame that has been converted into a handloom. In the frame, a pattern of triangles and rectangles emerges from the rough weave, interrupted by pieces of grass and other natural elements. She refers to these pieces as "playing around." They're the work she does when time and money affords, when she isn't producing pieces on commission or working toward a financial goal.

"I've always made my living freelancing, but it can be very iffy," she says. She recalls the financial crash of the 1990s. "When it happened, I had just bought a house. The whole interior design industry and architecture industry fell completely flat. People weren't sprucing up their houses. I had a thriving wholesale business selling to stores and galleries, and then, all of a sudden, I didn't. I had to scramble and figure out how to hold it together and keep my house." She survived that harsh time—and the similarly difficult financial crisis of 2009—by "hunkering down." She drove her car as little as possible. She turned down the heat in her house. And she budgeted very carefully. "I remember walking around the grocery store trying to find as much healthy, nourishing food as I could for $10. I ate a lot of rice and beans," she says. "It wasn't as horrible for me as it was for others, but it did give me a real appreciation for what people go through." For that reason alone, Sara is grateful for the difficult times in her life. Hardship has made her empathetic and kind, as well as extremely self-reliant. "It made me sensitive to how people with low incomes are valued in this country. It was an important experience," she says. She admits to feeling frustrated by American society's attitude towards creative work, particularly crafts that have been traditionally practiced by women. "I think people devalue what women do. If weaving were a male profession, prices would probably be higher," she says.

Although she has learned to price her rugs appropriately over time, she has never felt entirely comfortable advocating for what she's worth. An important factor in pricing artistic work is accounting for the passive hours. For Sara, this is the time she spends away from her loom, thinking about each piece to come and observing the outside world. "I think it's hard for our culture to understand creative time," she says, giving voice to a phenomenon many makers and artists have observed. "People think I'm not working when really I'm thinking about design or just looking out the window and observing things." But that, says Sara, is precisely when her creative brain is most fertile. "Every nanosecond, artists are taking in visual, auditory, and verbal information," she explains. "It all goes into our brains, and it does something up there. And you need to give it quiet time to form. Everything I experience, the things I see—it all comes out in my weaving."

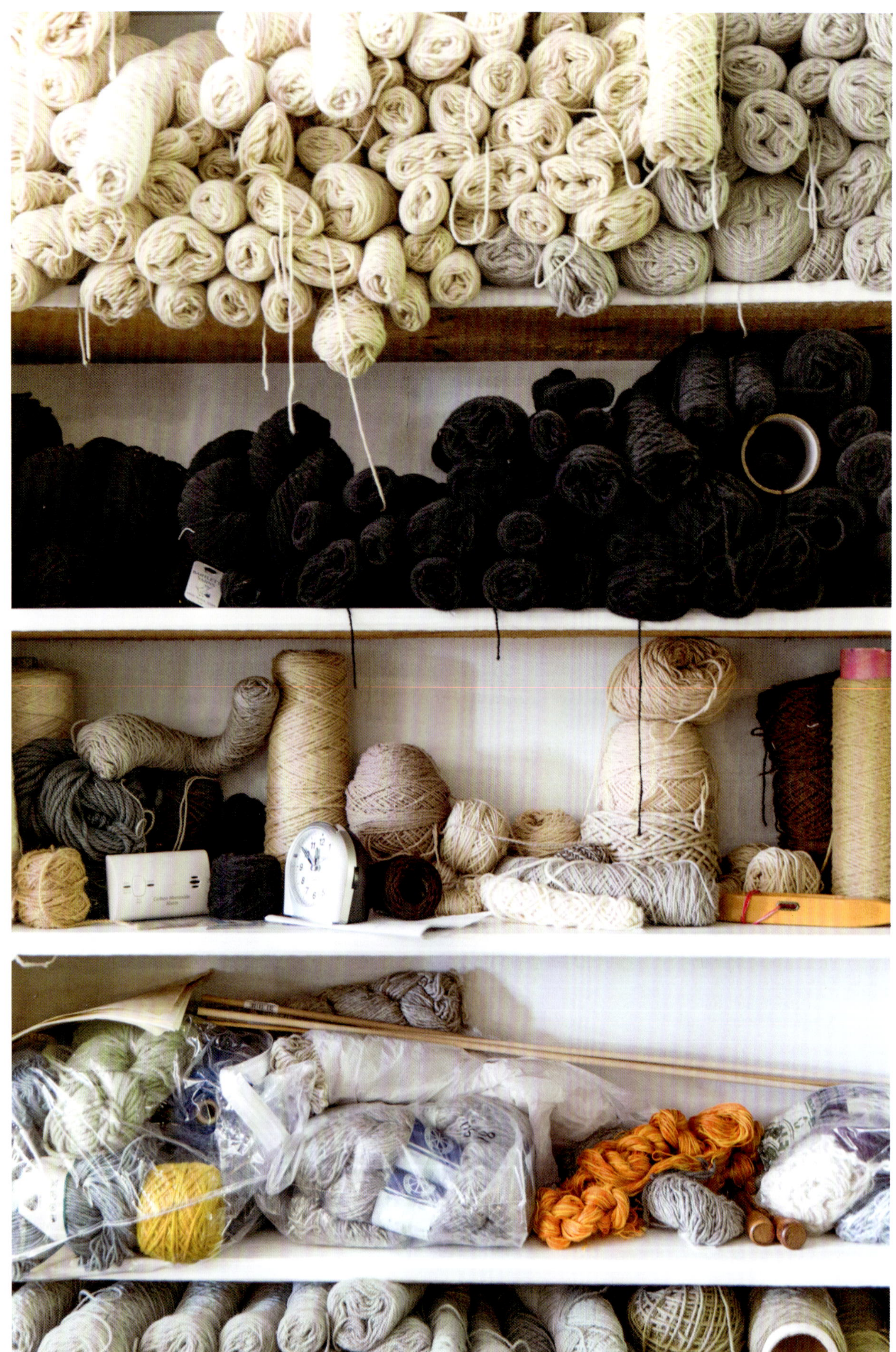

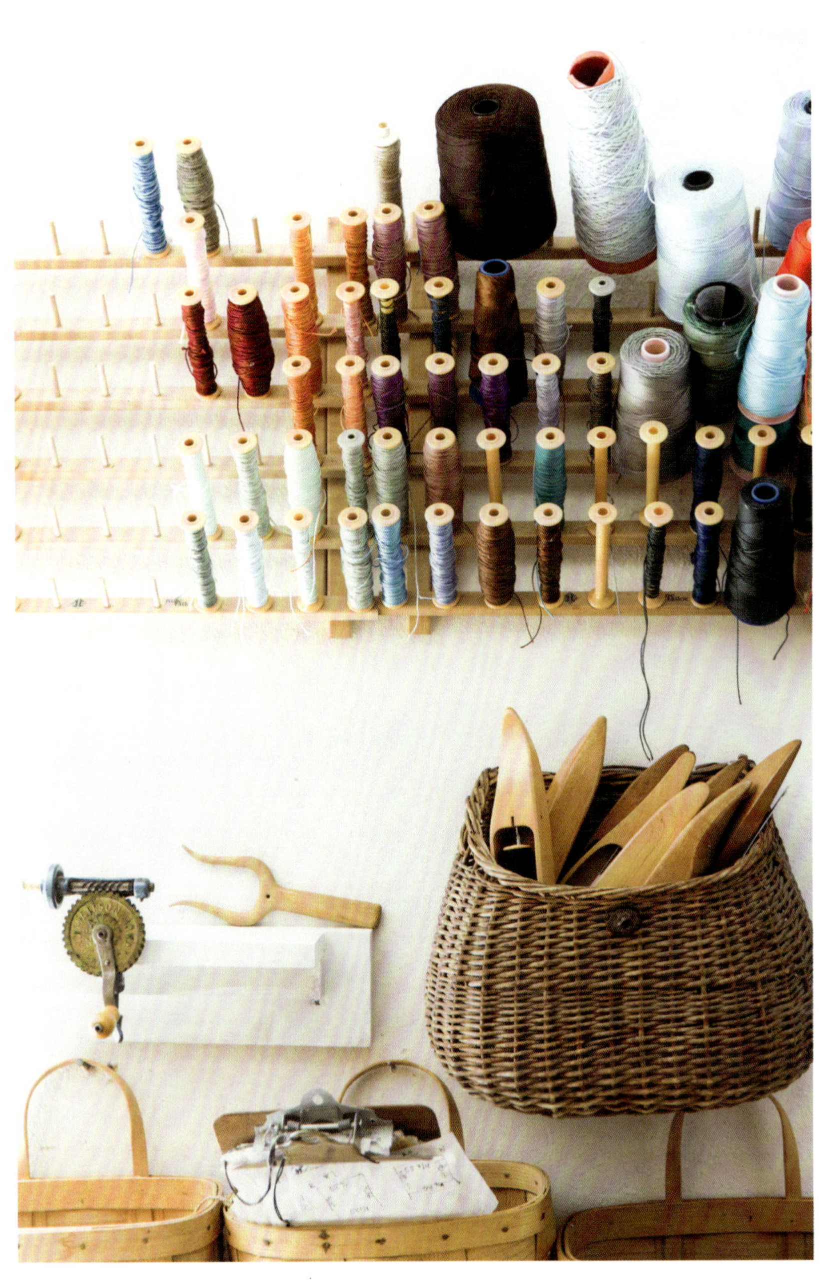

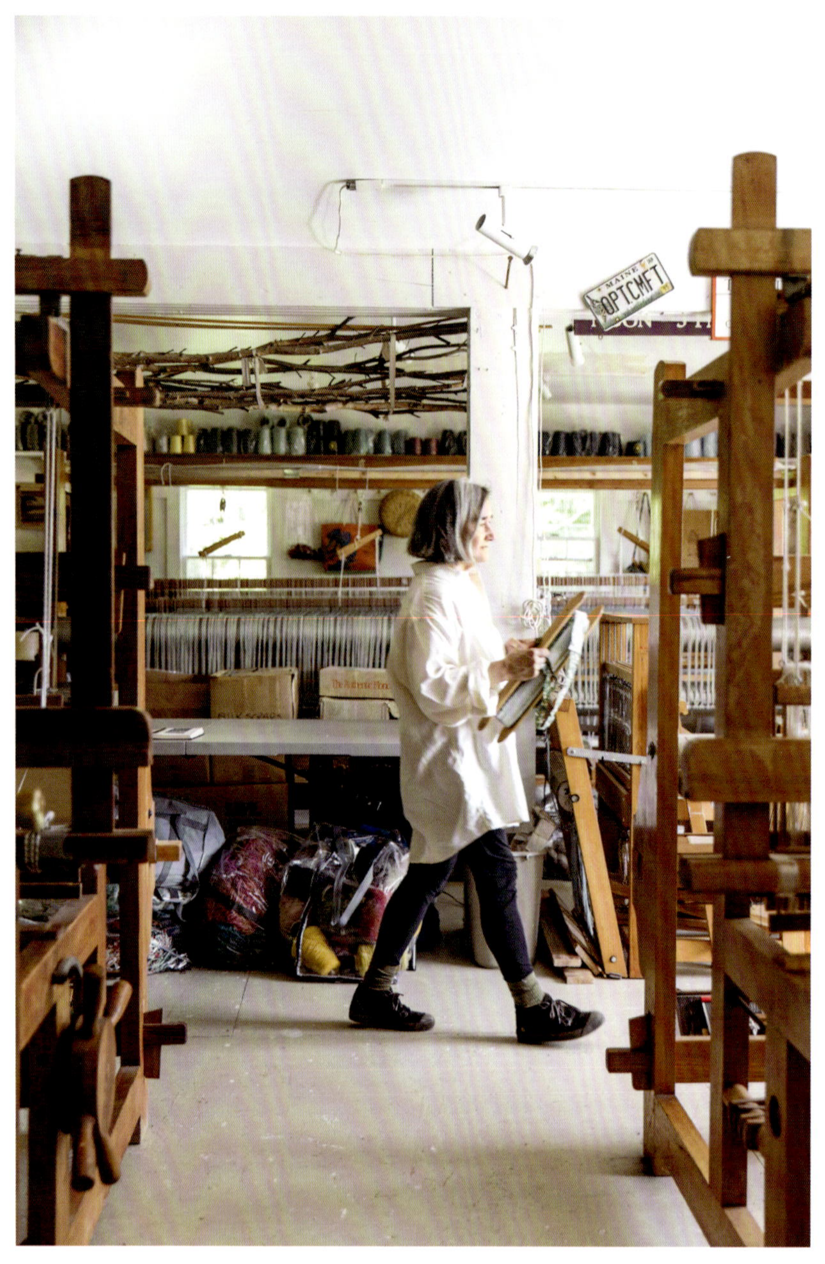
MAINE
OPTCMFT

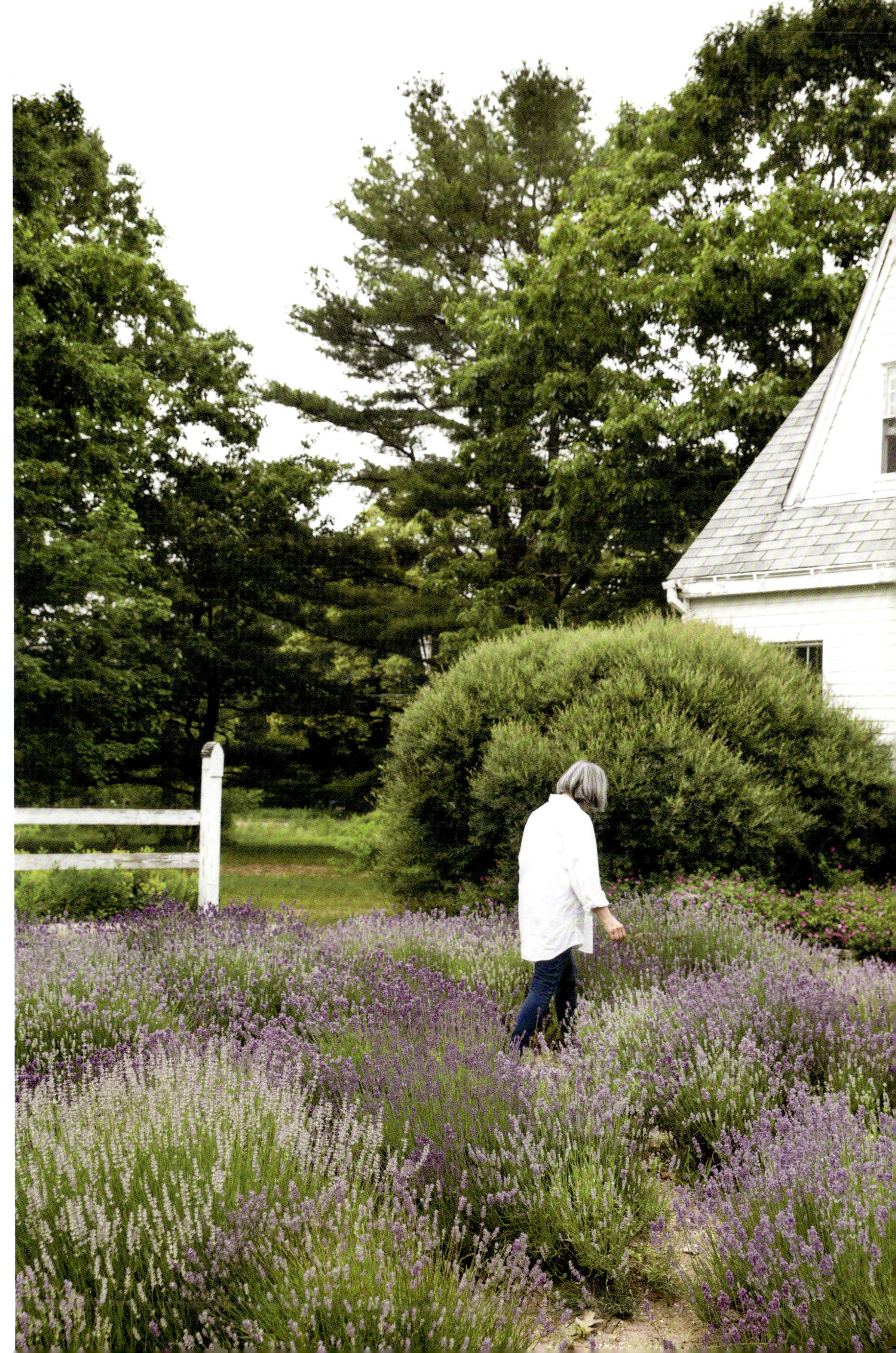

John Bisbee

Brunswick

"I find it very comforting to watch others make my art," says John Bisbee as his employee and former student, Elijah, manipulates a red-hot, twelve-inch nail into a series of corkscrew turns. After a moment, Elijah removes the nail from the clamp, places it on the workbench, hits it with a hammer, and dunks it in a bucket of water. The final product is a twisted piece of metal made up of two nails that spiral around each other like snakes. "It's not your best work," John says, leaning over the new creation. "This one," he points to the still-hot metal, "is too loose. The other one is too tight. They don't balance."

Elijah nods. He is clearly accustomed to John's sharp eye and judgment and appears unbothered. "John is the most popular art professor," he says. "Everyone wants to take his class. He's helped me figure out so much about my own work." Before leaving his post in 2016, John taught sculpture for twenty years at Bowdoin College and developed a loyal following among his students. It's easy to see why. He peppers his speech with jokes and references, moving quickly from one topic to another. His humming, high-strung energy bursts forth in frenetic movements as he speaks. He doesn't appear to sit still for long, and even when he does, he nods his head or taps his foot, jiggling his legs as though he is trying to keep warm.

John's artistic output reveals a similar kind of forceful, swift motion. Made entirely of nails, his large-scale sculptures reel between repetitive, Escheresque patterns (massive swirls or honeycomb shapes) and organic chaos (nails fused into haystacks or windblown lines). Surprisingly, he started his career as a potter, a much gentler art that failed to capture his full attention. He moved next to glass-blowing, but found the "overbearing machismo" of his instructors off-putting. Finally, in his final years at Alfred University in upstate New York, he started hanging around the metal shop and learning from the welders. "I was making these mediocre found-object assemblages," he says. "At the time, if you weren't working with stone and steel, you were doing feminine work." He doesn't need to scoff to convey his distain for this kind of thinking. John has never liked authority, bureaucracy, or social conventions. Liberal and outspoken, his offbeat manner has created some trouble for him over the years, particularly at academic institutions where hierarchy is imposed upon

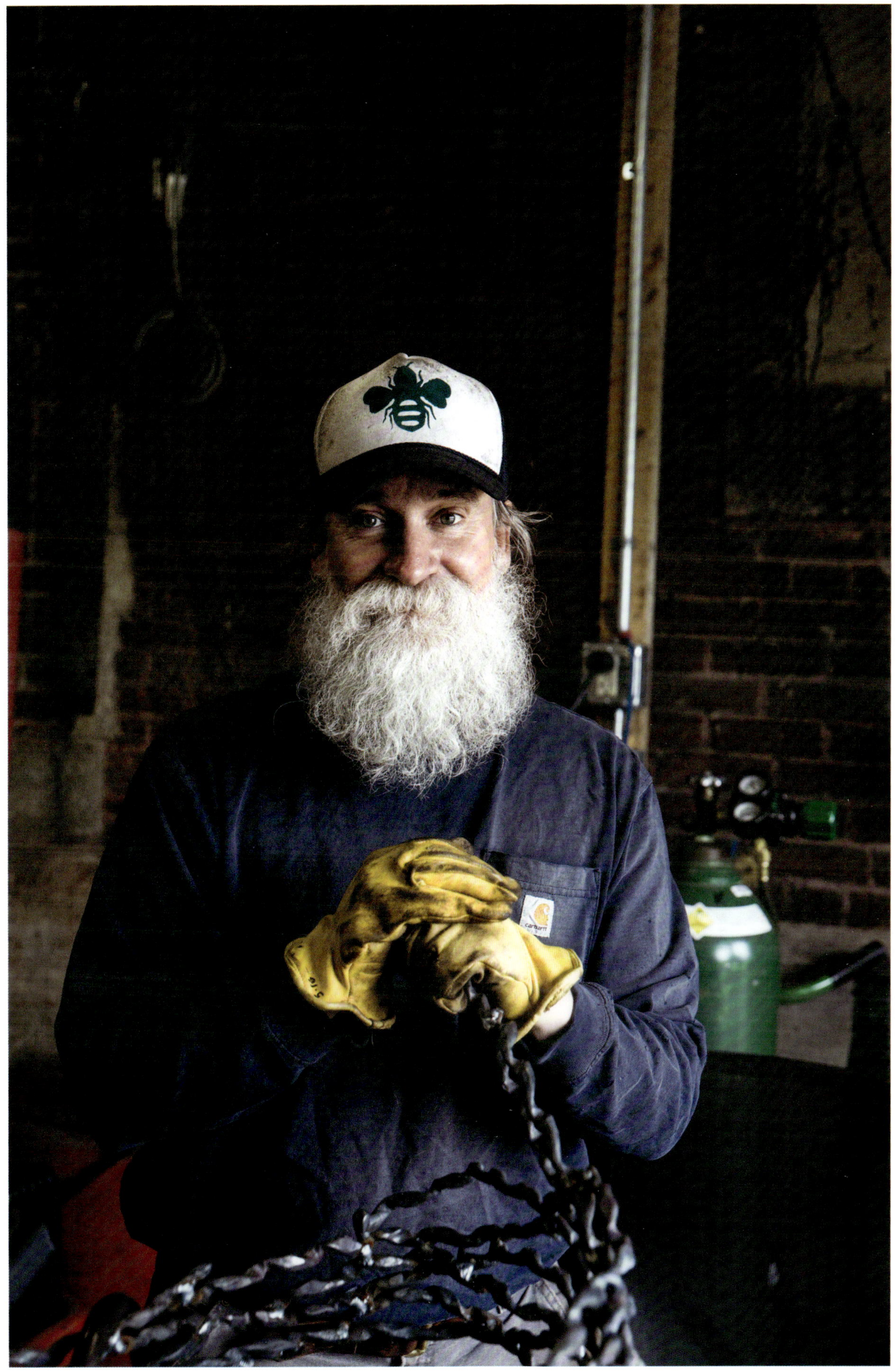

even the most popular professors. But if this bothers John, he doesn't let on. "Willy Nelson has this great quote: 'It's important to be hated by the right people,'" he says with a sly nod. "I think that's true."

John's massive, unwieldy sculptures are loved by the right people. Many pieces have been purchased by art institutions, universities (including the University of Notre Dame and Harvard University), private collectors, and corporations. But while these sales help pay the bills, John admits that he is most excited when his art appears in public spaces. His work has been shown at the Pennsylvania College of Art and Design Gallery, the Savannah College of Art and Design Museum of Art, the Shelburne Museum in Vermont, and Maine's Portland Museum of Art. In 2016, he was pleased to see a large, horn-shaped sculpture, *Heresy*, moved from an indoor gallery space, where docents would stop guests from touching or interacting with the heavy metal piece, to the freedom of the PMA'S garden. "I want people to have free, unplanned, spontaneous experiences with art."

John may be unpredictable and freewheeling in conversation and action, but his art reveals a brutal adherence to pattern and replication, planning and precision. Every piece comprises thousands of nails fused together using the process of arc welding, by which an electrical current is sent through the metal, heating the electrodes and fusing them at the point of contact. As he creates a metal column, sparks fly though the air of his small studio space in Fort Andross Mill. The musty smell of burnt dust mingles with the scent of a lightning storm—the sharp odor of ozone—as the metal slumps slowly and deliberately, conforming to a shape. "I can be too uptight," John admits. "I've killed things before by being too uptight." He places a hand on a cobalt blue machine that dominates one side of his studio.

"I bought this guy because of the name—power hammer," he says. "At the time, I felt like I was running out of ideas. I had been working with nails and I didn't know where to go next." He didn't want to abandon his material of choice, but he felt he was becoming static, rigid, and not as plastic as he needed to be. Then, like a bolt of lighting, he asked himself the right question: What does a nail want? "A nail," he says, "always wants a hammer."

He uses the power hammer to twist nails into spiraling spikes, manipulating the twelve-inch spears of metal into imperfect rods before fusing them together to create his massive sculptures. Some take the barbed spherical form of burrs or viruses, repeating patterns that are affixed to a wall; others are freestanding columns or spheres, hulking pieces that stand three or four feet tall. Still others seem to grow from the ground, hedges of nails that march, one by one, across his upstairs storage space, where dozens of finished pieces wait to be moved to their final homes. Today, he is creating a sculpture for an upcoming gallery show in New York. "I want this piece to be rough and honest," he explains, "A little slinky and unformed."

John is excited to find out what the finished work will be. Right now, it looks like a suspended fisherman's net. Unlike many of his sculptures, it is not densely packed or tightly constructed. "I'm getting a little panicked that I don't have an exact handle on this one," he admits, pulling off his leather gloves. He removes the dark lens shield from his eyes and walks to the other side of his cramped studio. On the nearby table sit several beer cans. He bypasses these for a large mug of coffee and sips quietly for a moment. "It's scary not knowing where I'm headed," he confides. "But that's the excitement and the thrill. I'm just jumping off a cliff and trying to do something new every time."

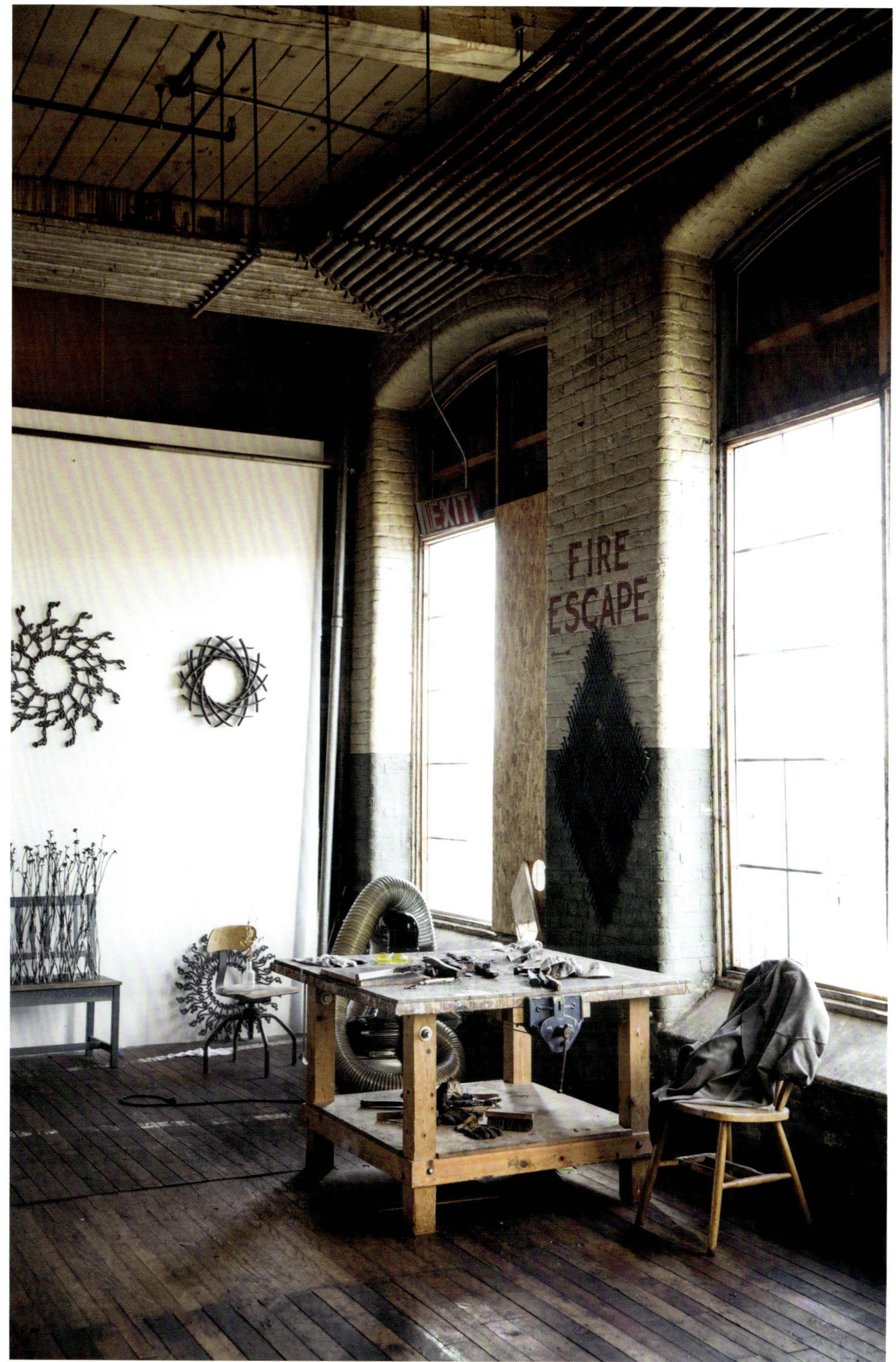
EXIT
FIRE
ESCAPE

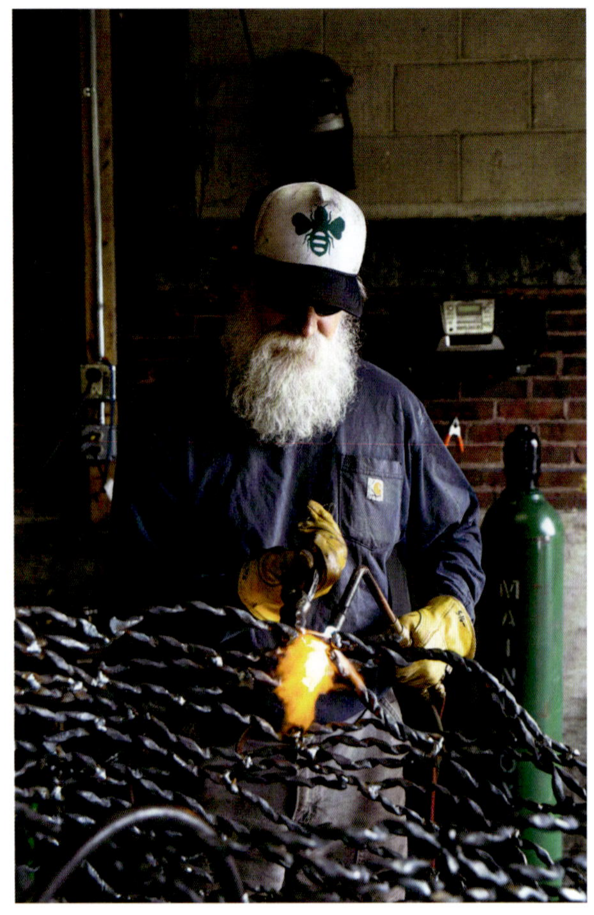

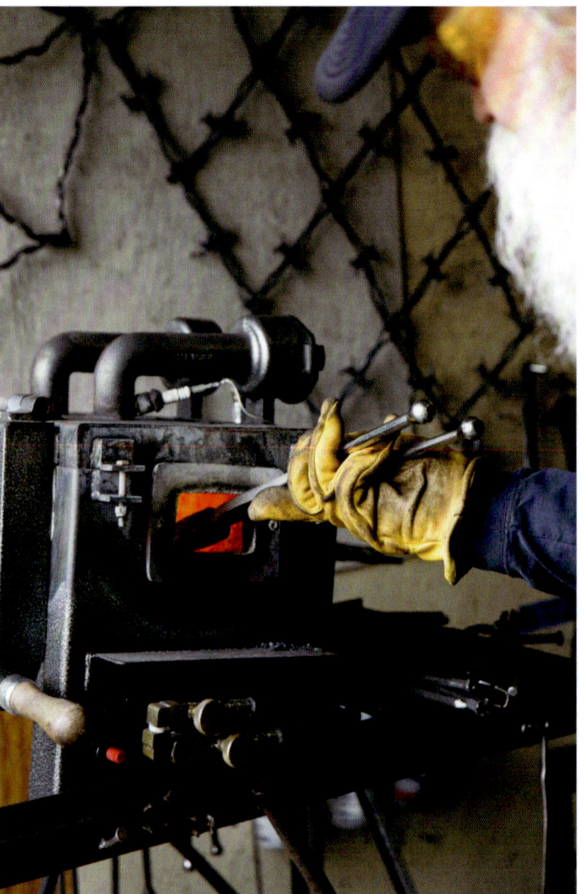

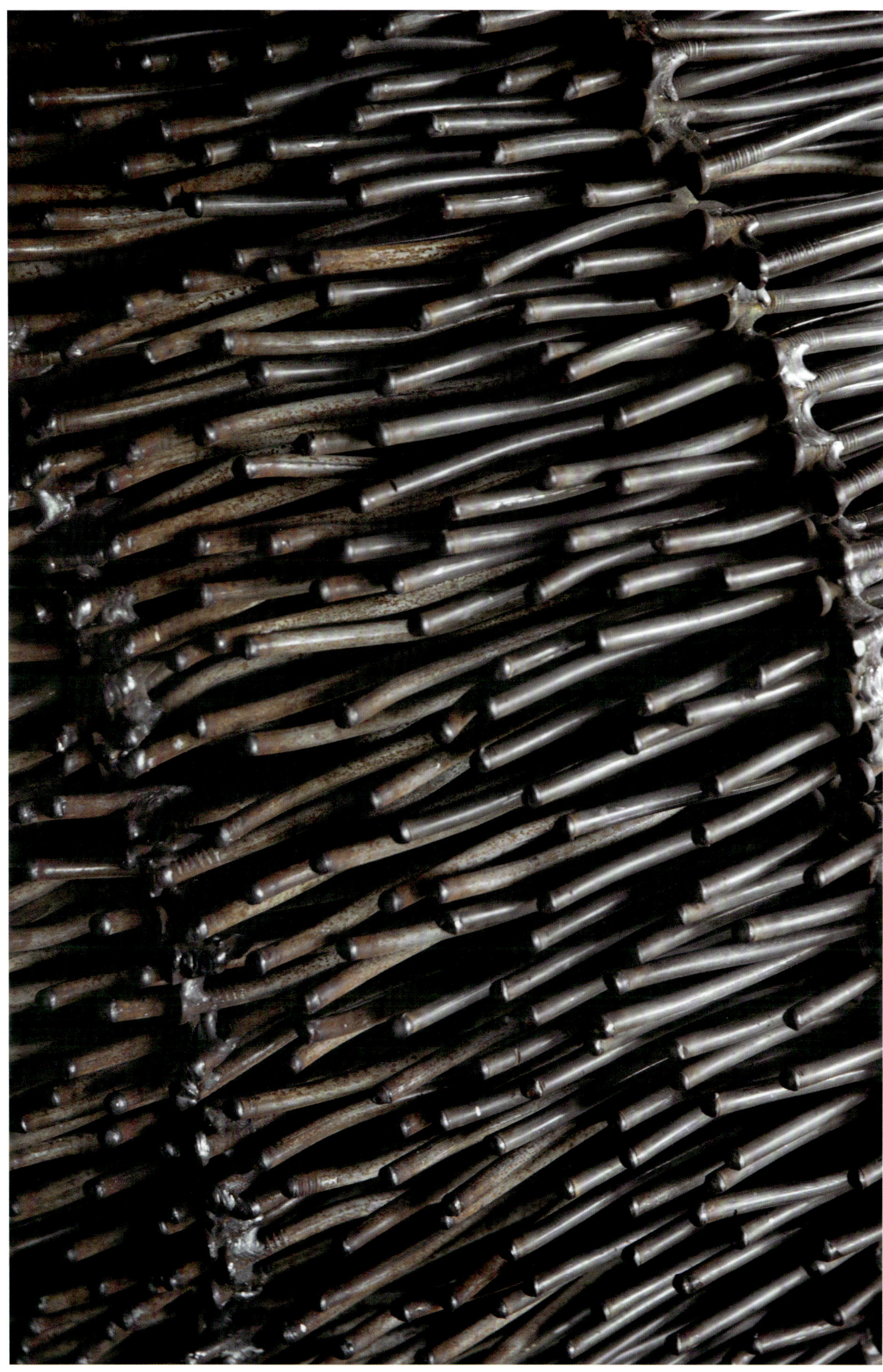

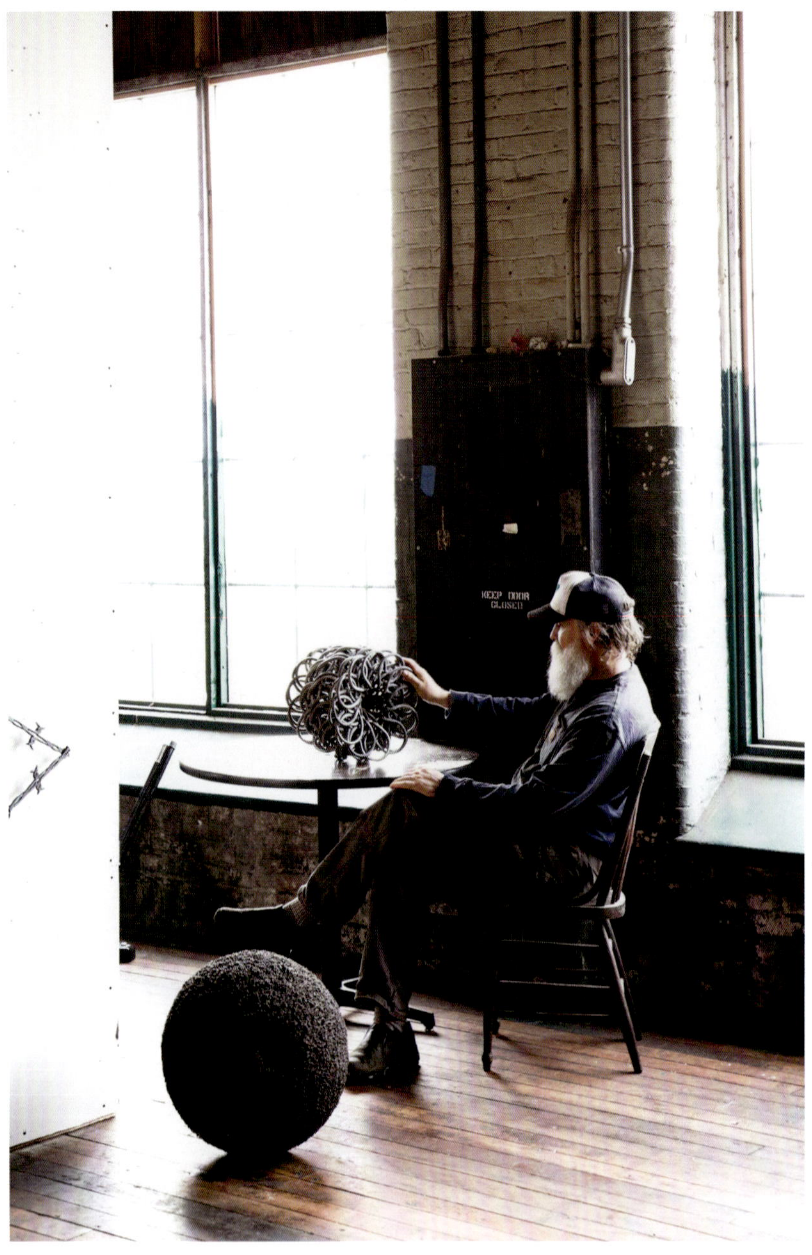
KEEP DOOR
CLOSED

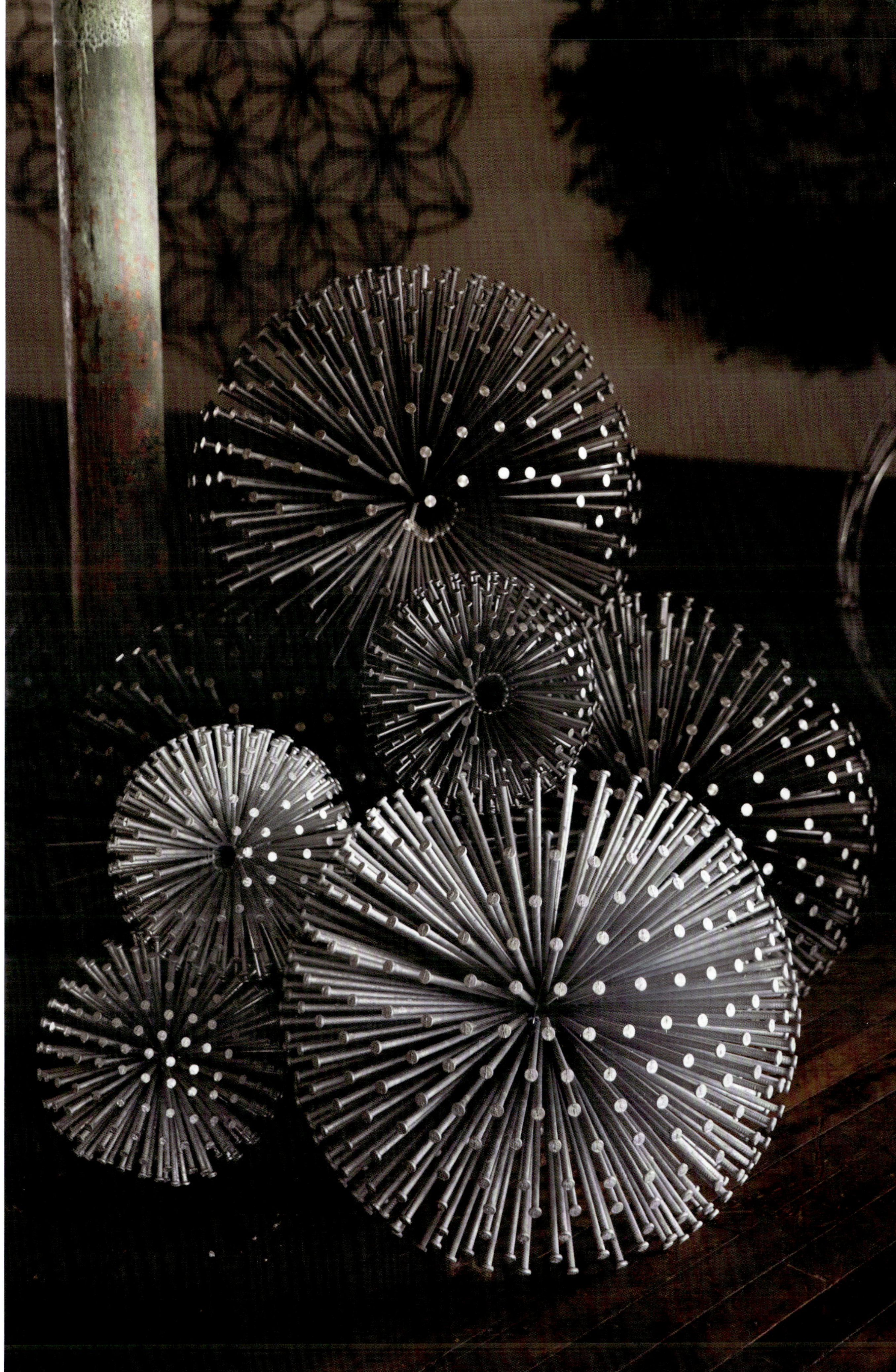

Farrell & Co.

Biddeford

Meg Farrell arrived at her creative destination after a series of twists and turns. The designer did not always know that her medium was leather. She was not a little girl dreaming of handbags. Farrell & Co. was born out of a practical demand rather than a romantic impulse: she needed a wallet.

At the time, Meg was living with her boyfriend (now husband), Greg Mitchell, on David's Folly Farm in Brooksville. The couple had left New York City, where they both attended college, to try the rural lifestyle. "I was in my early twenties and I was really struggling in New York. I was working as a nanny, but this was 2009. The country was deep in the recession. Though I loved the family I was working for, I knew I didn't want to be a nanny for the rest of my life," she explains. She knew she loved to make art—she had studied photography at Parsons School of Design and graduated at the top of her class—but a deep, painful feeling of discouragement had set in. She recalls receiving a packet with information about her student loans after graduating. "It was staggering," she says. "I lost my desire to practice photography. I lost my desire to do anything." And so rather than fighting to earn a living in a city crowded with young creatives, she and Greg decided to try farming.

The depression that had descended upon her in New York lifted in Maine, but unfortunately farming wasn't filling the creative void and she wasn't truly happy. "I was sewing my own clothes. I learned weaving and knitting. I loved it, but it didn't feel satisfying to me, not like photography did," she says. While she relished the opportunity to work with her hands, she didn't feel as though her artistic impulses were being channeled in the right direction. But Meg kept going, trying each new medium, hoping that she would find the perfect balance between purposeful work and expressive creation. When she picked up an awl in 2011, she didn't know where it would lead. She simply wanted a nice, well-made leather wallet, and she couldn't afford to buy one. "Even though the first few things I made weren't incredible—looking back, they're really pretty janky—I found working with leather so satisfying," she says. "It was the first time in years I'd felt happy with something I'd made. Photography is heady and conceptual, while leather is so hands-on. It's not as intellectual,

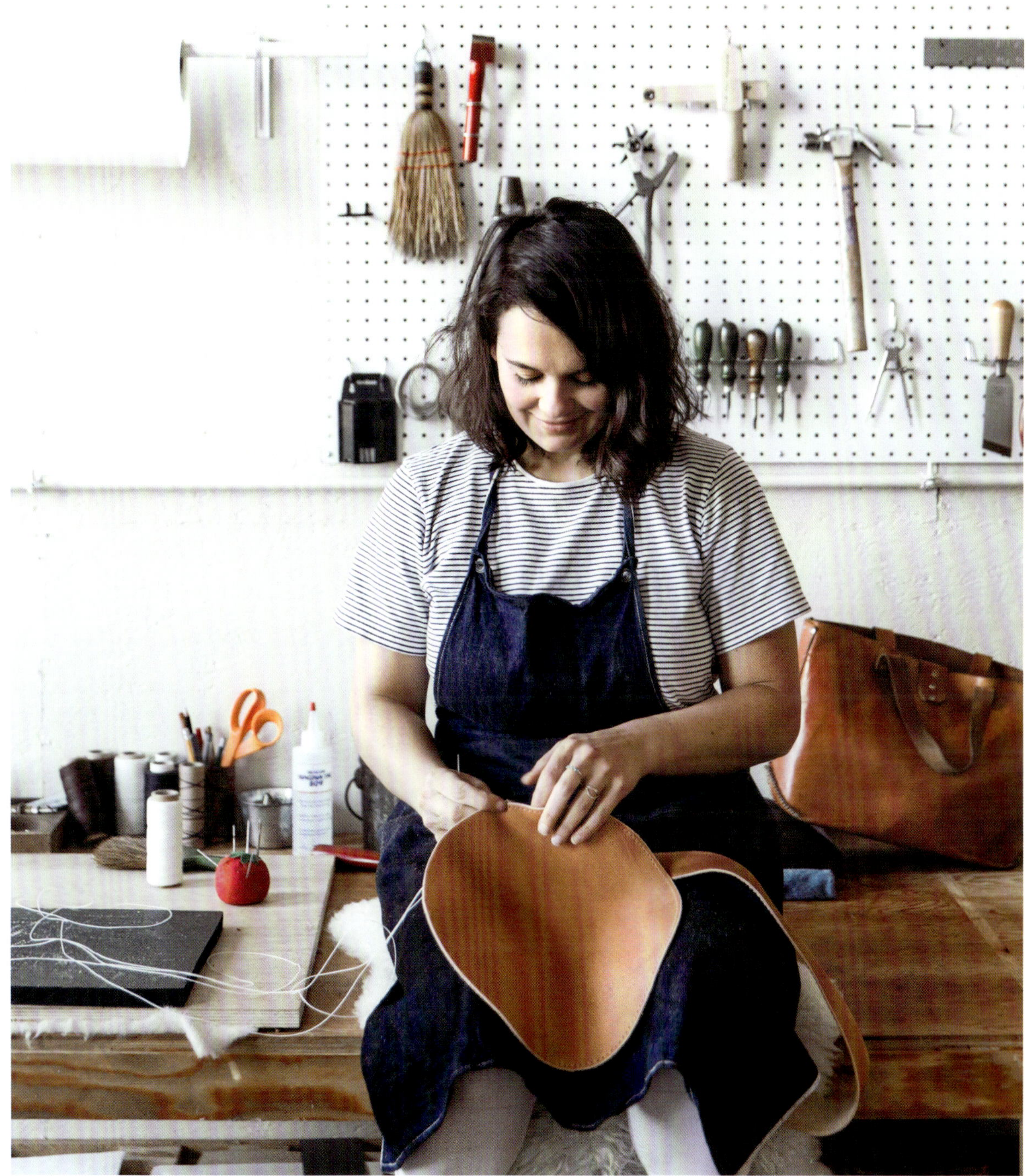

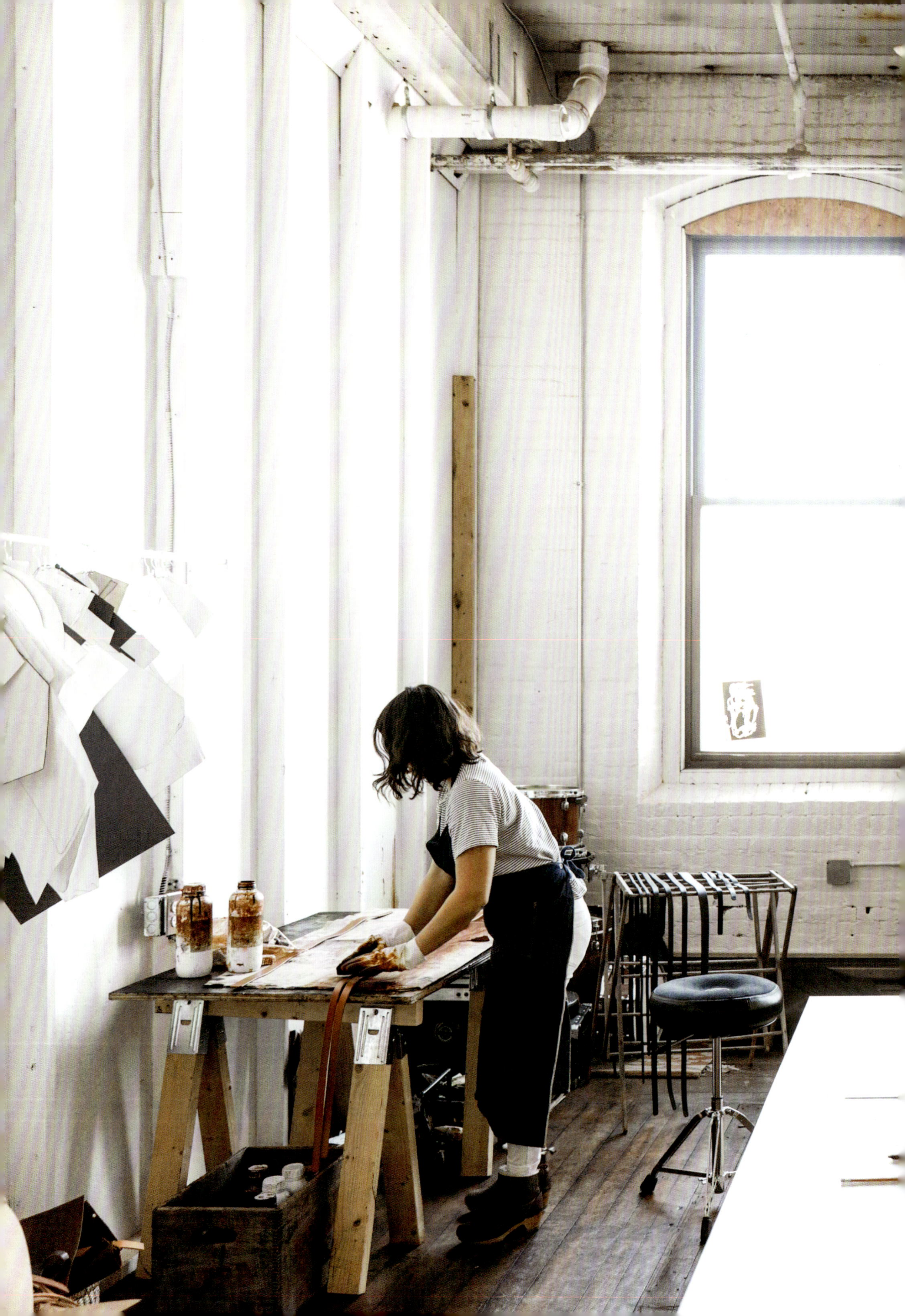

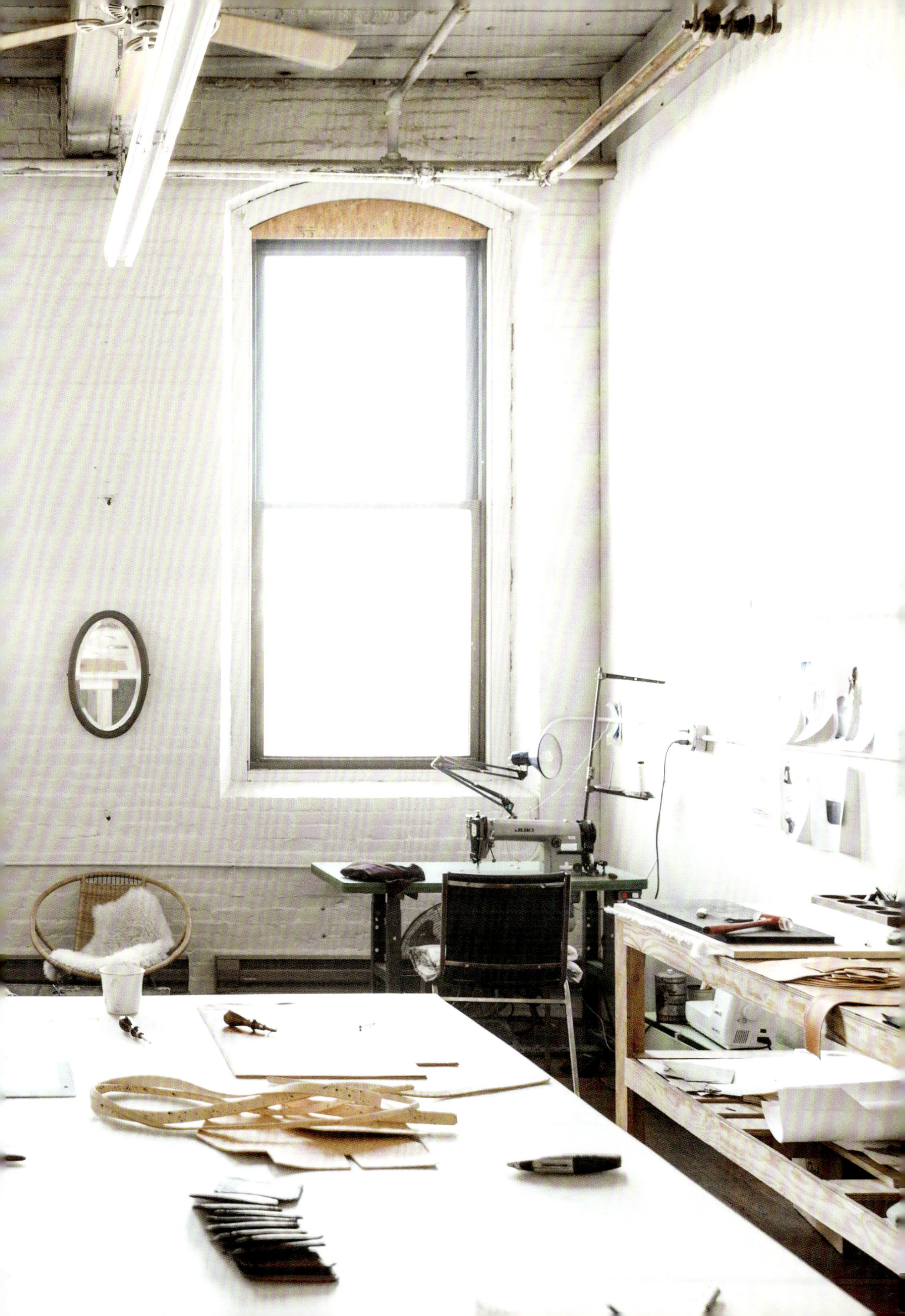

but I felt a similar sense of satisfaction from the work. And so I didn't stop."

Fast forward three years, Farrell & Co. occupies a studio in Biddeford in an old brick building with big windows and lots of light, Meg's bags can be found in boutiques around Maine and New England, and she is hard at work on a custom order, dying small pieces of leather for a series of wallets and cardholders that an unnamed client, a "successful yacht dealer," will gift to his best customers.

Meg's work is deceptively simple but it has progressed substantially since she began working with leather. While her early bags reveal the restrained elegance that still characterizes her creations, they do not display the same deft workmanship. Over the years, she has learned which awls are most effective, which snaps and rivets hold up under heavy wear, and which threads work best for stitching leather (Meg prefers nylon to linen, which she feels isn't as durable). While her bags aren't entirely unisex, the former tomboy strives to make subtle, geometric designs that wouldn't feel out of place with a suit or blazer (or in Maine, a flannel work shirt). Her most immediately recognizable item is a semicircular handbag that closes with a snap flap. Spend enough time in Portland on the weekend and you're bound to see these distinctive leather moons hanging from the arms of well-dressed city dwellers.

Meg is the first to admit that she's not going to create the next "It Bag." Although she follows fashion—and has a great sense of personal style—she doesn't want to create a status bag. For inspiration, she turns to "vintage bags and timeless, classic, natural leather items" rather than the current issue of *Vogue*. She works primarily in shades of tan, black, and occasionally oxblood red. "Leather has a beautiful texture and look to it. The way it ages is wonderful. It gets a lovely patina, a rich color and smooth texture," she explains. Anyone who has handled a well-worn leather purse knows the buttery soft feeling of aged leather. With time, Meg's bags will acquire that same look and feel—or so she hopes. "I will always fix my bags for free. I want these to be heirloom pieces. I want moms to hand them down to their daughters, and for them to hand them down to *their* daughters." For a moment, the bright and cheerful young woman turns uncharacteristically serious and says, "I want my pieces to last forever."

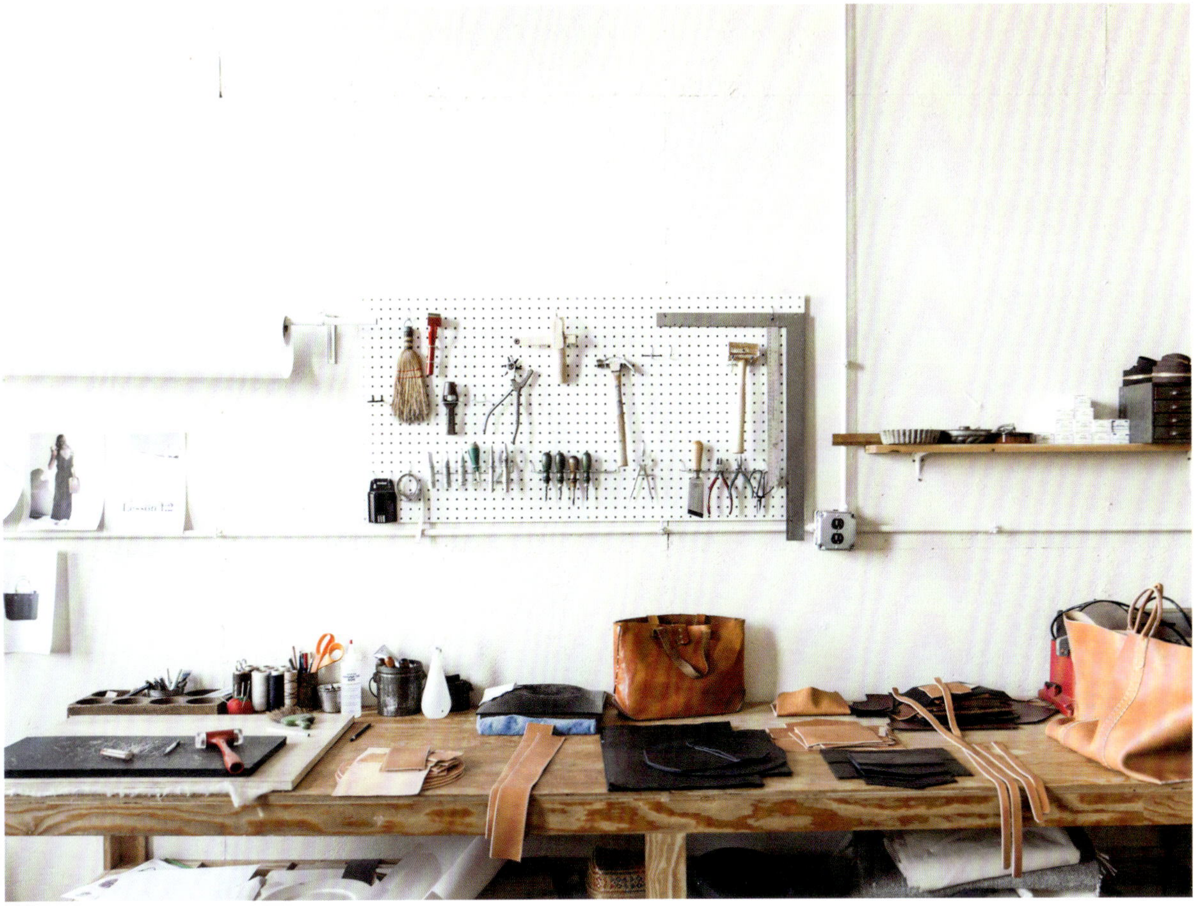

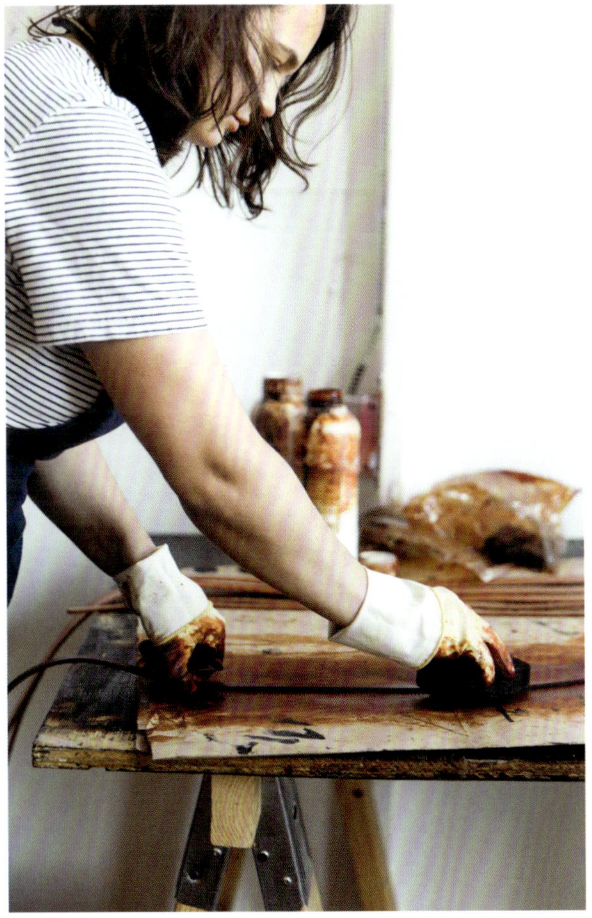

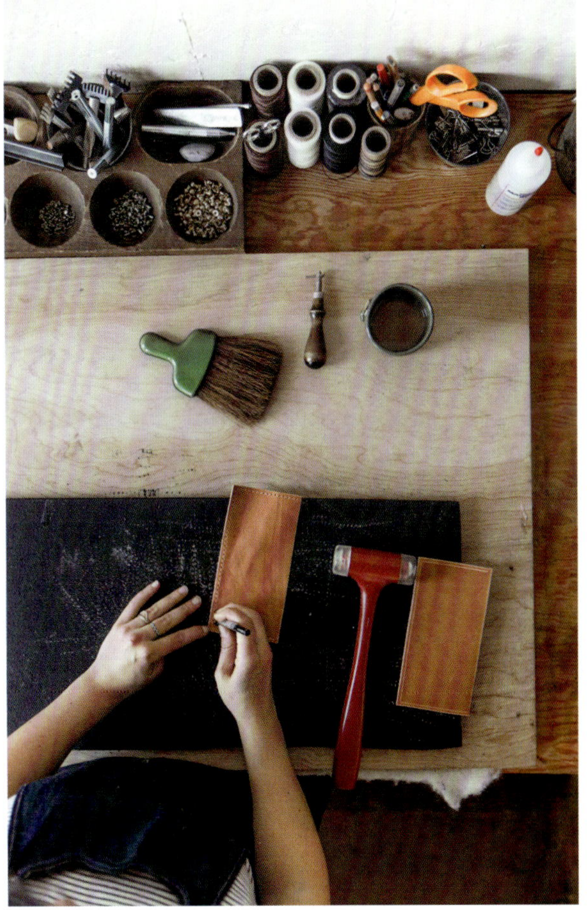

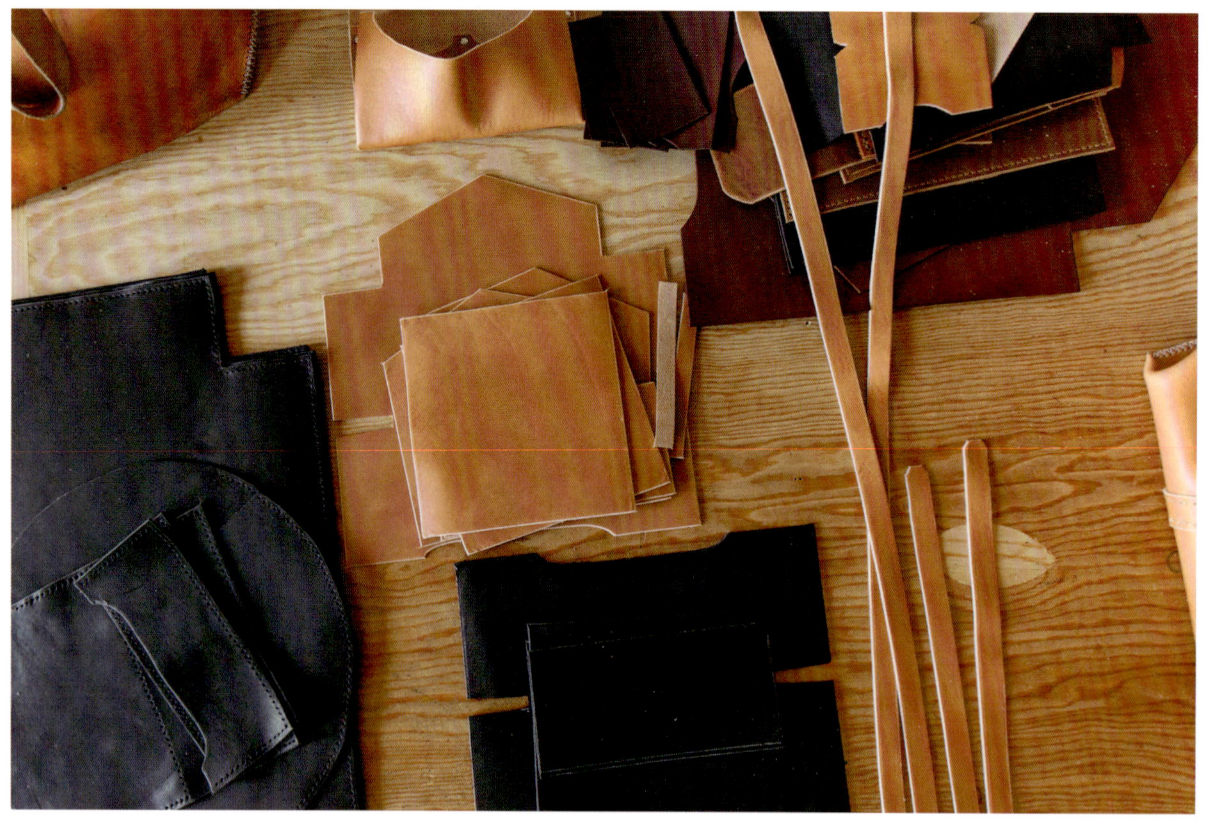

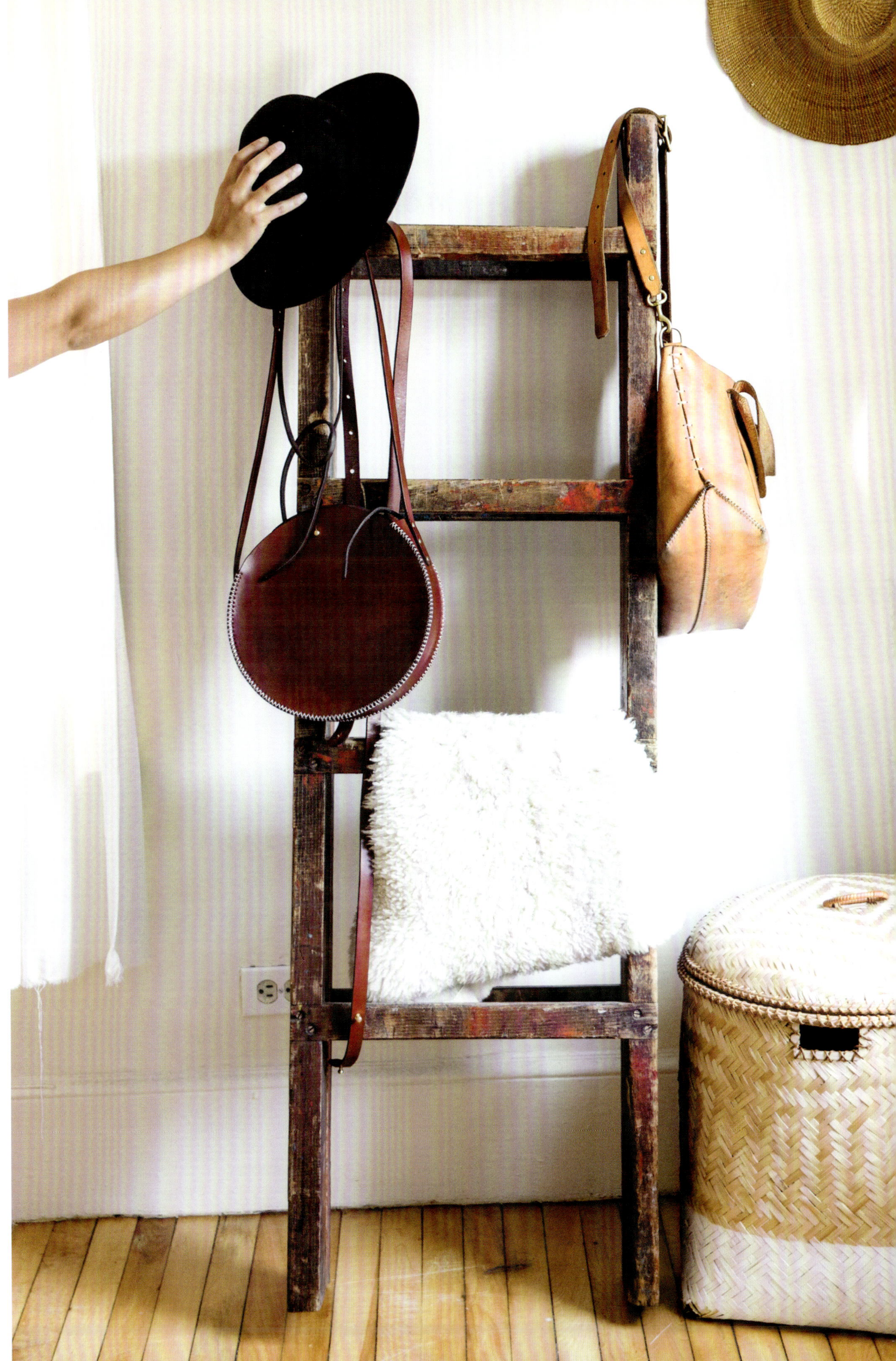

Ray Murphy

Hancock

As Ray Murphy creates his chainsaw sculptures he alternates rapidly between short, intentional movements and wide, sweeping gestures. The chainsaw looks like a toy in his hands as he bobs and weaves around the tree trunk, pulling new life from within its cylindrical shape. The harsh buzzing of the chainsaw fills the air and small pieces of wood fly up to land in his beard and wild gray hair. He tips the end of the saw into the trunk and slices sections of hardwood as easily as you might slice a carrot. From the trunk emerges a sitting bear, a massive lobster claw, or a spread-winged eagle displaying chiseled, stylized feathers. Later, he will return to these large wooden sculptures to add color, sometimes with a paintbrush or a spray can, and sometimes with a blowtorch, turning the blond wood first earth-brown, then a deep, carbon black.

Ray is not a shy man. He's a natural performer with a wicked sense of humor and a rough sort of charisma that has earned him a following among visitors who drive this commercial stretch of Maine's Route 1 to visit his woodshop. And you can't miss it. Large sculptures sit alongside thick tree trunks and piles of lumber. The roughly hand-painted sign on the side of a long, rustic warehouse—CHAINSAW ARTIST LIVE SHOW—beckons the curious into Ray's handmade theater, the stage set for nightly performances choreographed by Ray himself to a soundtrack of classic "rock 'n' roll." A spotlight shines on the artist, goggles covering his face, white beard catching flying flecks of sawdust, as he saws stumps into animated wooden animals—open-jawed bears, graceful whales, even goofy, cross-eyed clams. He cautioned, "Don't call it carving. I've had many an inept scribbler call it that, but I don't carve. Period. I saw."

Modern road trippers are familiar with chainsaw art but that wasn't always the case. When Ray first began creating his unusual pieces he was the only sawyer on the scene. "I was ten years old when I discovered the chainsaw," he remembers. "I got a spanking." His wince turns to laughter. His parents weren't pleased that their ten-year-old son was playing with such a dangerous tool. But Ray wasn't deterred. "I was the founder of this art and the first one to ever do it." His early work was "crude stuff," he says. For his first sculpture in 1952, at age ten, Ray sawed his name into a piece of firewood.

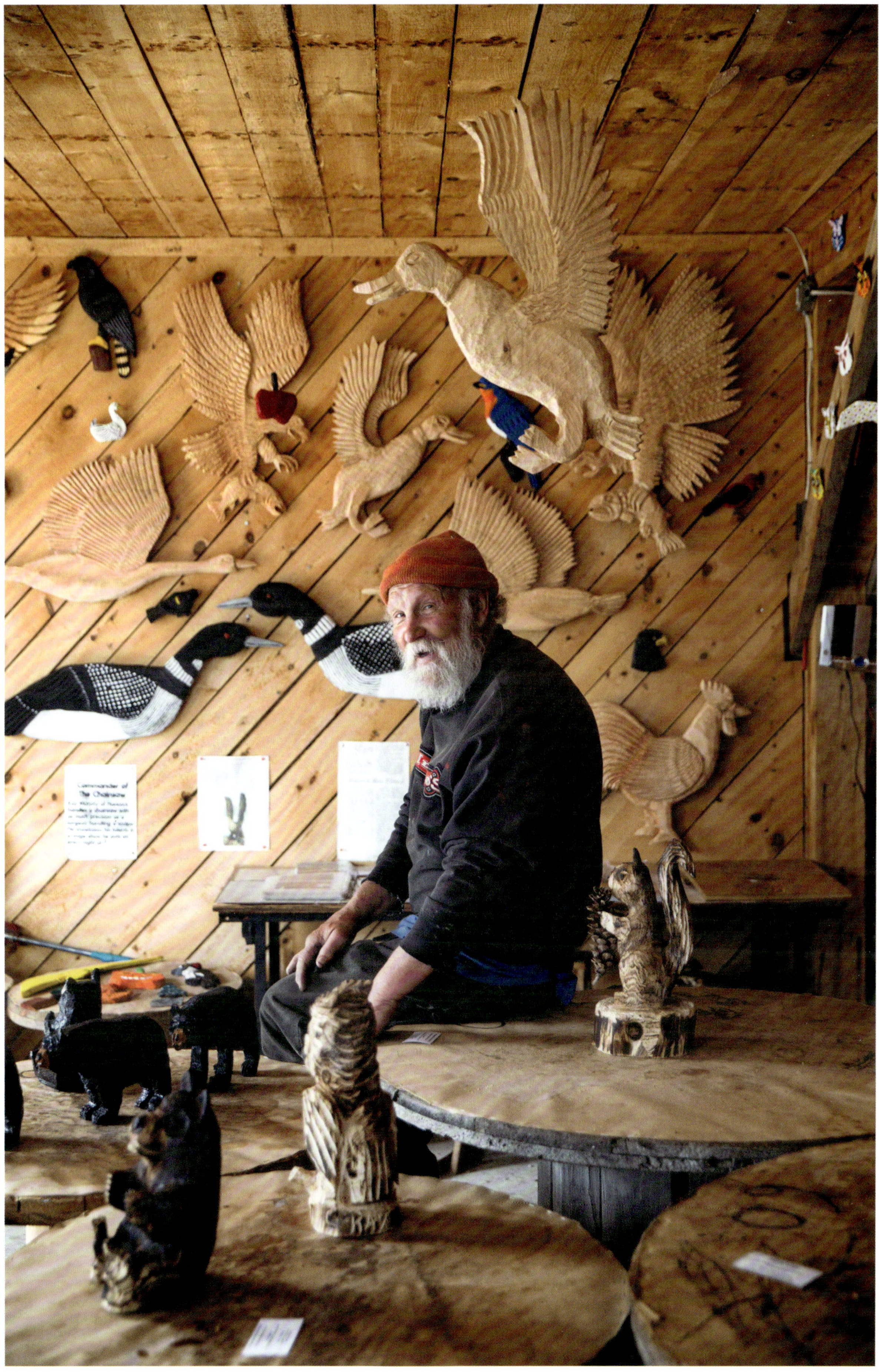

(Ever since, the signature "RAYe" authenticates each piece.) At age eleven, he began making three-dimensional sculptures of animals and a year later he mounted his first performance for an audience of siblings and neighbors. Half Shoshone and one of twelve children, Ray was born and raised on a Wyoming reservation where he observed first-hand the pain and addiction that continues to plague his people. He also learned a fierce sense of pride. "Think about this," he says, using the chainsaw to punctuate his point before setting it back on the ground. "Lewis and Clark never would have made it to the west coast if they hadn't taken Sacagawea. And would you believe it? Sacagawea was the sister to my great-great-grandpa!"

Now much of his art references his native heritage, from freestanding totem poles to two-dimensional hawk-nosed figures wearing elaborate headdresses. "Life on the reservation was hard," Ray says later, growing somber for a moment. "There's not much there and drugs and alcohol are very prevalent. The thing is, the apple don't fall far from the tree. My dad was a drunk. My grandfather was a drunk." Ray has been sober now for thirty-nine years. His preferred tool hasn't just shaped his life; it also saved him from alcoholism. "The chainsaw sobered me up," he confides. "I spent forty-seven hours straight behind a chainsaw just south of Rapid City, South Dakota. It kept me from drinking."

Although his insistence on using the term "saw" may be confusing at first, there is something deeply human and relatable about his desire to control his own narrative. Ray, for his part, views himself as a mythological figure of sorts and he has worked hard to become the man he is today, the first of a kind: the Shoshone chainsaw artist. The artist is also a masterful storyteller. And his optimism, expressed in the soft, gravely tones of the former smoker, is part of what makes Ray such a compelling character, a self-described "wild mountain man" with a big heart. Sentences punctuated with hyperbole and the occasional curse, and fantastical displays that toy with the truth convince the listener that he is the kind of man who could tell a tall tale. Honestly, it is hard to tell whether or not his tales are tall. His life has been strange enough that it is possible that all his eccentric stories are true.

Chainsaw in hand, Ray Murphy hacks away at the stuff of life and forces this world to make space for his big personality, his daring visions, and his savage chainsaw creatures. And, when some part of it or another no longer suits him, he pulls out his blow-torch and burns it away until nothing is left but ashes and smoke.

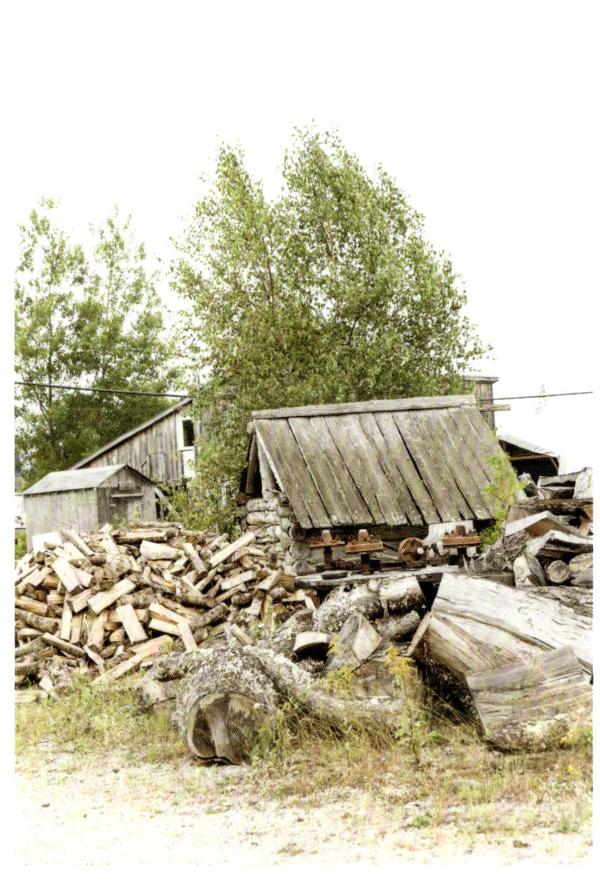

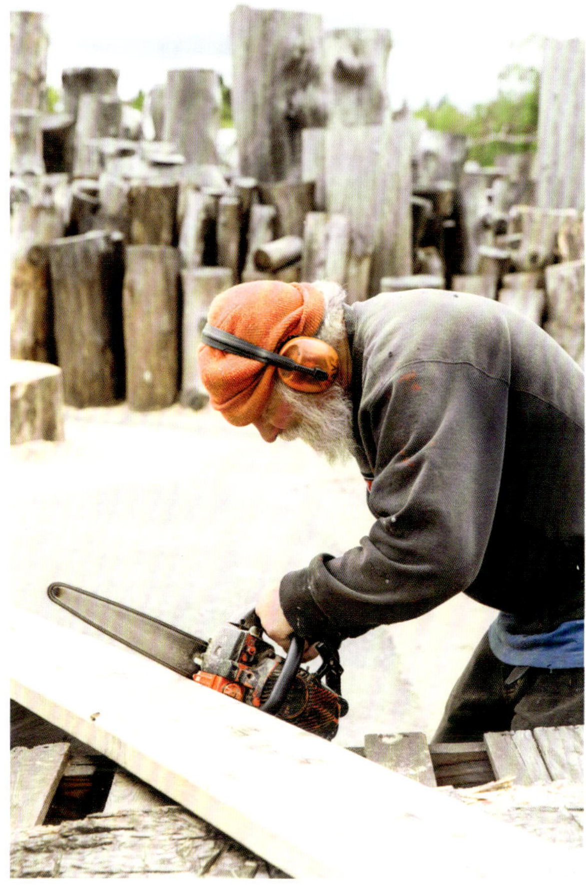

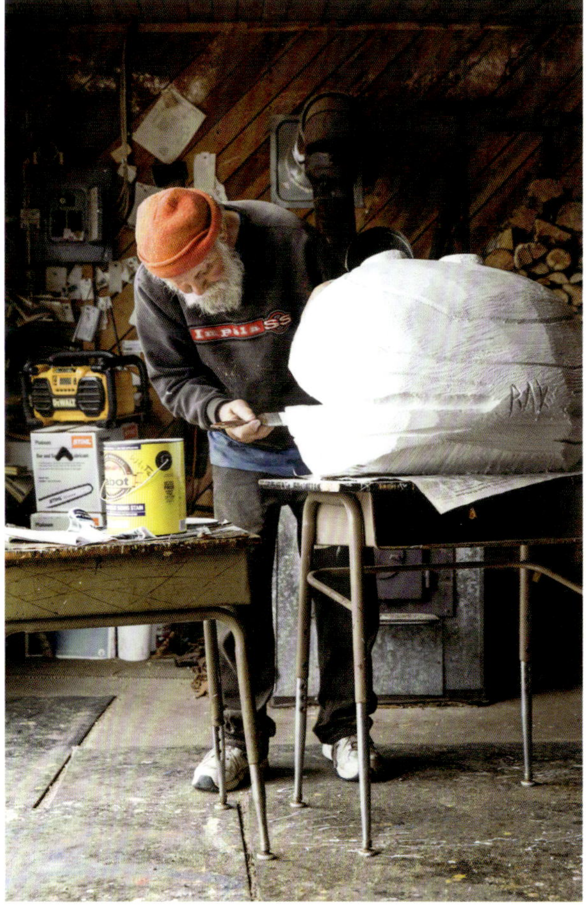

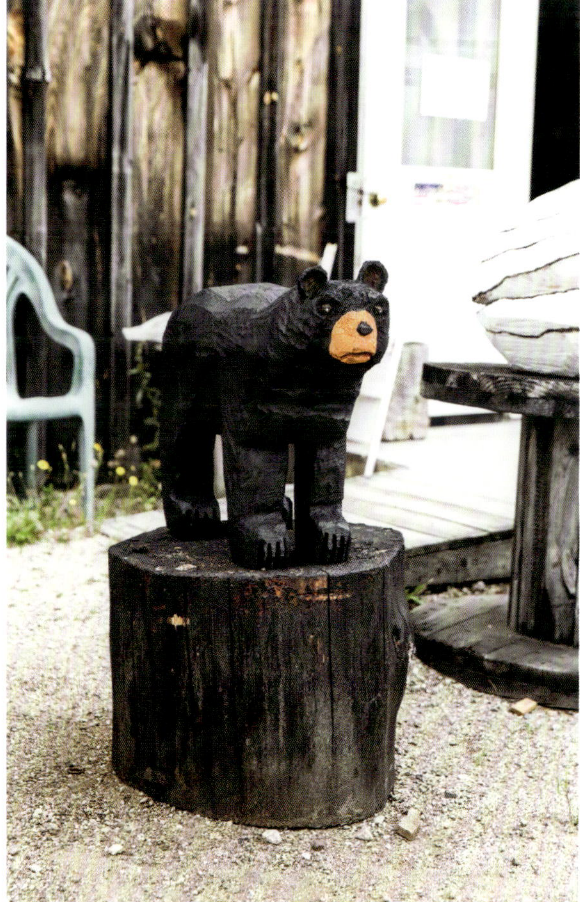

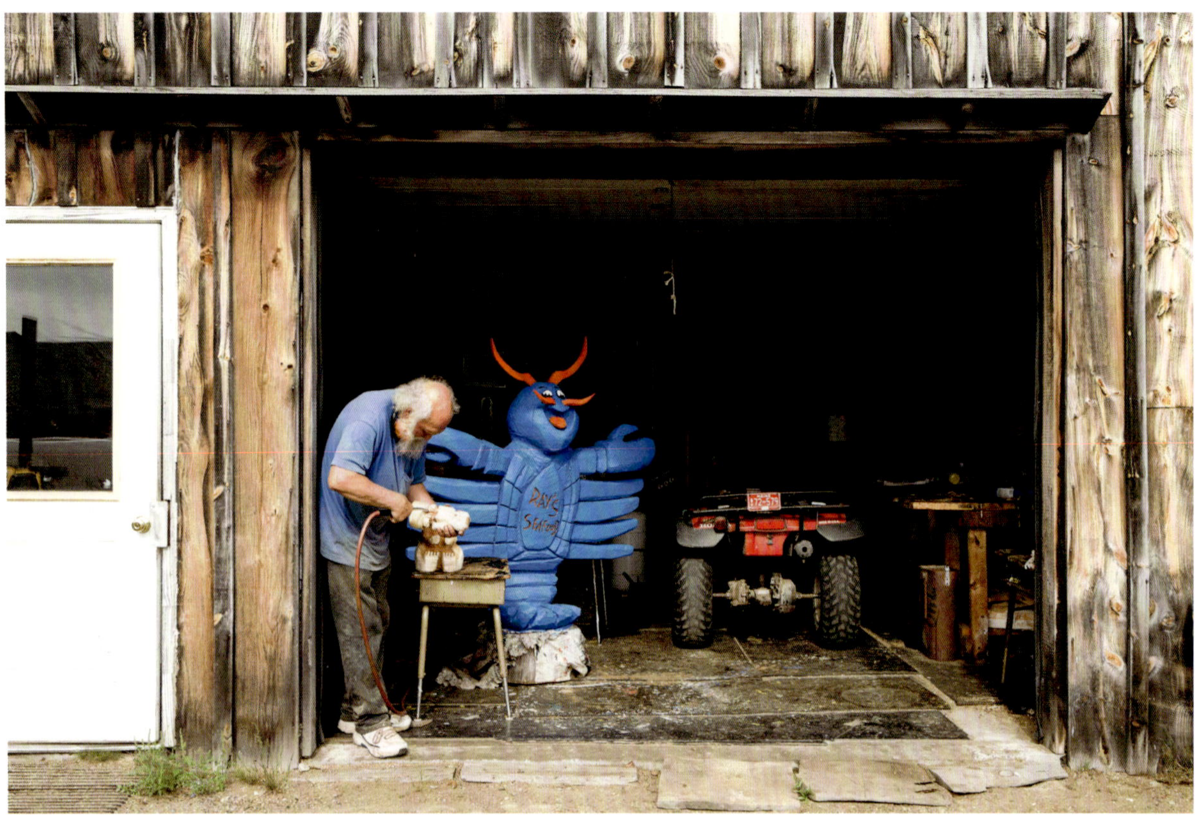
RAY'S

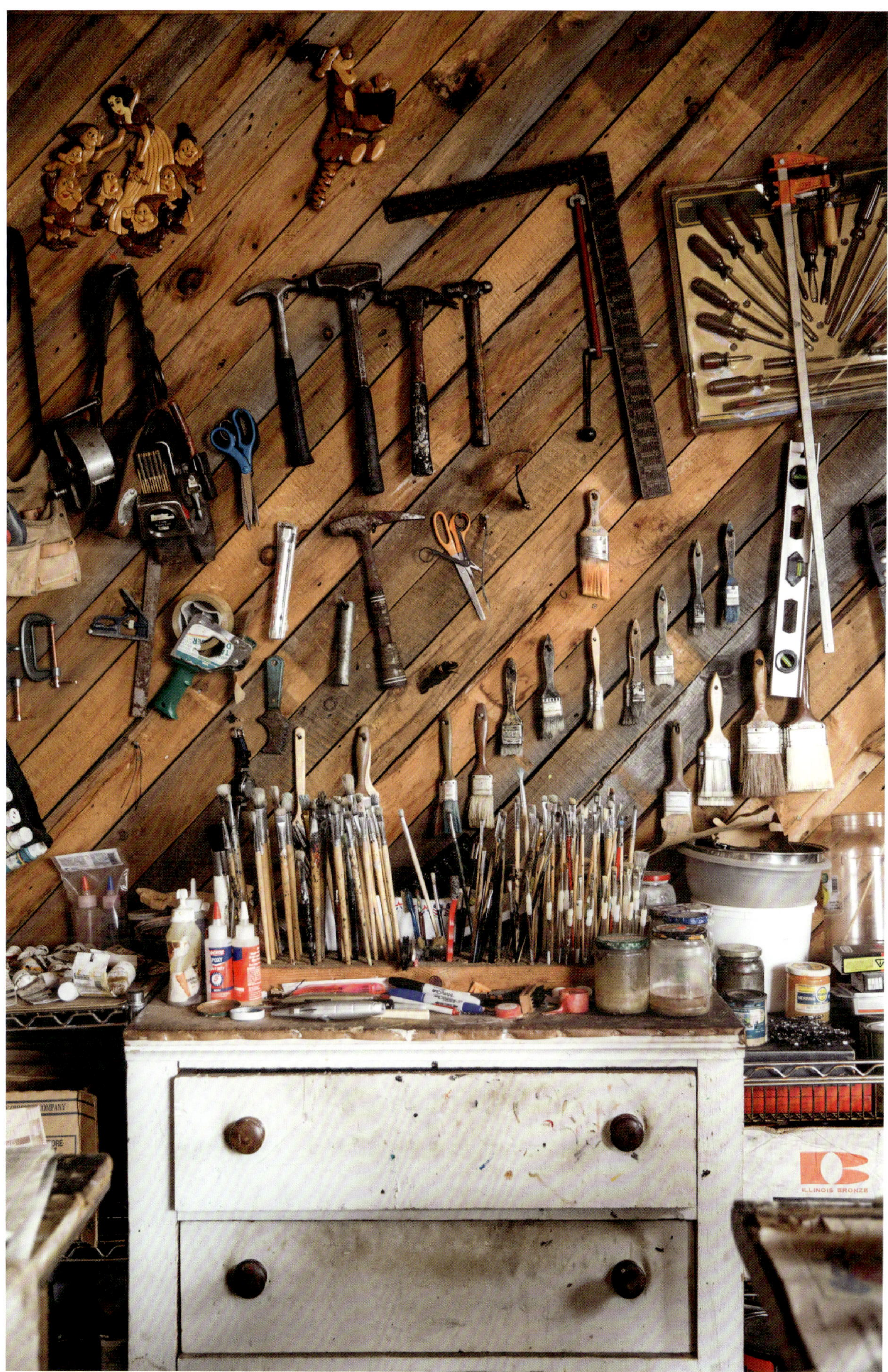

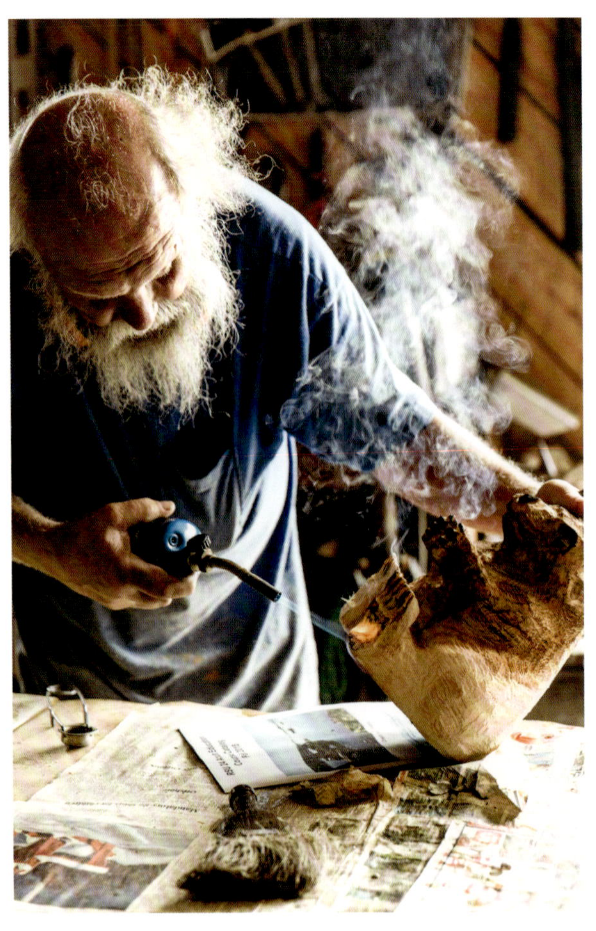

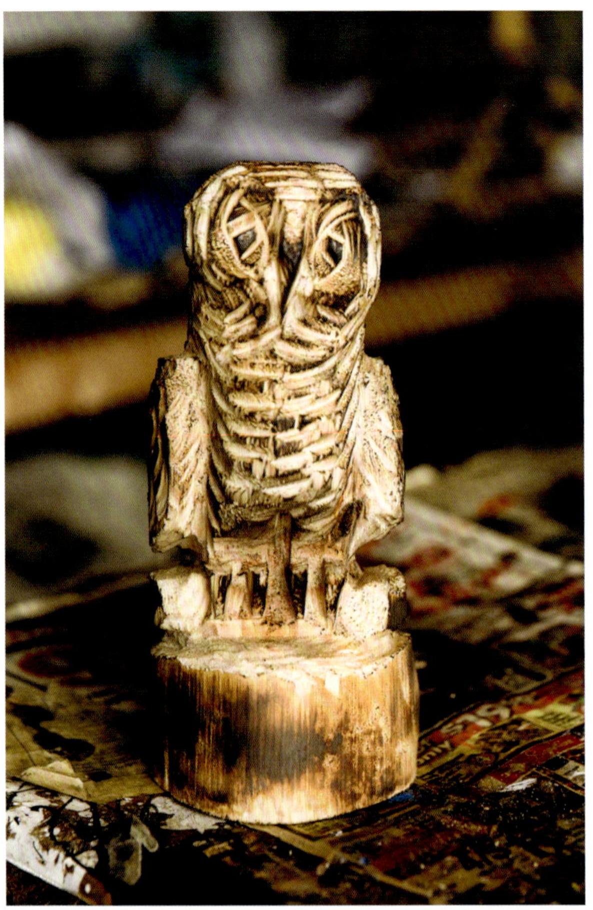

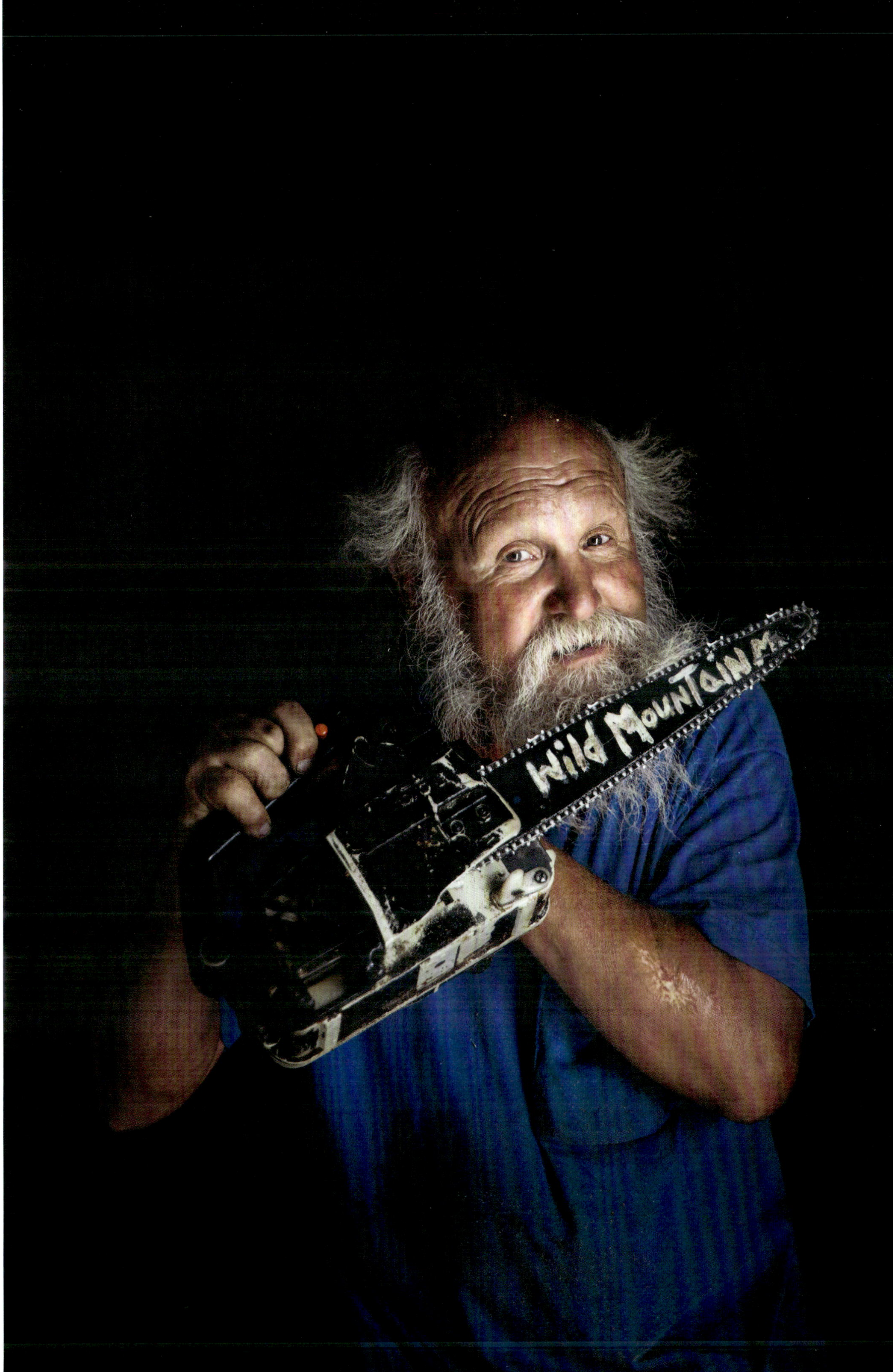
Wild MOUNTAIN

Swans Island Company

Northport

A Swans Island blanket is immediately recognizable, if not by its rectangular logo, then certainly by its tight weave and meticulously hand-stitched details. Over the past three decades, the company has become a brand trusted by interior designers and lifestyle bloggers. The soft wool wovens can be found on beds and couches throughout Maine—as well as in upscale boutiques around the country. Lucky treasure hunters might even stumble across a vintage one at a local Goodwill.

Swans Island has become as famous as photographer Peter Ralston's gray-toned images of the Atlantic. Like Ralston's image of sheep crowding into a boat on their way to the eponymous island, these blankets have entered into Maine iconography. But while Swans Island's aesthetic feels familiar to locals, few realize the changes that the company has undergone, the necessary compromises that have been made to keep this high-end maker in business. "When Swans Island started out, we were using only natural dyes and making everything by hand in Maine," explains owner Bill Laurita. "We still do that, but over the years we have had to make some changes. Now we have two different types of products: our traditional products and our entry-level products." Bill, who purchased the company in 2003, explains the difference between the categories by holding up a soft gray shawl. It's the color of a Maine winter sky and features an intricate, lace-like pointelle pattern. "This piece, like everything on this table, is one of our second-tier products," says Bill. "We designed the piece and hand-dyed it, but we didn't use natural dye on this one." The shawl, like many of the products in this range, was made in the United States by a knitter contracted by Swans Island, but unlike the pieces in their premium line, it was not made in their Maine facility.

Spread over a nearby bed in the showroom is a queen-size wool blanket. It's a similar grey hue and feels every bit as soft as kitten's fur. The fibers are long and luxurious, tightly woven to form a durable, naturally insulating layer. "This piece," Bill explains, "was made on our looms. The wool was dyed out back with all-natural dyes." These blankets, which range in color from beetroot to marine blue to ivory, are the classic products. Swans Island's gently weathered clapboard building, which looks more like a house than a studio, is located on a rural stretch of Route 1

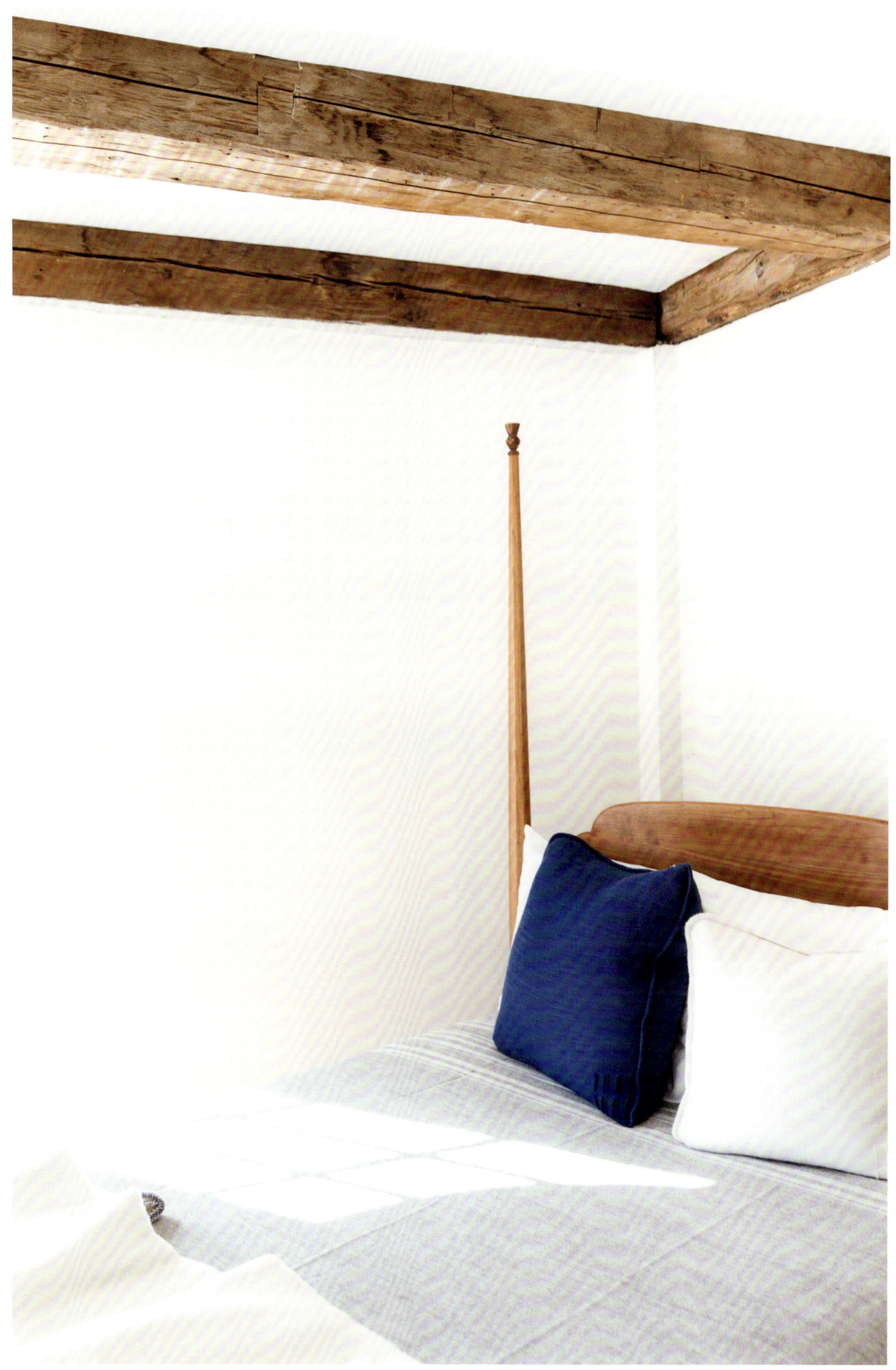

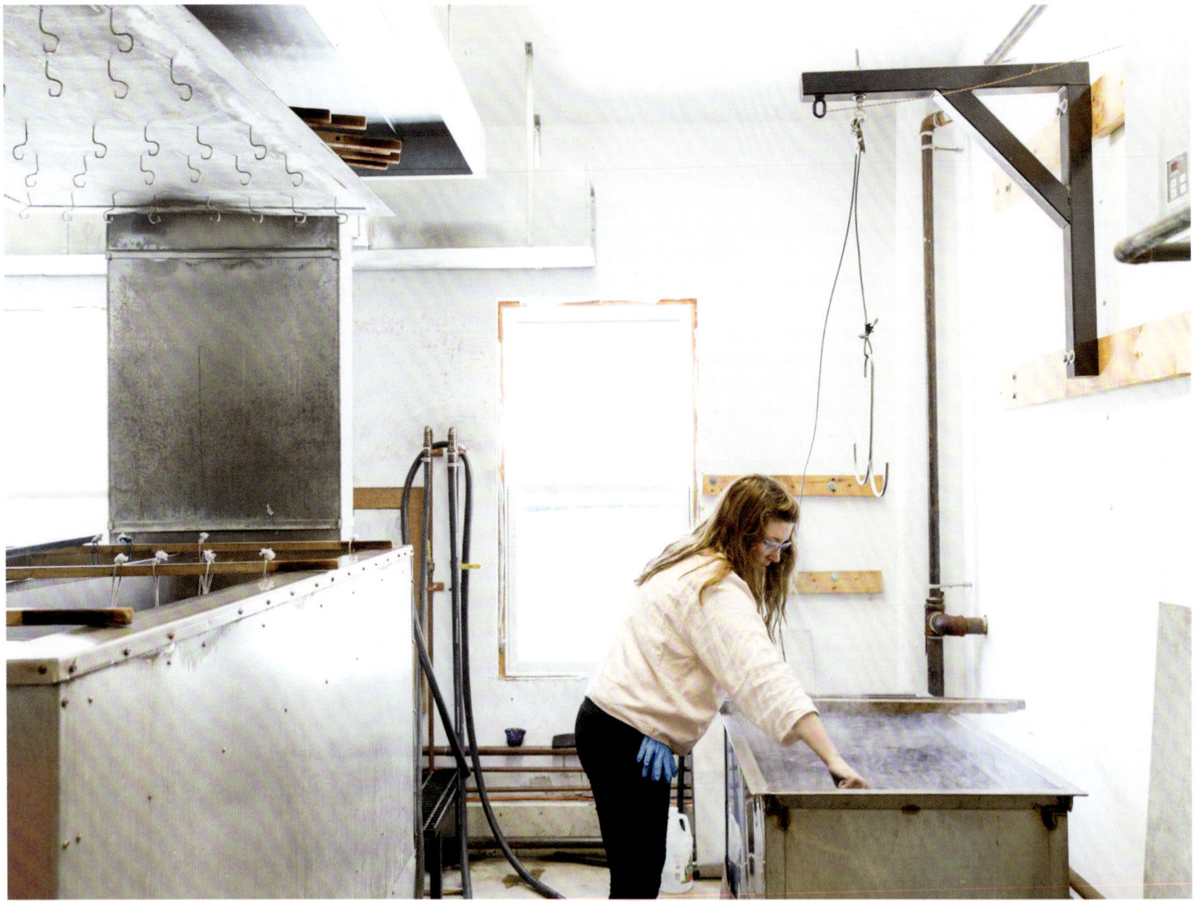

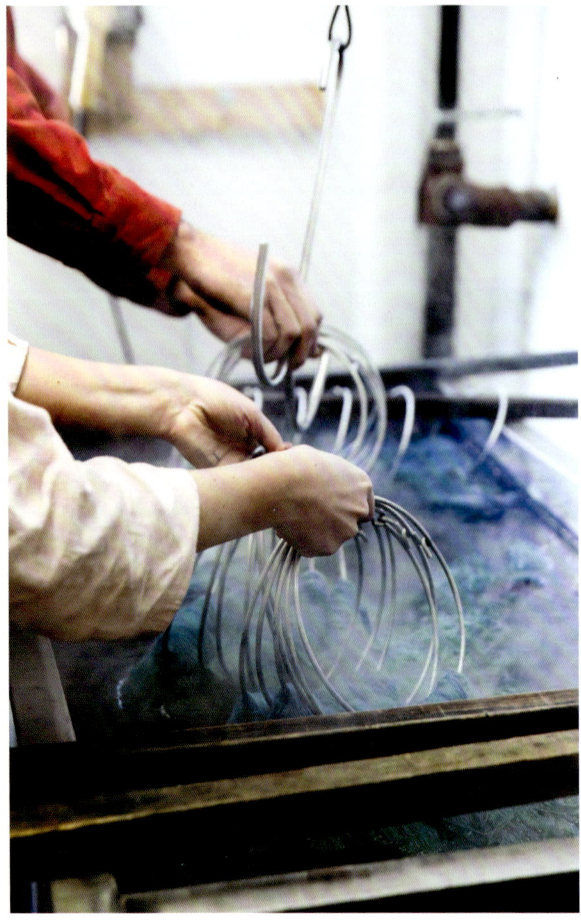

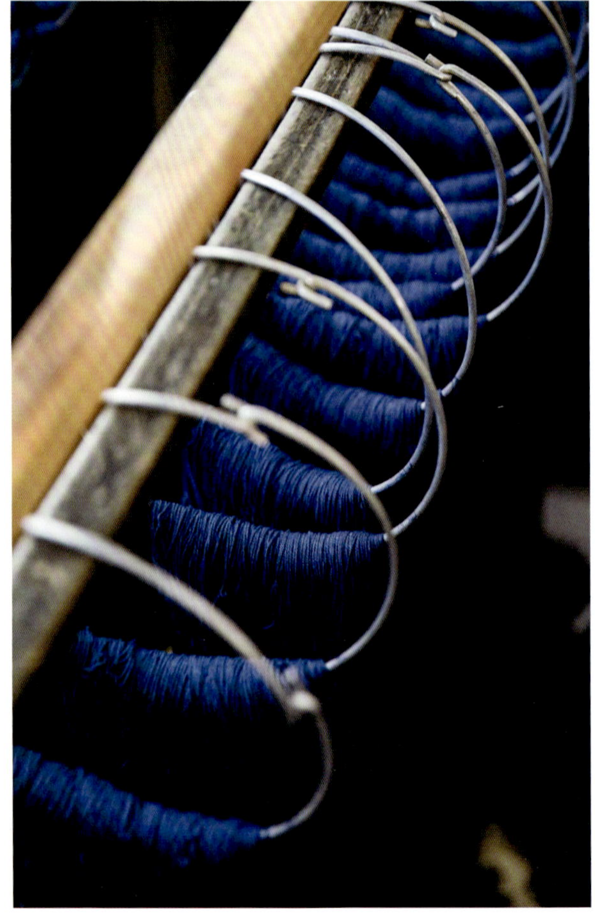

in the small town of Northport. The retail showroom, open daily to visitors, fills the front portion of the building. "Out back," as Bill puts it, is where the team weaves, dyes, and finishes the blankets.

In one room, weavers push shuttles swiftly through the warp threads on massive looms. These wooden machines are "torturous to set up," one weaver explains, as she strings and ties thousands of warp threads. Her hands move quickly and deftly, as industrious as a spider building its web. The summer-weight blanket will have over three thousand warp threads, and the process of preparing it for weaving will take days to complete. The finishing work happens upstairs, where the wool is cut and sewn. This is where they add monograms, the Swans Island logo, and other details.

Past the weaving room lies another large workshop, but this one is quieter. No looms are clacking here. The air is steamy and warm, filled with scents that are difficult to place. Mist wafts from a large metal vat, into which dye master Tony Vinci is preparing to dunk a rack of wool. On the wall nearby hang several skeins, some white and clean, others striped with deep blue. The latter have been bound tightly and dyed with indigo, creating an uneven, yet pleasing, pattern that is reminiscent of the Japanese dyeing method *shibori* (Swans Island calls these "ikat," though that borrowed term doesn't quite describe the free-form results). Today, Tony is planning to create a watercolor-like pattern by dipping skeins of wool that have been tied and dyed grass green (thus creating white and green stripes) into a bath of hot indigo. "This is something we're playing with now," he explains. "This wool has been washed and mordanted, and dyed green. This morning, we untied all the ropes and washed the wool, and now it's ready to go into the blue. Hopefully, we'll get a good color out of it."

There's a little guesswork that goes into each product, but for the makers at Swans Island that keeps it interesting. "We don't know exactly how the wool will come out," says Tony. This is especially true with natural dyes. "I've found that lighter greens actually get more grassy, bringing out a nice yellow hue, when you overdye them." To create a soft, Monet-like color palette of greens and blues, Tony has brewed a weaker batch of indigo. (Swans Island uses organic indigo sourced from India. It arrives in powder form and requires precise handling according to chemical specifications for pH and oxygen levels.) "You have to watch closely now," he says as he lowers the wool into the vat. "Indigo does something curious when you take it out." Moments later, he lifts the wool from the vat. It hangs in the air, dripping wet and strangely fragrant. "As the indigo reacts with the oxygen in the air, it turns from bright yellow to dark blue." The colors transform quickly, and behind his bushy beard, Tony grins. His eyes crinkle and he says, "This is the cool part of my job, when I get to play around with colors and experiment. Every day is different here—you never know what you're going to make."

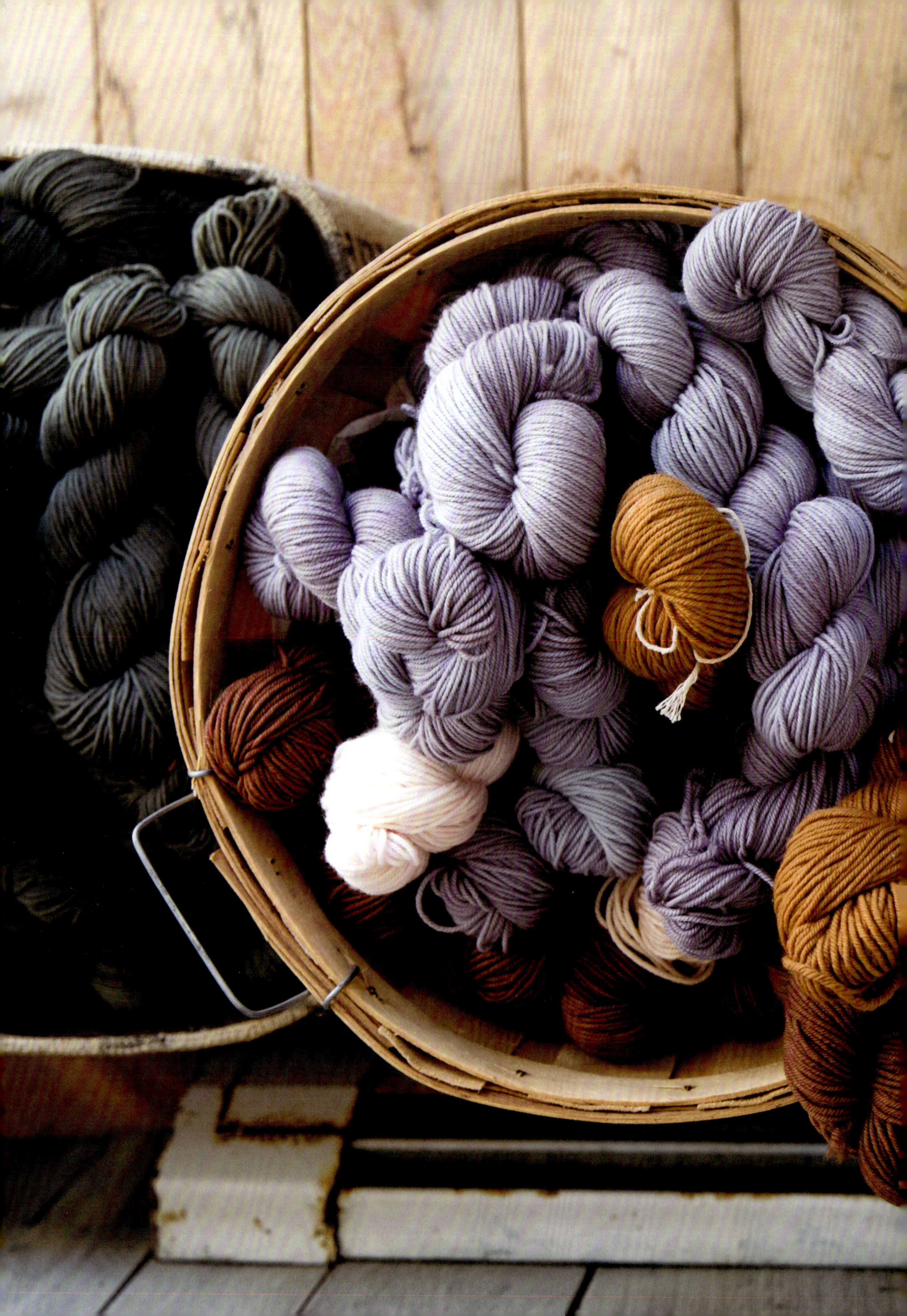

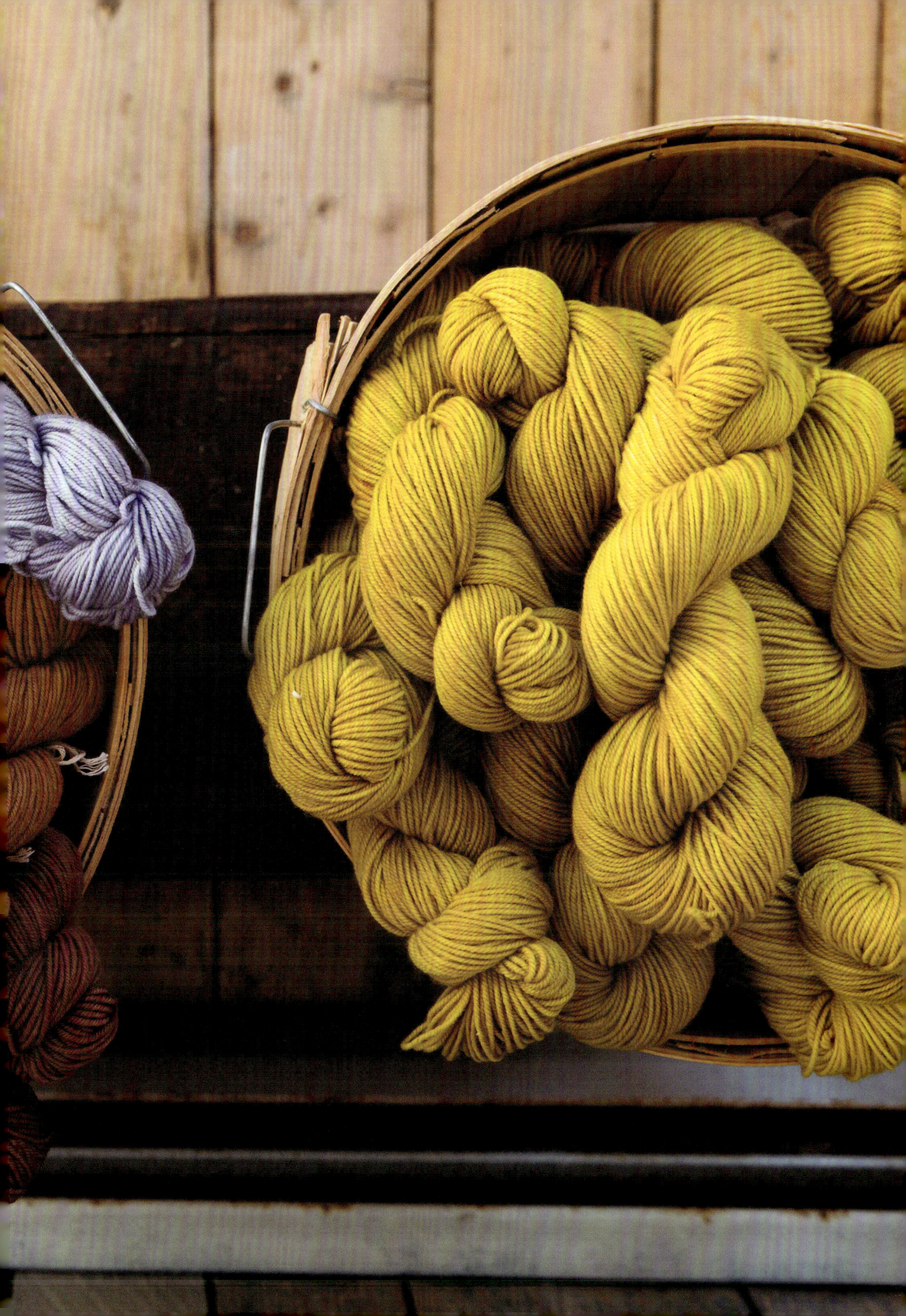

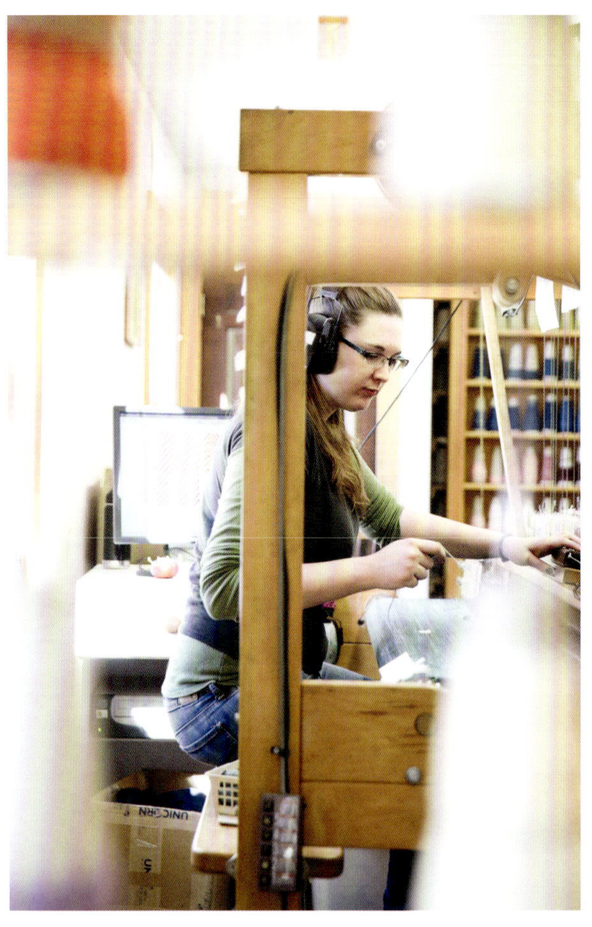

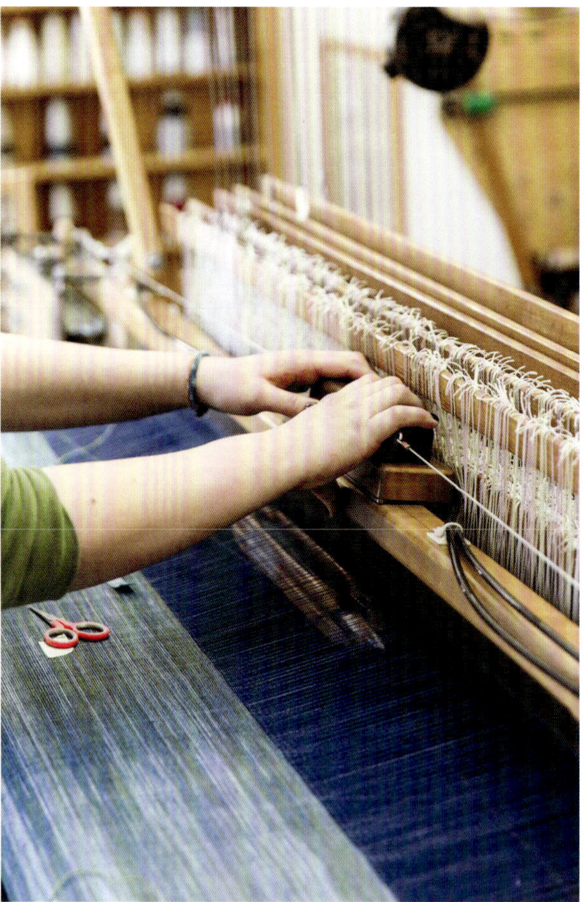

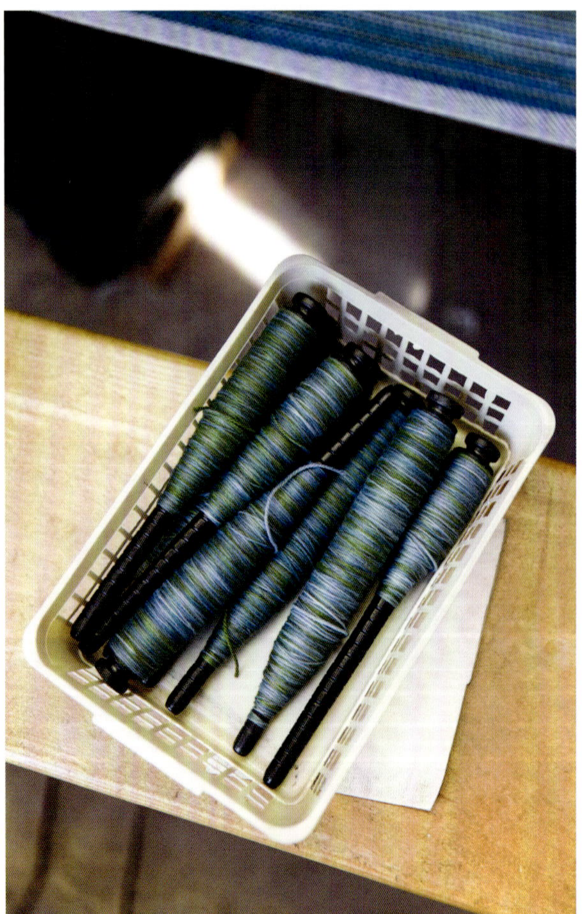

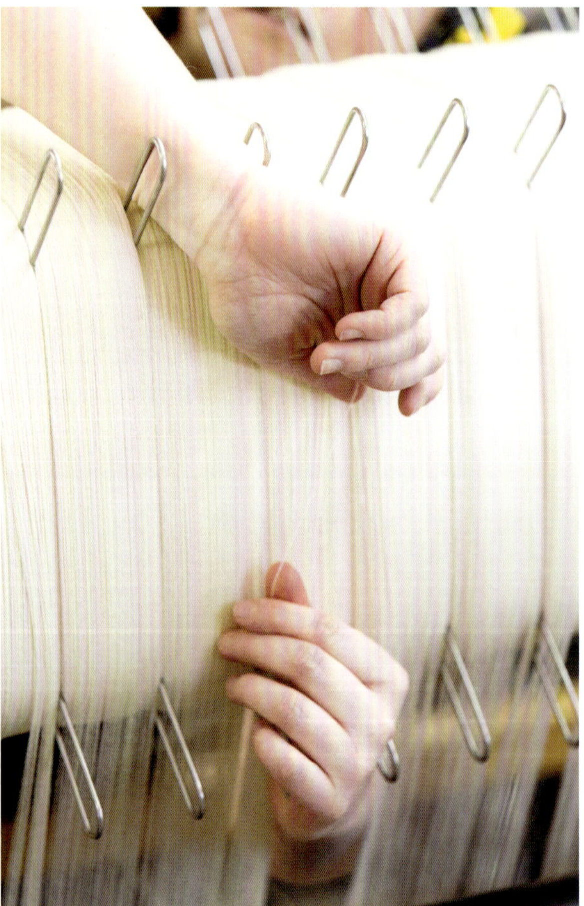

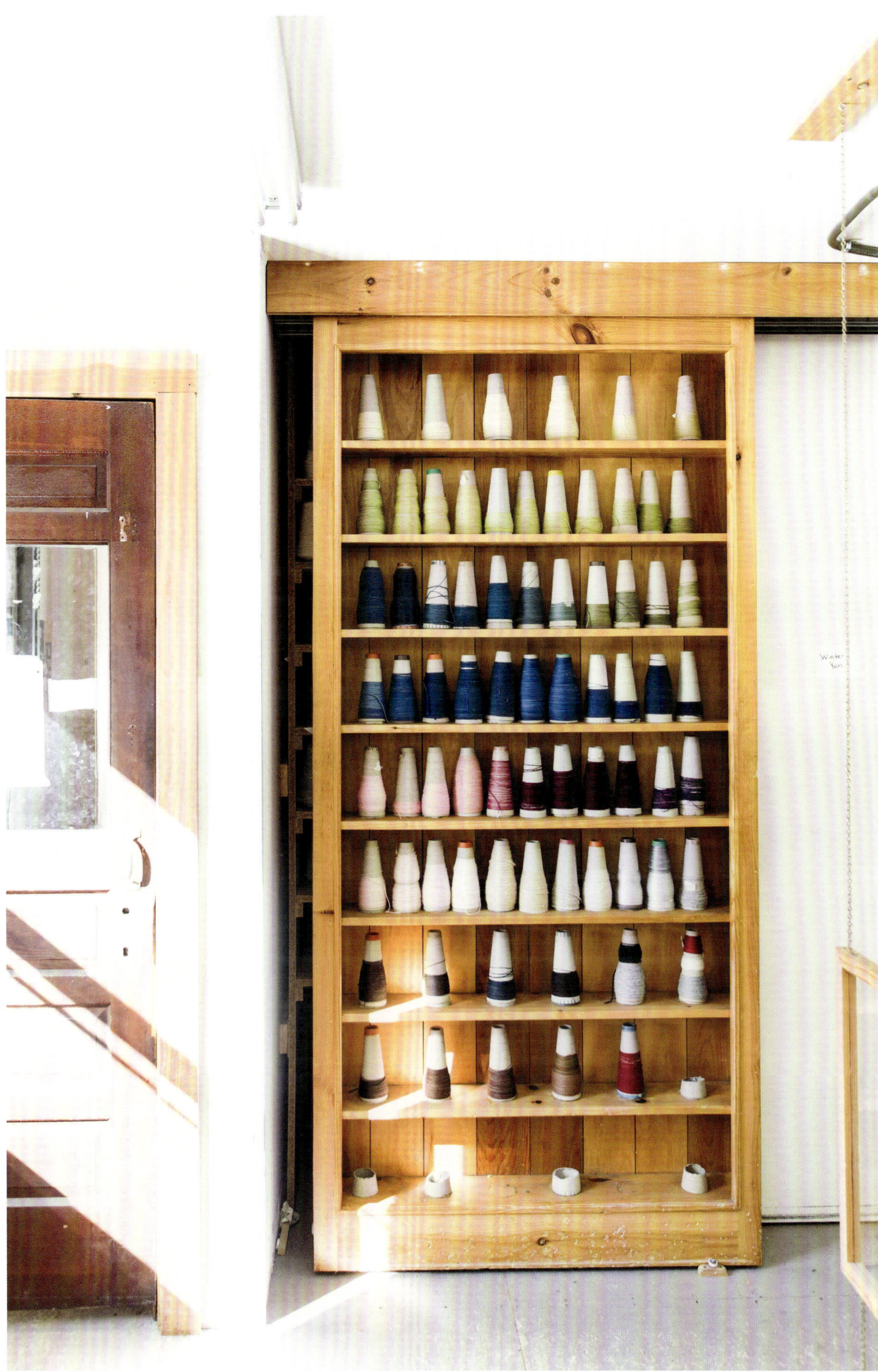

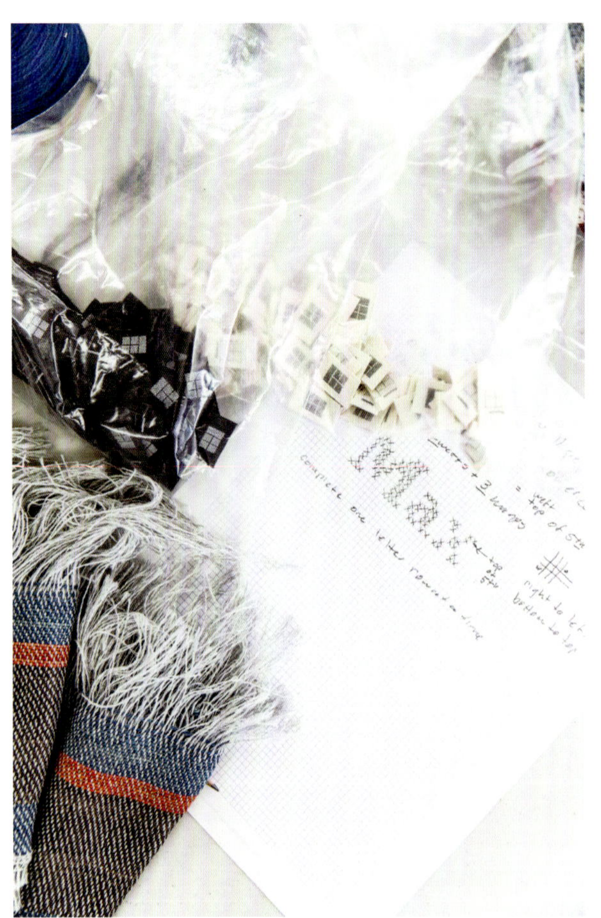

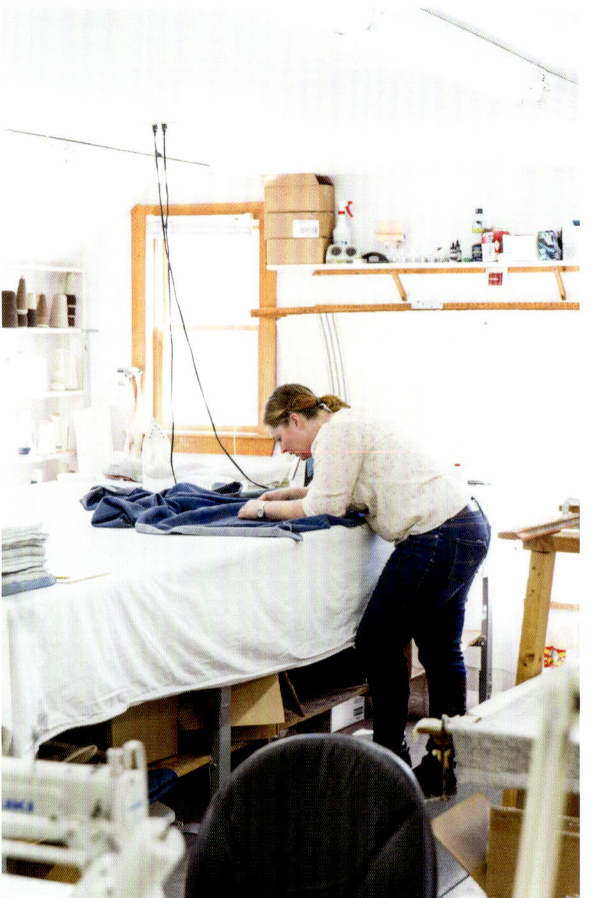

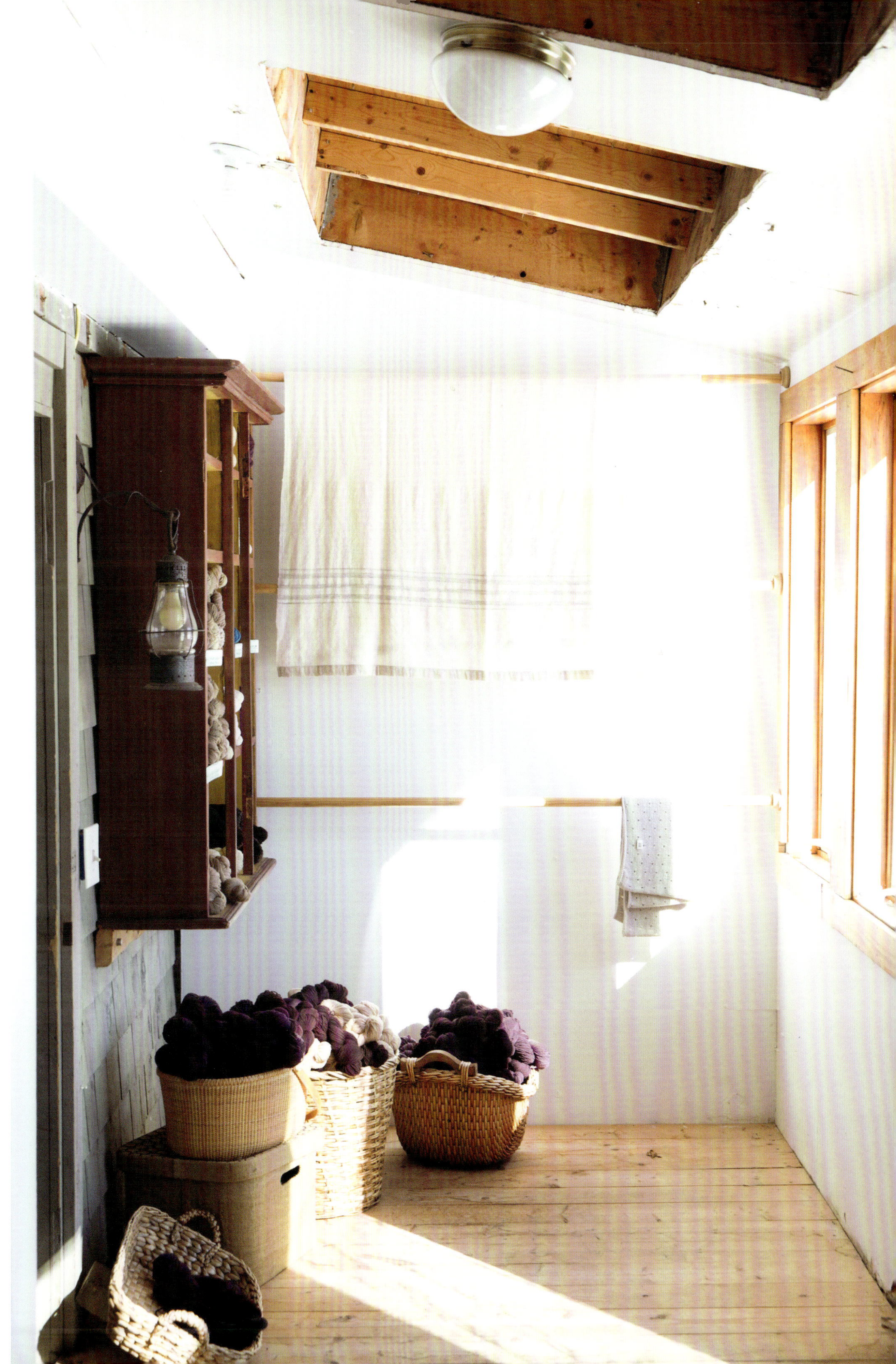

BUILDING
&
LIVING

Will Winkelman

Portland

"I haven't taken a shower indoors in months," says architect Will Winkelman as he leads us across his Peaks Island property. He is barefoot on the mossy groundcover as he shows off his "tree house shower," a compact little structure built around and into several tall trees. "It was a slapdash job," he says, "but it's so much fun to use." Nearby is his home. From where we stand, we can see the scrubby low-bush blueberries that grow on his roof.

Will loves building small, unusual structures that utilize every square foot of available space. His living roofs, which typically feature local plants, both ground the structure in the landscape and provide garden space where one may not typically expect it. "The only drawback is that you have to weed it," Will says of his elevated plot of greenery. He grabs hold of a long chain that runs from one corner of the roof to the ground. "This is a clever bit of problem solving. It helps the roof drain, and in the winter, it creates these amazingly cool structural shapes as the ice adheres to the metal."

They say a carpenter's house is never finished, and that appears to be true of architects as well. Will is continually tinkering with new, whimsical structures, creating airy workshops for his wife, Kathy, or fun playhouses for his kids. "I reached out to Will after I found his website. He had all these beautiful restorations and big lovely homes. But what really got me was a play structure he built with all these funny angles," remembers John Bullitt, a sound artist and former client of Winkelman Architecture. "I saw it and thought, Yes! That's the kind of designer I want. I want someone who doesn't think in terms of boxes." But John is an artist and as such he has particular ideas about what his home should look like—and some specifics for how it should function. He needed a sound studio with good acoustics. Since much of John's work involves listening and recording the sounds of the natural world, he wanted a quiet space, one that blended into the natural landscape. John is also a practicing Buddhist, and he wanted his house to have a sense of peaceful cohesion—to "respect the world around it," he explains. "I wanted to be set at a respectful distance from the ocean," says John. "I didn't want to be right on top of all that power, all that noise."

In order to best realize John's vision, Will scheduled a small charrette to take place on the land.

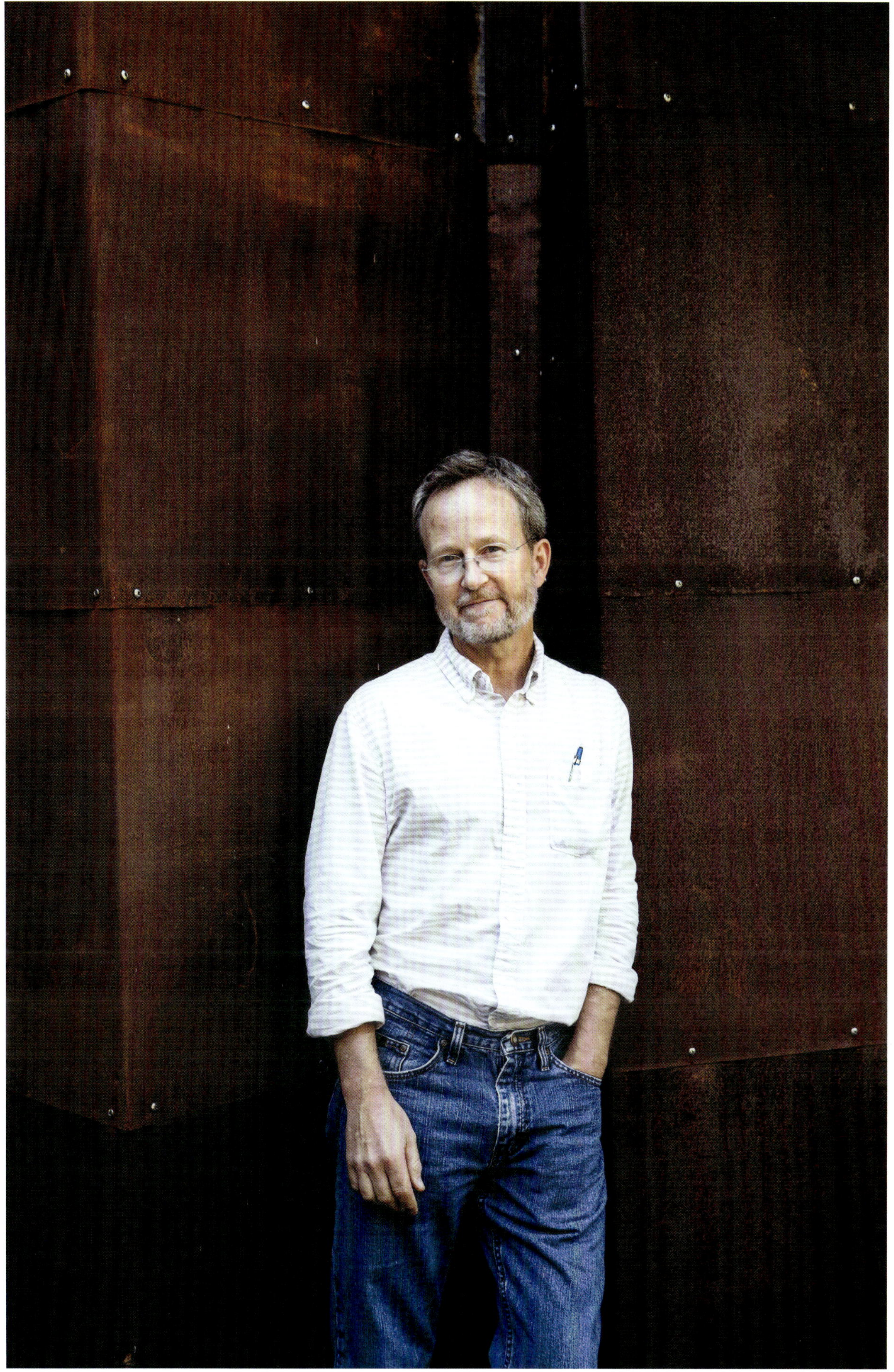

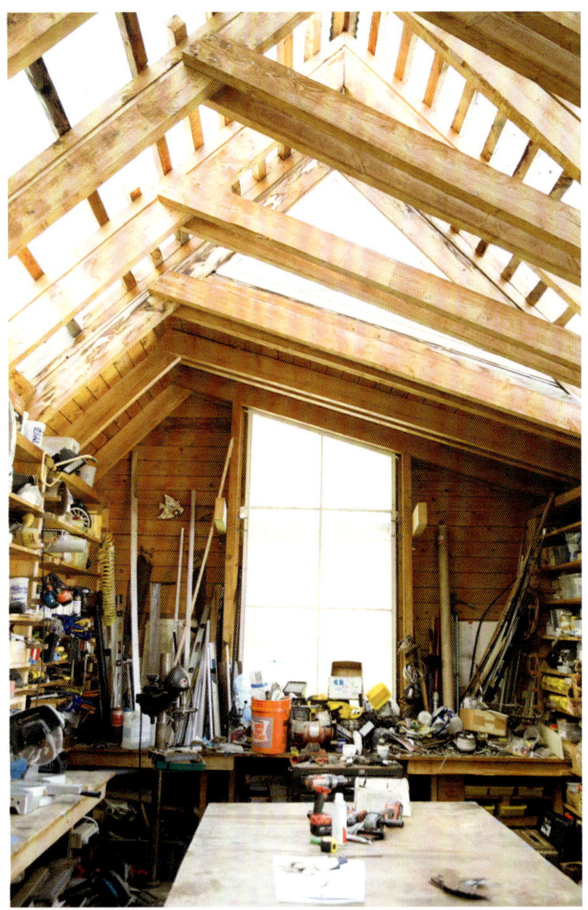
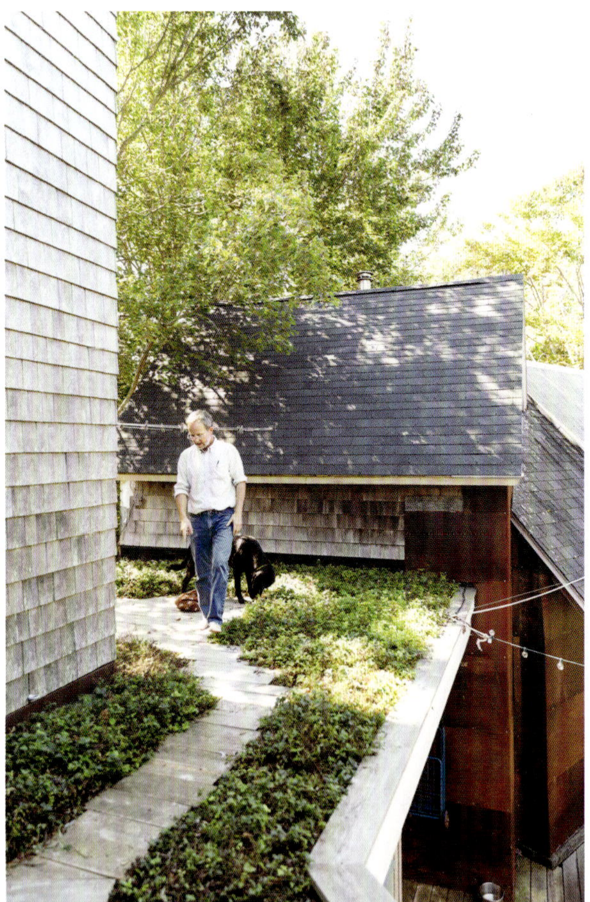
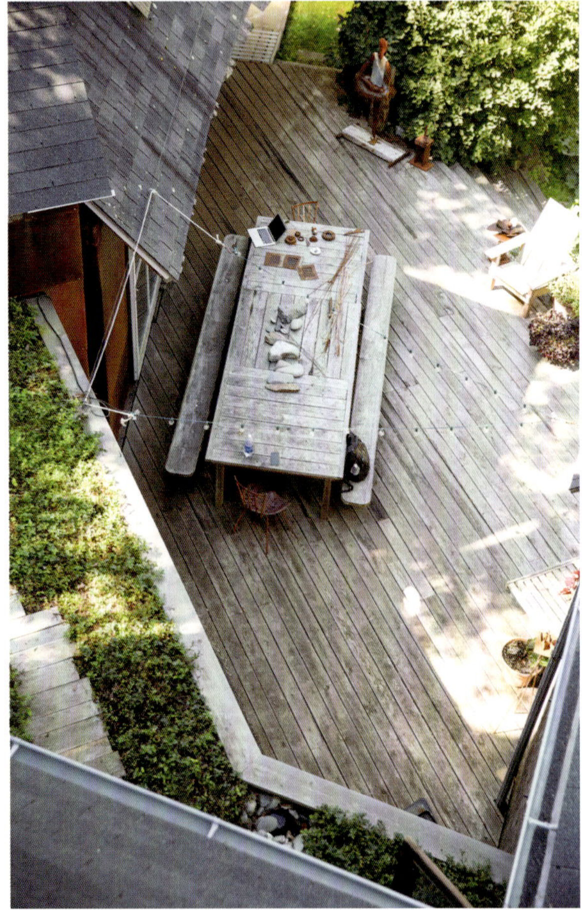
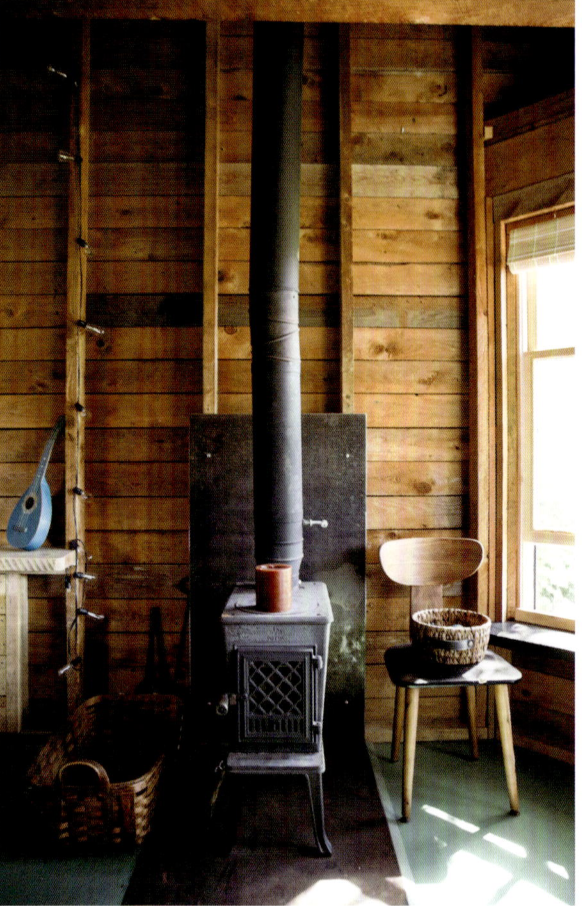

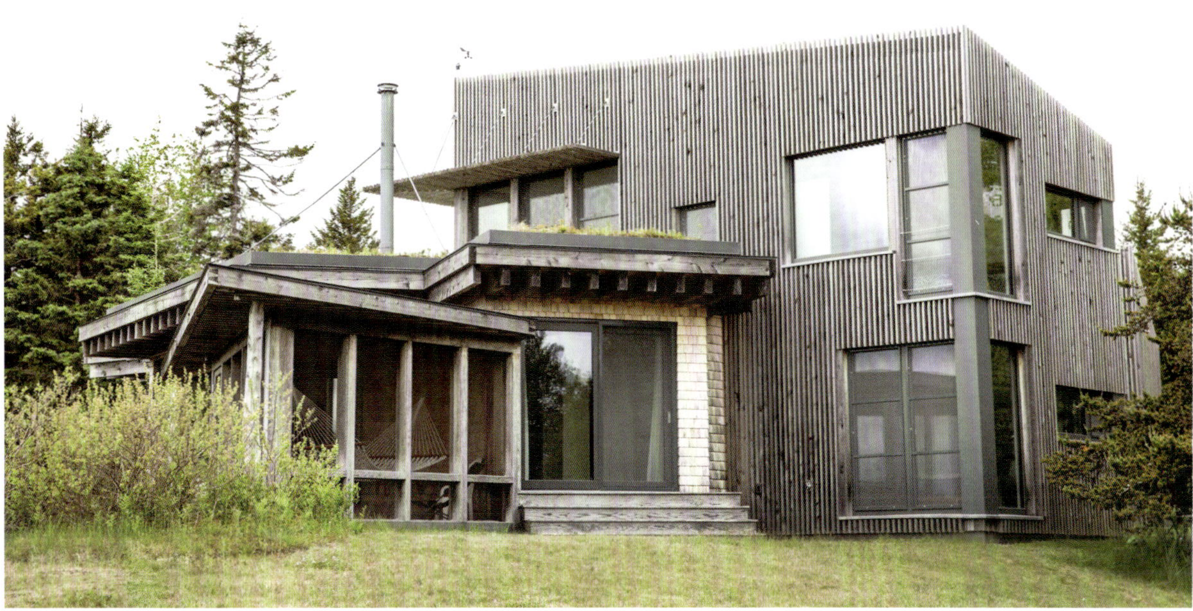

Will credits the collaborative nature of his team for much of a structure's success. "Mature designers are able to check their egos," he says. "It's never all about me and my vision. The house should be all of ours." Will and Eric Sokol, a lead architect at the firm, traveled north from their Portland office to meet landscape architect Todd Richardson and landscape designer Ken Studtmann (of Saco-based Richardson & Associates) at the Steuben site. "We spent two or three days together, walking around the land, talking about our ideas, and brainstorming," John remembers. "It was this open-ended, blue-sky thinking, which really appealed to me. We talked about what the land was asking for and what I needed. Working with Will felt like play to me."

The resulting home has a living roof, large windows, and a freestanding studio with walls that splay outward as they rise up. "You think acoustics and sound engineering is some sort of magic, something no one can understand," says Will later. "But really, I just called up a sound engineer and told him what we needed. He knew right away the best way to do it, at what angle to set the walls, and how the sound would function within the space."

When Will looks back on that project, completed in 2013, his face still lights up with excitement. "It flows with the landscape, as if the field were jumping up onto the roof. In the summer, when the grasses are three feet tall, it melds right into the surrounding area," he says. "And we built in this great little surprise for John. I designed the placement of the windows so that you can still have a view of the lighthouse, even if you're standing outside, behind the house, away from the ocean." John didn't notice this precise framing until months after he had already moved in. "I'm always discovering something new, partially because Will has this amazing attention to detail," he says. "Just the other day I saw how the light comes in through the skylights through the network of woven beams—it creates this wonderful changing pattern. These things are little Easter eggs that I find unexpectedly as I'm walking around the house." Toward the end of construction, Will added another small, personalized touch for John—brass disks set into the wood floorboards. "We made him a walking meditation path," he explains. "The little bronze nickels are the pivot points."

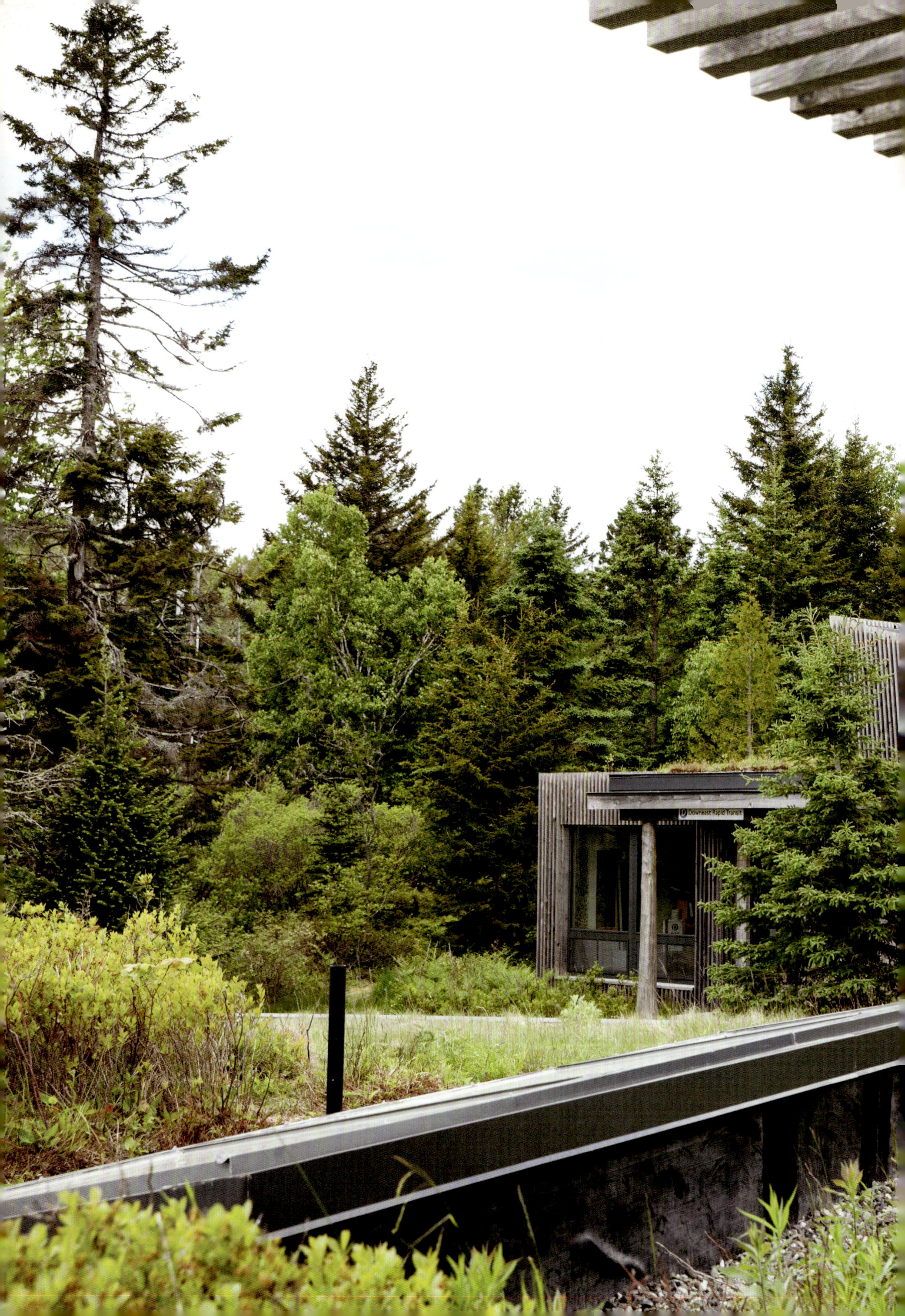
Downeast Rapid Transit

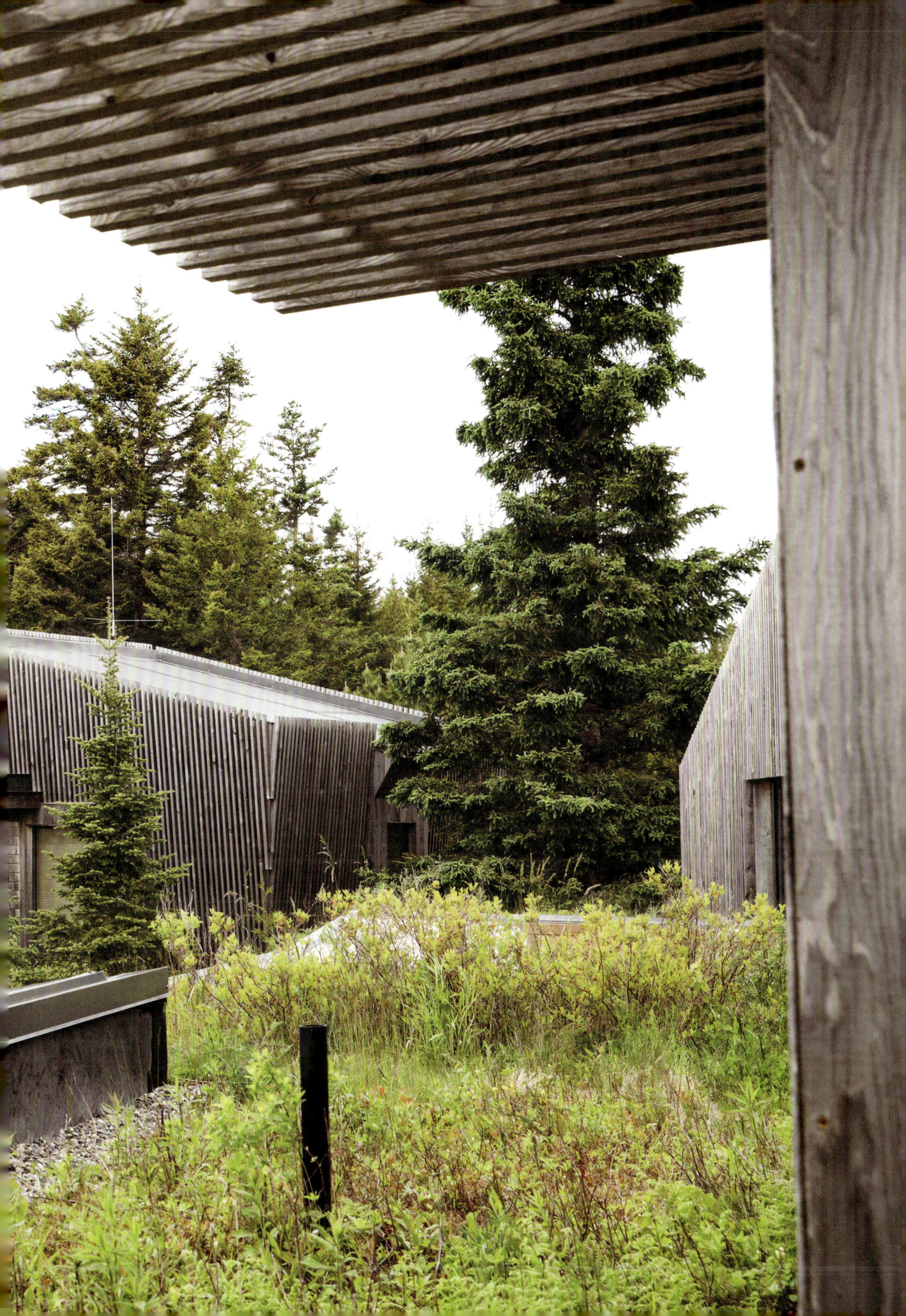

Months after our first meeting on Peaks Island, we join Will on the shores of Sebago Lake where he is working on a vacation home for Karen Burke, owner of Portland boutique K Collette. "I feel like I got the A Team," says Karen, who, like John, has also chosen Richardson & Associates as her landscape designers. "I wanted Will because he knows how to work with a small space, and I wanted this to be a functional, compact camp. It's a retreat and a place to step away. It's all about living with less—no dishwasher, no TV, no microwave. Just small and simple." Sebago Lake holds a special place in Karen's heart. As a girl, she attended summer camp at nearby Wohelo Camps. Years later, she married her husband at nearby Migis Lodge. "I wanted this house to be a part of the forest, to feel like the Sebago I remember from growing up," she says. "Most importantly, I wanted it to meld into the land. I want to preserve the original landscape as much as possible." To that end, Todd has decided not to remove most of the plantings on the property, which means Will and his team must figure out how to set the foundation without damaging the roots of nearby trees. (Carefully placed concrete pylons were the solution.) They were also tasked with designing an exterior that harmonized with the surrounding homes while incorporating mid-century modern elements.

"This book was our bible," says Will, as he flips open *Norwegian Wood: The Thoughtful Architecture of Wenche Selmer*. This copy is Burke's and it's bursting with yellow sticky notes. Inside, she has highlighted entire passages, circled pictures that she loves, and written small notes to herself that read simply, "color!" or "living room." For Will, Todd, and Karen, the book provided a visual vocabulary for the project, one full of raw wood, modern shapes, and sophisticated, muted hues. "What's really cool is that this is a book I discovered ten years ago. Wenche Selmer was on my radar, and I've used this as inspiration for other projects," Will says. "But Karen found it separately and brought it to me. She said, '*This* is my vibe.'"

For the Sebago Lake retreat, Will combined elements of classic camp architecture, like exposed beams and a large gable at the front of the house, with modernist touches, including flat roofs that link the gables (which will be covered with small stones and forest duff), irregularly dimensioned vertical siding, and updated, scaled-down rafter tails that reference Japanese architecture as well as post-and-beam homes. "We used traditional forms and materials, and then gave it a little edge with deliberate, subtle tweaks on proportion to make the entire structure feel special and detailed," Will says as he walks around the half-finished house. He points to the windows as an example. "They're ordinary windows, but we didn't use regular trim on them. Do you notice how they're aligned with the gaps on the siding? To make that work, Eric drew every side of the house, with every board, and placed the windows exactly. Although you don't notice it at first, it gives a calmness to the house," explains Will. "And Karen is smart, she feels it. She's a vibrating force. The moment something is off, she knows."

Todd Richardson's landscape design highlights the natural serenity of the region. Instead of planting a traditional lawn, Todd used squares of local moss and groundcover that the landscaping team transported from a wooded corner of the property. Any trees that were removed during construction were replaced with tall, white birches. "What we are doing here is stitching the landscape back together," explains Todd as he walks through a hedge of highbush blueberries, mountain laurel, and huckleberry bushes. "We aren't even making true trails down to the water, just little sneak-downs covered in pine needles where the plants part enough to let you through." "If we do our job right," adds Will, "you won't be able to tell that this has been landscaped. You will feel as though the house just flows with the land. Like it belongs here."

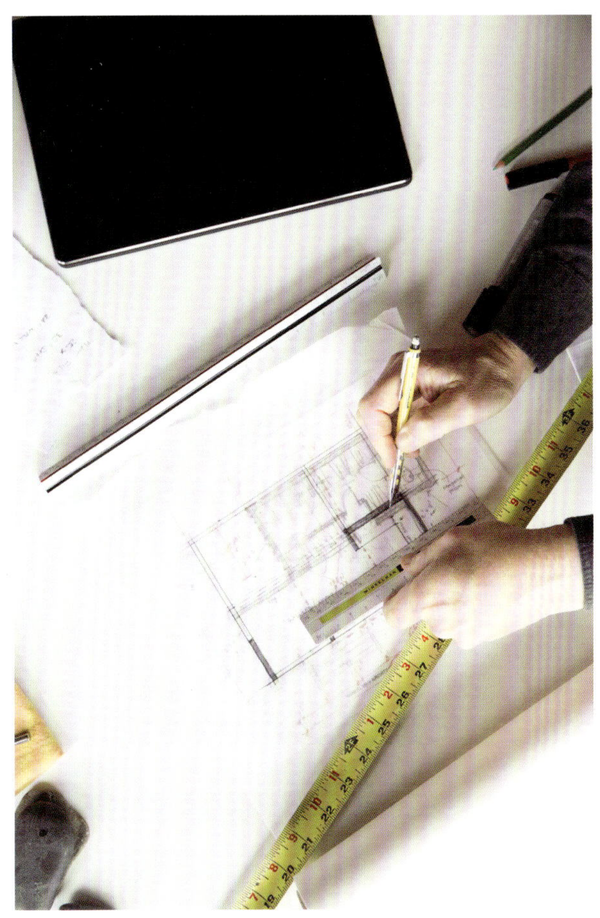

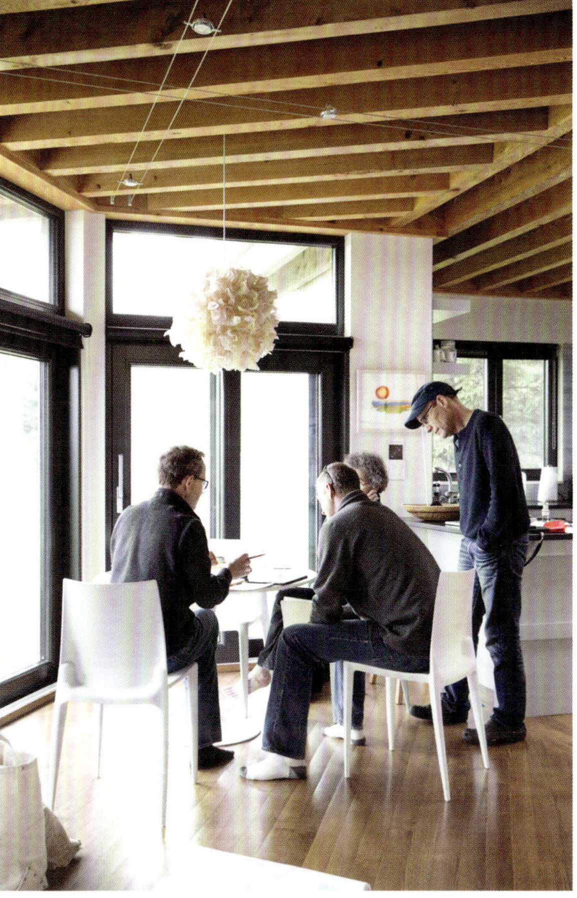

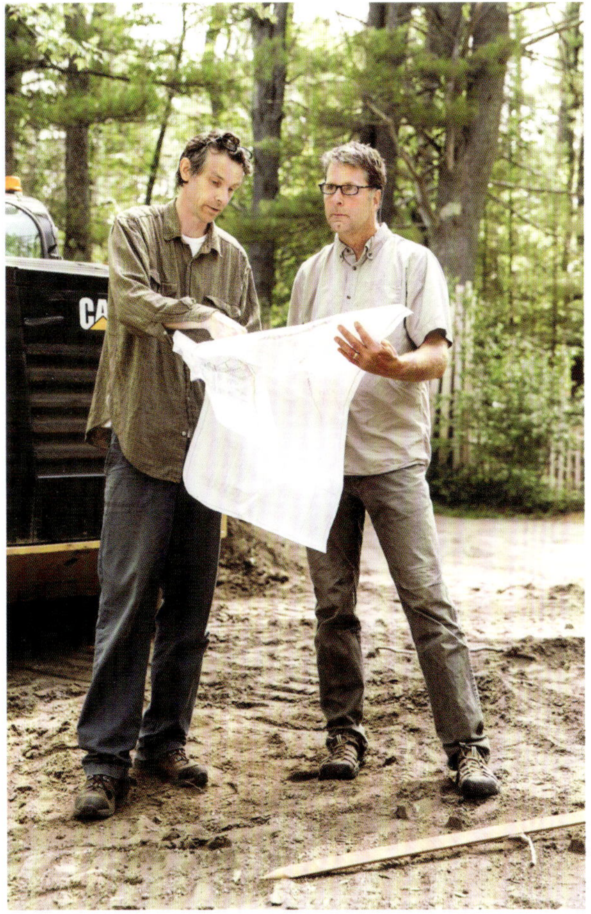

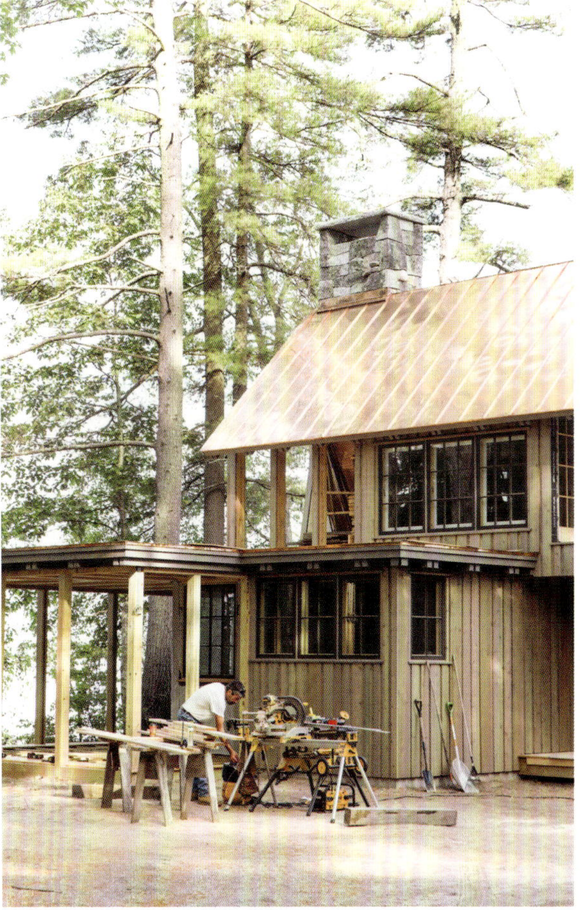

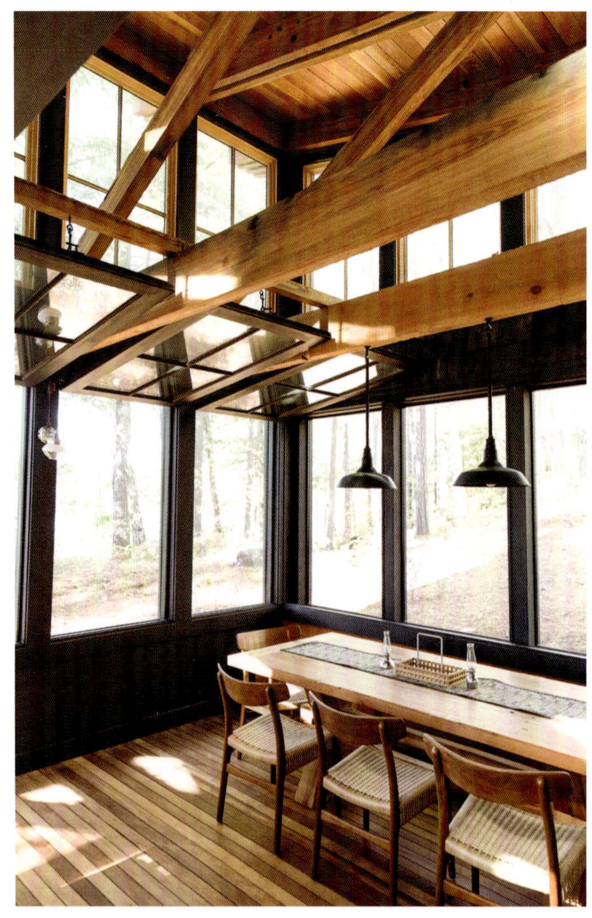

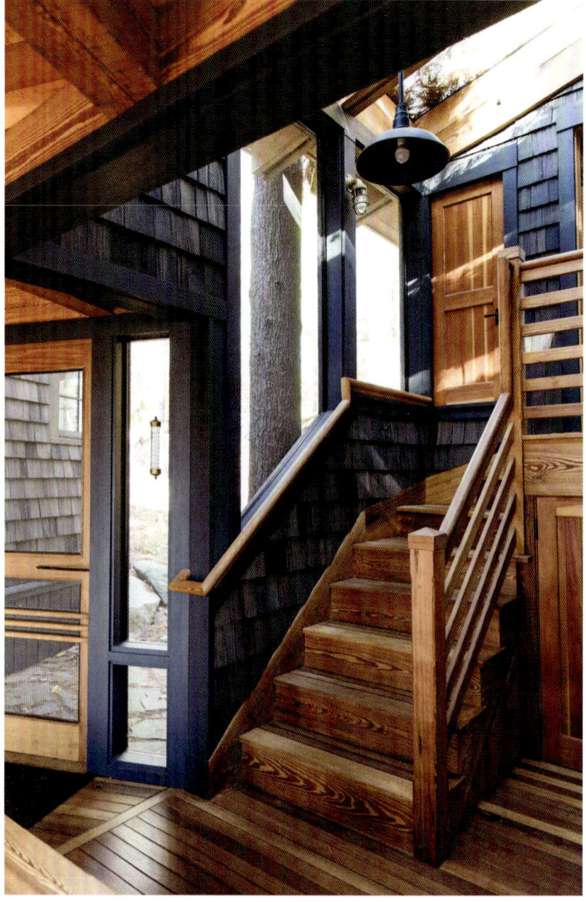

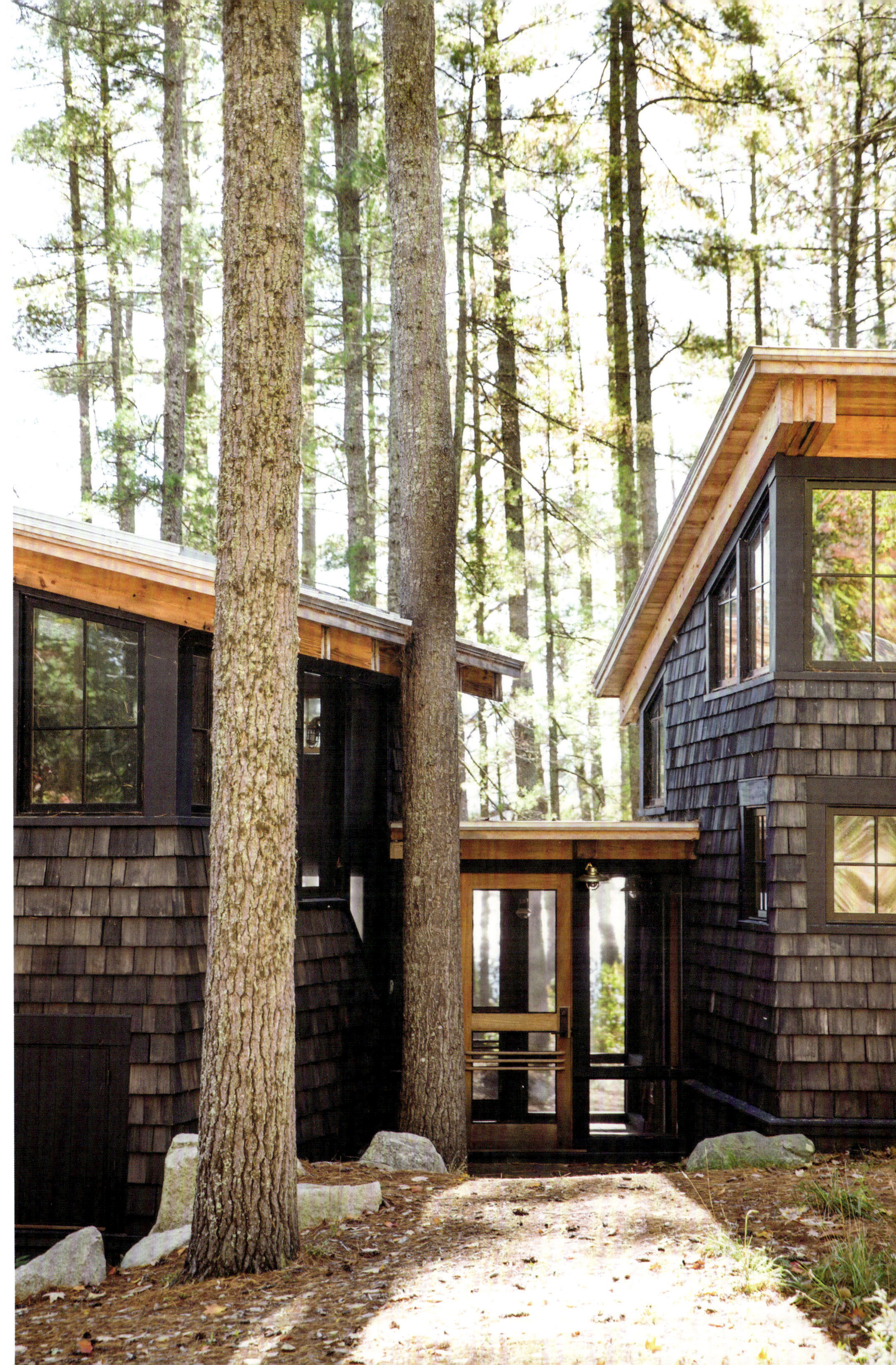

Lunaform

Sullivan

Phid Lawless had a problem. He had built a beautiful, Japanese-style concrete lantern urn for his father's ashes. But the top was so heavy that he was unable to install it himself. Naturally, he called a friend, a ceramics professor at the nearby College of the Atlantic in Bar Harbor, to help. "But we needed three men to lift it," Phid recalls. "And so he brought along Dan, who was one of his students." It was this day in 1992, when Phid and Dan Farrenkopf first met. Neither one had any idea what would come of their chance meeting or of the strong relationship they would build or of the successful business that would grow out of this one urn by Phid, this one favor from Dan.

At the time, Phid viewed Lunaform "more as an experiment than a potential business," but Dan immediately recognized the skill behind Phid's monumental designs. Dan was majoring in human ecology and studying garden design, sculpture, and architecture at College of the Atlantic. Phid had been working in creative industries for decades, first as a painter, then as an architect, and later as a graphic designer. On the side, he experimented with large concrete shapes, building planters to complement the granite surroundings of his wooded homesite in Sullivan, Maine. Dan was studying concrete and its applications in school. "And suddenly here was this guy," he recalls, "who simply said, 'I love concrete.'"

"We didn't realize we were building a business," Dan explains. "We were simply trying to build something that hadn't been built before, to answer questions that we had just begun to ask." Despite their twenty-two-year age difference, Dan and Phid were partners from the start. It has been twenty-five years since they sold their first planter and Lunaform has grown from a backyard operation to a well-regarded studio that produces large-scale concrete planters, lanterns, and garden features for private gardens and major public spaces, including the Smithsonian Institution, the New York Botanical Garden, Rockefeller Center, and airports in San Francisco, Chicago, Memphis, Detroit, and Baltimore. Lifestyle authority Martha Stewart has called Lunaform pots "extraordinary," going on to praise their shapes as being "reminiscent of vessels found in ancient Greek and Roman gardens." (Skylands, her summer house on Mount Desert

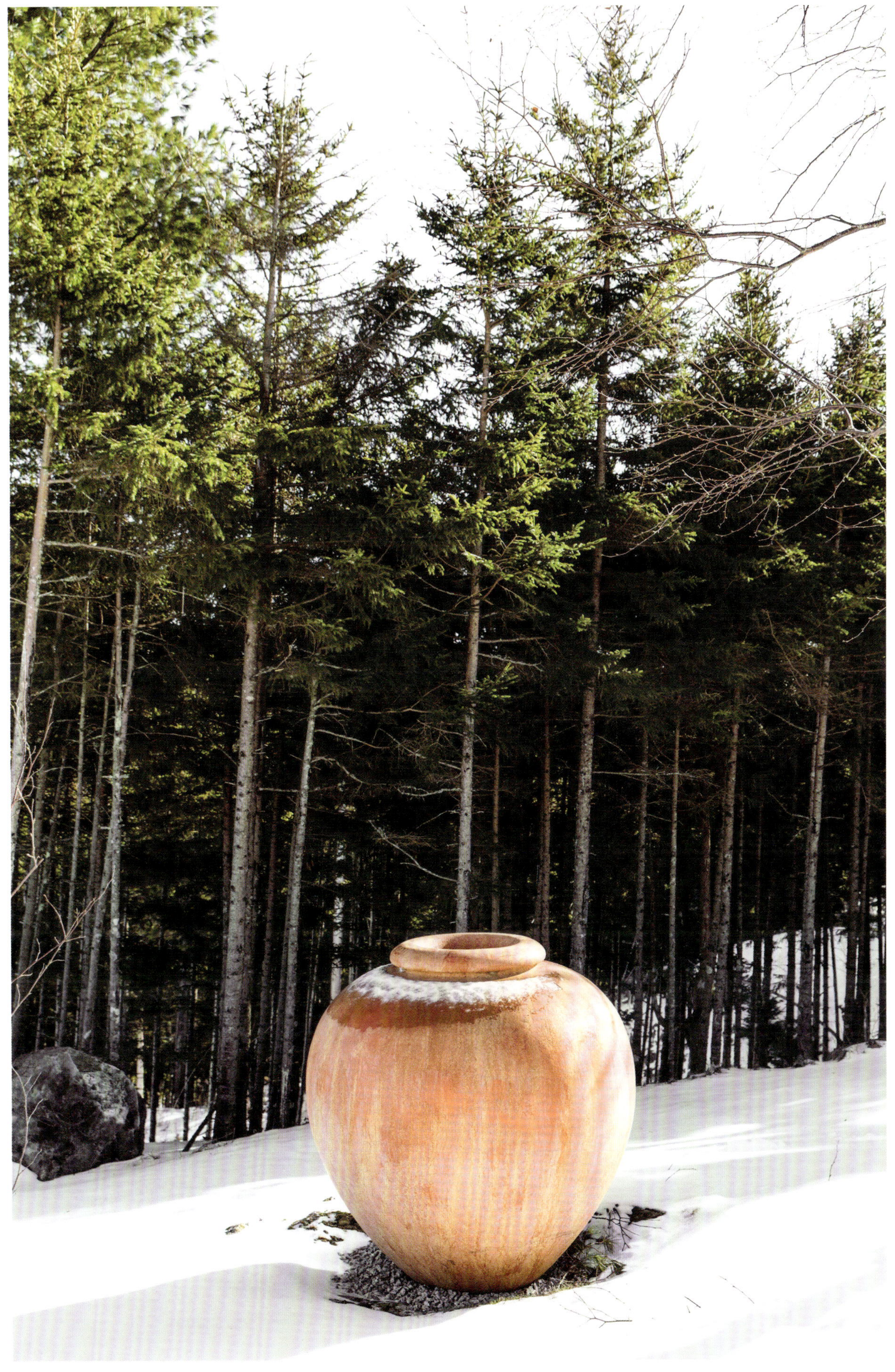

Island, features several Lunaform pots on its elegantly landscaped grounds.)

Phid and Dan's success lies not only in the grace of their designs, but also in the remarkable scale. "I think to most humans, that grand scale is appealing," Dan says. "You don't always see things of this size on a day-to-day basis, and it makes the pieces feel special." The owners of Lunaform also work closely with their customers which allows them to influence the design of their own pot, creating a planter that will fit naturally into its intended landscape. Often customers arrive at Lunaform with an idea of what they want—size, shape, color—but the final designs are achieved only after much collaborative discussion.

While there are many makers creating cement pots, no other manufacturer can match the size and durability of Lunaform's products. In a workshop that smells of concrete and earth, cool scents that match the muted tones of the walls, Phid creates the unique interior structure that will support each Lunaform pot. Concrete is subject to weathering and erosion, but steel skeletons in Lunaform's planters reinforce the concrete and enable them to withstand Maine's harsh winters—wind, snow, ice, and subzero temperatures. "Concrete is really good under compression but it has no real strength under tension, so you need to give it something to keep it from cracking," Phid says. "Each one of these strands"—the steel wires—"has a tensile strength of a thousand pounds; the steel provides the needed support against a freeze-thaw cycle." Dan adds that Lunaform's unique process allows them to work with concrete that has a consistency more like a toothpaste than a liquid. "By molding our pots in the round, we're able to change the shape easily, but we're also able to take advantage of concrete's natural abilities and forms," he explains. "By adding less water during the early phases of construction, we create a stronger final product."

While other manufacturers of concrete planters use two molds, pouring the liquefied concrete between the shaping shells, Phid and Dan do things differently. They start with a frame mold, which they design and construct, then apply layers of concrete onto it. They then attach a cage of steel wire to help hold the concrete paste in place. The pot is finished with multiple layers of concrete, added in the same way that a plasterer might spackle a wall. The basic form is then rotated through a steel screed to shave off the rough edges and mold the pot into a smooth, graceful shape. "It's almost like we're clay potters working on a wheel, except we're using concrete," Phid explains, weaving his hands through the air to reflect the turning of a wheel.

Although the screed creates a uniform shape, it removes some of the texture of the concrete. "It's just too smooth," says Phid, who prefers natural, rough textures and soft, neutral colors. And so, from there the pot moves to the lower studio, where workers sandblast it to produce a pitted texture (many of their pots have little craters and valleys, which make them look like the surface of the moon). Finally, a painter applies layers of pigmented concrete, in shades of gray, terracotta red, and forest green (and any other color a customer desires).

Landscape designer Todd Richardson has placed Lunaform pots in many of his clients' gardens, and even his own gardens, at home and outside his Biddeford office. "The beauty of Lunaform is that when you see one of their pots in a landscape, your eye believes that it should be there," Todd says. "They exist in the Maine landscape in a way that's sympathetic rather than dominating." Todd also cites the versatility of the pots as a major draw. They can be used in water features, as planters, or as stand-alone structural pieces that punctuate the organic shapes of the landscape. He also frequently employs several Lunaform pots in a single space, creating "echoes of graceful forms" throughout the design.

The harmony with the natural surroundings is something that Dan and Phid have strived to achieve over decades of continual work. "I believe strongly in Malcolm Gladwell's ten thousand hours rule of achievement," says Dan, referring to the guidelines for mastery put forth in Gladwell's book *Outliers*. "That's the gestation period for real professionalism. We've split the hours, Phid and I, and now we no longer have to play at anything." Dan continues: "In college, I called myself a painter. I was pretending, playing at professionalism. You pretend and you pretend until one day, you no longer pretend. You just are." After years of building their business, and layer and layer of concrete, Lunaform has become a valued and integral part of the landscape, blending seamlessly into the wild, natural world of Maine.

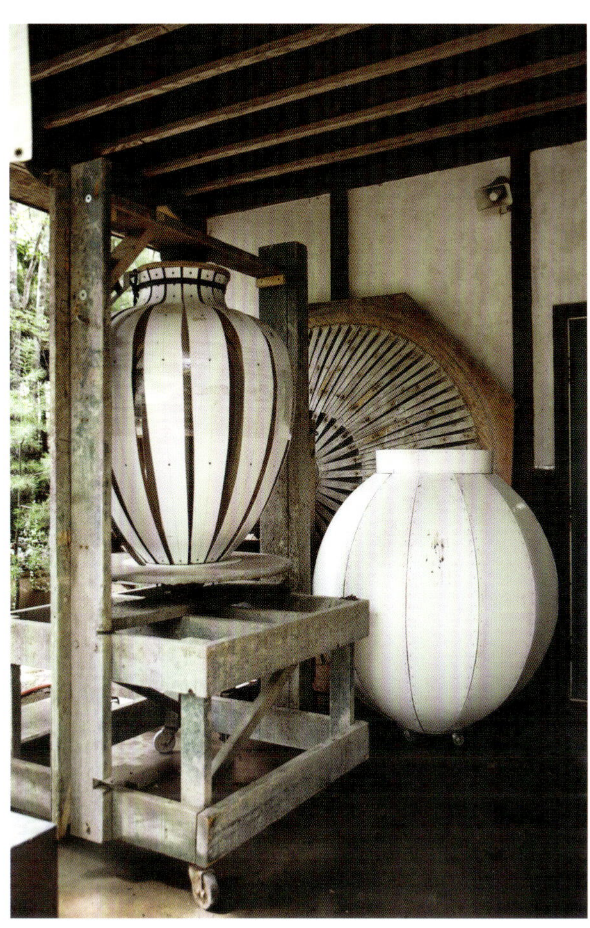

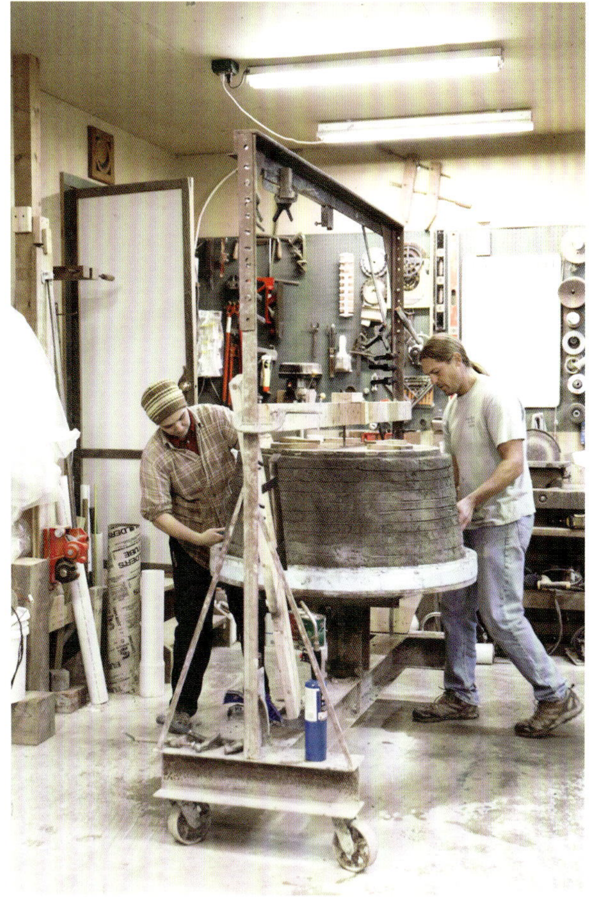

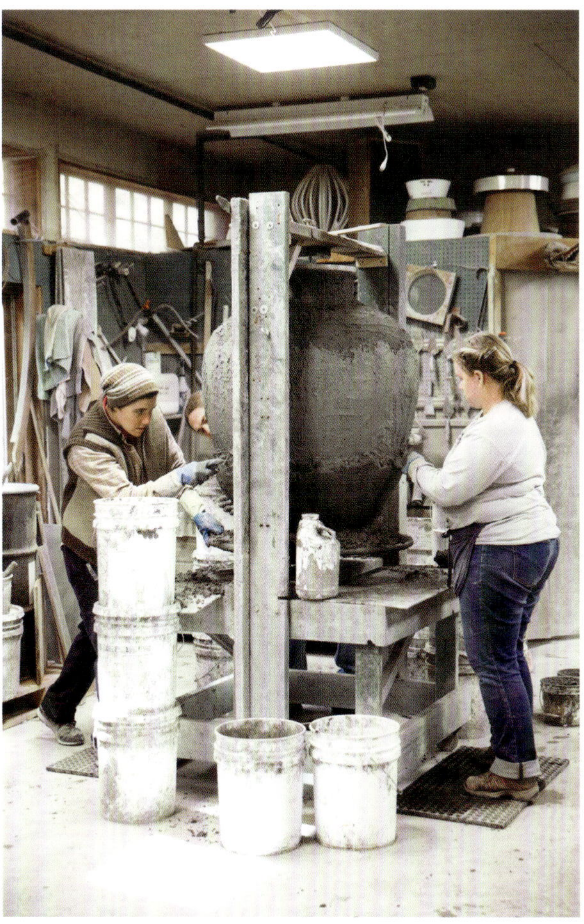

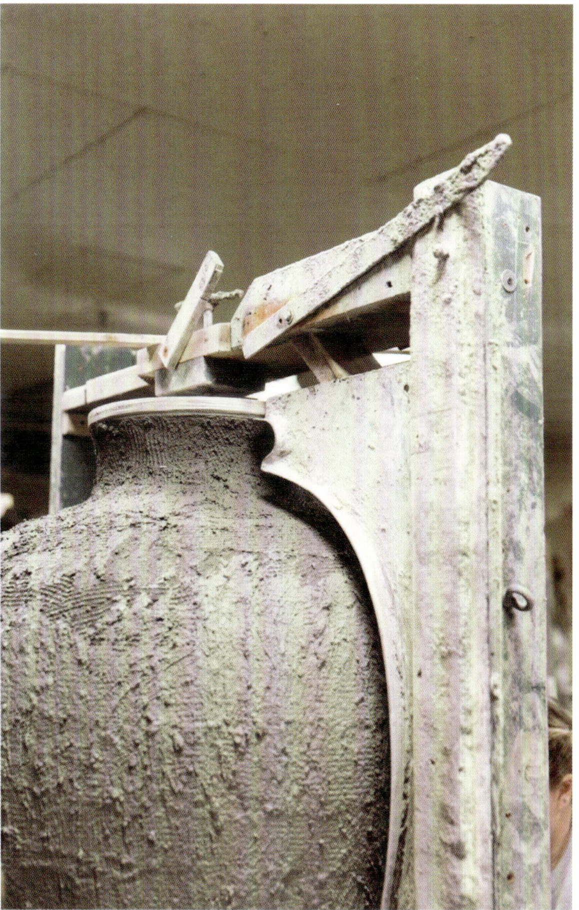

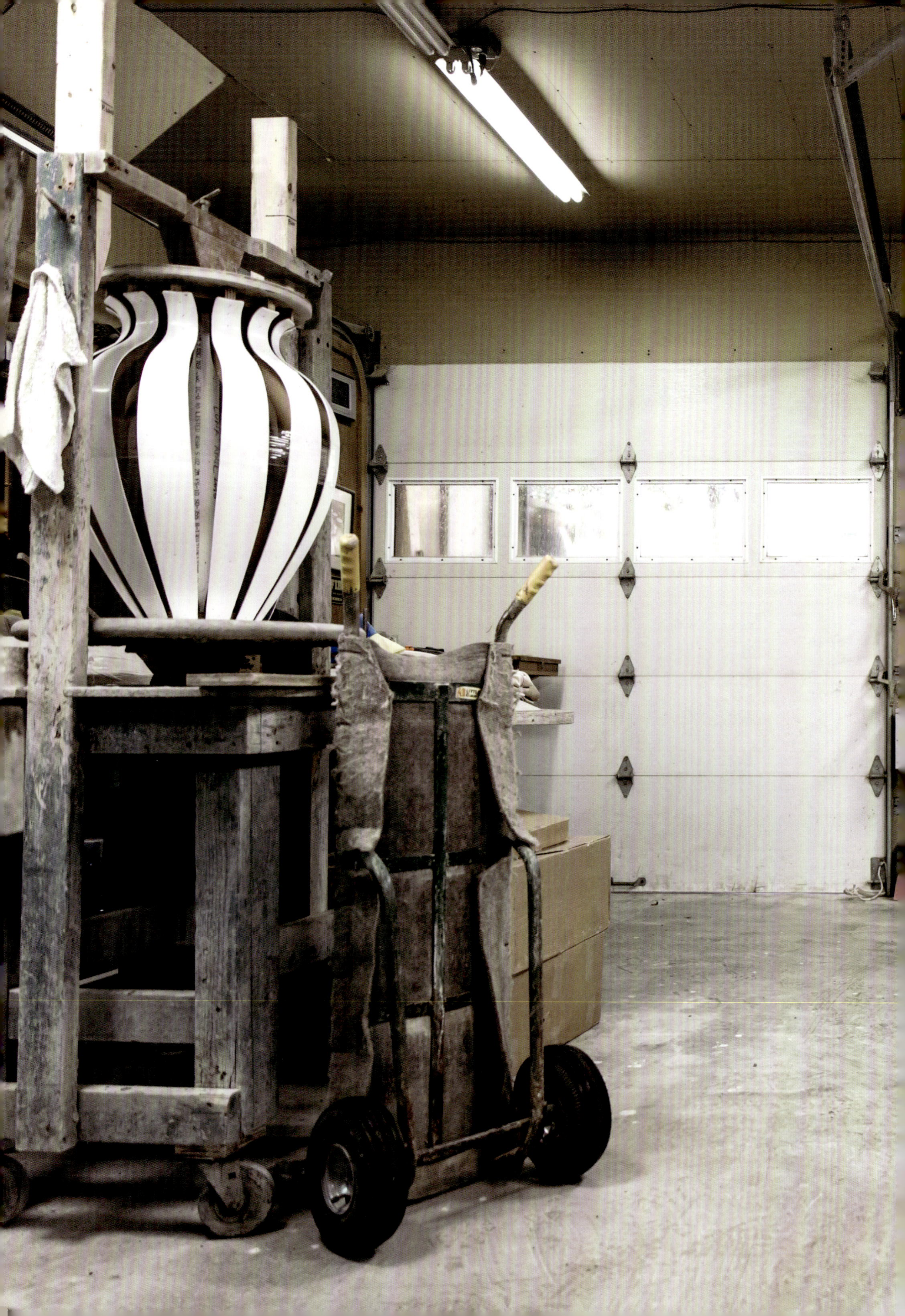

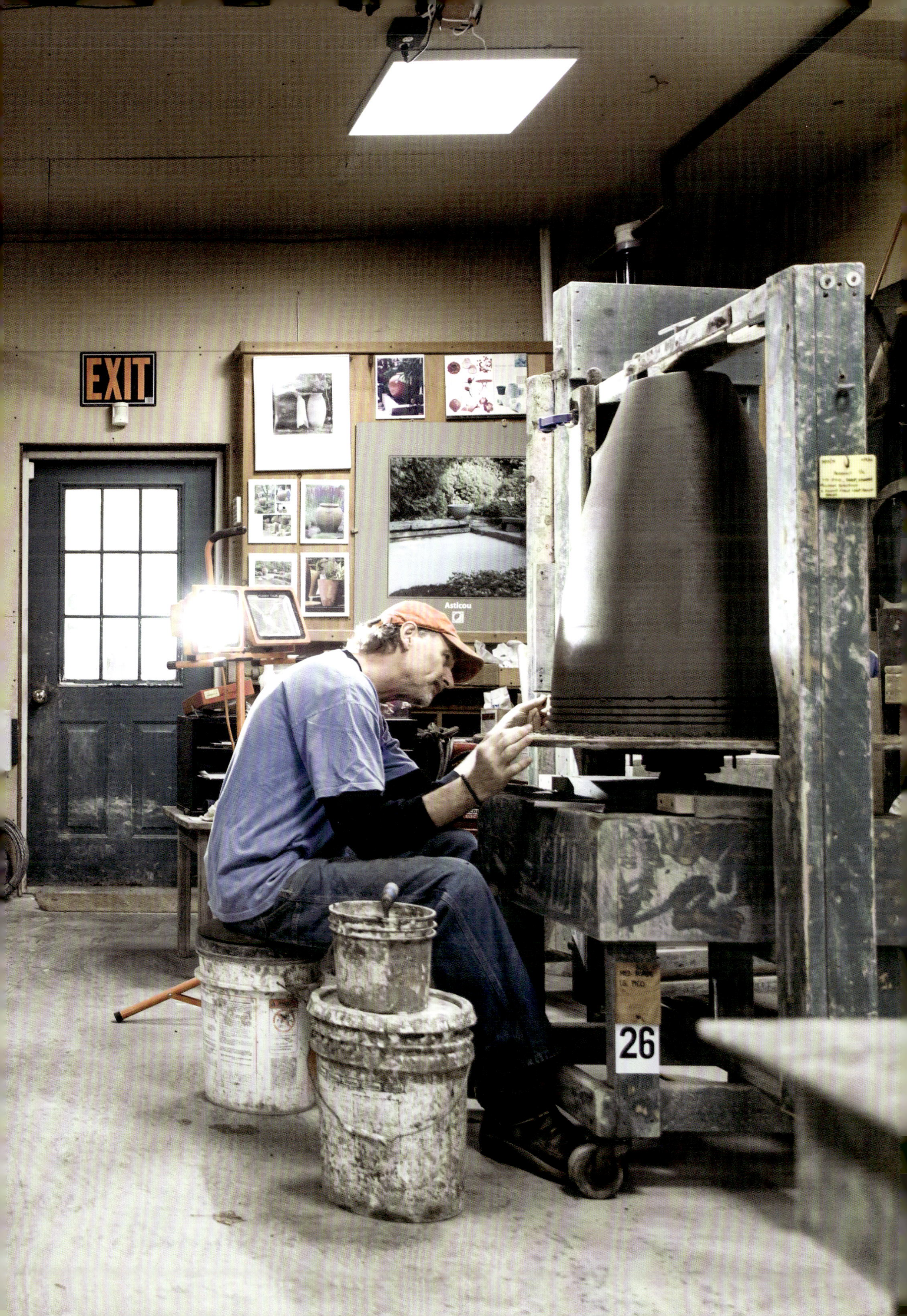
EXIT
Asticou
26

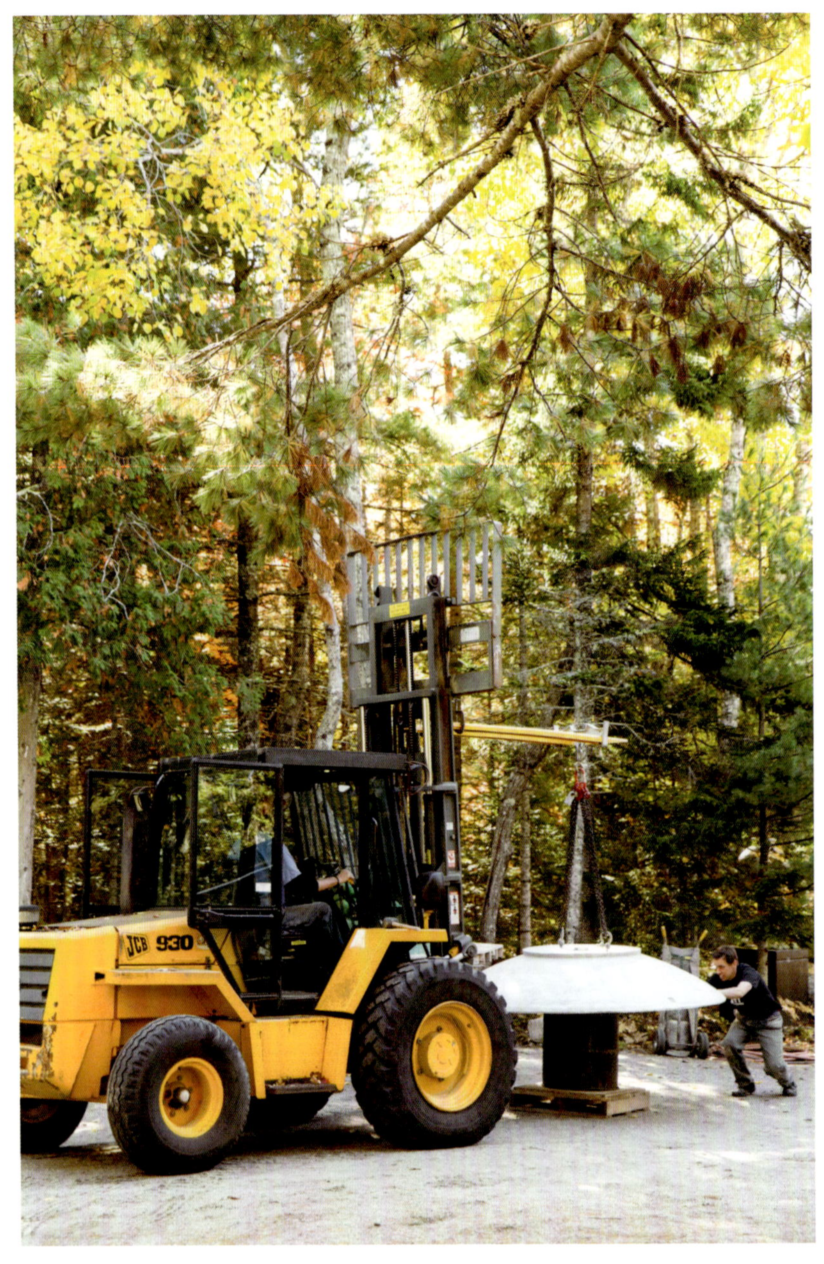
JCB 930

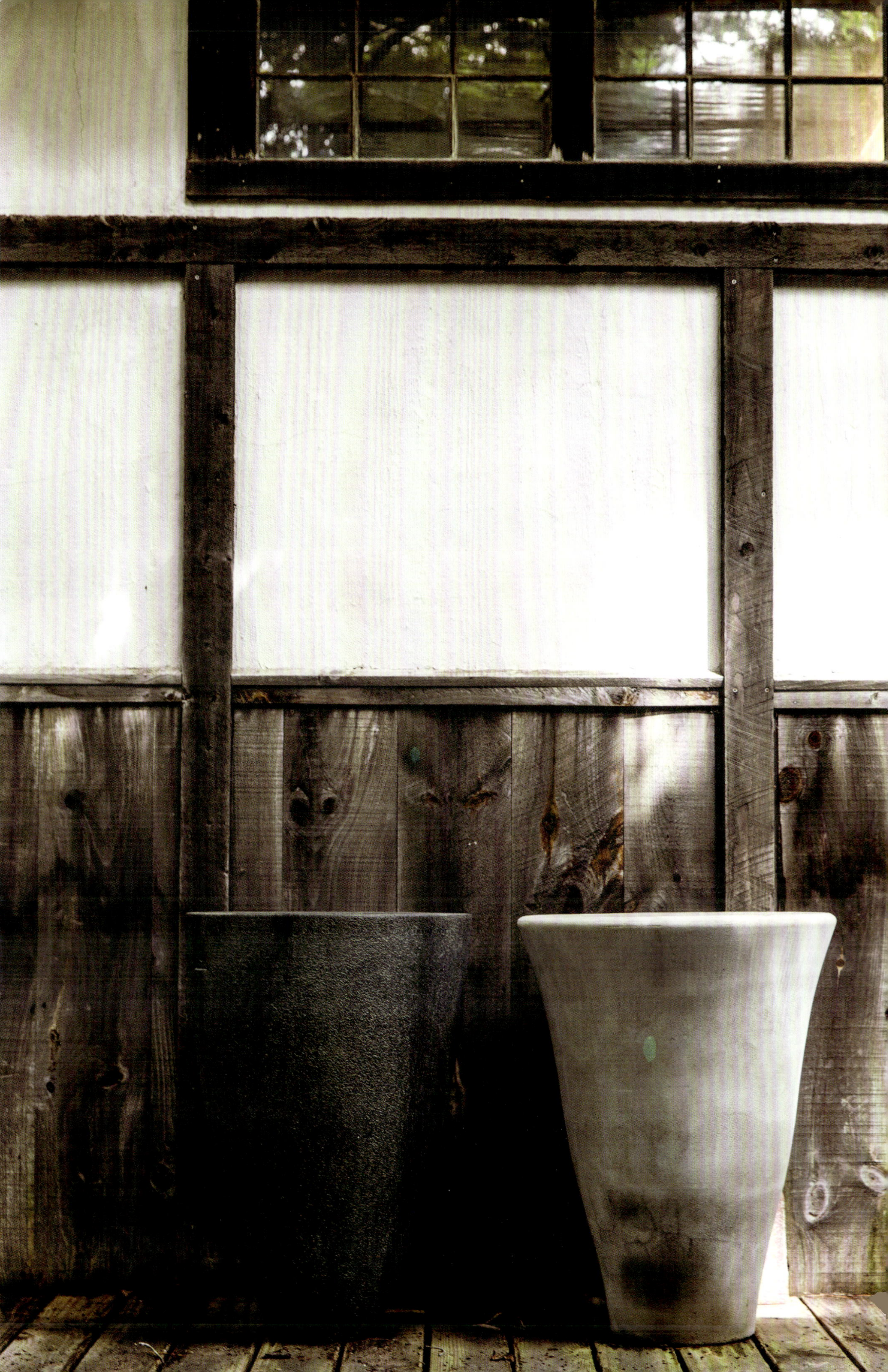

Mahoosuc Guide Service

Newry

Before anyone mounts a sled, Kevin Slater asks for silence. "Please, do not talk while riding on the dogsled," he says. Then the bearded guide does something strange: he leans over and begins to breathe heavily while patting his knees quickly, rhythmically. "That's the sound you'll hear," he says. "There's an Inuit word for it." And with a vapor of breath escaping his mouth, he utters a series of guttural syllables: *Iv-ak-kak*. This, he explains, is the noise of the dogs running and painting. It's the sound of trail, snow, and speed.

Minutes later, a reverent calm comes over the group, broken only by Polly Mahoney's shouts of "Gee!" "Haw!" and "Good girl, Amber! Good baby, good girl!" Amber, the dog leading Polly's team, is a two-year-old Yukon husky, a regal creature with honey-colored fur and a strong, lean body. Michaela O'Connor, an apprentice dogsled driver, or "musher," follows closely behind with her team. Kevin brings up the rear with five large, broad-shouldered, black-and-white dogs. The February frost obscures the faces of the mushers, and the rhythm of the dogs' paws as they fly over the snow is like a heartbeat.

Kevin and Polly have been driving sleds and guiding wilderness adventures in Maine for over four decades. Together they run Mahoosuc Guide Service, a small company based in Newry, Maine, near the White Mountains of New Hampshire and the seemingly endless white expanse of Umbagog Lake. They are also partners in life, although they have never married. ("We don't need a piece of paper to tell us what we already know," Kevin says.) In the winter, they lead guests on day-long and overnight wilder-ness expeditions, the longest lasting two weeks. In the summer, they guide groups down the rivers of northern Maine in handmade canoes built by Kevin in his cavernous workshop, where the dogsleds are also made. During the shoulder seasons, Polly and Kevin train their dogs, repair their sleds, and teach the occasional wilderness course. Their business comes piecemeal, as it does for many of Maine's self-employed craftsmen, and they take an income where they can.

Dogs, Kevin explains, are expensive to care for, particularly in their final years of life. "We have forty dogs right now. We raised them from puppies and we'll keep them until their final breath," he says.

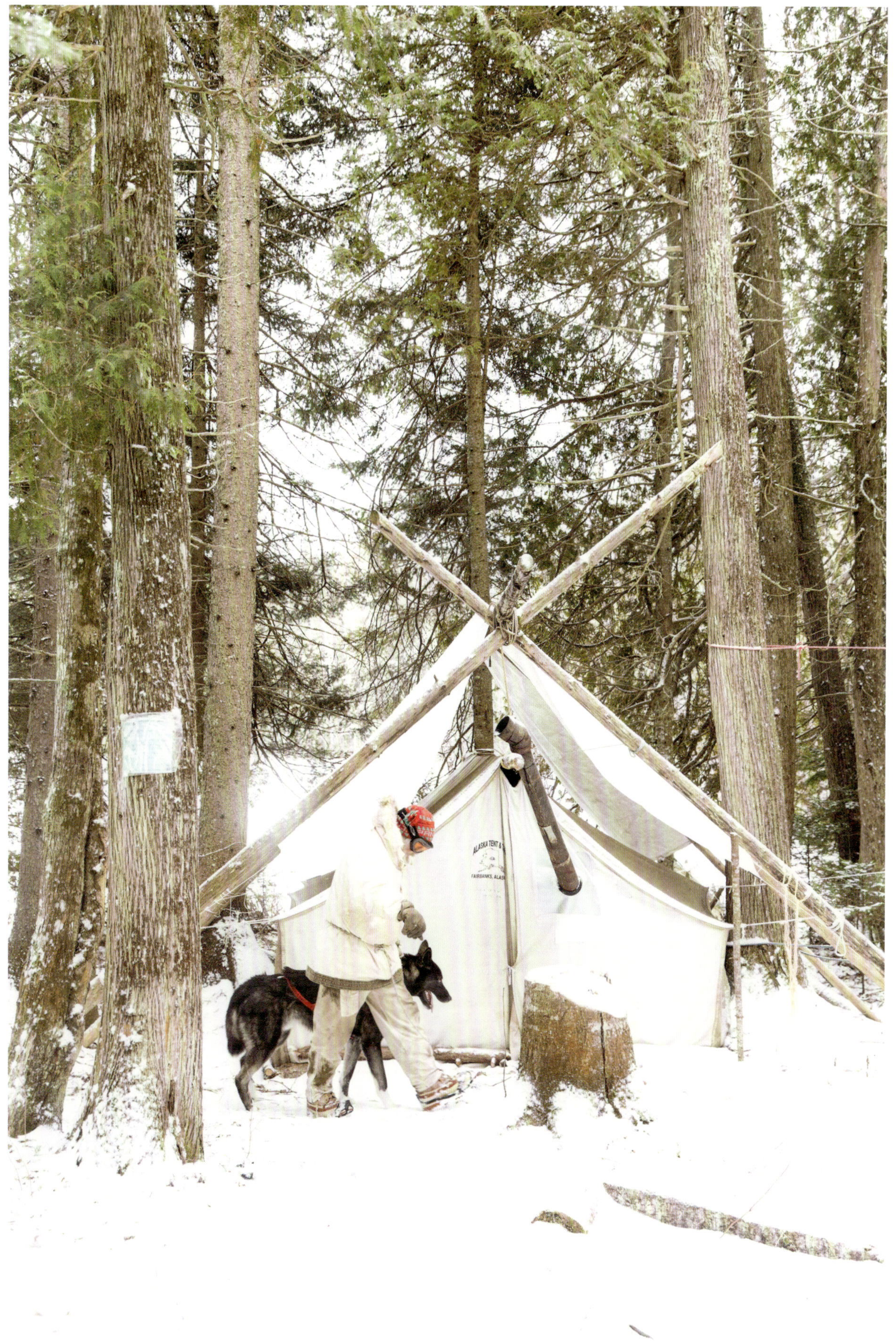

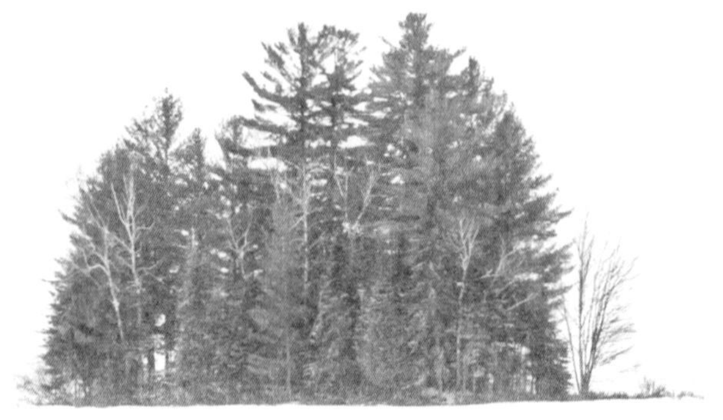

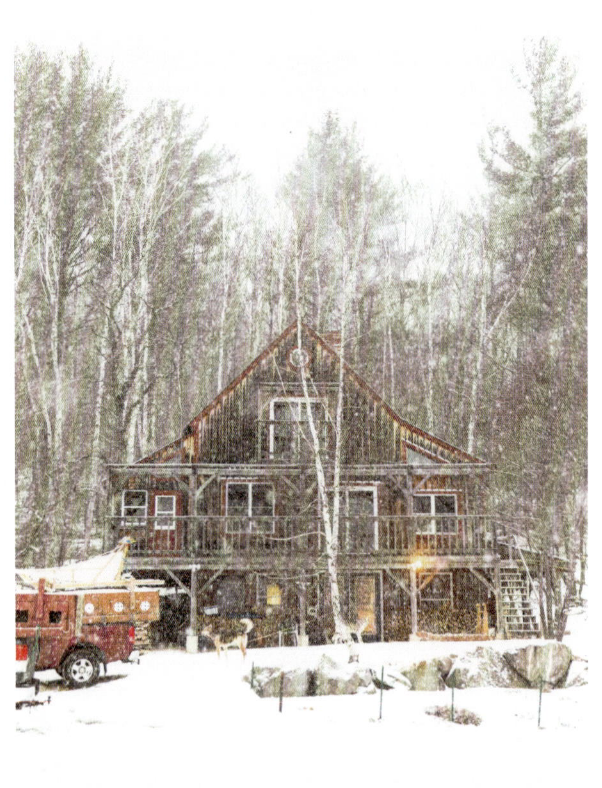

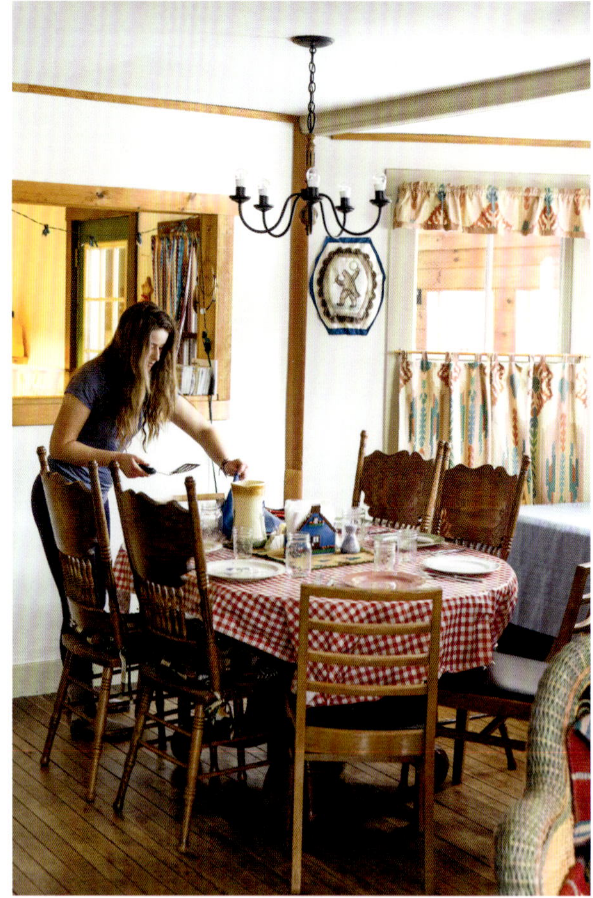

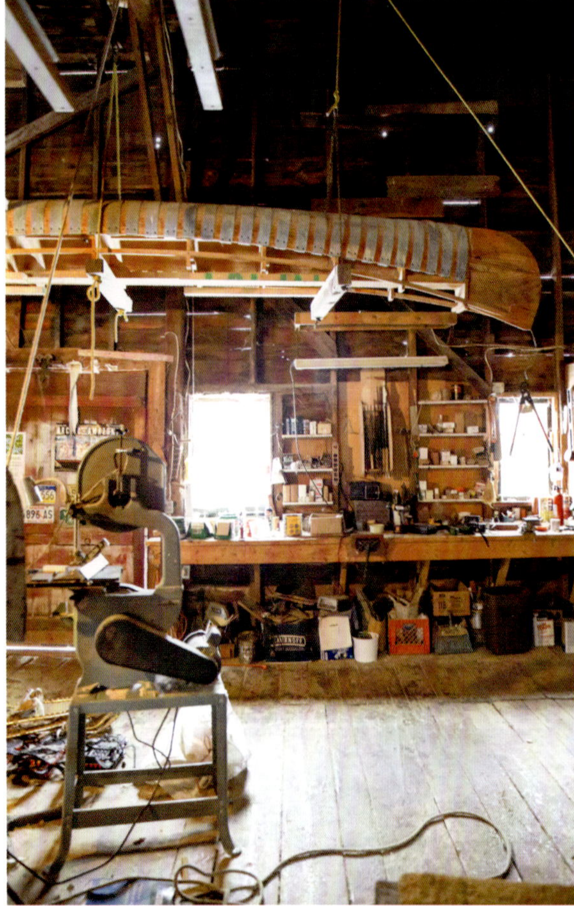

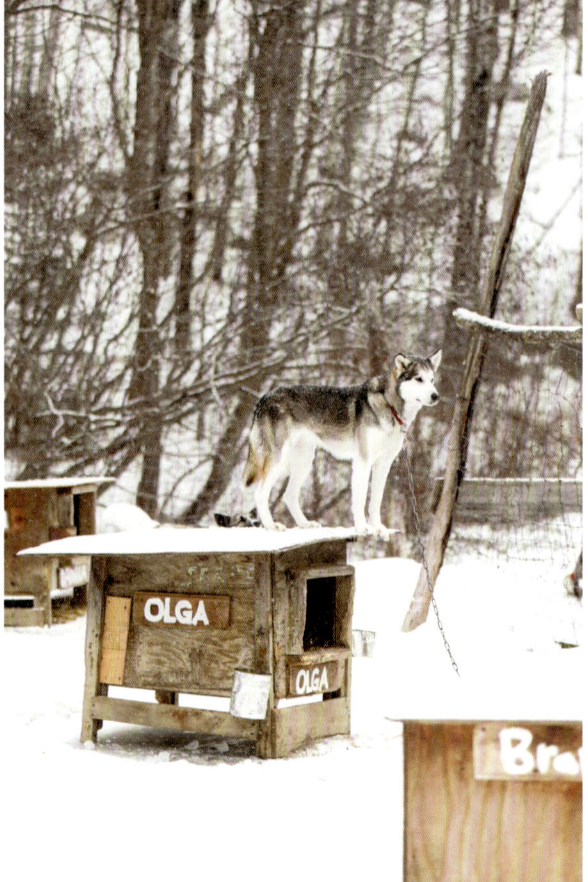
OLGA
OLGA

"Most of their expenses come in the final months of their lives. A lot of mushers will dump dogs when they can no longer run, but any dog that works for me for ten years is going to get a full retirement." Polly adds later that some mushers will shoot their dogs once they're no longer useful; this happened up in the Yukon, where Polly learned to mush, but not at Mahoosuc. "They're our family, our children," she says. "They have their own personalities, their own spirits." In the past, Polly has taken her dogs to an energy healer, where she learned that two of her pups, sisters who were attached at the hip, have been companions through several lives. "Those girls are one soul in two bodies," she says. Polly and Kevin have no children of their own. "It was never the right time," explains Polly. And yet their life has been filled with the love for each other and their dogs. Like the sister-dogs, Polly and Kevin believe they were destined to meet. To put it simply, they make perfect sense together. Polly is a softer personality, yet she came to their relationship with years of dogsledding experience. Kevin can be gruff, but he tempers his brusqueness with a wicked sense of humor and a broad smile.

Polly and Kevin lead a life filled with physical labor, early mornings, and sacrifice. Often, they put the needs of the dogs before their own. It would be easy to idealize their lives, to gloss over the smell of dog shit and the challenges of their work, and focus on the serene beauty that surrounds them. Or cast them as trailblazers rejecting the stresses and pace of twenty-first-century life. But Polly and Kevin have worked hard to learn the history behind their skills and to respect the guides who came before. "If you go back one hundred years, a guide who needed a pair of snowshoes or a toboggan for their winter trap line wouldn't go to L.L.Bean," observes Kevin. "They would go into the woods, cut down a tree, and make a toboggan themselves. I want to keep that tradition alive." It also brings him great joy to do this work himself. "When I realized I could live my life outside, spending every day in the woods, it was a no-brainer," Kevin says, using a favorite term. Build your own canoe instead of buying one? No-brainer. Keep your dogs after they're useful? No-brainer. Stay with the one woman who matches your stamina, who is the yin to your yang? That's a real no-brainer.

Due to their busy schedules and the needs of their dogs, Polly and Kevin spend quite a bit of time apart. They can't always guide together, but when they do, the chemistry is palpable. They work seamlessly, communicating with a look; and when that doesn't cut it, with shouts that ring across the ice. As the morning turns to afternoon, they take the small group of first-time dogsledders to a wooded camp on the shores of Umbagog Lake. From afar, the tree line appears unbroken. Up close, glimpses of canvas are visible through the pines. The guides have built a small campground here with four huts (and, nestled out of sight, an open-air composting toilet). Polly and Kevin tie up the dogs and begin preparing lunch. The dogs pant and bark joyfully before settling down into a bed of straw. They've been running all morning, and they too are ready for a rest.

Inside a tent, Polly ladles out steaming bowls of corn chowder. She toasts bagels in a cast-iron pan over a wood-burning stove, and passes each one to the next hungry sledder, along with a tub of cream cheese. The food is filling, warm, and good. The sledders chat about jobs and politics and movies. It's strange, this talk of modern life when all around are the trappings of tradition: tents and sleds and snowshoes that have been made by hand, built to withstand the weather. Outside, a dog named Olga stretches her back, rolling around in the straw, with her belly offered to the sky. Soon, under the guiding hand of her owners, she will run again.

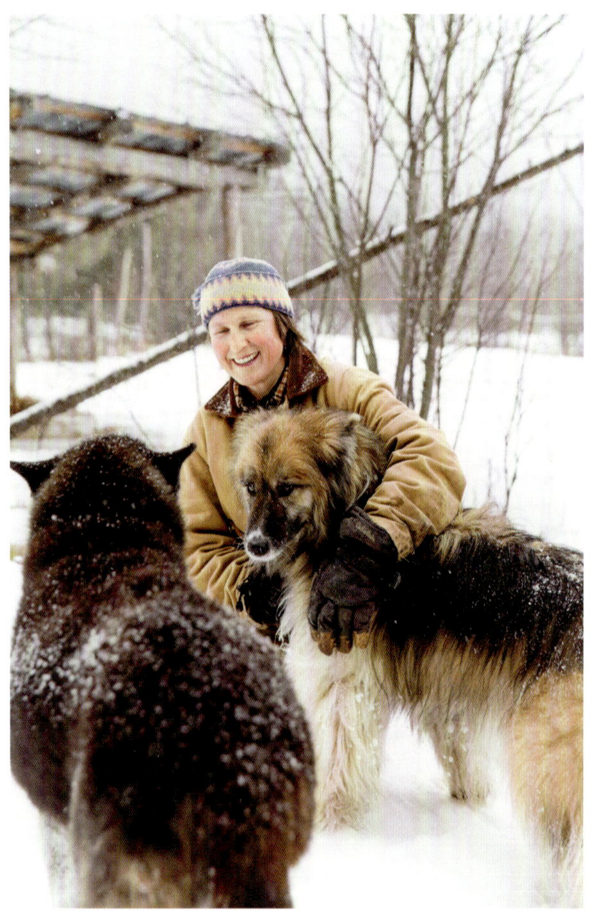

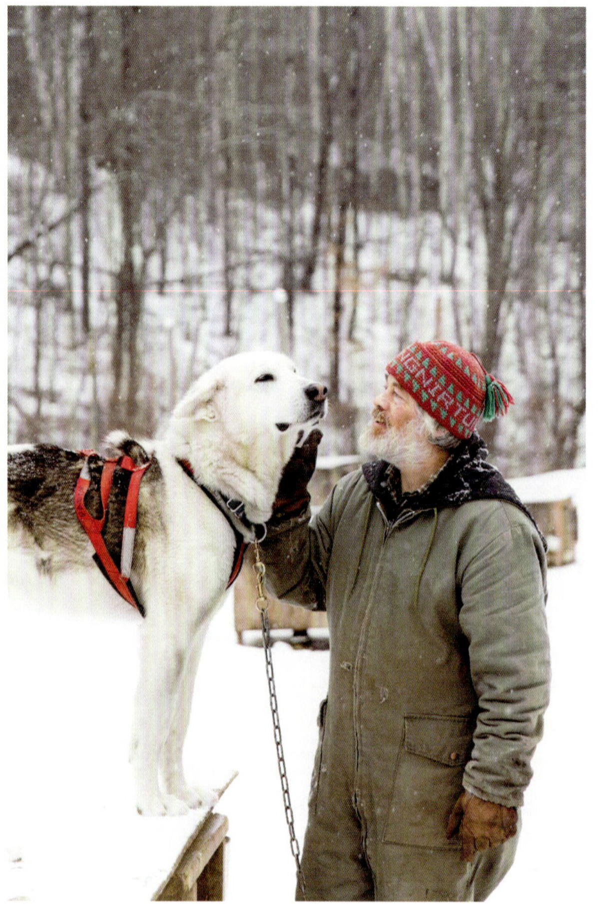

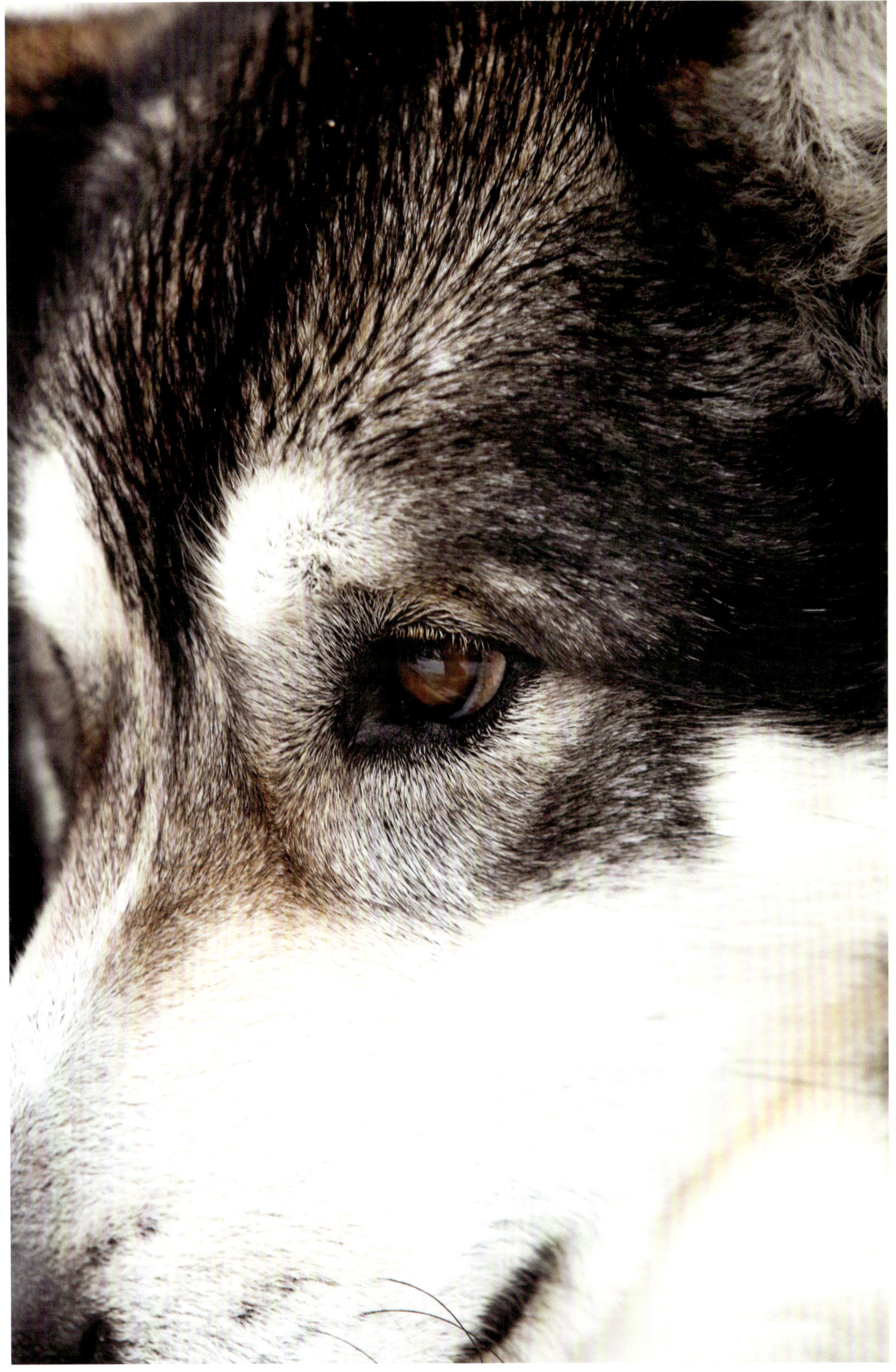

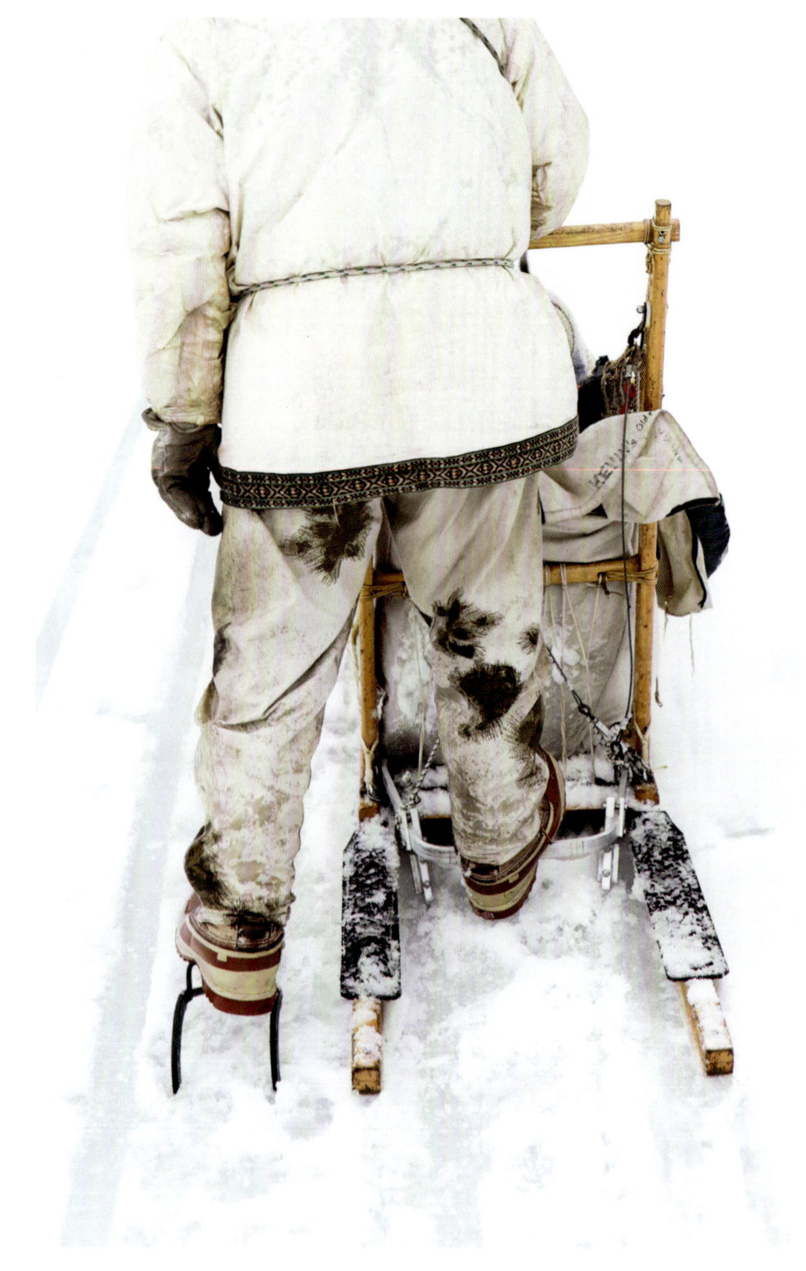

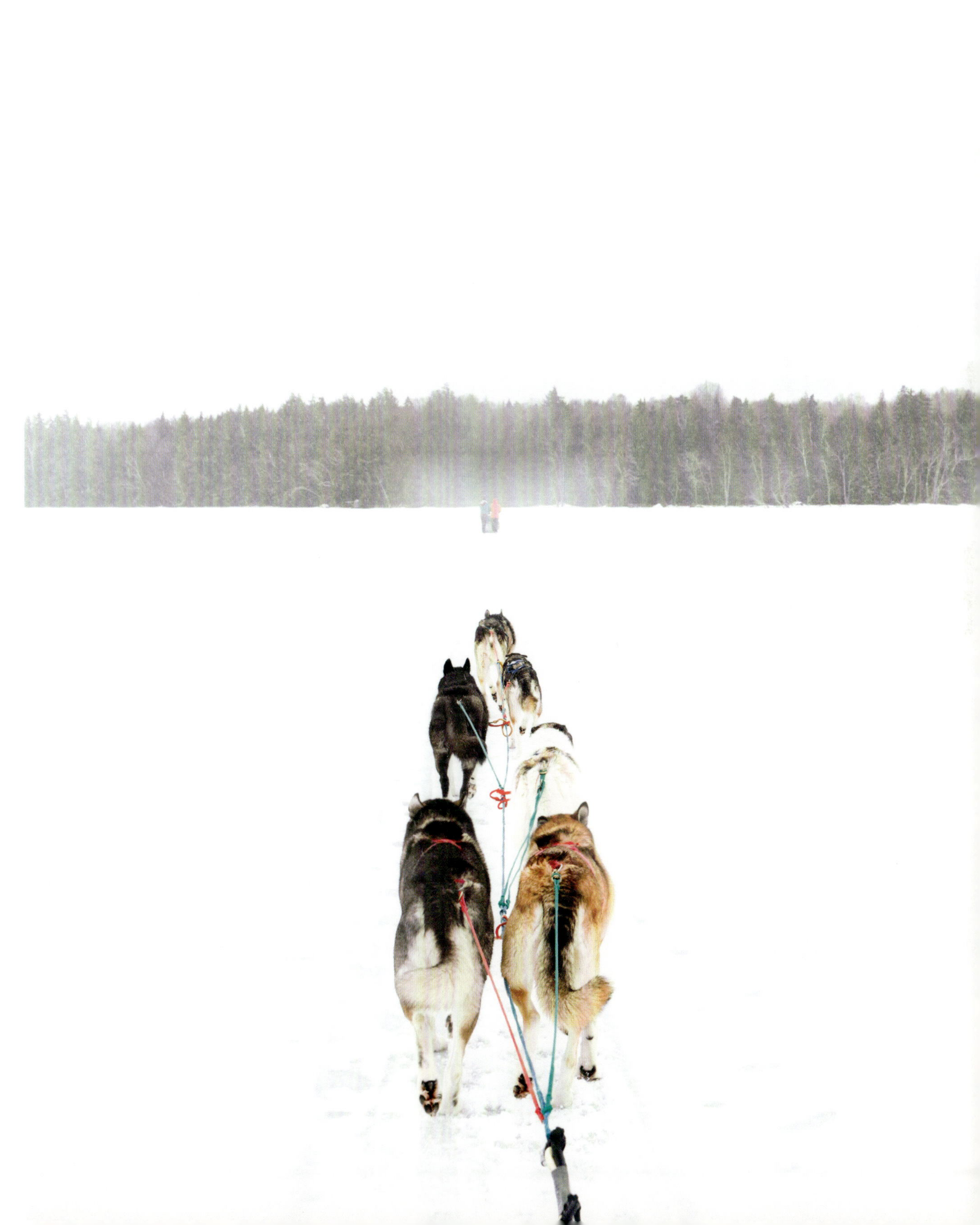

Artisan Boatworks

Brunswick

"A lot of small businesses in Maine fail because their owners are too passionate about their craft and not passionate enough about the business and they end up essentially giving their product away," says Alec Brainerd, founder and owner of Artisan Boatworks. Alec is determined not to make that mistake. Passion may have launched his career, but practicality keeps it going.

It's a busy day at Steamboat Landing in Camden, where Artisan Boatworks is launching two wooden sailboats, the *Mariah* and the *Silk Purse*. The summer sun beats down on the *Mariah*. Alec Brainerd's muscular arms are reflected in the gleaming blue hull as he inspects the mahogany rudder. The carpenters who built the boat take it for its inaugural sail and then it's ready for delivery. Alec and his crew move fast, attaching the boom and unfolding the ivory-colored sails, which crackle and snap as the wind tries to pry them from Alec's hands. Few sailboats in the yard are as popular as the *Mariah*. A Subaru drives by, and the driver slows to shout, "Beautiful boat!" Sailors and kayakers walking by on their way to the ocean stop to ask, "Is she for sale?" "Where's this one headed?" "What kind of boat is *that*?" She's not for sale and she's headed to Solomon's Island in Maryland, where her owners will take possession of the sixteen-foot (twelve-and-a-half at the waterline) vessel. Based on plans from 1914, she's a little slow for Alec, but he calls her a "great learner boat." Originally, he explains, this model, produced by the Herreshoff Manufacturing Company on Narragansett Bay in Rhode Island, to teach kids how to sail, was perfect for novice sailors or older yachtsmen looking for an easy boat that's nearly impossible to capsize.

Adherence to historic practices is a cornerstone of Artisan Boatworks's business. It's also the facet of boatbuilding that excites Alec the most. A Maine native and lifelong sailor, Alec founded his Midcoast boatbuilding company after learning how to build and restore wooden boats at Seal Cove Boatyard in Brooksville, then at Rockport Marine. These early experiences gave him a keen appreciation for wooden boats, while providing him with the practical skills he needed to create artful vessels. In 2002, he established Artisan Boatworks. "I had the stamina at the time to work eighty-hour weeks," he recalls. "I founded the company because I wanted to work on smaller boats and to build according to the old

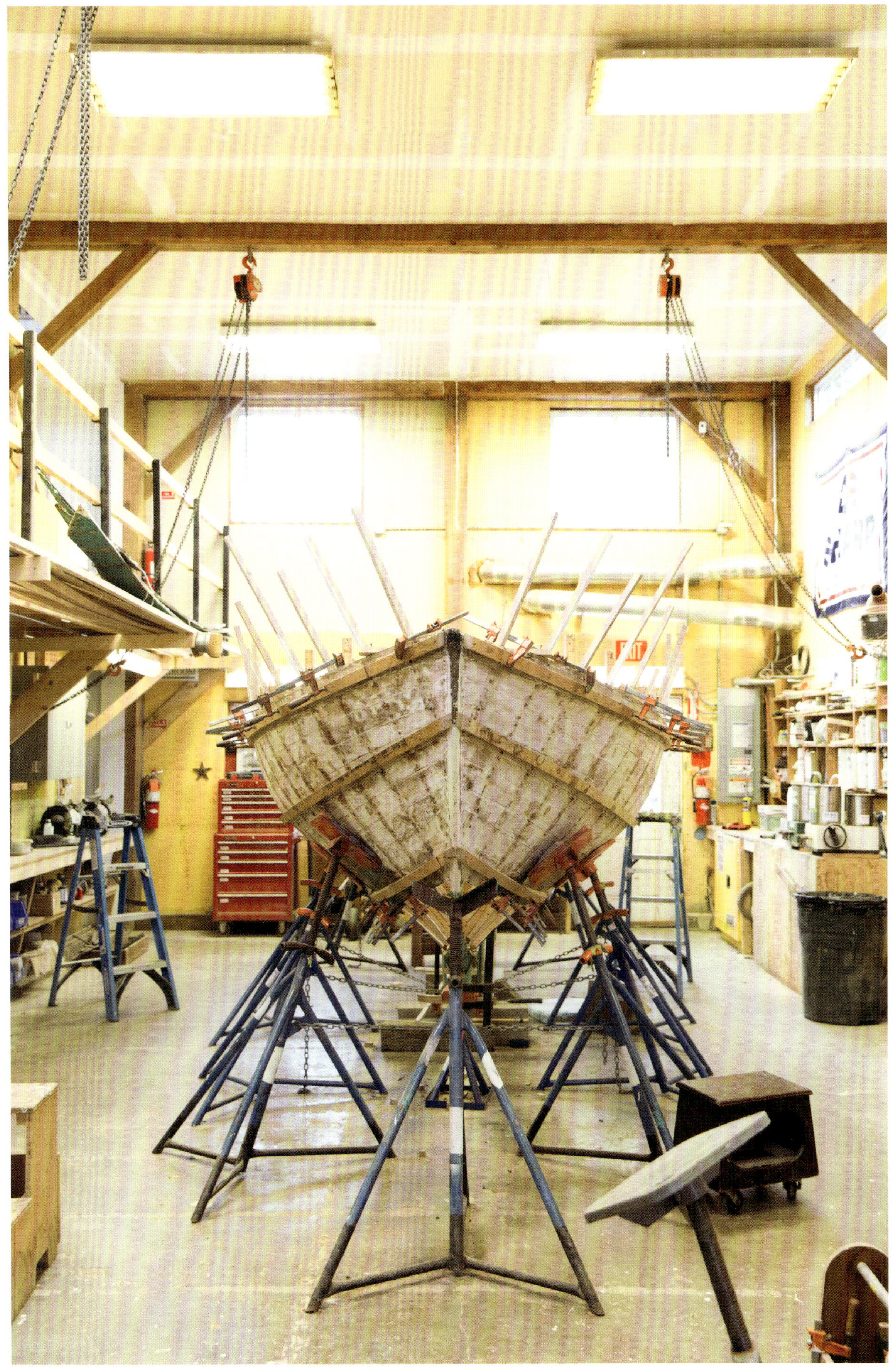

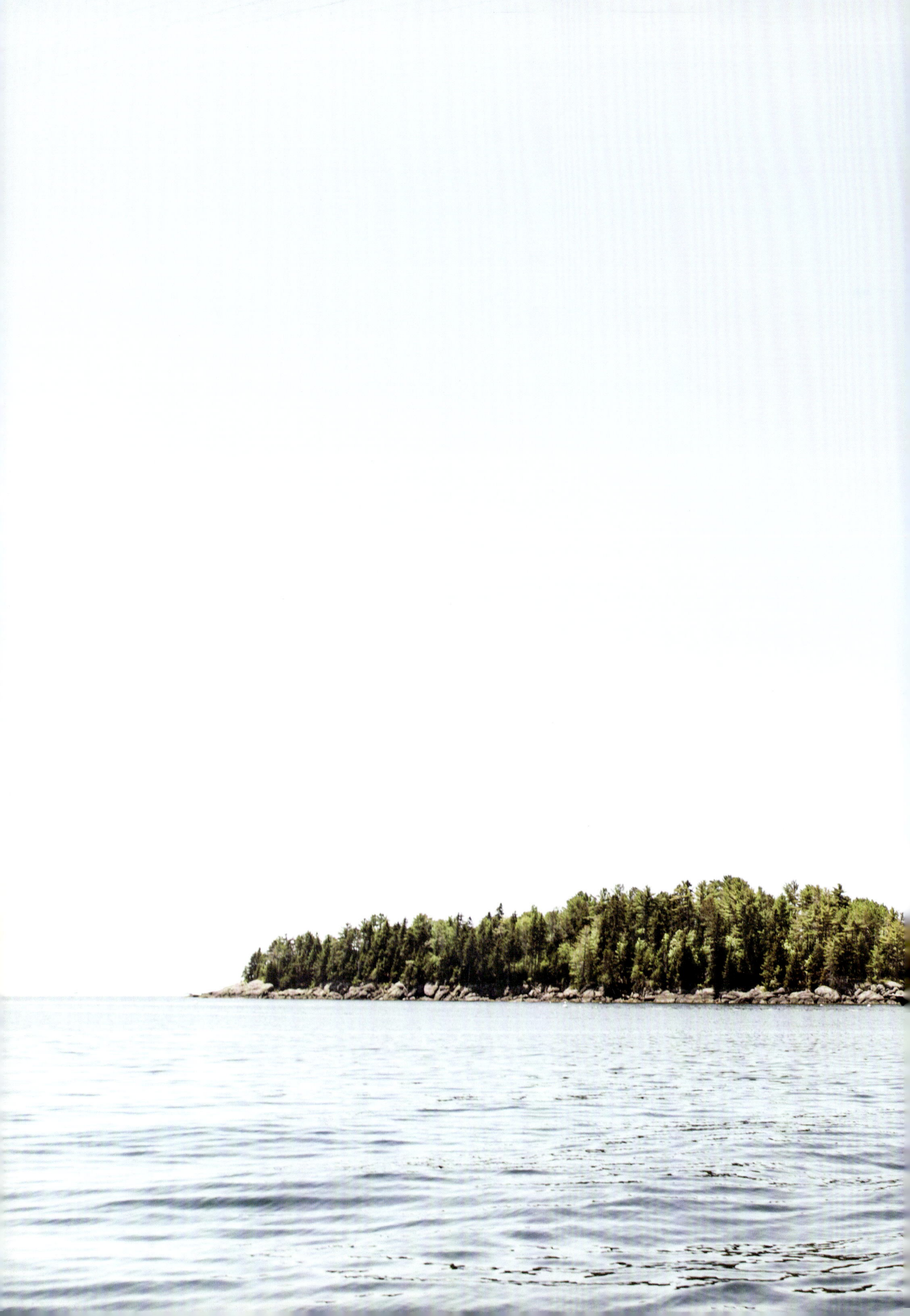

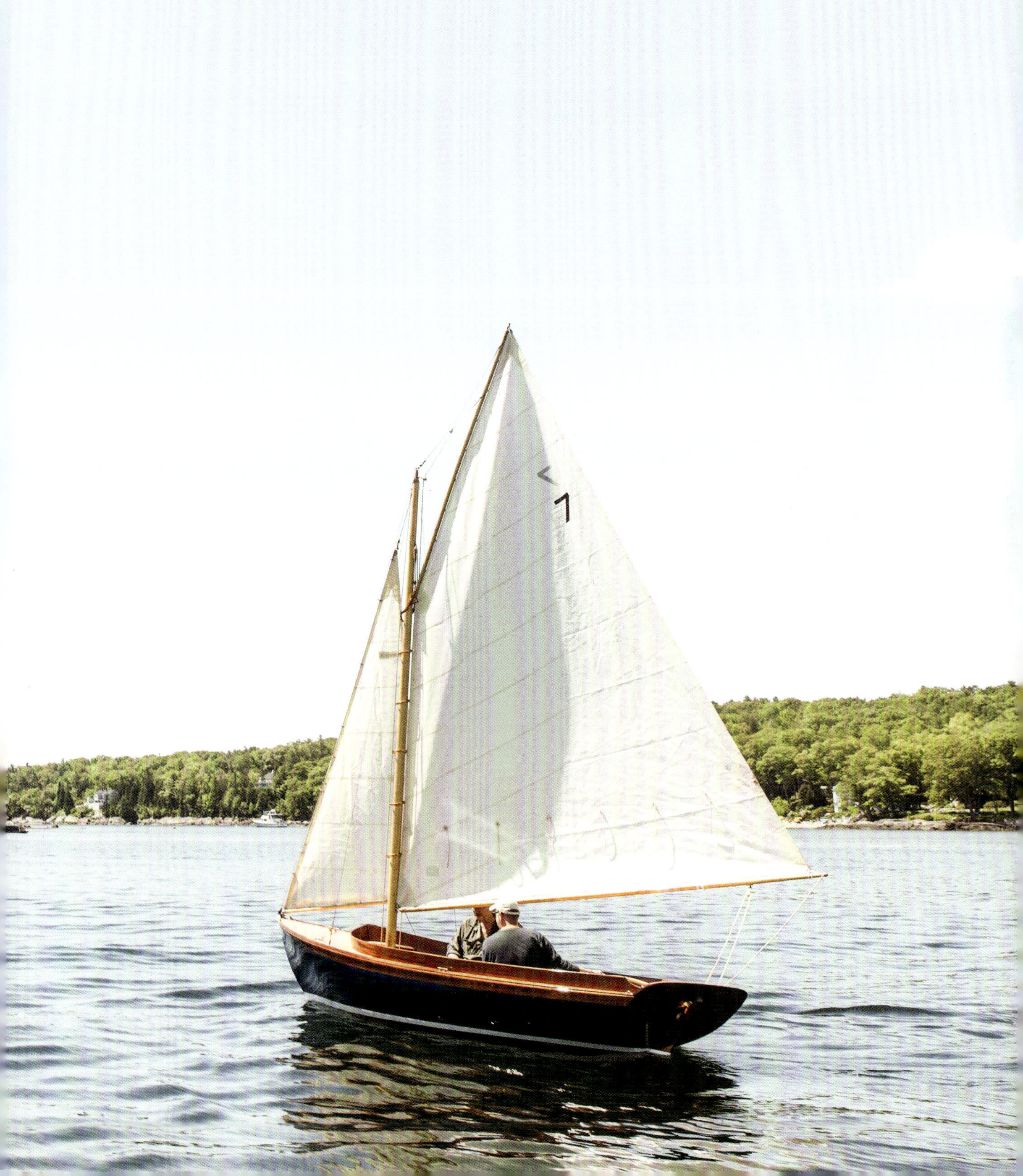

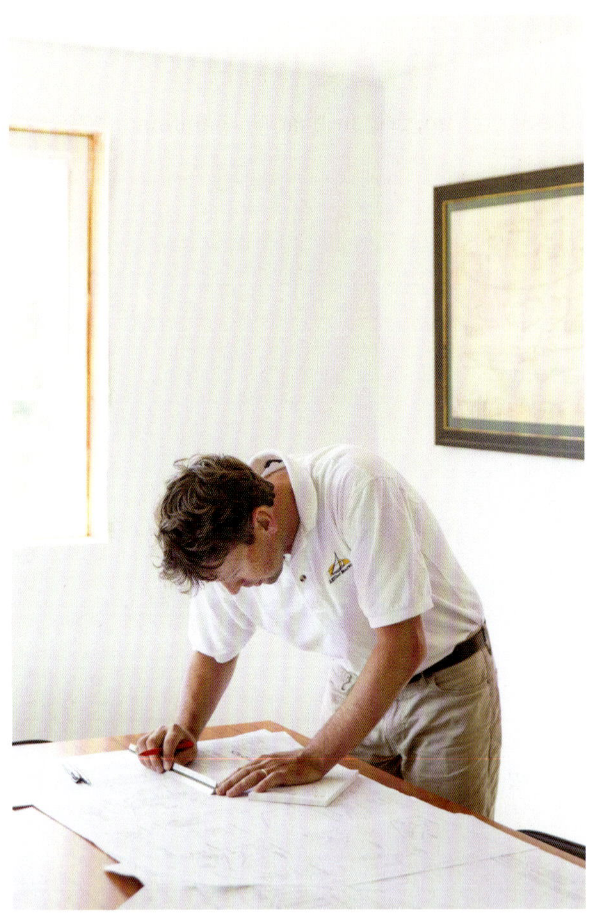

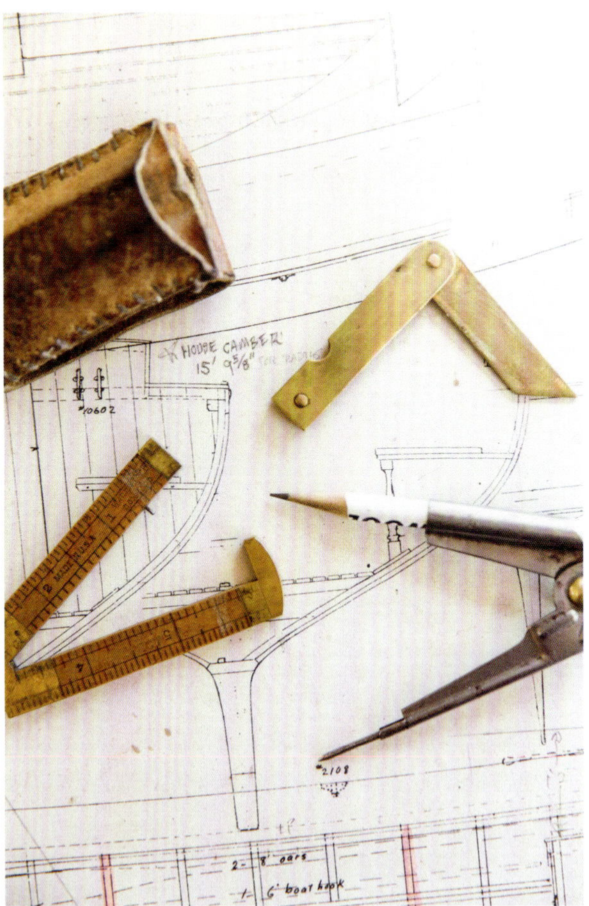
HOUSE CAMBER
15' 9 5/8"
10602
2108
2- 8' oars
1- 6' boat hook

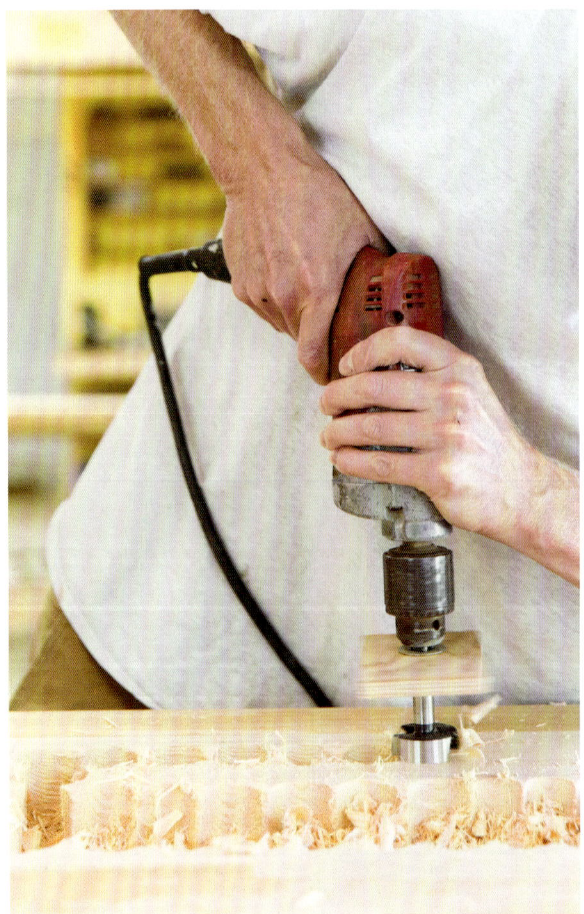

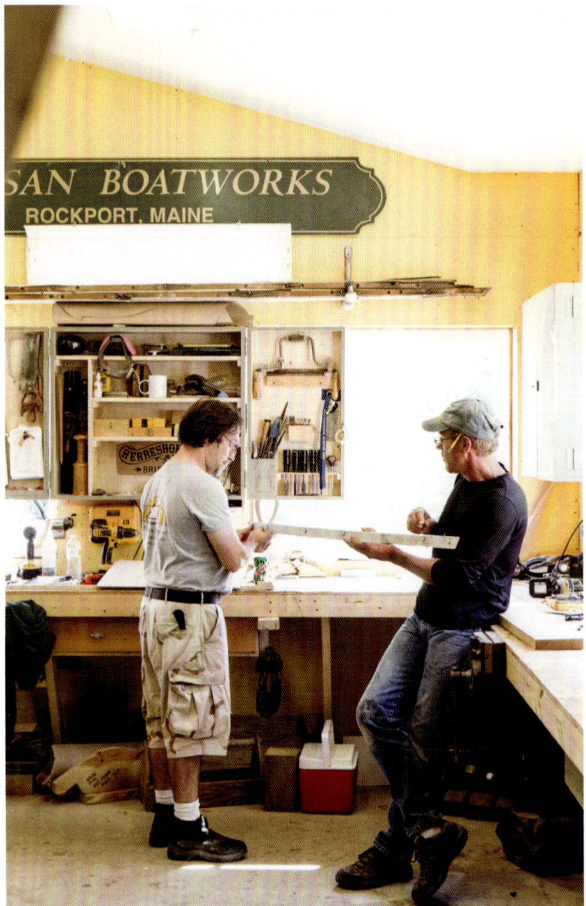
SAN BOATWORKS
ROCKPORT, MAINE

plans. I've always been drawn to boats that were designed in the 1920s or 1930s. I think there's been a resurgence in that aesthetic, and an increased desire to have boats that are timeless, true to the originals." For Alec, wooden boats also provide a value that is unmatched by smooth fiberglass. "One of the reasons that classic wooden boats last so long is that they're infinitely repairable," he explains. "It's like the grandfather's ax, which has had three new handles and a head that's been replaced twice, but it's still the same ax. As long as you keep putting new parts on it, it's still the same as it ever was."

While Alec's passion for boats and the hands-on work of construction compelled him to establish his own company, his focus has shifted over the years. With a young family at home, Alec is no longer excited about putting in eighty hours a week. He wants to make a viable business so that he can afford to continue living in Maine and provide a stable future for his children. Over the past decade, Alec has realized that the best place for him to be is in the office, not the workshop. He's recruited a skilled crew to build his boats, but he no longer spends nights working late with a hand planer. "At this point, I'm an aspiring businessman who happens to have a boatbuilding business. Like everything else, it's a matter of finding a balance," he says.

Today, Artisan Boatworks remains true to the original vision. "Our main mission is building, restoring, and maintaining classic wooden boats. We squeak in a few fiberglass ones here and there, but I personally like working with wooden boats," says Dan MacNaughton, service manager, longtime yachtsman, and coauthor of *The Encyclopedia of Yacht Designers*. With almost six decades of sailing experience, Dan has spent time on many different boats and observed how materials and design affect how a boat sails. "There's something really special about wooden hulls," he says. "They have a much different feel under sail and under foot. You get the feel, from the bottom up, that the boat was handmade." He goes on to explain that even a handmade fiberglass boat can't match the design and craftsmanship of a wooden boat, particularly an old one. "They might go through the water the same way, but there's a different sound inside the hull," he says.

Watching the *Mariah* cut through the water of Camden, it's easy to understand how Alec fell in love with these historic vessels, with their graceful curves and simple shapes. It's also easy to understand why Alec and his employees have devoted their lives to restoring and recreating vintage boats—and sailing them off the Maine coast. "Sailing here is just unparalleled," Alec says as he shields his eyes from the sun, staring out at the horizon. Even from the calm waters of Camden Harbor, it's possible to see the rugged appeal of the region. Geography has conspired to create a rough and brutal coastal landscape, with jagged rock cliffs and finger-like peninsulas, not to mention the thousands of islands that jut from the water. Sailing in Maine is an endless adventure. There are always new harbors to explore, new inlets to navigate, new beaches to visit.

Sailing provides a much-needed break from the demands and fast pace of daily life, from long workweeks and constant business calls. "These things," says Dan, gesturing toward his phone, "stop working on the other side of those islands. Out of touch, you can decompress and recenter. It's just you and the boat and whoever is with you. It gives you time to appreciate the company that you're in." He pauses a moment, and then speaks for every sailor who has fallen in love with the freedom of open water: "It's really something. It's meditative. Out there, it's like going to church."

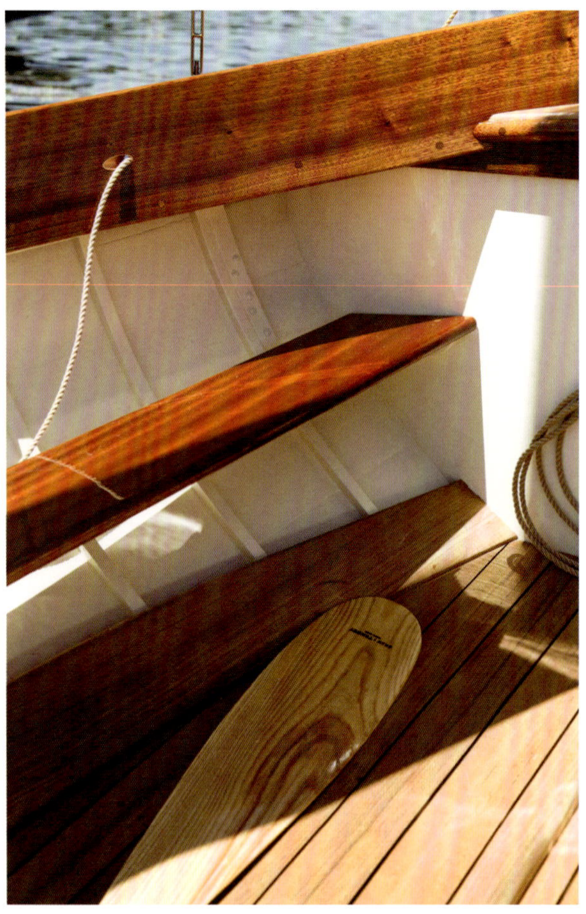

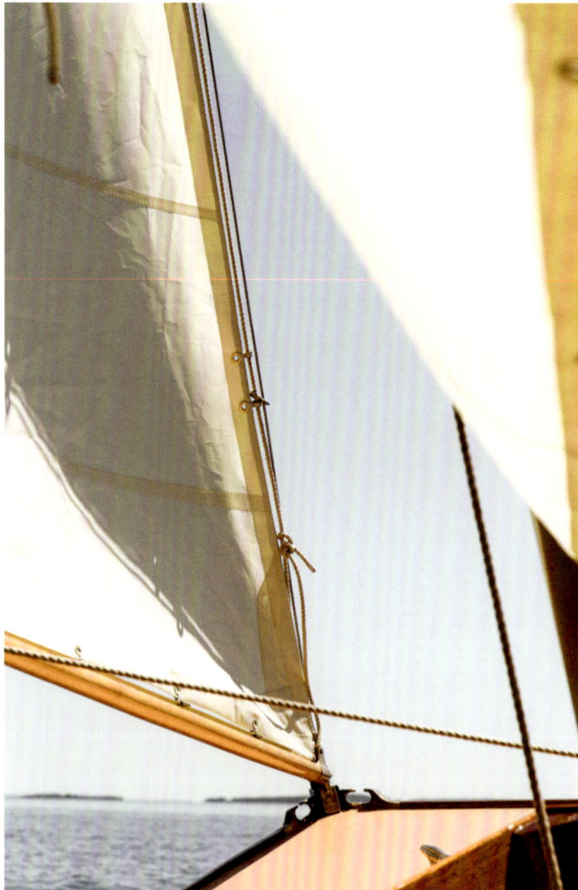

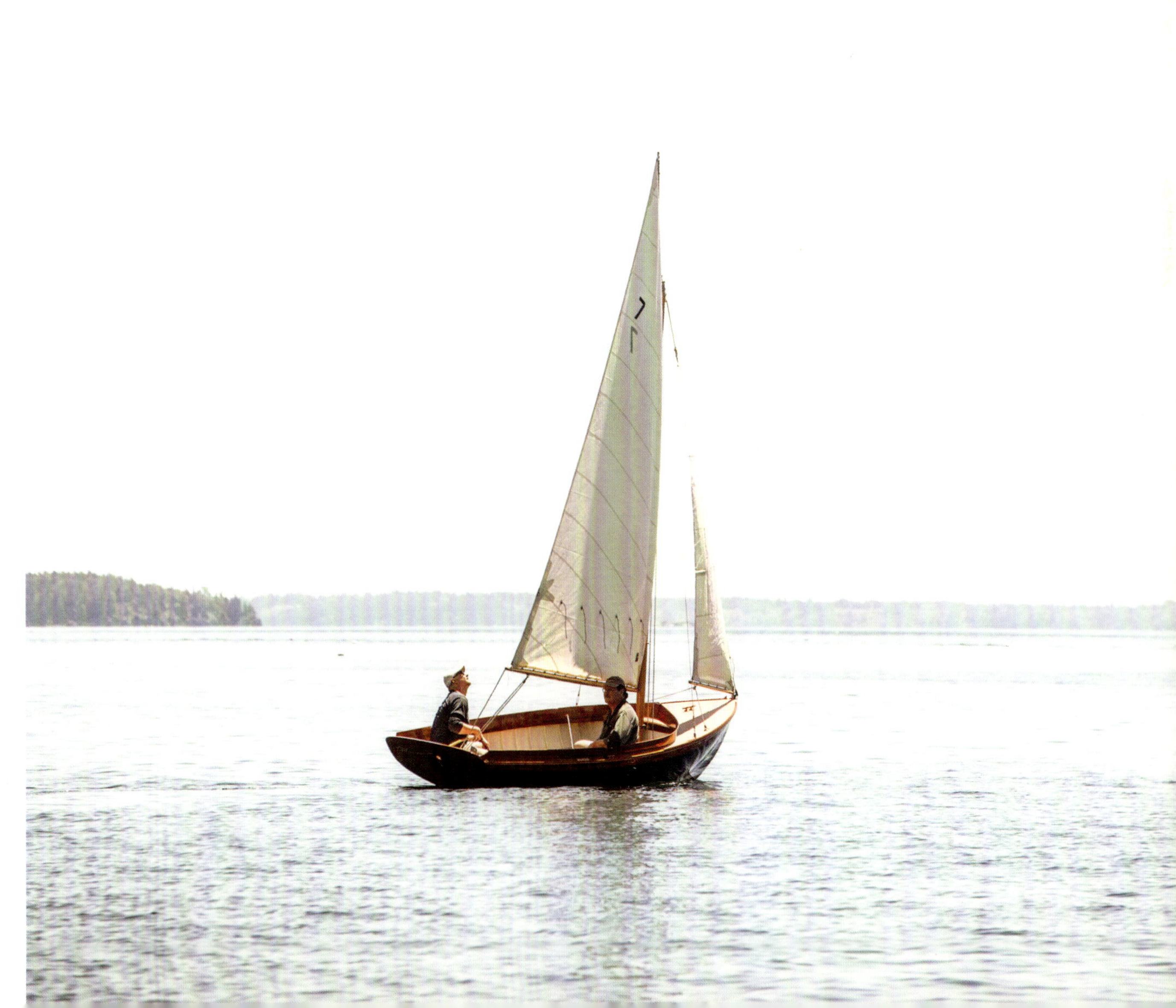

Red River Camps

Portage

The traditional image of a Maine fishing guide is a gruff man with a white beard and mud-crusted L.L.Bean boots, a knife in his belt and fishing flies on his vest. Against this, Jen Brophy may seem an utter anomaly. A young woman with pixie-short hair and a wardrobe of brightly colored tank tops, she stands out from her fellow guides. She's a former engineer with an interest in circus arts, and a well-educated young woman with a passion for theater. Yet she moves through the woods swiftly and surely, stopping here or there to point out a poisonous plant or evidence of a beaver's powerful teeth. She is at home in the woods—as are the best guides—and it shows in her confident stride across rugged terrain, the smooth cast of her fishing line, and her strong, even paddle strokes.

Red River Camps is located seven hours north of Maine's southern border, deep in the sparsely populated region of Aroostook County. Its driveway is a long dirt road that takes an hour to travel and is used primarily by loggers who barrel down the gravel path at breakneck speed. Arriving at Red River Camps feels like stepping back in time or finding yourself in the pages of a Jack London novel. The view from the road is picturesque, from the campgrounds to the large, rustic lodge to the idyllic lake. As you step from your car, you are greeted by the silent acknowledgment of Chaos, a black-and-white cat with an all-knowing air. Moments later, Jen Brophy and Gloria Curtis emerge from the great post-and-beam lodge that houses the dining room, where they have been preparing dinner. These two women run the seasonal business, welcoming fishermen and hunters to their eight thousand–acre wilderness retreat, a remote naturalist's paradise offering outdoor instruction, home-cooked meals, and a disarming dose of Maine hospitality.

Jen and Gloria are far from any true city, but their life isn't lacking in excitement or company. While Jen admits "it can be real hard to date up here," she says it lightly. The rewards of running a sporting camp far outweigh the disadvantages (she beats winter loneliness by planning trips to visit friends in Massachusetts and Washington, DC, where she takes classes in circus arts or dance or whatever strikes her fancy). Over the years, Jen has grown accustomed to the solitude of her unusual life—not to mention the skeptical looks occasionally thrown her way by

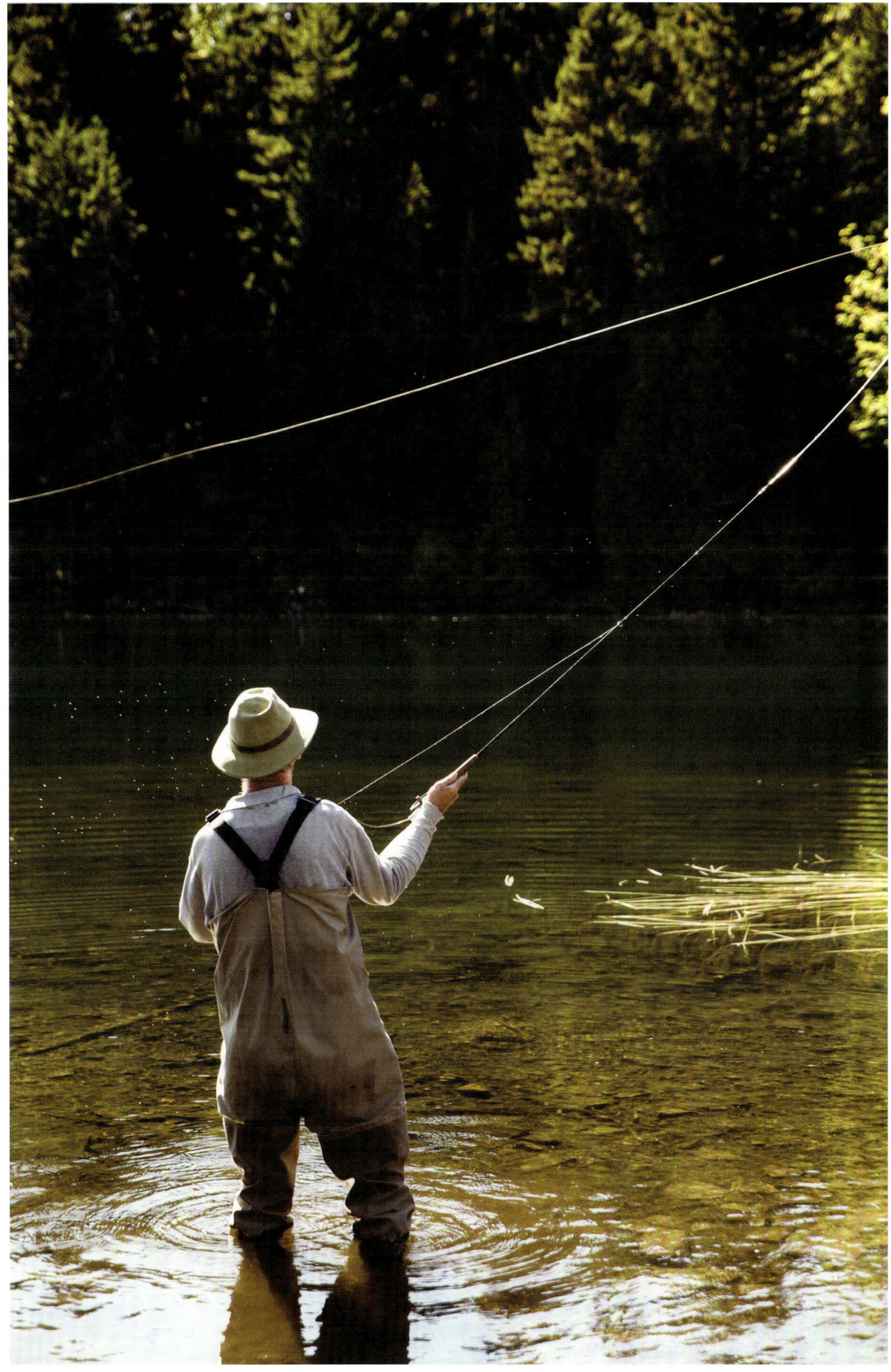

would-be fisherman. "Sometimes a group of men will arrive and Gloria and I will introduce ourselves," she says with a mischievous grin. "With some guys, I can see them looking around, and they keep the conversation going, but they're working up to the question. Finally they'll say, 'So it's just the two of you here?' Yup! And they wait another minute, 'No one else?' Nope. Then they'll pause before asking, 'Well, if something goes wrong, who fixes it?'" This time she doesn't supply the obvious answer; she just raises her eyebrows.

Jen learned how to manage and guide the camp the way many outdoorsmen, and outdoorswomen, do—from firsthand experience and know-how inherited from her parents. She grew up at Red River Camps alongside her two brothers. "I had the best childhood," she says. Her parents were hunters and they taught their three kids to fish, hunt, and find their way in the wilderness. Red River Camps is situated deep in a protected area known as the Deboullie Unit of Maine Public Reserve Land, which brushes up against the Canadian border. Technically, the camp owns only the cabins and buildings and leases the land from the State of Maine. While they may not own the land, the Brophy family has uncontested access to the thirty miles of trails, seventeen ponds, and three mountains that sprawl across the eight thousand acres of reserved landscape. The massive tract of wilderness that was her childhood playground is now her dominion.

After years of exploring, Jen knows the Maine wilderness like painters know their brushes. She understands each natural feature and how to best enjoy and respect it. She knows where you can find the talus slopes, massive accumulations of rock that have crumbled down a cliff face and come to rest on the side of the mountain. These slopes give the region their name: "Deboullie is an Americanization of the French geology term for a talus slope, *d'éboulis*," Jen explains as she leads hikers through woodland toward the shores of Gardner Pond, where an impressive rock formation cascades into the deep water below. In the summer, the pond becomes a swimming hole where swimmers step gingerly from rock to rock and jump into the clear, cool water of northern Maine.

Jen also guides hikers to hidden ice caves, small pockets of rock in which ice remains year-round. She instructs her guests to place their hands near the mouth of a cave. The musty air feels fifteen degrees cooler than the balmy September day—a refrigerator hidden under the soil. She knows where to find brook trout and arctic char, and the best times of day to fish for them. She knows where and how to hunt for partridge and moose, deer and bears. These days, though, she prefers to hunt with her camera.

Gloria, however, has no such qualms and has hunted for years. Her kind eyes belie her fortitude. She is spry and funny, with the sarcastic sense of humor common to Mainers and a penchant for repeating local sayings—with colorful vocabulary fully intact. Gloria is a "master fisherwoman," according to Jen, who has immense respect for the older woman's outdoor skills. Gloria can skin a deer and track a moose. She has accompanied biologists to tag hibernating bears and bagged her own bucks. "Gloria's been fly fishing longer than I've been alive," Jen says. "Whenever we have people who want to learn to cast, I send them to Gloria."

The affection between the two women is most palpable in the kitchen. While there are creative elements to every aspect of their camp work, from repainting the cabins to blazing new walking trails, the kitchen is the place where they can play with new recipes and tinker with old favorites. They work side-by-side to make nourishing meals for their guests, but their skill elevates each dish beyond the typical campsite meat-and-potatoes fare. "We run our kitchen like an olive-oiled machine," Gloria says as she slides a metal spatula under a crispy piece of trout that she caught just hours before. "Trout for breakfast, 'cause that's how we do it here," Gloria explains, her "here" arching upward with a slight Maine accent. The trout is silvery in places, crispy brown in others. Topped with butter, the flesh flakes off in steaming chunks. It might appear unorthodox on the breakfast table, served alongside muffins and pancakes. "Some guests think it's weird to have fish so early in the day," Jen admits, "but then they try it and they don't care." And just like that, Jen Brophy sums up the experience of Red River Camps: a little different, and all the better for it.

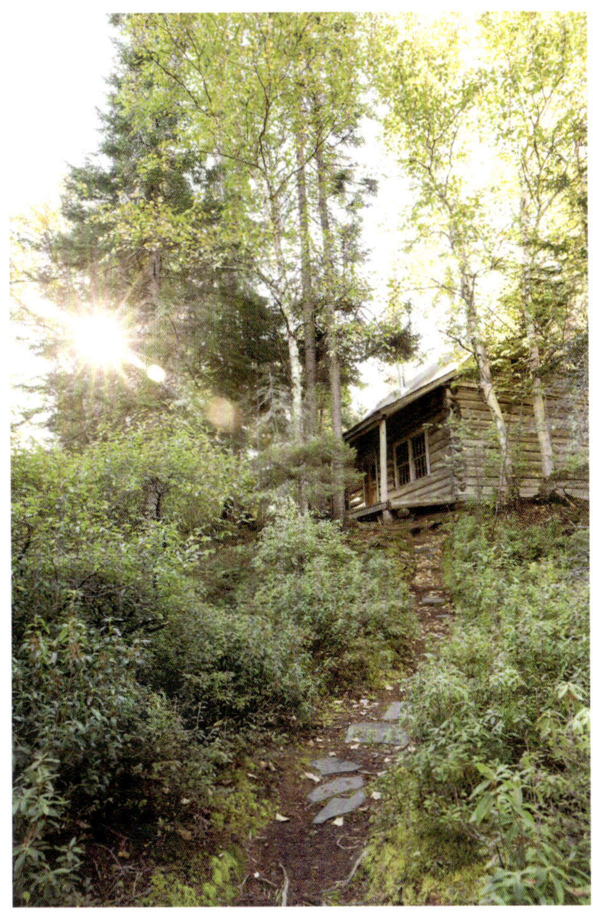
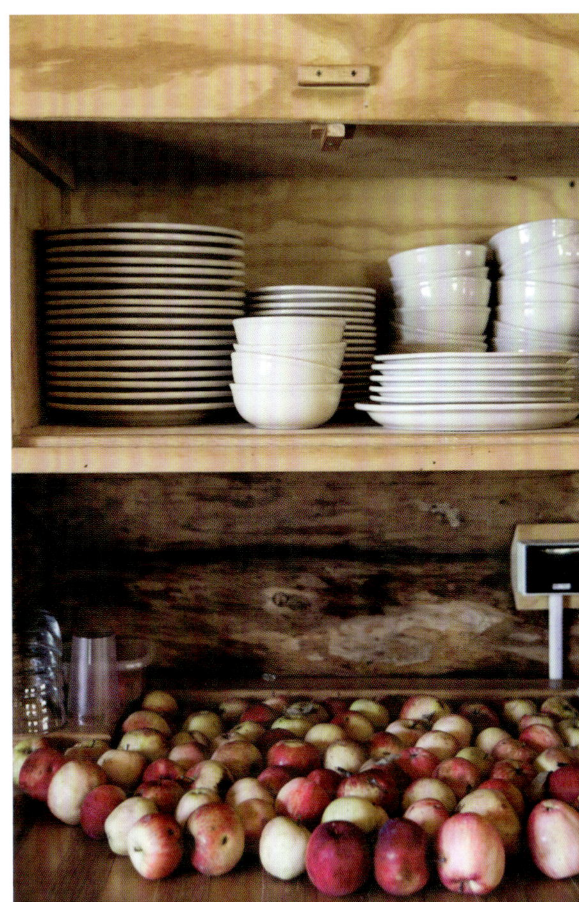
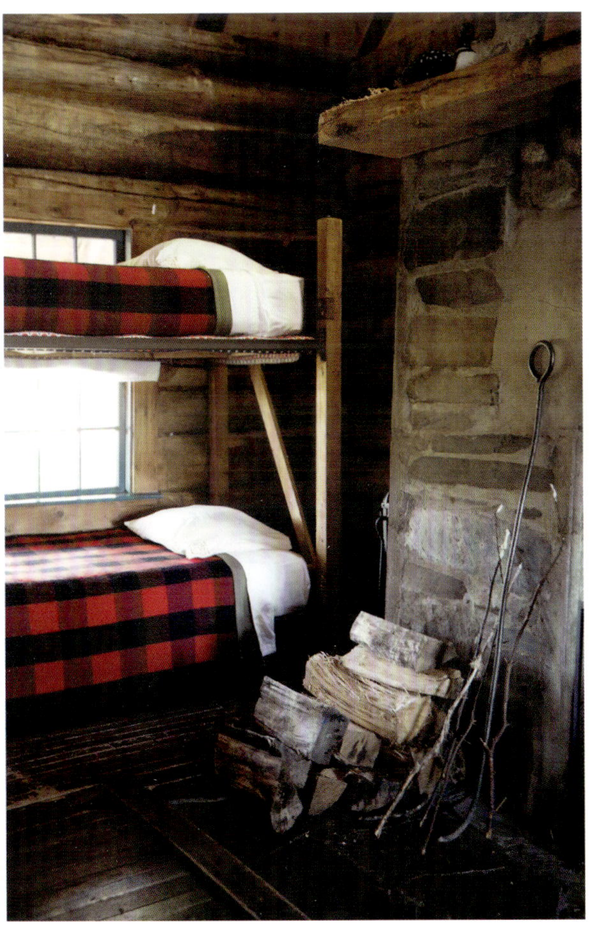
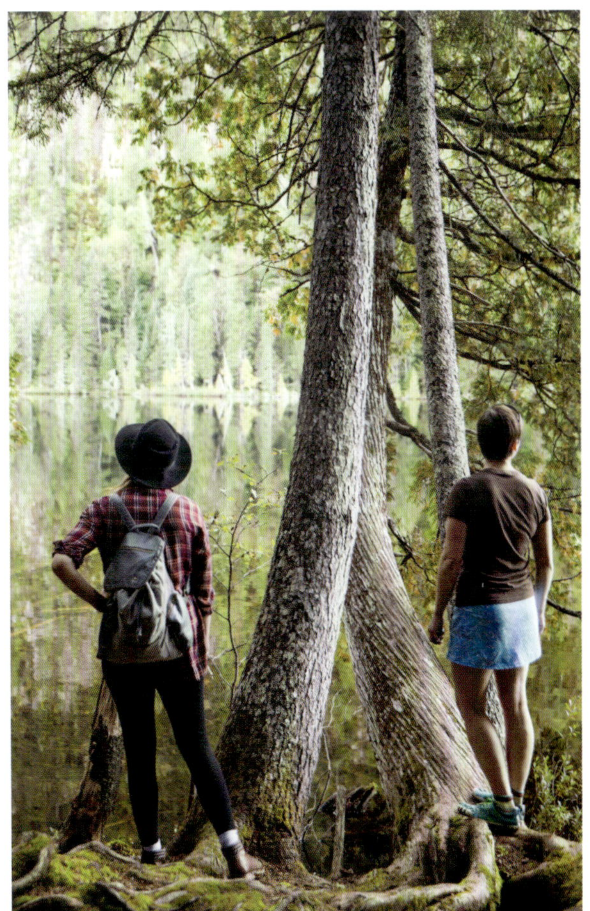

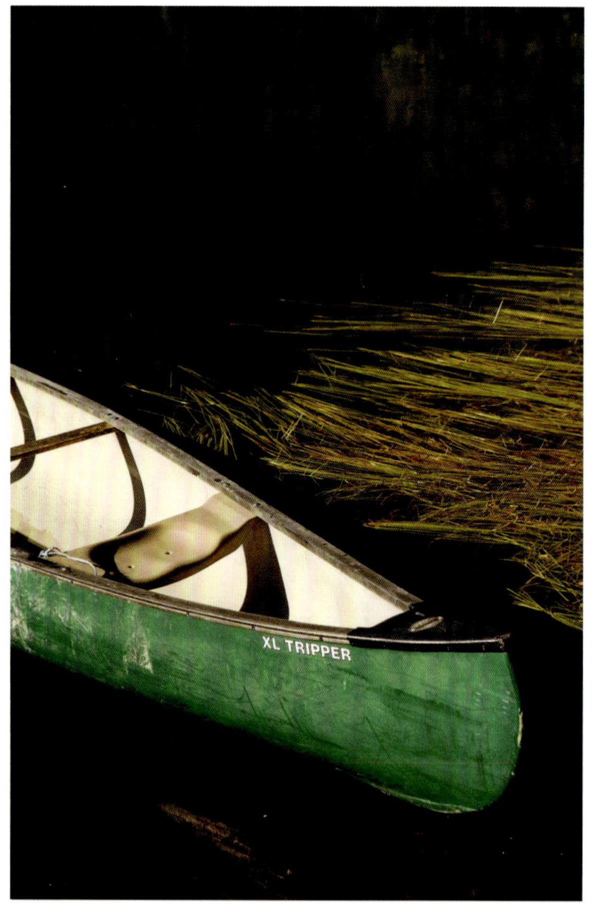
XL TRIPPER

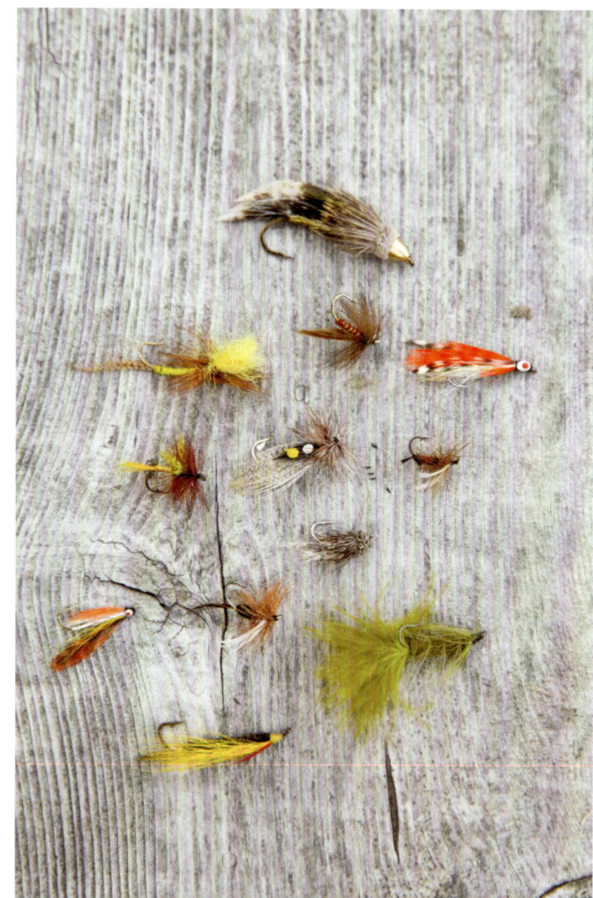

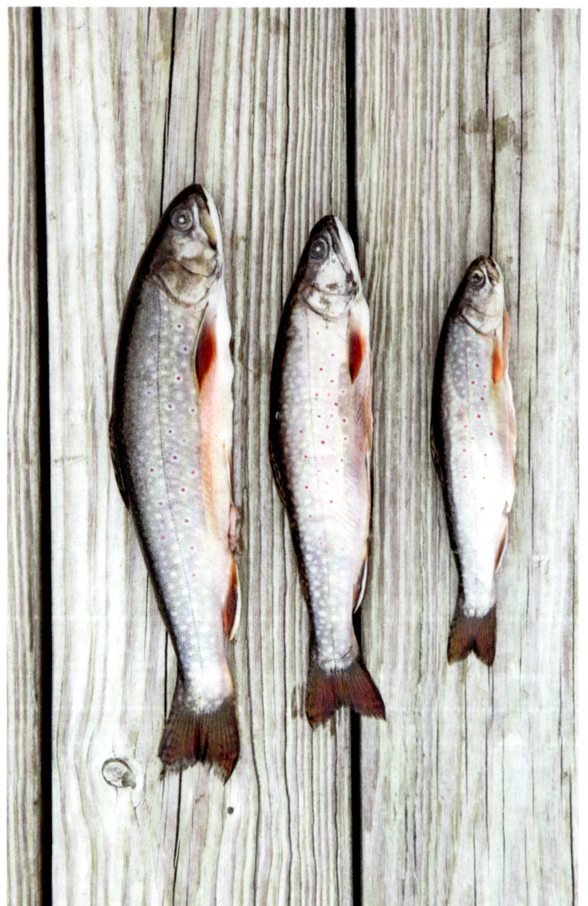

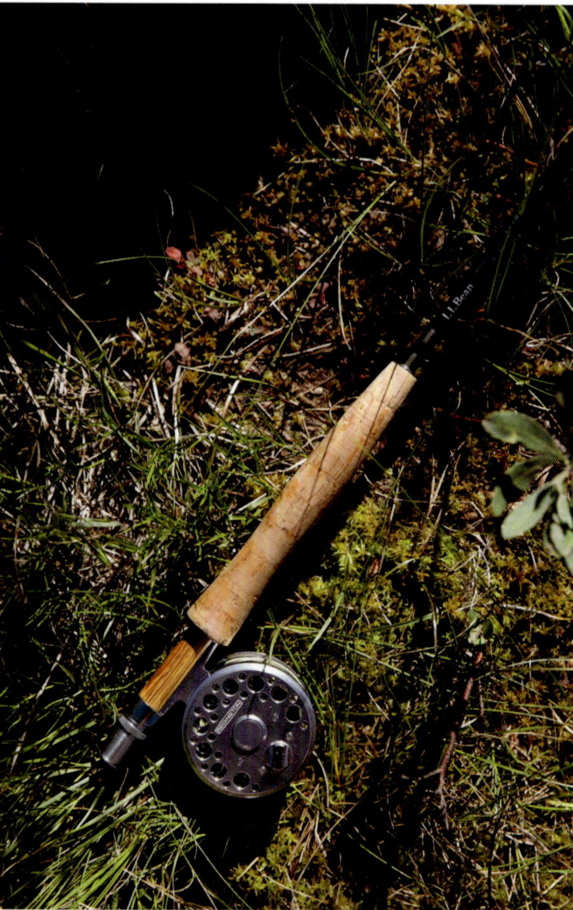
L.L.Bean

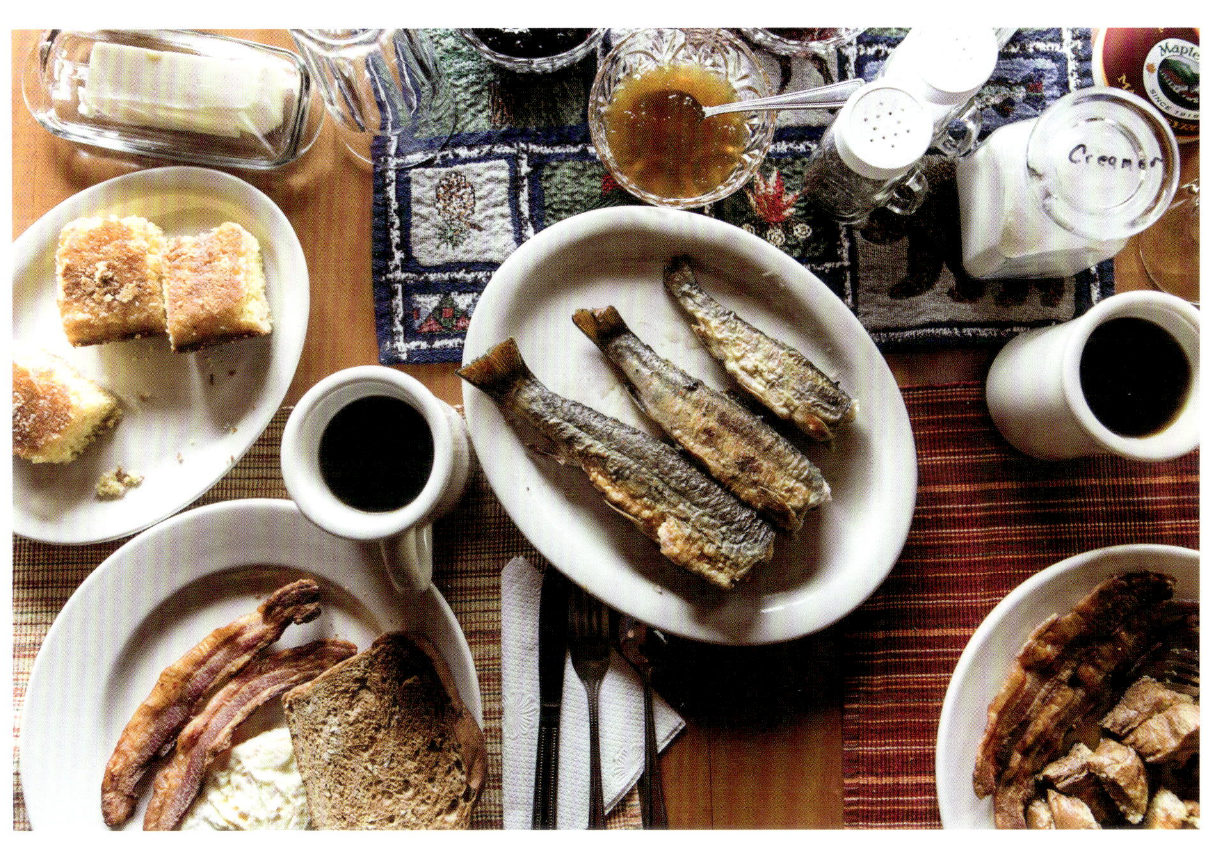
Maple
Creamer

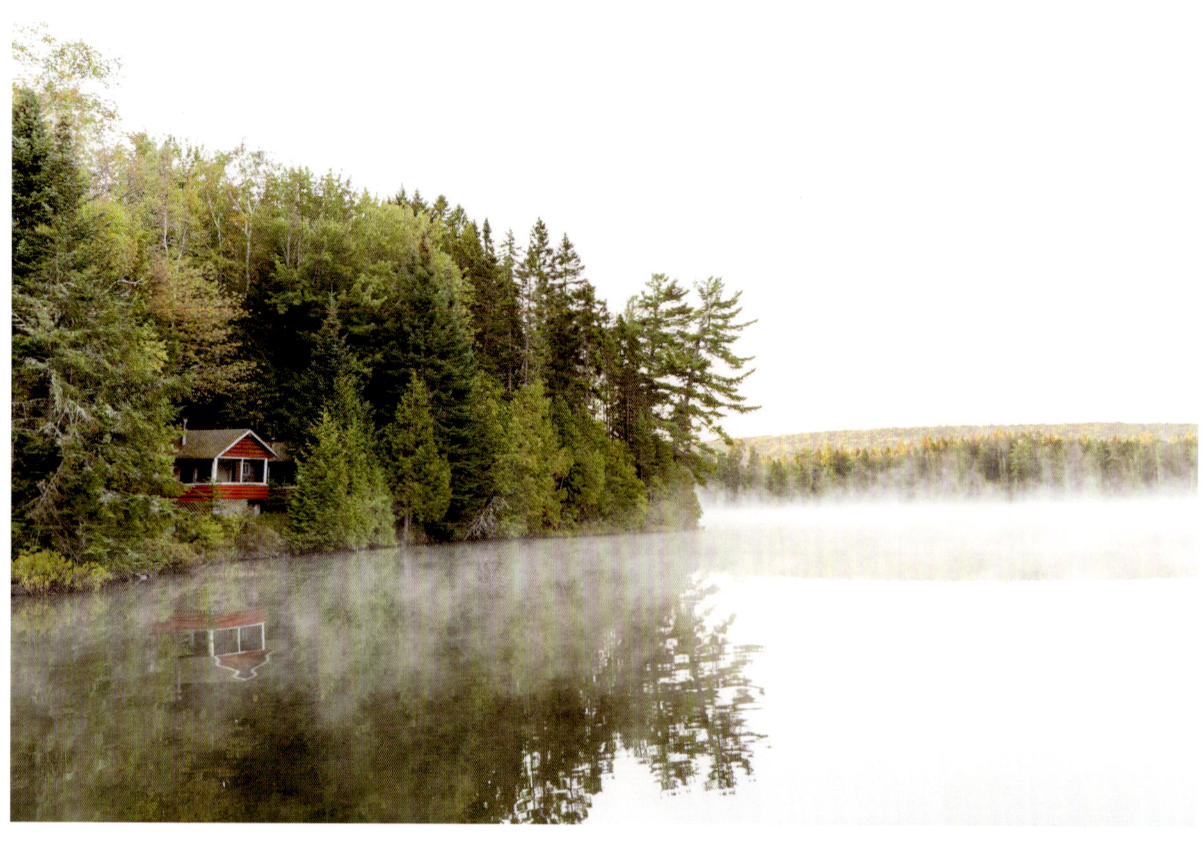

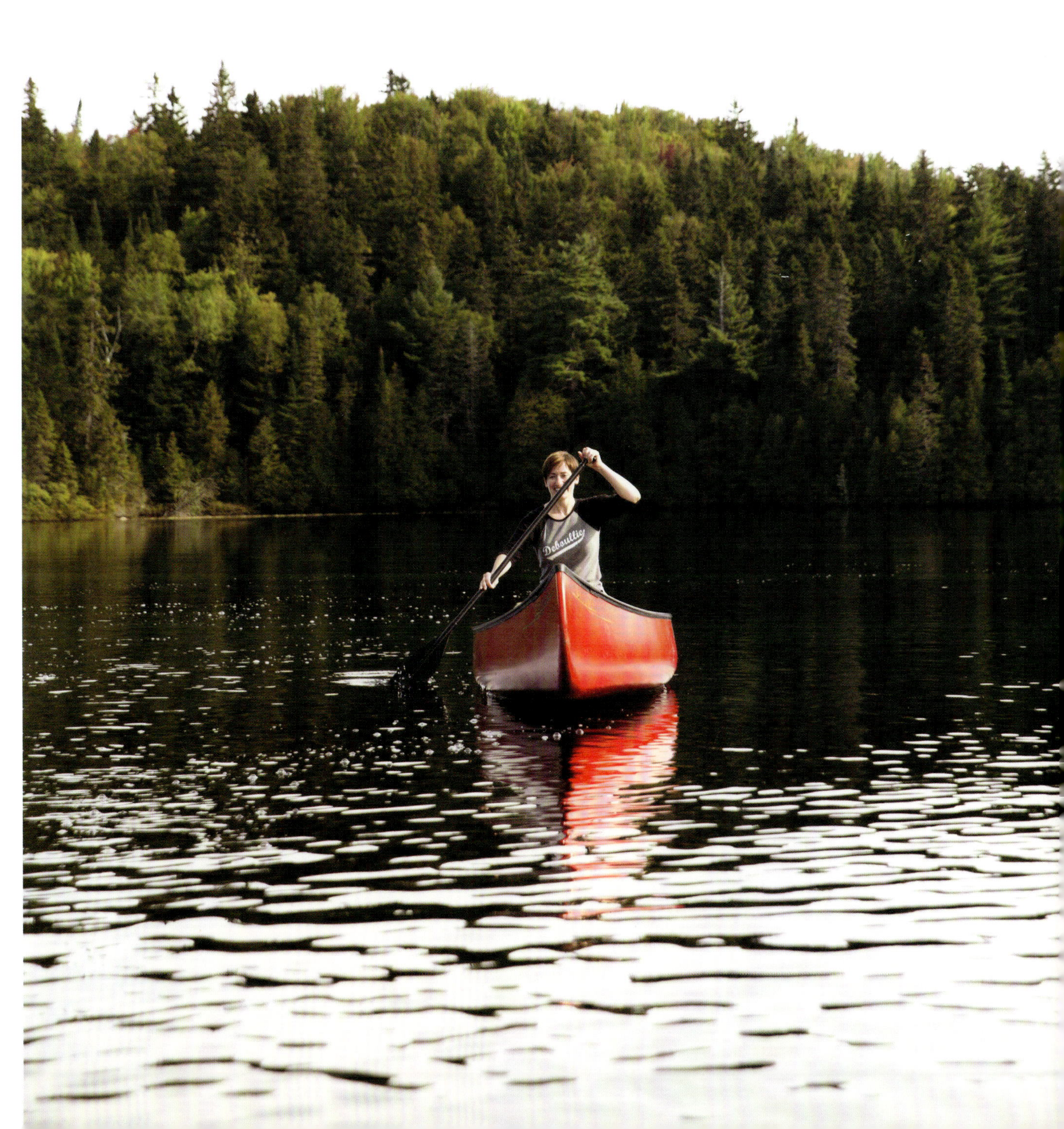
Deboullie

Grain Surfboards

York

"When we started our company, we knew we didn't want anyone to have set hours. We didn't want nine-to-five for ourselves *or* for our employees," says Brad Anderson, co-owner of Grain Surfboards. "All they have to do is make sure their shit gets done. I don't care when they do it."

On a blistering summer day, Brad has been up all night working in the woodshop. "Sure, I'm a little tired, but I do it all the time," he says. "I actually love doing it. There's nothing better than being up when the sun is coming up and the birds are singing, and I think, 'All these people are sleeping and they're missing this!'" Sometimes, he caps off his all-nighters with an early morning surf off the coast of southern Maine.

Grain Surfboards started as a passion project of Mike Levecchia's. "When I met Mike, he was doing this out of his basement," Brad recalls. "We weren't friends or anything, but we both had the same ideas about life. We want it simple and we don't want a lot of stuff." They had a few other things in common, too—both had backgrounds in boat building, believed strongly in the DIY movement, and were ardent environmentalists. And they both love to surf.

Maine surfers are an anomalous breed. They go out in winter, frozen sand crunching underfoot, to catch waves in wet suits as snow falls around them. They are protective of their surfing spots, often a little secretive—Mike and Brad are downright evasive about their favorite places to surf. They are dedicated to the sport, perhaps even a little fanatical. This trait is especially true of the younger surfers, like the guys who work in the Grain shop, sanding and cutting and fitting the various pieces that make up each board.

Now the company is over a decade old and the Grain cofounders have mellowed. They no longer work out of a basement; Grain is headquartered in a large and rustic white barn on a country road in York, Maine. Much of the work crafting boards is done here. A Grain surfboard is hollow inside and constructed around a frame composed of small pieces of wood. Precision-cut on CNC machines and then shipped to Grain, the interior scaffolding is assembled by Grain workers who add a cedar skin. The resulting boards are lightweight, durable, and uniquely beautiful, thanks to the natural variation of the white and red cedar planks.

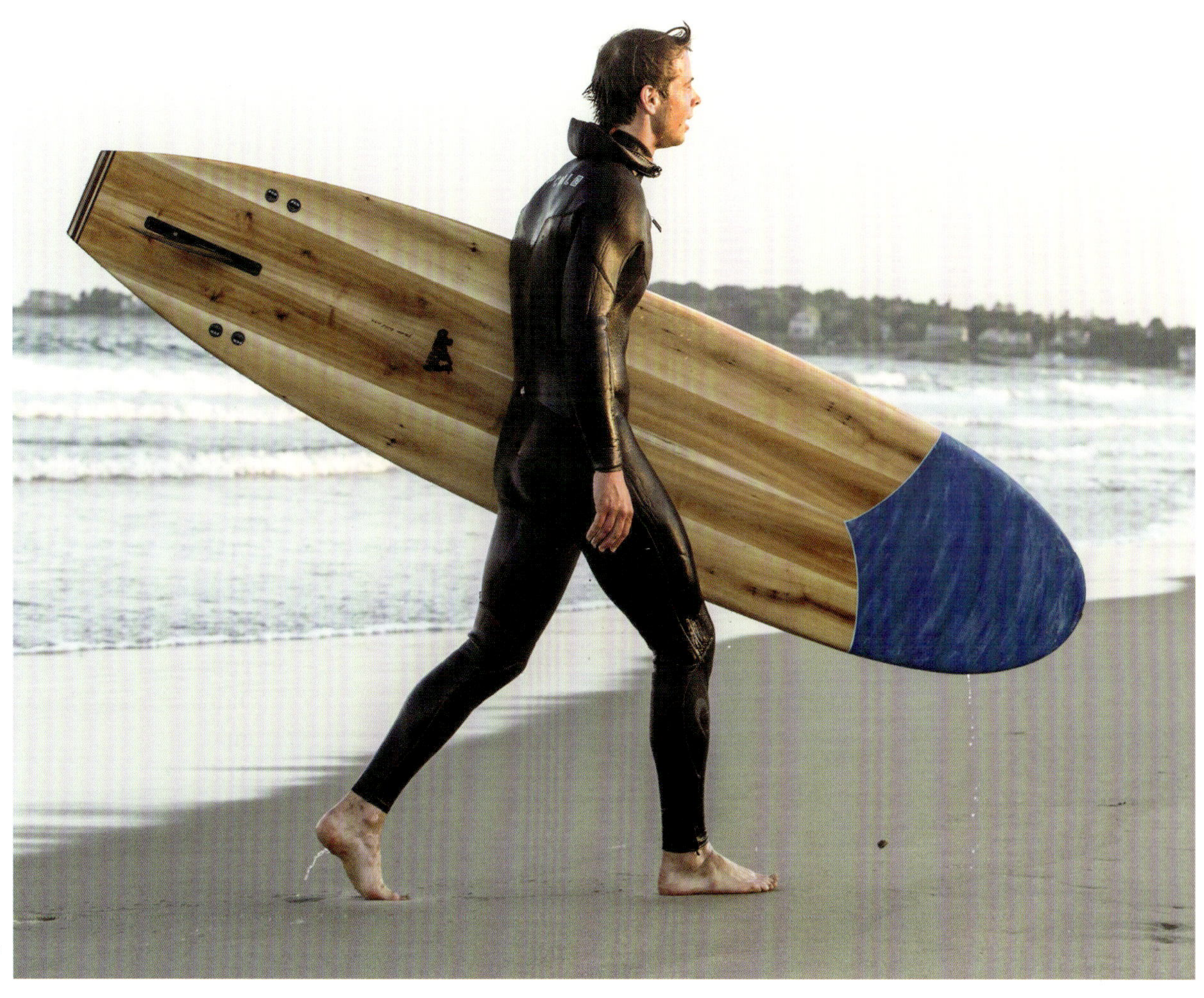

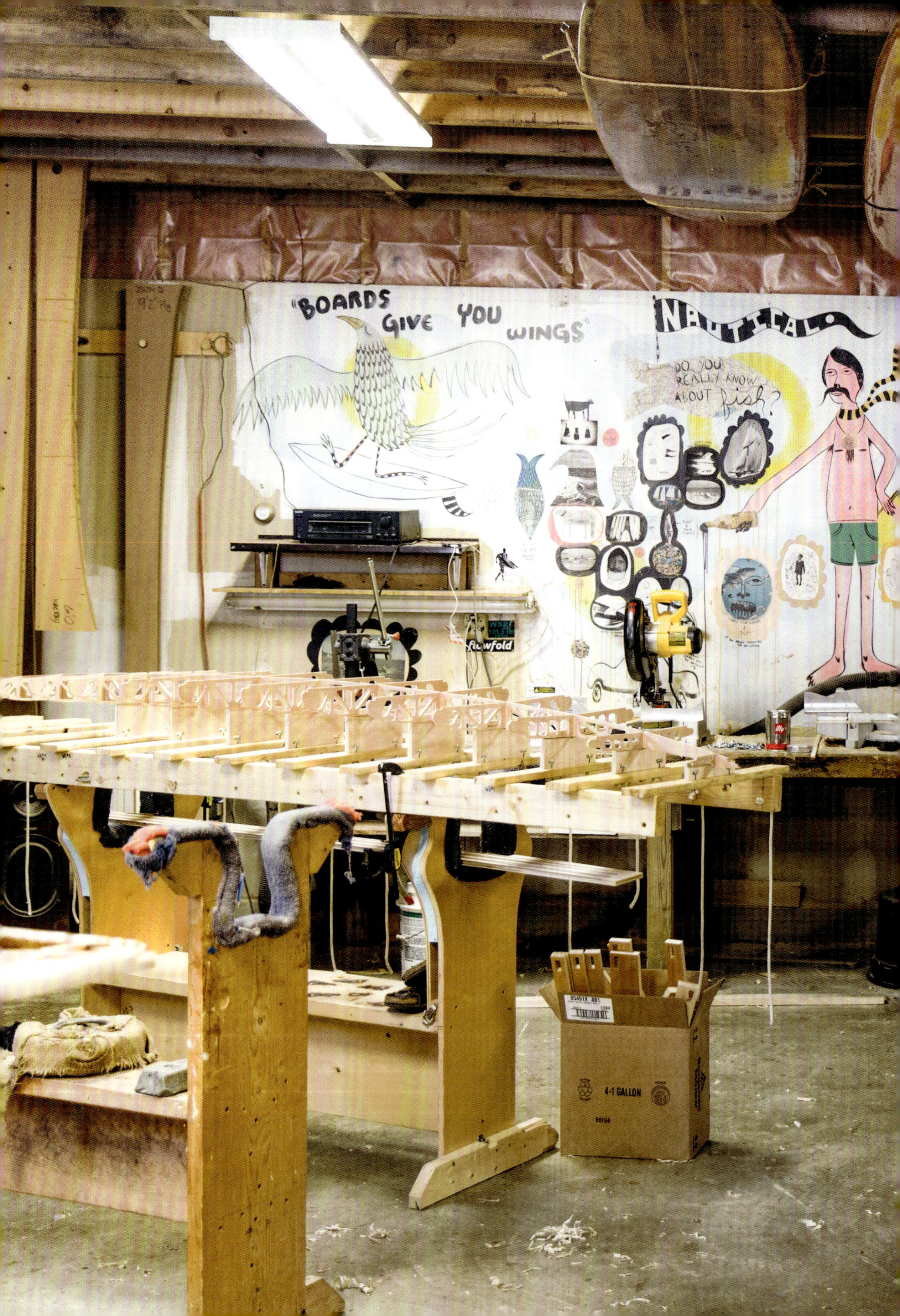
"BOARDS GIVE YOU WINGS"
NAUTICAL
DO YOU REALLY KNOW ABOUT fish?
flowfold
4-1 GALLON

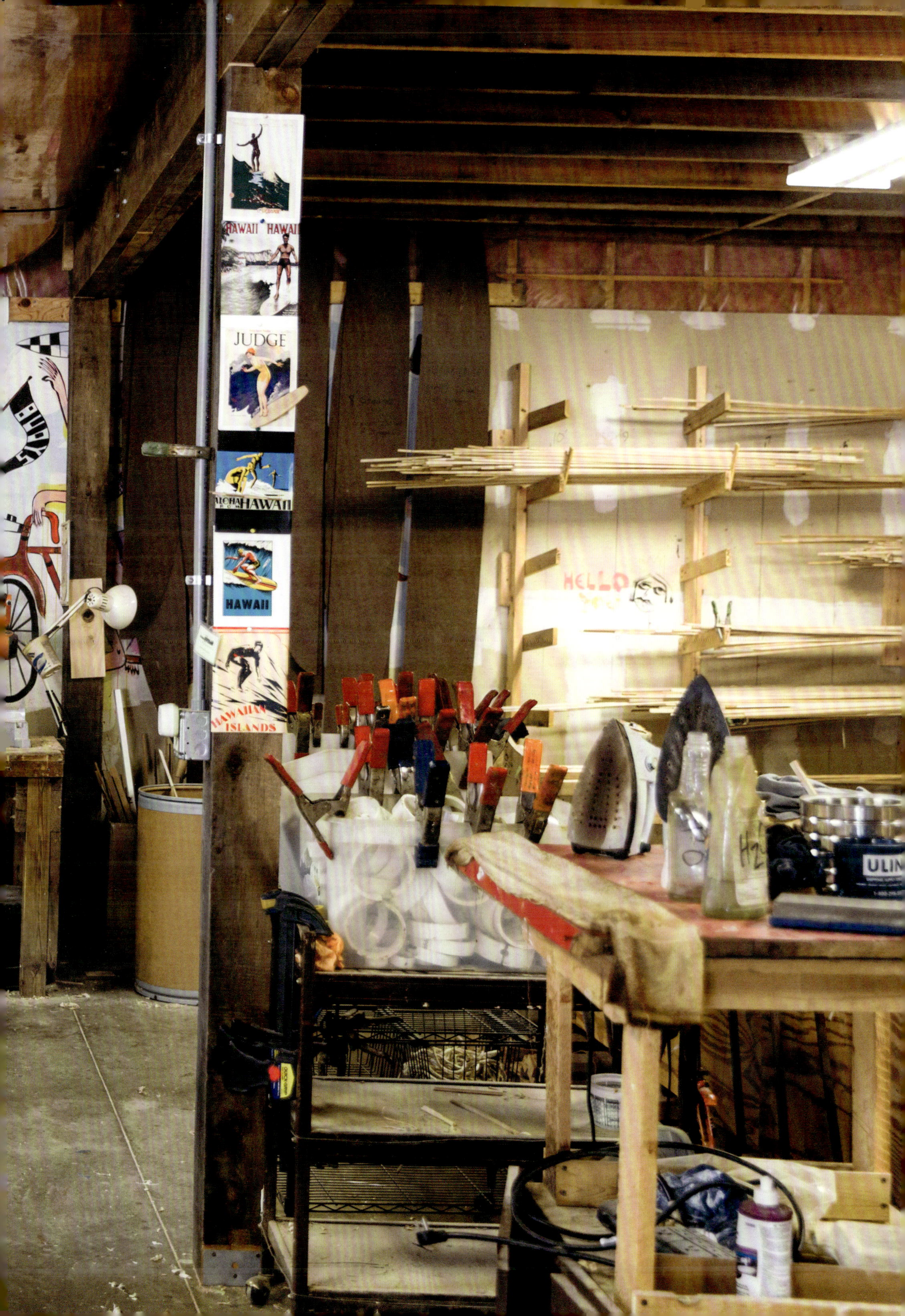
HAWAII HAWAII
JUDGE
HAWAII
HAWAII
HAWAIIAN ISLANDS
HELLO

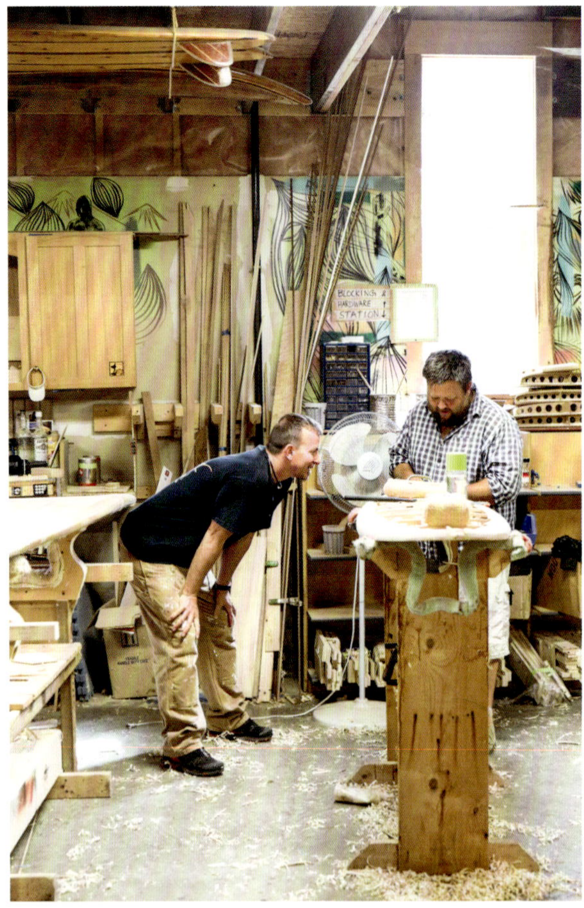

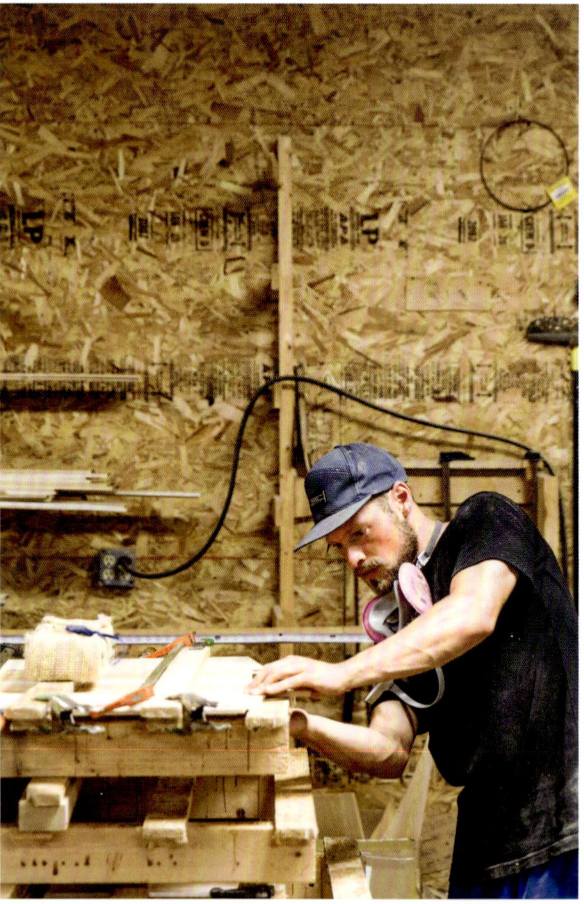

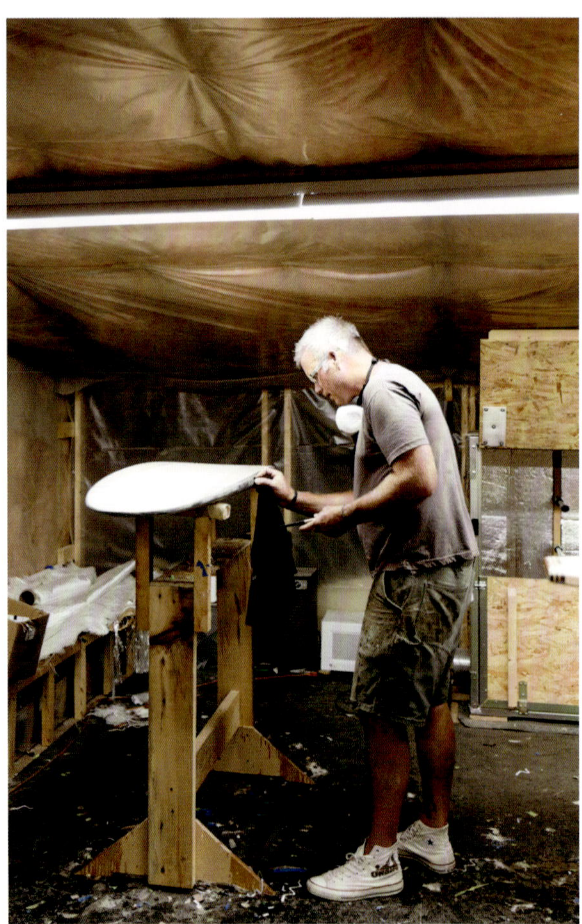

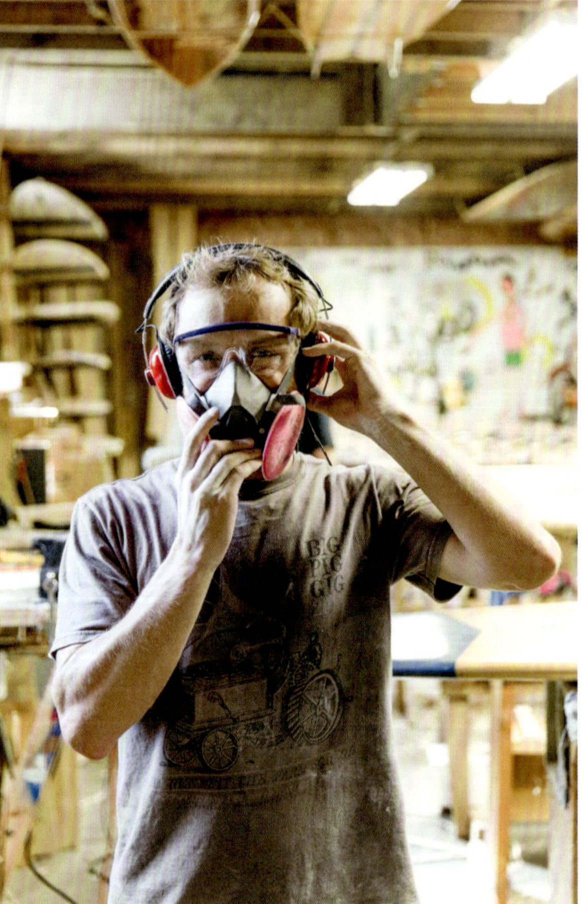
BIG PIG GIG

Grain surfboards perform differently in the water than the foam boards that most modern surfers use (the earliest surfboards were made of wood; it wasn't until the 1970s that foam and fiberglass boards began to dominate the market). "Even though our boards are heavier than foam boards, surfers remark that they actually feel livelier in the water," explains Mike. "Real wood boat enthusiasts say that a wooden boat doesn't wear them out the way a fiberglass boat does, and I think that's true of our surfboards. Wood has memory. It always returns to its shape. Not all materials do that."

Each Grain surfboard takes approximately fifty hours to make, and the Grain guys claim that they can last a lifetime (with occasional repairs). "Part of our sustainability ethos is to build something that lasts forever," Mike says. "There are faster and cheaper ways to build wooden boards, but I don't think they're better. When we first started, we spent a ton of time researching the history of surfing and the evolution of construction and materials. The way we build boards is similar to how you build boats, but we modified techniques to work better with the tighter compound curves of a surfboard."

From the beginning, it was important to Mike and Brad to share their knowledge with fellow surfers. Much of their business comes from the surfboard-building kits they sell online. While they require some woodworking skill, the Grain kits are accessible, even for surfers with few tools and minimal workshop space. "We had a guy build a ten-footer in his apartment in Brooklyn," Mike says. "We really want people to be able to make their own boards. Back in the day, everybody built their own boards. It was part of the experience." Grain also offers on-site four-day workshops that generally run from Thursday to Saturday ("Just tell your boss you need a long weekend!" their website suggests). Students learn to construct their own surfboards, from building the rails and installing the hardware, to attaching the top planks and sanding them down. It's an experience that Brad believes helps surfers better connect with their boards, which leads to better surfing—not to mention righteous bragging rights. "They can walk down to the beach, and whenever someone goes, 'I like your board,' they get to say, 'Yeah, I made it,'" he says.

The workshops also offer a chance to experience the lifestyle enjoyed by the Grain co-owners, which includes lots of time outdoors, farm-fresh food served by an on-site chef, and working with their hands. "We've had all kinds of people come through, people on their honeymoons, retired guys, fathers with their sons. But my favorite students are the young guys, kids who are still trying to find their way in the world," Brad says as he leans against the barn. Green fields stretch out before him and sawdust clings to his T-shirt. He doesn't look like a man who has stayed up all night. He looks content, relaxed. It's easy to see why a young surfer might envy his life. "When I meet guys who are a little lost, I tell them, 'Look fellas, it's not that hard. You don't have to sign up for all the shit, all that quiet desperation. You can follow your passions. It may not pay you back in money, but it will pay you back in literally every other way. And that's what matters.'"

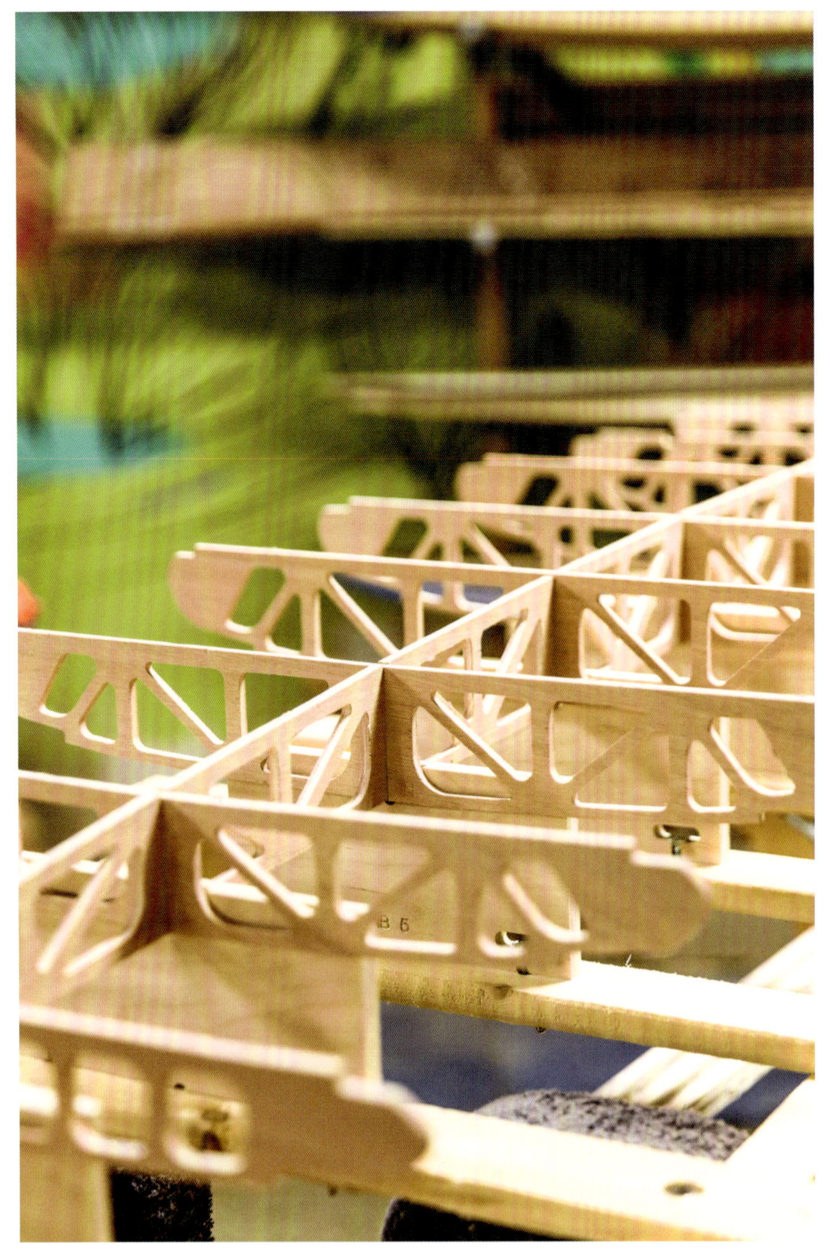

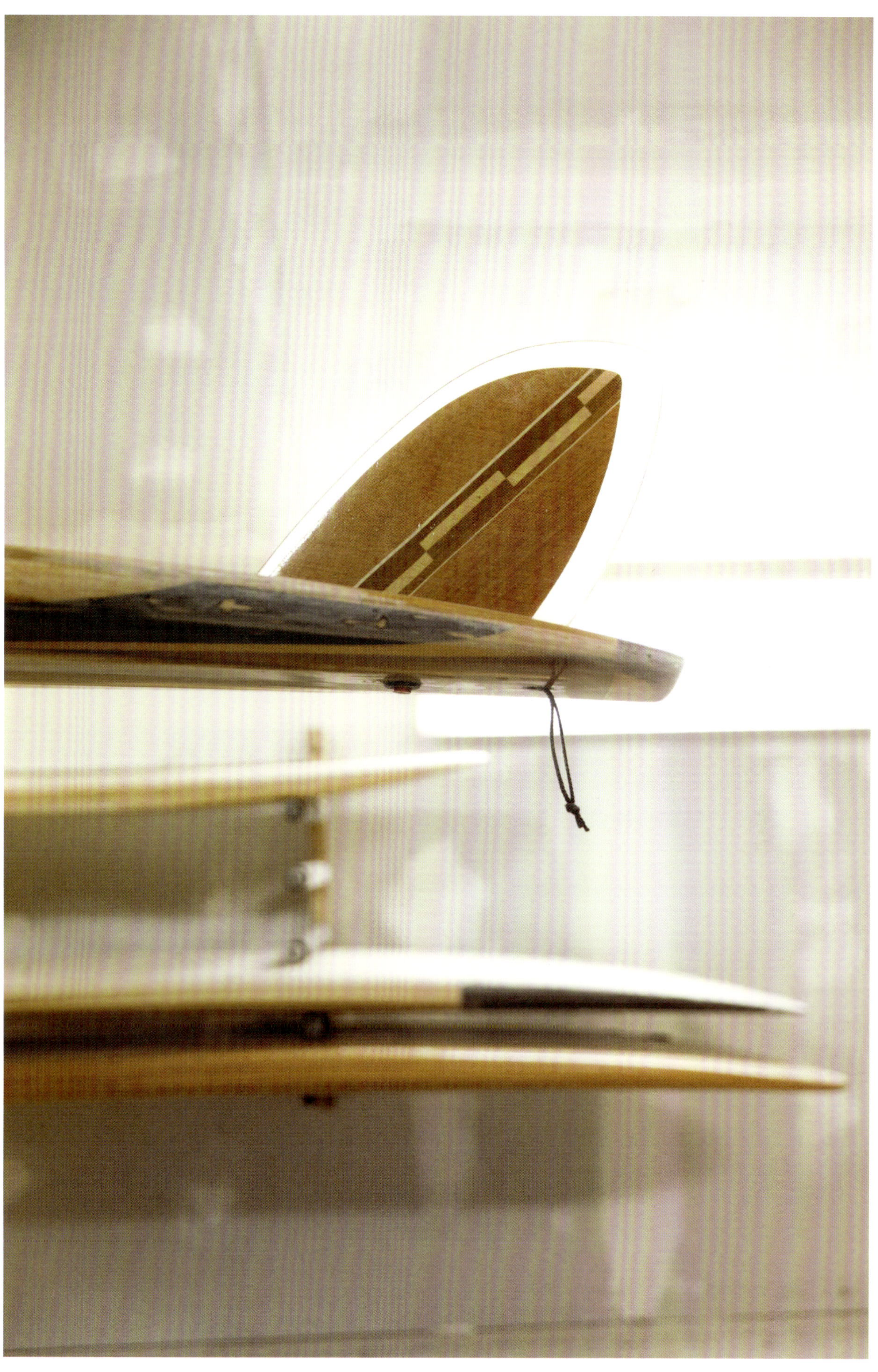

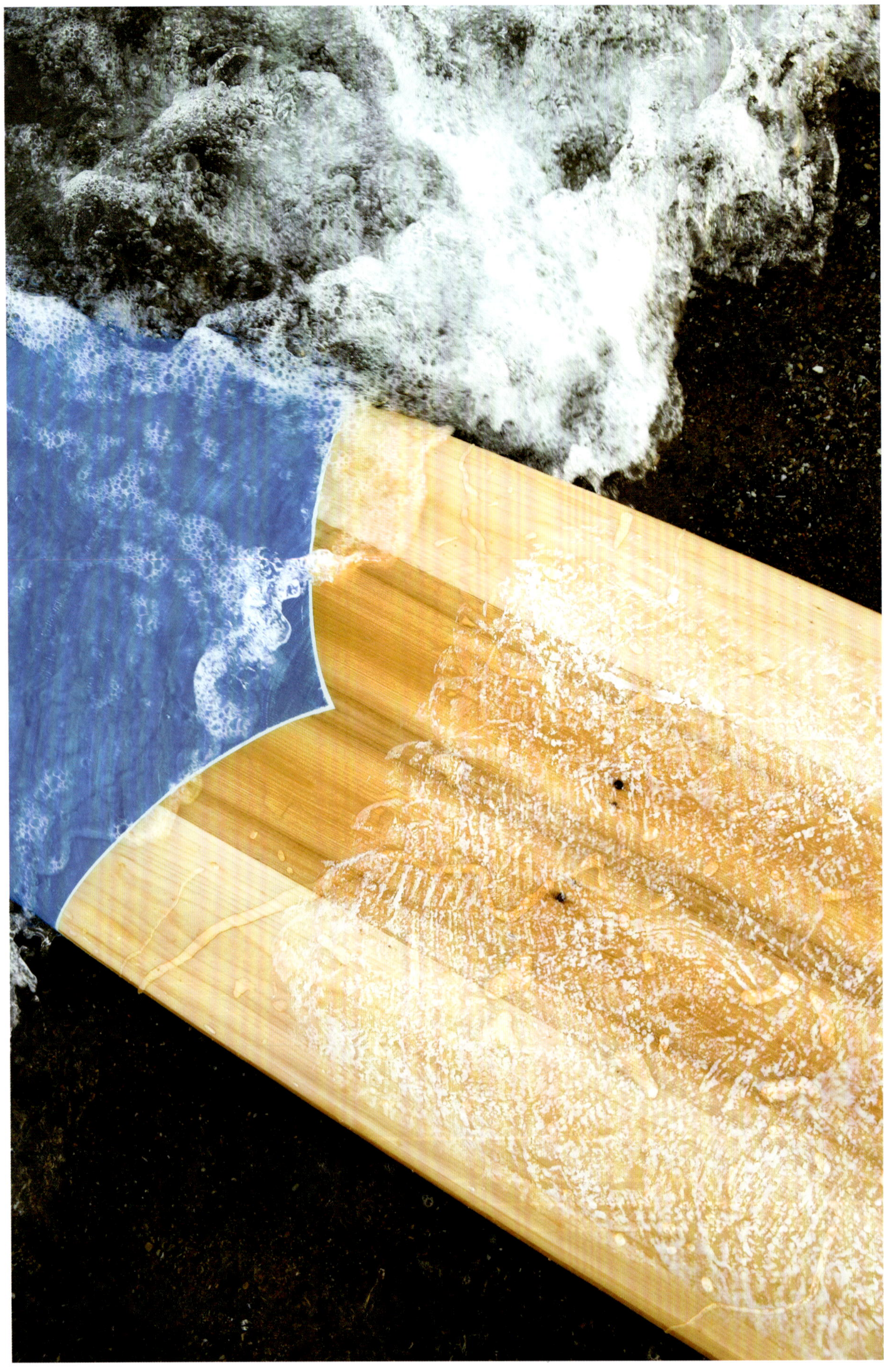

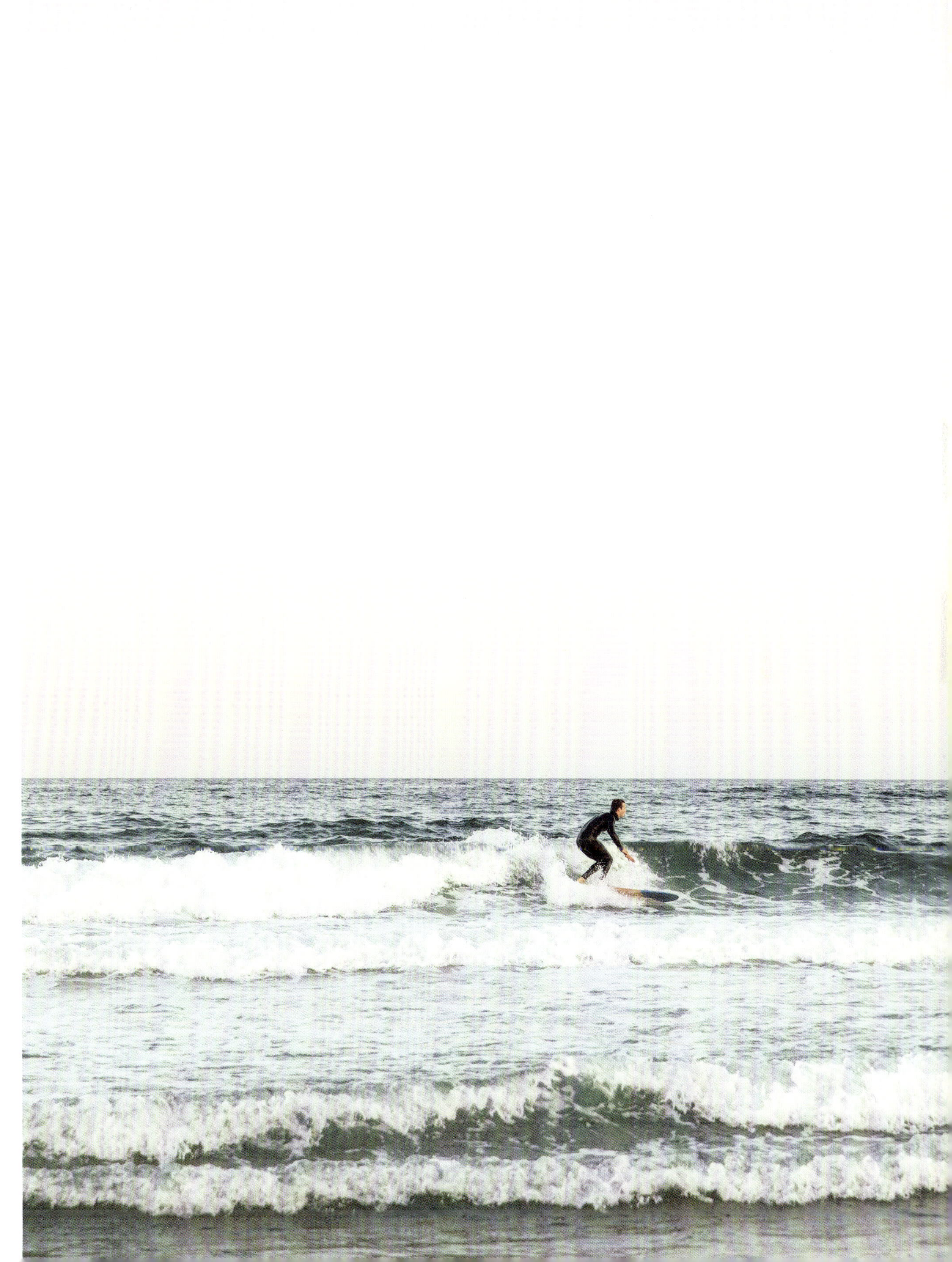

FOOD
&
HARVEST

Chase's Daily

Belfast

"The seeds for inspiration come from all over," says Freddy LaFage as he sits in one of the booths of his family's Belfast restaurant, Chase's Daily. He lays his palms flat on the varnished wood of the rustic booths—booths he built himself, though he claims to be "no great carpenter"—as he searches for the words to describe his cooking style. "Much of the produce we feature on the menu comes from the farm, harvested at the height of flavor and freshness. Much of the time, our job in the kitchen is just to deliver it to the plate," he explains. "I'm not into transforming one thing into another. I like things to be as they are, to let the produce retain its character." As he speaks, his serious brown eyes remain level and focused, but his rough worker's hands continue to move across the table. "I'm better with images than I am with words—or with food," the painter, carpenter, and chef adds a moment later. "And food is a form of communication, too." Food, he knows, is a way of showing love, a powerful tool that binds communities. It's also a creative genre all its own.

In their casual sit-down eatery, the Chase family has created a community of cooks, servers, farmers, and patrons, people drawn together by the power of simple, fresh food, much of which is grown nearby at the family's vegetable, fruit, and flower farm. As Freddy begins prepping for lunch service in the kitchen at Chase's Daily, his partner, Meg, is twenty-two miles away in Freedom, hard at work harvesting greens, strawberries, and flowers. Meg's sister, Phoebe, is tucked away in the Chase's Daily bakery, where she makes tarts, pastries, and breads. Meg and Phoebe's father, Addison Chase, is at the farm, and Penny Chase, his wife and mother of the Chase sisters, is working in her charming upstairs apartment, which is full of Meg and Freddy's paintings. Every member of the family, including eleven-year-old Romy (daughter of Freddy and Meg), is busy on this Thursday morning. It's not even nine o'clock and the entire clan has already been working for hours.

The results of their labor can be tasted at their daily breakfast and lunch service, and at the weekly Friday night dinner service. The menu, which is created by the family during weekly meetings, changes regularly but features certain staples, like inventive salads (incorporating whatever is fresh, tossed in simple, homemade dressing), bean

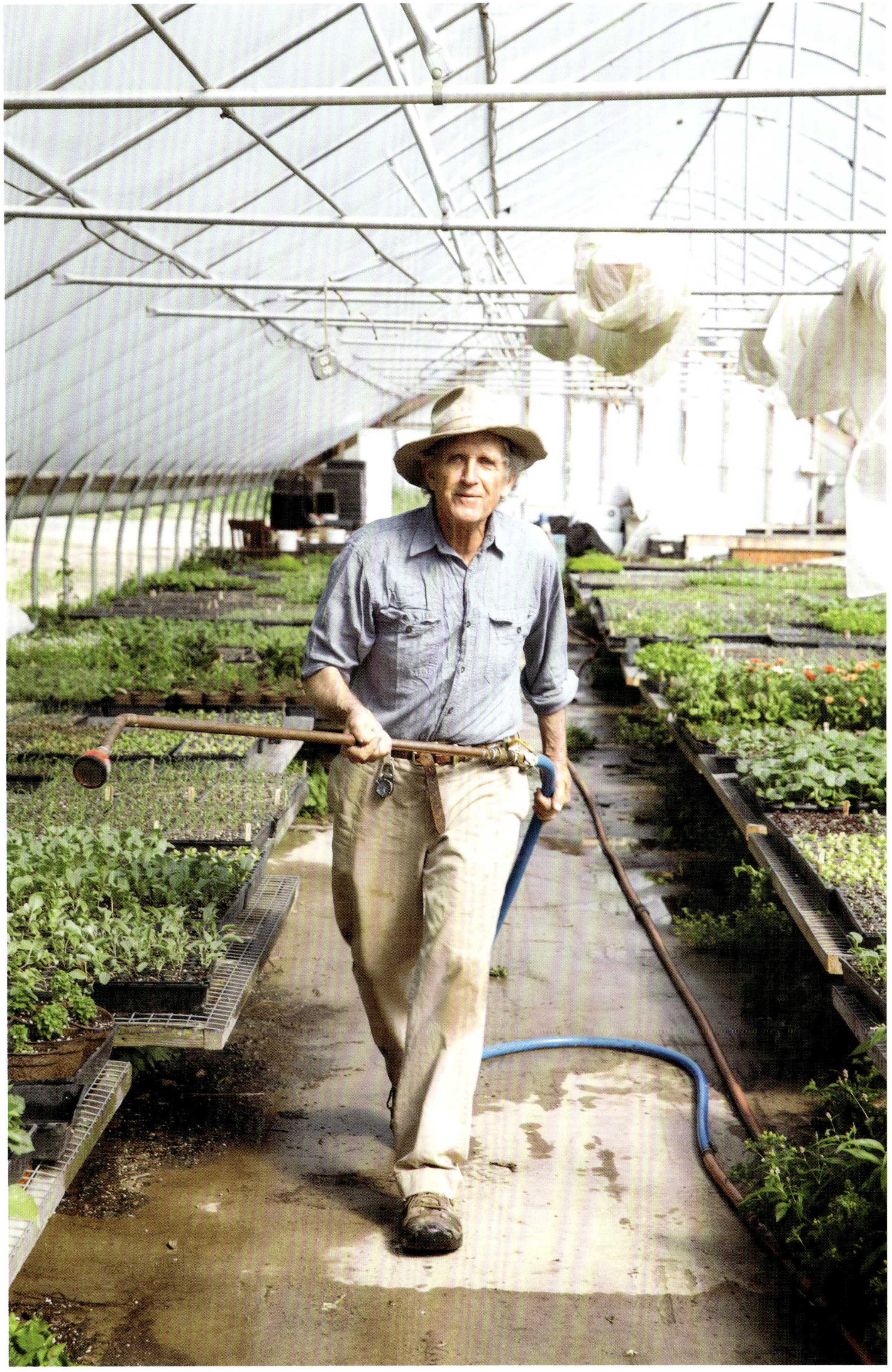

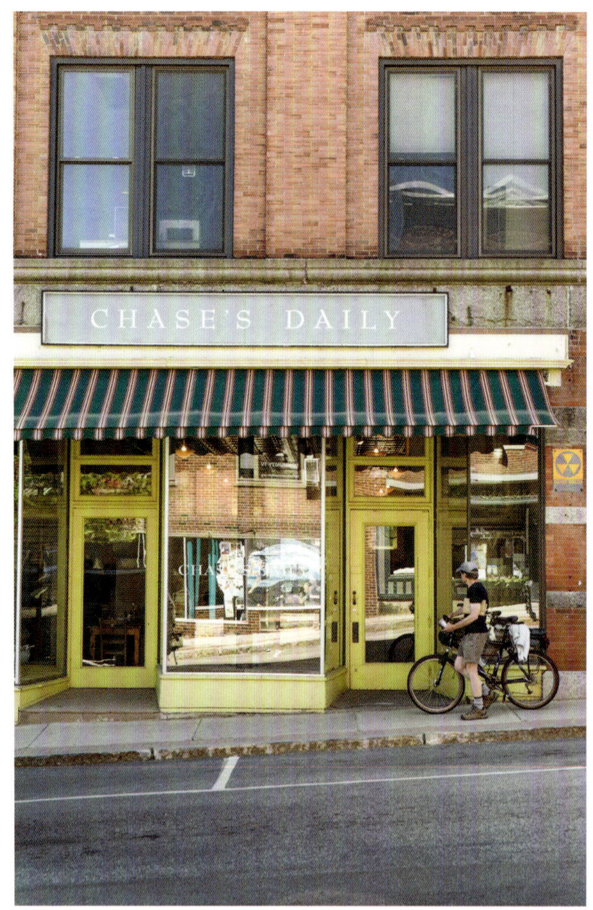
CHASE'S DAILY

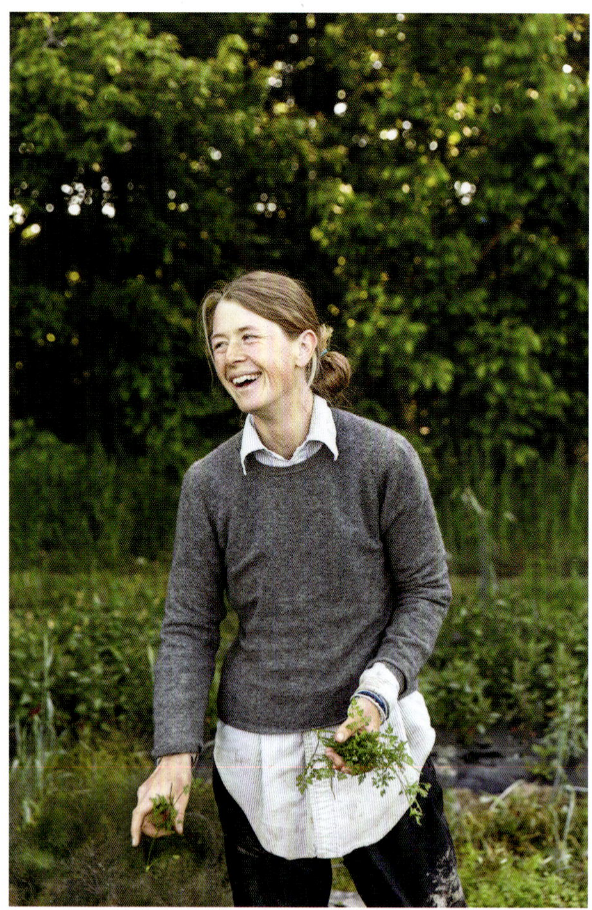

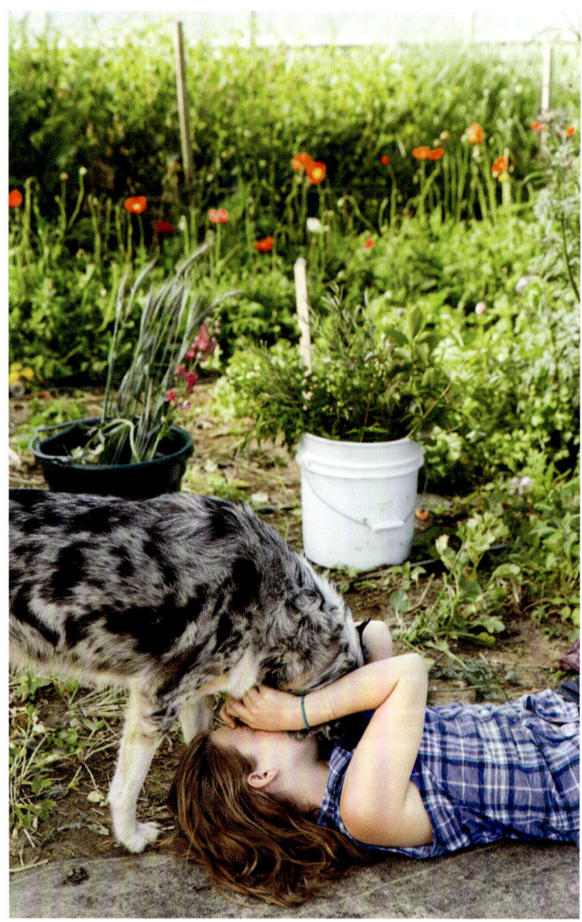

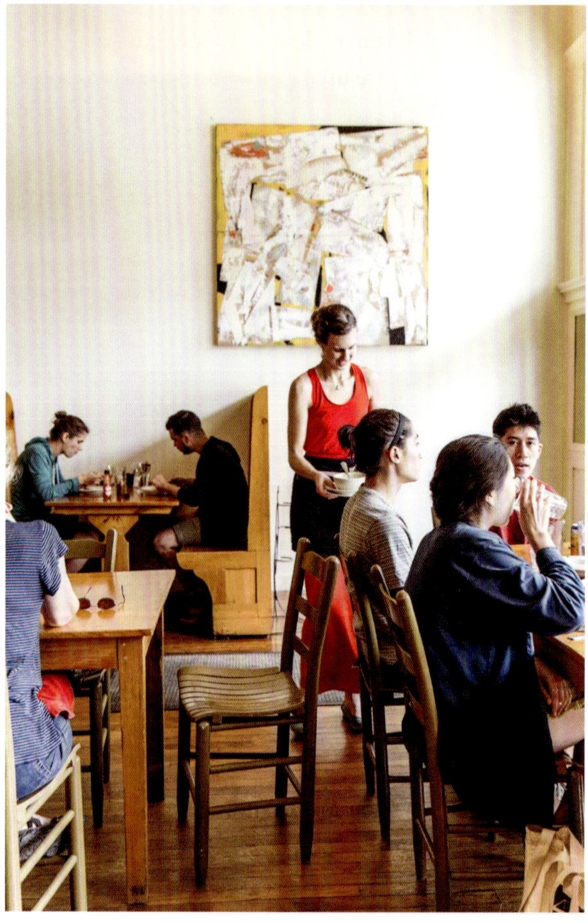

bruschetta, and generous plates of pasta. In the past, the menu has included a vegetarian version of Vietnamese *bánh mì*, Italian-inspired flatbreads, and savory bowls of borscht. Inspiration can come from around the globe, but the dishes are unified by their simplicity, their wholesomeness, and their emphasis on fresh produce above all else. "There are so many cuisines in the world that have wonderful vegetarian options," says Penny. "What we serve is just good food, real food, hearty, simple food."

Like the rest of the family, Penny Chase has the quiet confidence of an innovator who knows her mind. While the family works hard to ensure their restaurant and farm's success, they have never placed advertisements or welcomed reporters. In true New England fashion, they are reserved and humble. They prefer working in the fields or in the kitchen to answering questions or marketing their business. At Chase's Daily, the food is intended to speak for itself. However, Penny is willing to discuss her daughters, and when she does, she allows her pride to shine. "From the very beginning, the girls have always had a clear idea of what the restaurant would be," she says. Although Addison originally intended to use their land as a cattle farm, after Meg and Phoebe returned from college as vegetarians, the family decided to give up livestock and focus solely on produce.

For Meg, choosing seed varieties is one of the most pleasurable aspects of her work. "It's fun paying attention to each plant," she says. "I can walk through the field and taste each one as it grows to figure out exactly the right time to harvest. Right now we have greens, lots of greens—kales and mustards, broccoli rabe, Aztec spinach, lettuce and chicory, beets and chard and agretti." Freddy has been cooking and serving greens like these for years. "When we first started out, back in 2000, no one was serving greens like we did," he says. "Culturally, people in America weren't used to having a side like that. Even though it's a very simple dish—just greens, garlic, olive oil, and lemon—it wasn't something people were used to." Some of the greens, like agretti, an Italian vegetable that looks like—in Freddy's words—"a succulent crossed with dill," were foreign to the family, too. But this is a family that believes in trying everything, tasting everything, and pulling inspiration from both trips abroad and to the garden. "When Meg and I first encountered it in our travels, we liked it a lot, but we didn't know how to cook it," Freddy recalls. "So we had to experiment. Like everything else, it was a process of trial and error."

Chase's Daily has built a devoted following of customers who trust the menu, no matter how unfamiliar the ingredients. In return, the Chase family has committed to staying open year-round for their local patrons (as well as for their employees, a rare thing in such a seasonal, tourist-driven economy). "We're not really joiners," says Phoebe, "but I do think it's important to all of us that we're part of the local community." Even when storms are raging outside and other businesses have closed, Freddy, Meg, Phoebe, and Penny will make their way to the brick building to serve breakfast and coffee in the morning, and soup and sandwiches for lunch. "We have a responsibility to our town," Phoebe says. "We love to feed people, and we want to be there for them, to be consistent, no matter what."

For the entire family, consistency and quality go hand-in-hand. "From the very beginning, quality was so important to us," says Penny, recalling the days when Meg and Phoebe were teenagers selling Chase family produce from the back of a pick-up truck. "Even before we had a restaurant, we made sure our produce was top quality and that it was arranged beautifully, too." "We know what we like, and we have very specific ideas about the quality of the food, how it should look, how it should taste," adds Meg. "The kind of food we grow is special. It's rare. And I think people appreciate that."

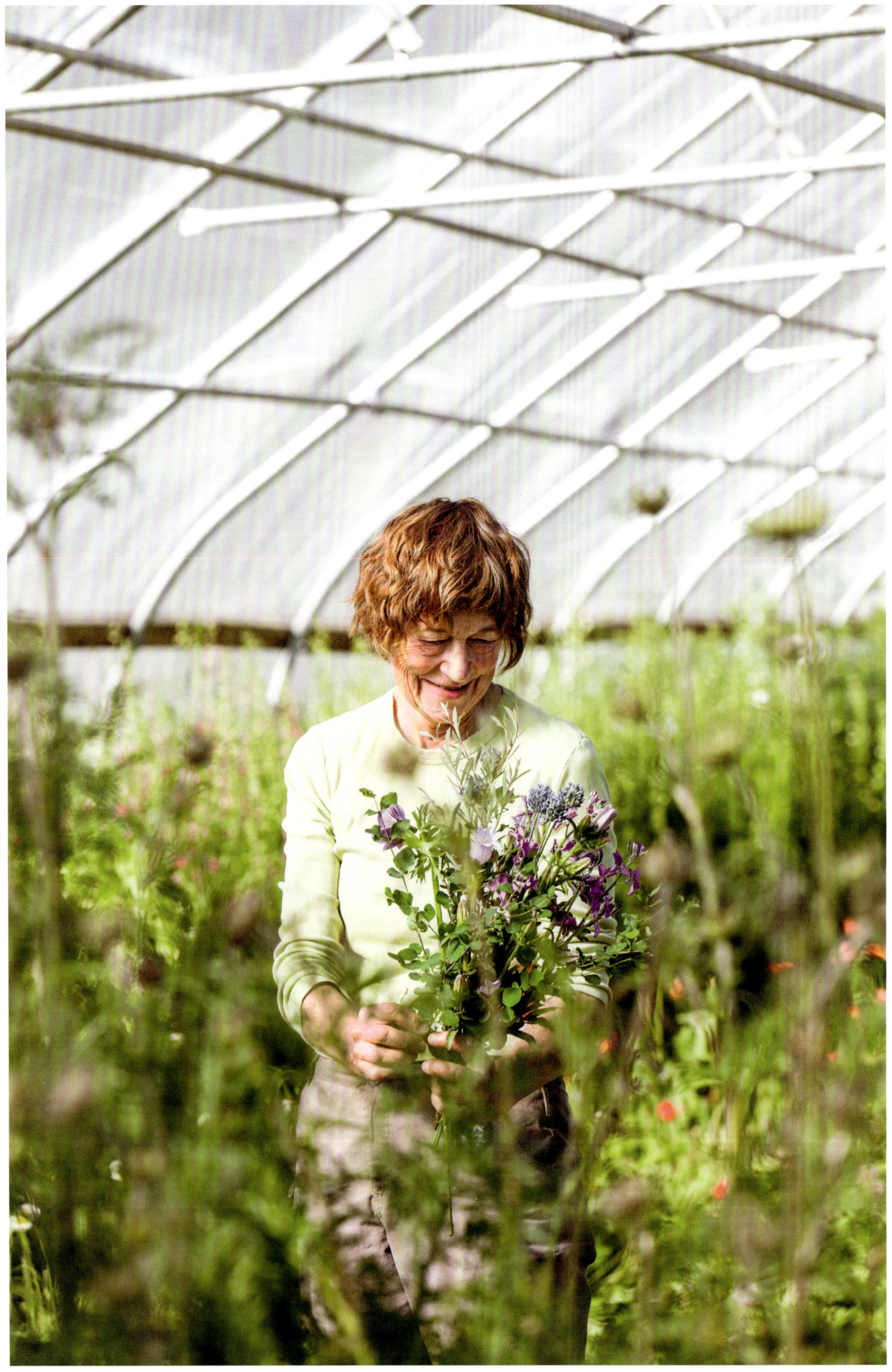

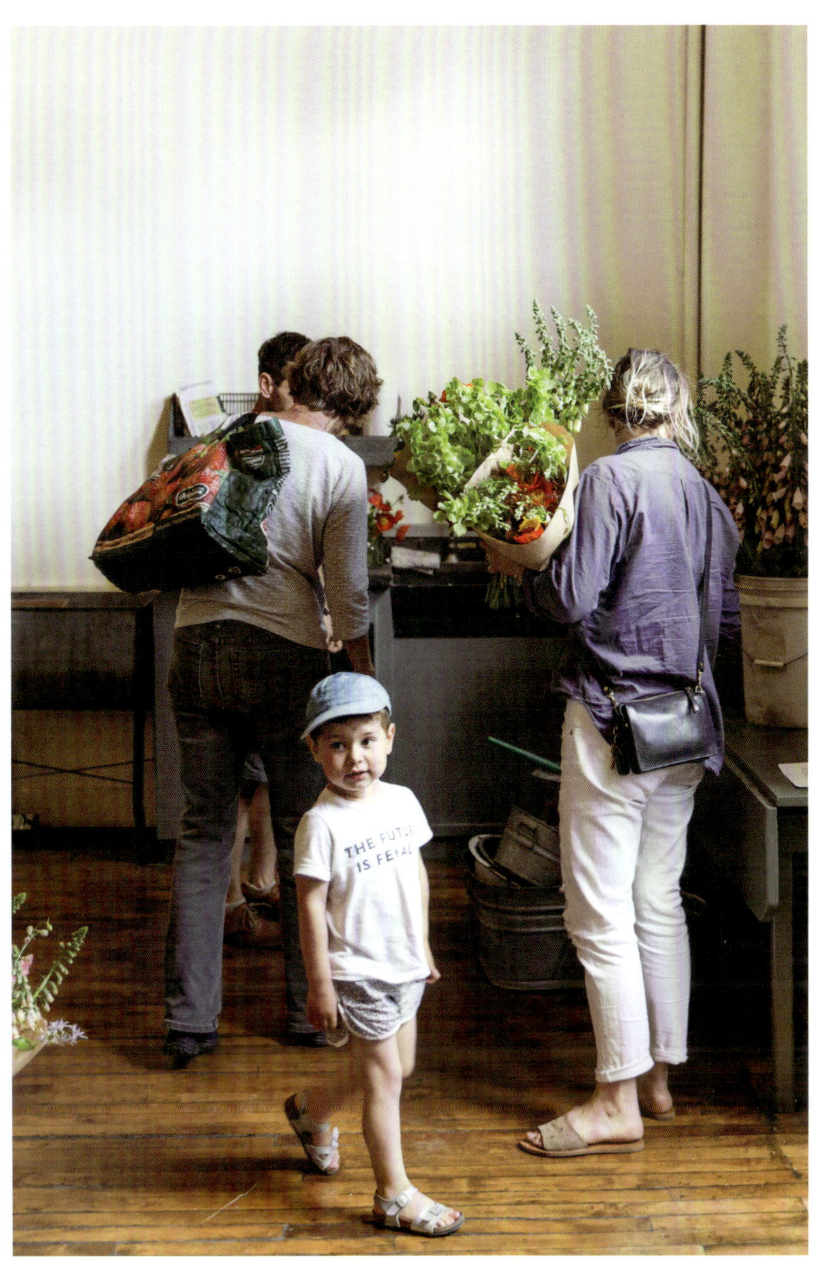

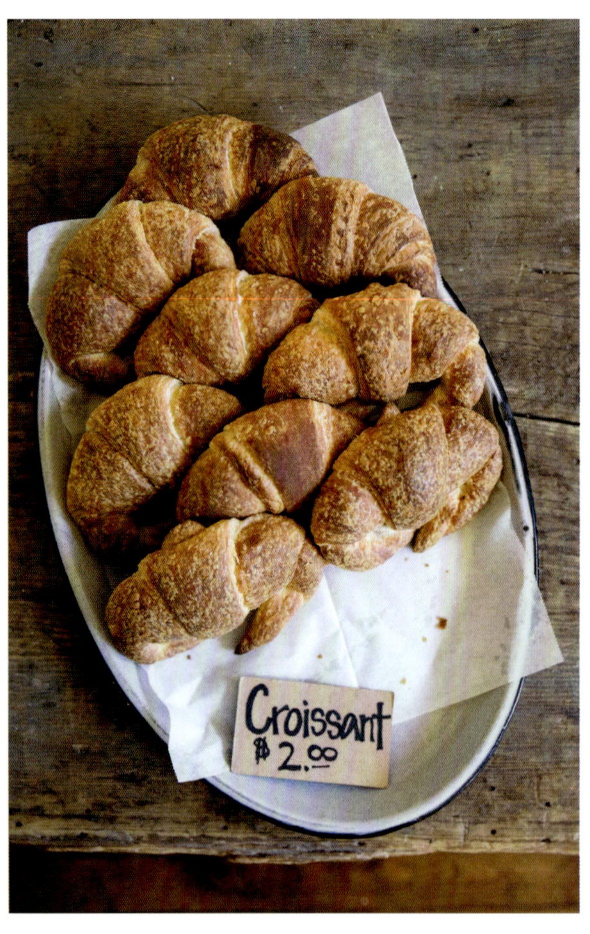
Croissant
$2.00

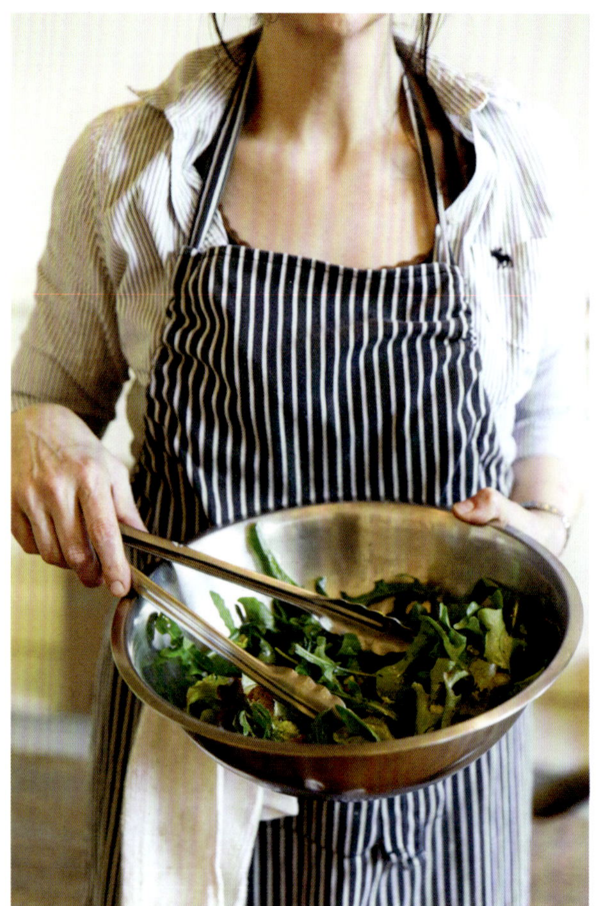

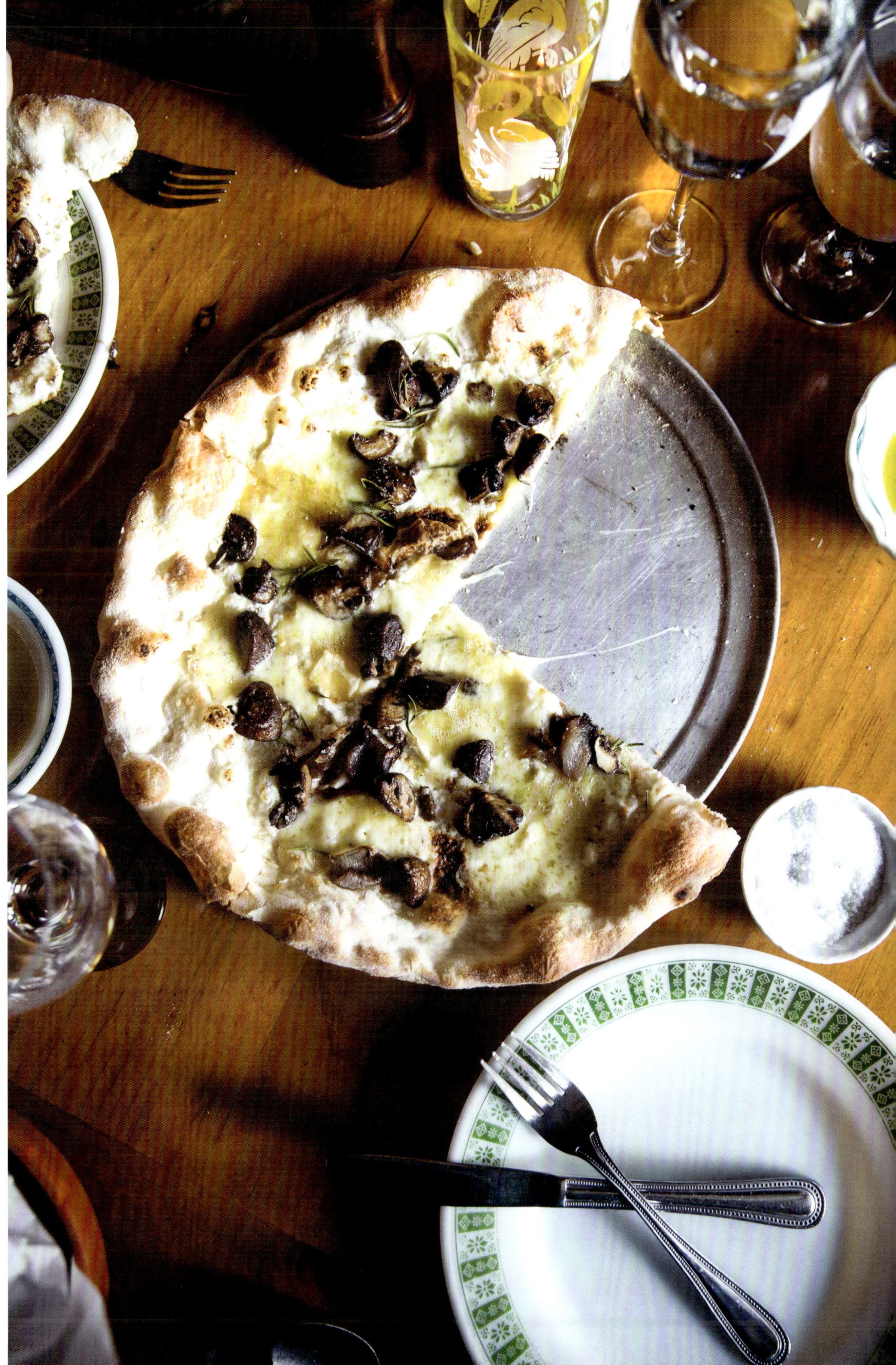

John Williams

Stonington

The sun is hours from rising and the sky is overcast and black. It's frigid, a typical January morning in Maine, and each breath forms clouds in the air, obscuring the faces of John Williams and his crew as they climb aboard his lobster boat, the *Kristy Michelle*. A light snowfall muffles the sounds of the water and the engine as John pulls up to the Little Bay Lobsters warehouse. Over the radio he alerts Little Bay of his arrival. Minutes later a group of workers who have been packing chum since three that morning lower heavy crates filled with silvery frozen herring onto the boat. Under the yellow glow of florescent lights, Alvin Jones and Zach Carter parcel the fish into mesh bags for bait. In the summer, the herring is sharply pungent, but for now, the winter air tamps down the scent of fish and sea.

The men don't talk much as they work, but every now and then Alvin, the youngest of the crew, breaks the silence. "You haven't seen a sunrise until you've seen one out at sea," he tells us. The nineteen-year-old Stonington native has been working on fishing boats since the days before he had whiskers, but he has yet to tire of the sublime scenery. The boat pitches wildly, but Alvin and Zach are undisturbed. Their hands work rapidly, mechanically, to create the dozens of "fish packets" they'll need today. A few feet away, John Williams stands at the helm, as straight as a mast.

Over an hour later, the *Kristy Michelle* arrives at its destination. We're seven miles off the shore of Stonington and the sky is rosy pink and light blue, delicate as an opal. The waves buffet the ship violently, their colors no less impressive than their force: glassy navy blue, cresting to a soft, translucent turquoise. The closest landmass is Isle au Haut, but it's soon lost in the fog. The ocean stretches endlessly, and the lobstermen begin their true labor. A whirring of motors fills the air as they haul trap after trap from the ocean, checking each one for lobsters. John has eight hundred traps laid out in lines, linked by metal cables, baited with herring and, he hopes, filled with red and blue lobsters with fat claws and plump tails.

Many of the lobsters John and his crew catch today will be released back into the water; since the near-collapse of the lobster fishery in the 1920s, Maine's strict regulations have imposed minimum and maximum weight and size restrictions on the crustaceans. Scientist and lobsterman Ted Ames,

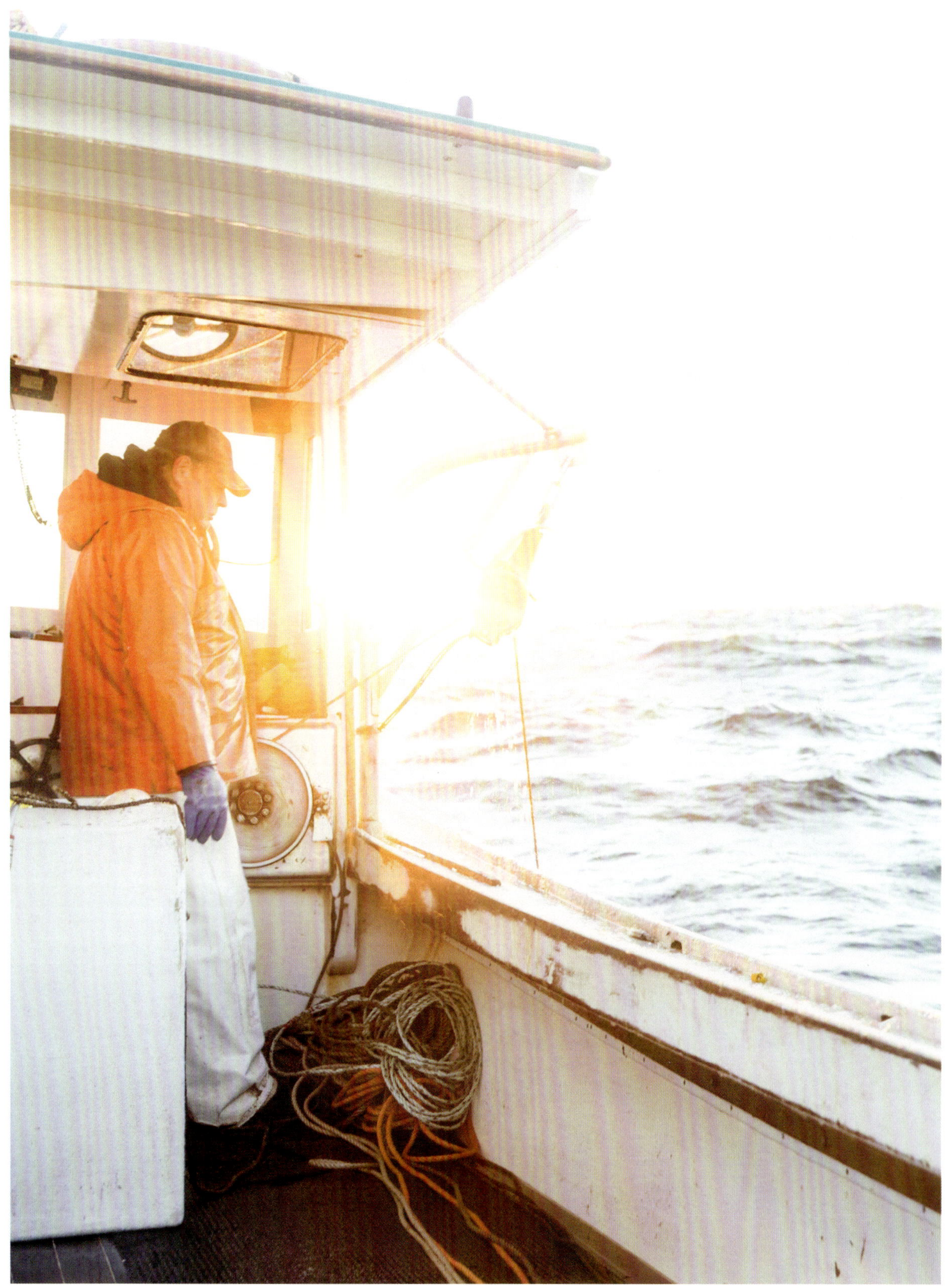

a 2005 recipient of a MacArthur Genius Grant for his work on Maine fisheries, argues that, over the past century, the lobster industry has been transformed into one of the "most dynamic and sustainable fisheries" in the world and the "backbone of the coastal economy." "We protect oversized lobsters, which can be up to seventy or eighty years old, because they have the healthiest eggs," he explains. "Every fisherman out there throws more over the side than they bring home. But most fishermen get it. It's a complicated fishery, and if we catch and eat them all before they can breed, there won't be any left in the future."

While John admits to occasionally feeling frustrated by how few lobsters he can keep—he estimates they throw 90 percent of their catch back into the sea—he understands why these regulations are in place. The laws protect future generations so they may live and work as he does. "You can't make a living as a wild fisherman in many places anymore, but I can," he says. "My father was a fisherman. My grandfather was a fisherman. If we catch all the young lobsters, there won't be any left for our grandkids. Most lobstermen understand that."

While state regulations have helped solve the problem of overfishing, John explains that drug use and cutthroat competition pervade the industry. "One of the biggest problems I've seen in the past ten years is drugs. Kids will leave school, take a job on the boats, and get hooked on heroin. And within two years they will have lost everything," he says. It demoralizes him to watch young lobstermen burn out this way and he enforces an anti-drug policy among his own employees. He shakes his head. The young people of Maine, he says, "have got the world by the ass and they don't even know it."

John tries to instill strong values in his younger crewmen—particularly Alvin, who in his two decades hasn't seen much of the world yet. "Alvin's been brought up alongside some of the harder fishermen, the guys who will cut other people's trap lines or go offshore where they aren't supposed to place lines. I'm trying to teach him that there's a better way to live." Cutting trap lines is a grievous offence; each trap costs $100, and cutting just one string can set a fisherman back $1,000. Unfortunately, it's still a common method of retaliation practiced by territorial lobstermen. "It can get violent," Ted Ames agrees. "Most guys start with a warning, like a 'Matinicus cocktail.'" Named for the downeast island, a Matinicus cocktail involves hitching the trap line around the wooden handle of a buoy so that it stands upright (rather than across the surface of the water), protruding from the ocean "like a thumb."

Despite the difficulties of lobstering—the brutal weather, the territorial disputes, and the long days on the water—John can't imagine doing anything else. "Lobstering is easy compared to the ground fishing I used to do," he says. "It feels like I've been on vacation since 1990." Recently, he was out on the water with his son, who remarked that John "makes a hard job look easy." John thought about that comment, only to realize that yes, for him it is easy. Years of fishing, of watching the waves, steering the boat, placing traps, and hauling lines has soaked into his blood, turning it to saltwater. Now, he explains, "Lobstering is not my job—it's a habit. It's a rhythm. It's ingrained in me."

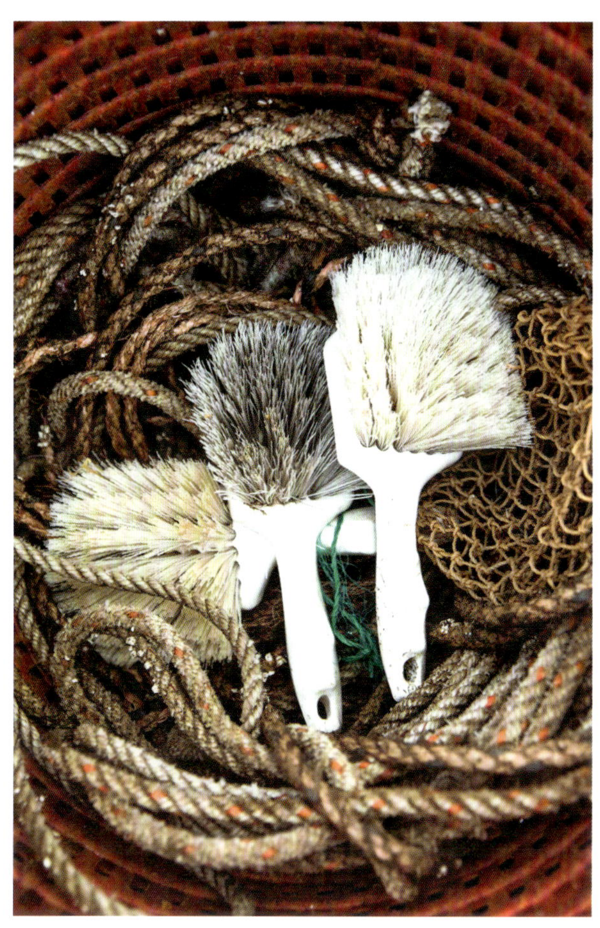

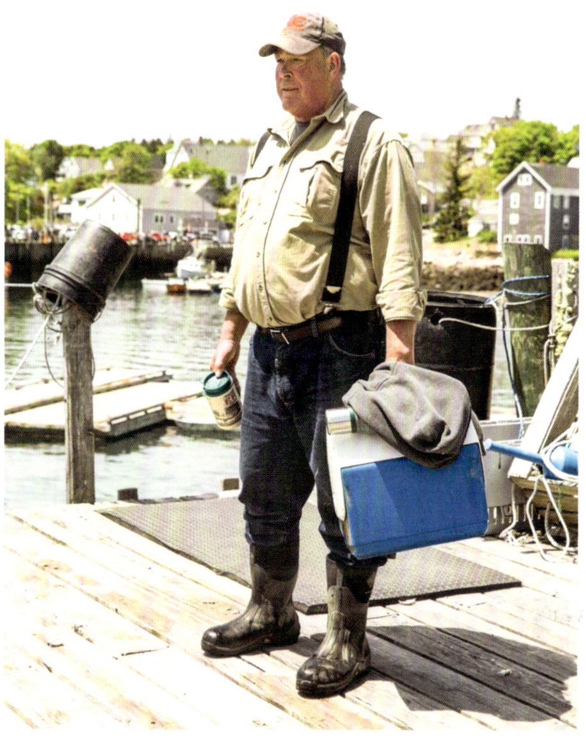

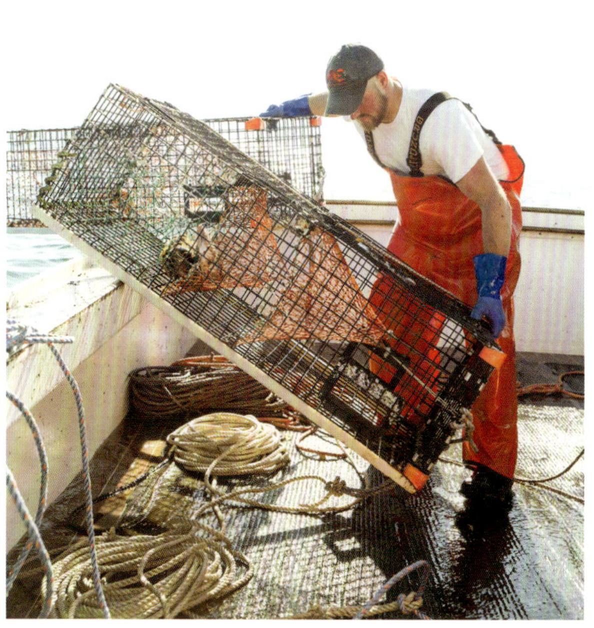

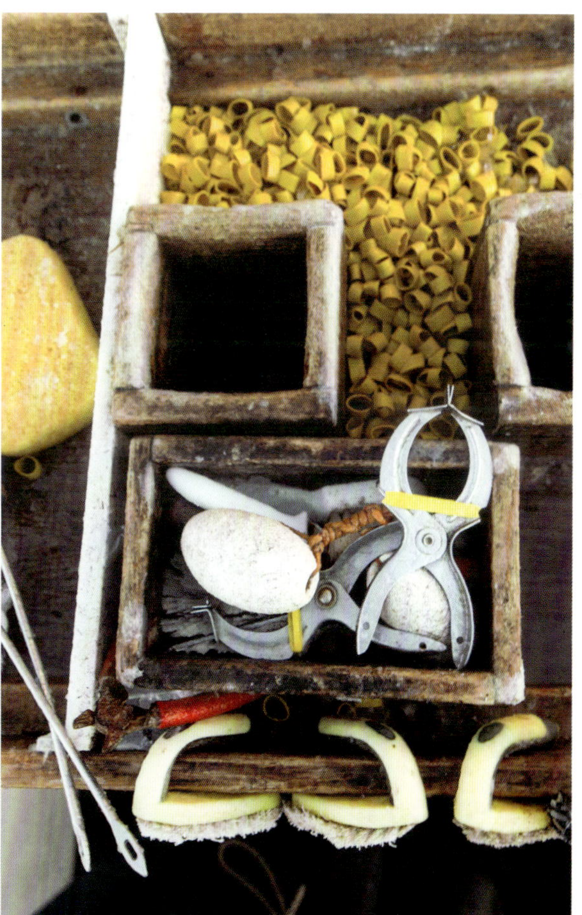

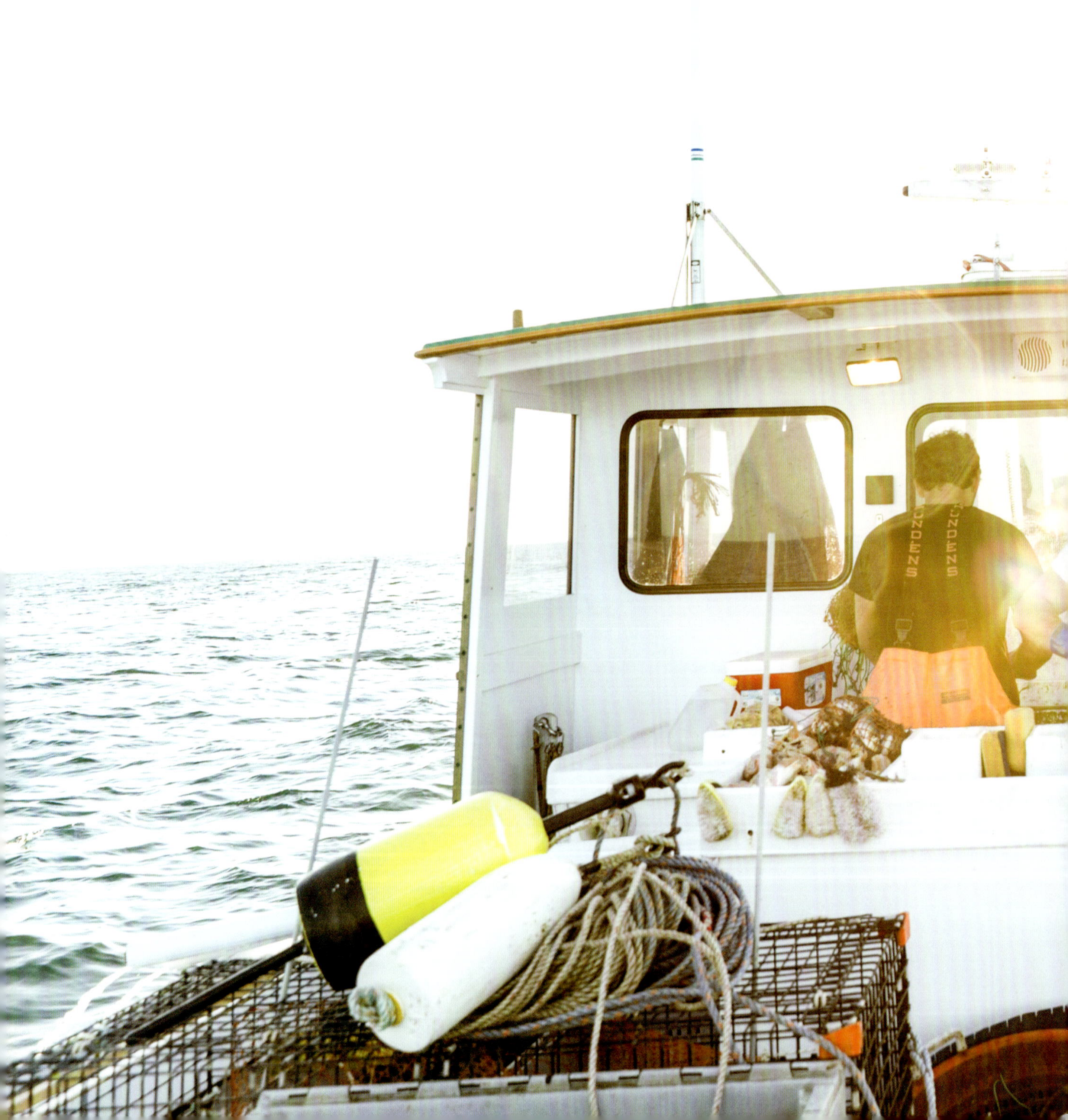

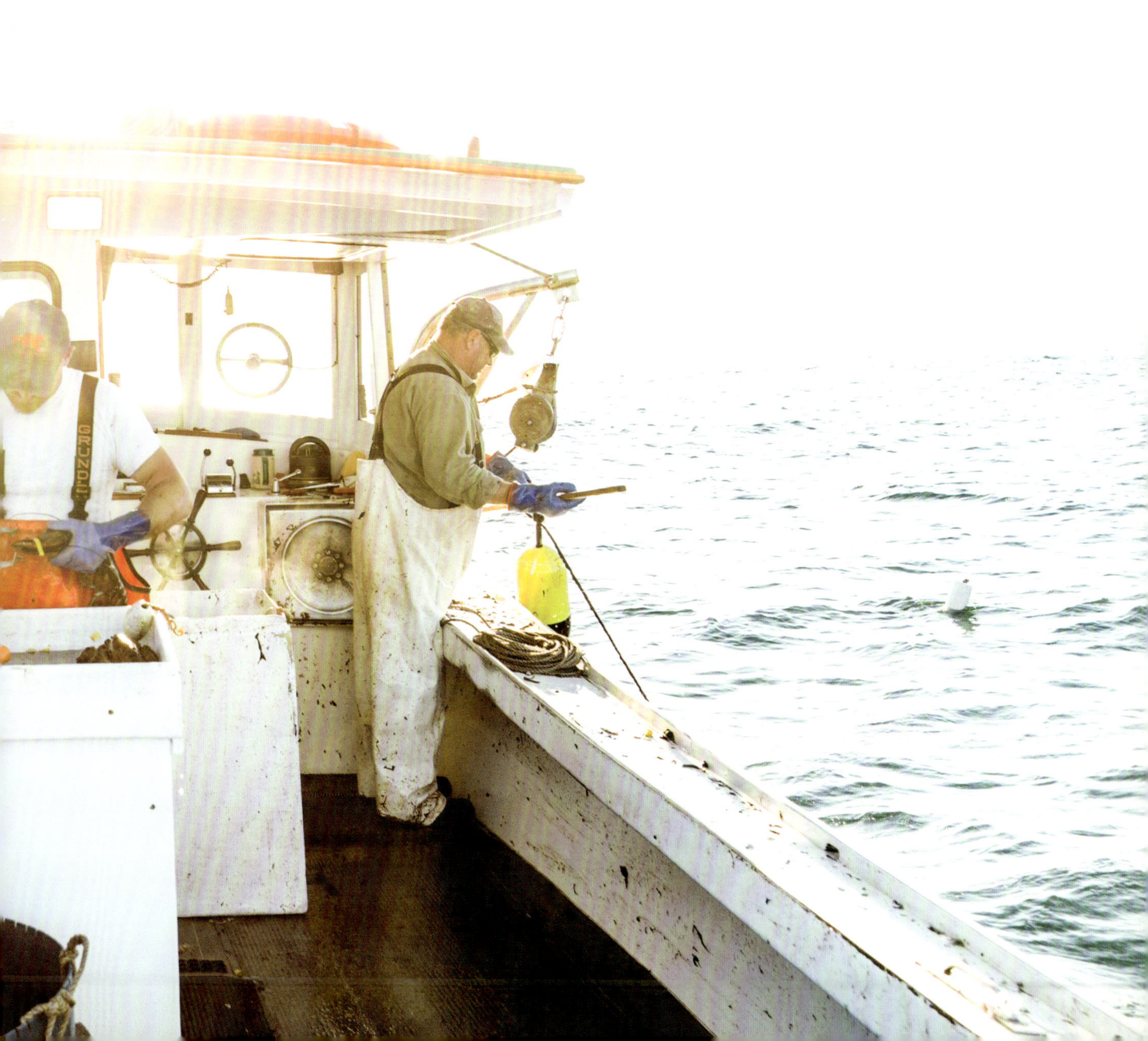

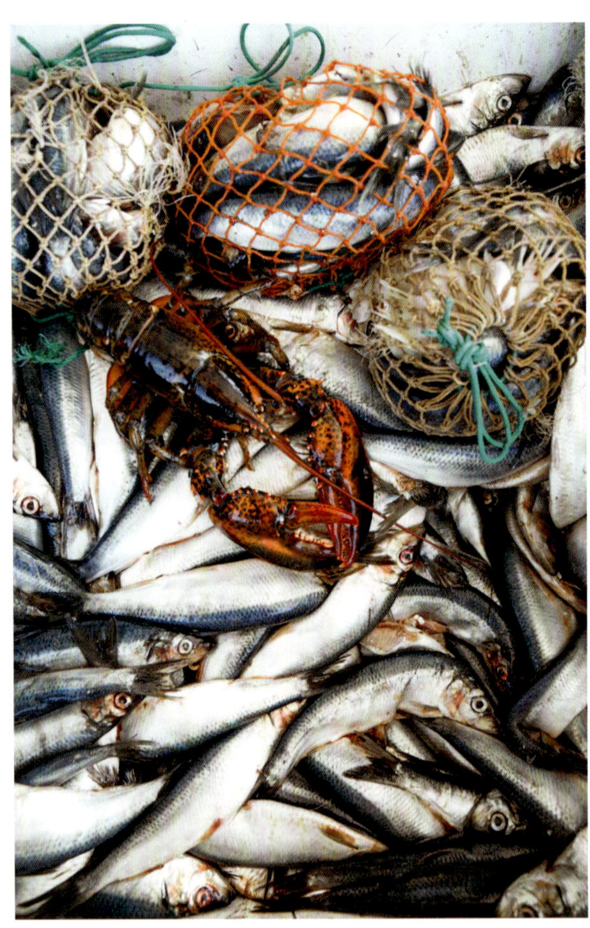

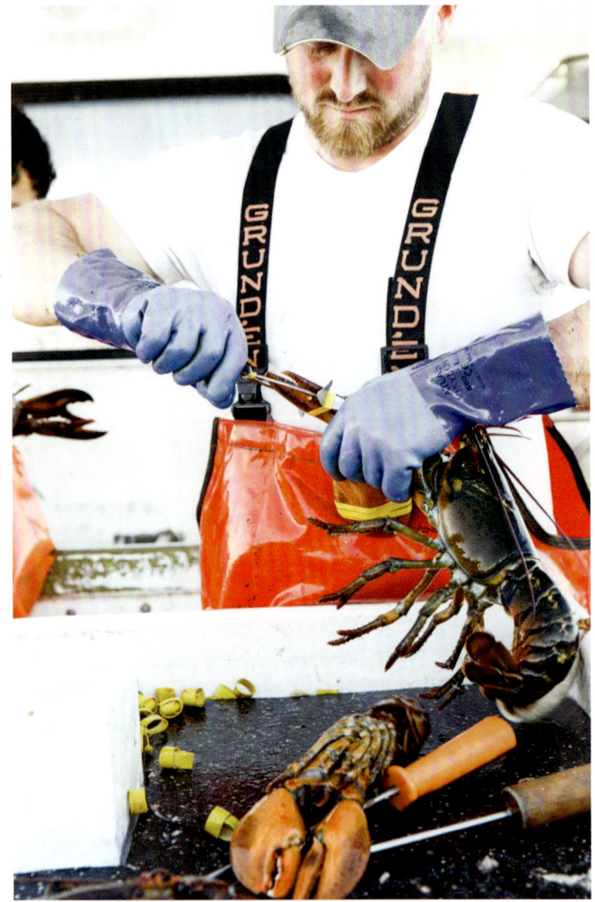

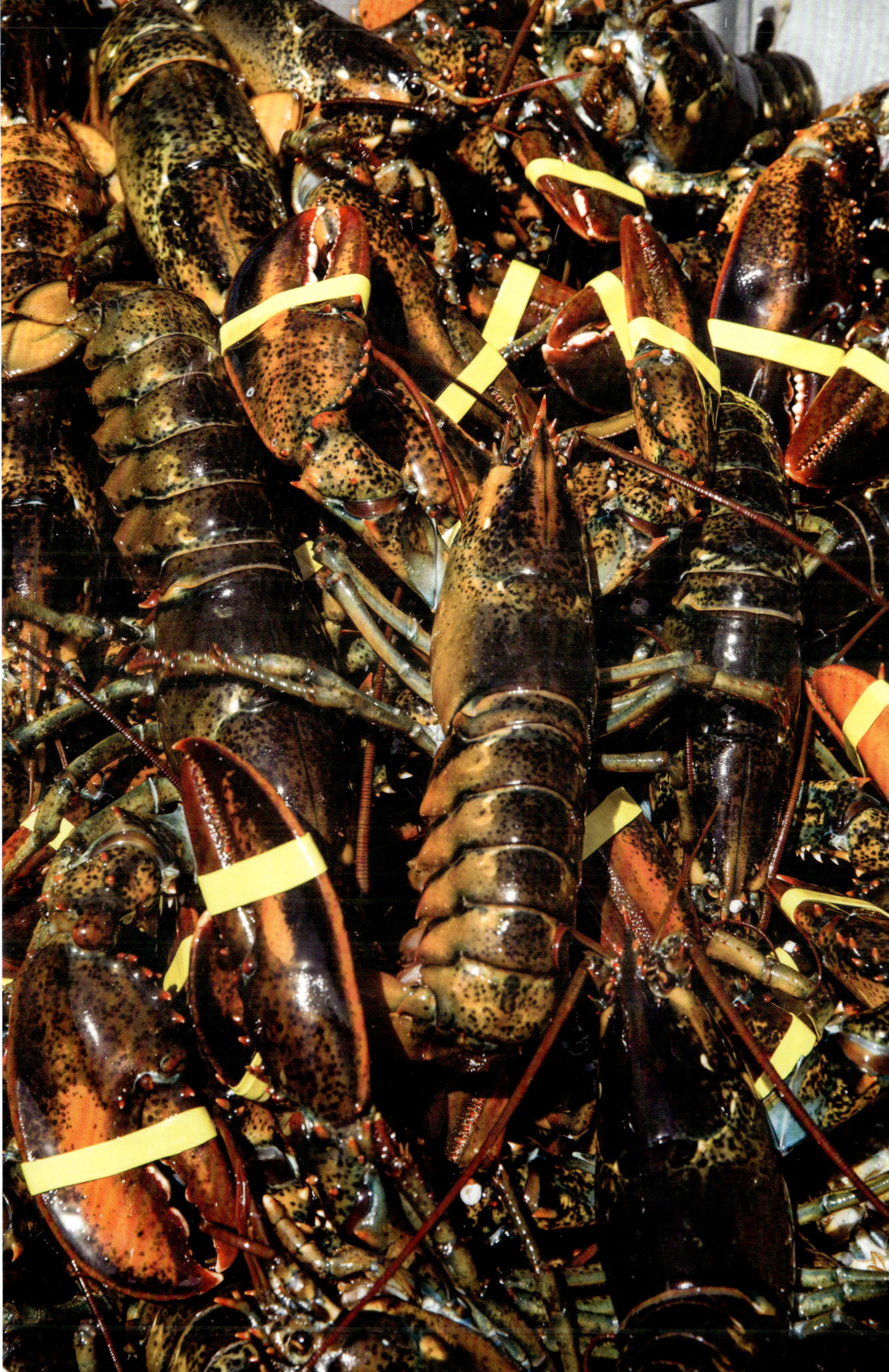

Oxbow Beer

Newcastle

Few states can rival Maine when it comes to craft beer—the sheer number of breweries, the variety of beer available, and the innovative and experimental blends. It's not easy for a brewer to stand out when the competition is of this caliber, but Oxbow beer manages. By adopting traditional European techniques, local production, and international flavors, this American farmhouse brewer has become a staple in the beer snob's pantry, a must-know name for chefs, and a popular tourist destination for out-of-state visitors.

Drawn from the tap with a perfectly proportioned head of foam, it's easy enough to understand why this beer tastes better than its peers. Founded by Tim Adams in 2011, the Oxbow brewery is based in a picturesque wooden farmhouse in Newcastle, a town so small that it barely has a downtown. The brewery is tucked away down a long driveway lined with pines and other conifers. Marked only by a wooden sign emblazoned with their trademark owl symbol, it's appealingly remote (but thanks to GPS, it's also easy to find). In the winter, the brewery's isolation is enhanced by the quiet cold that steals over the farm. The guinea hens in their roost are quiet, and snow covers the small cherry orchard. (It is filled with young trees that have yet to bare fruit, but someday these stone fruits will lend their tart, sweet juice to Oxbow's sour lambics.) The raised garden beds resemble puffy white mattresses. Near the brew house, steam curls out the glass doors and the smell of yeast and fermenting grains wafts over the snowdrifts. It's a warm scent, reminiscent of baking bread, and it beckons us in to have a taste.

But before tasting, a tour. Like most visitors to Oxbow, we take a tour of the brewery and observe each step of the process. Founder Tim Adams is not usually the guide—his company is growing, and he spends less time brewing and more time managing—but today he insists, to our good luck, as he knows this process and this place better than anyone. "The decision to locate our brewery up here was an easy one," he explains as he strolls amongst the industrial tanks. "The water here has a really unique mineral content that makes our beers taste so much better." He speaks over the sound track of fermentation: bubbles pop and fizz as the beer releases its gasses through the shining steel pipes into a small bucket that jiggles as it fills with foam and froth. Despite the

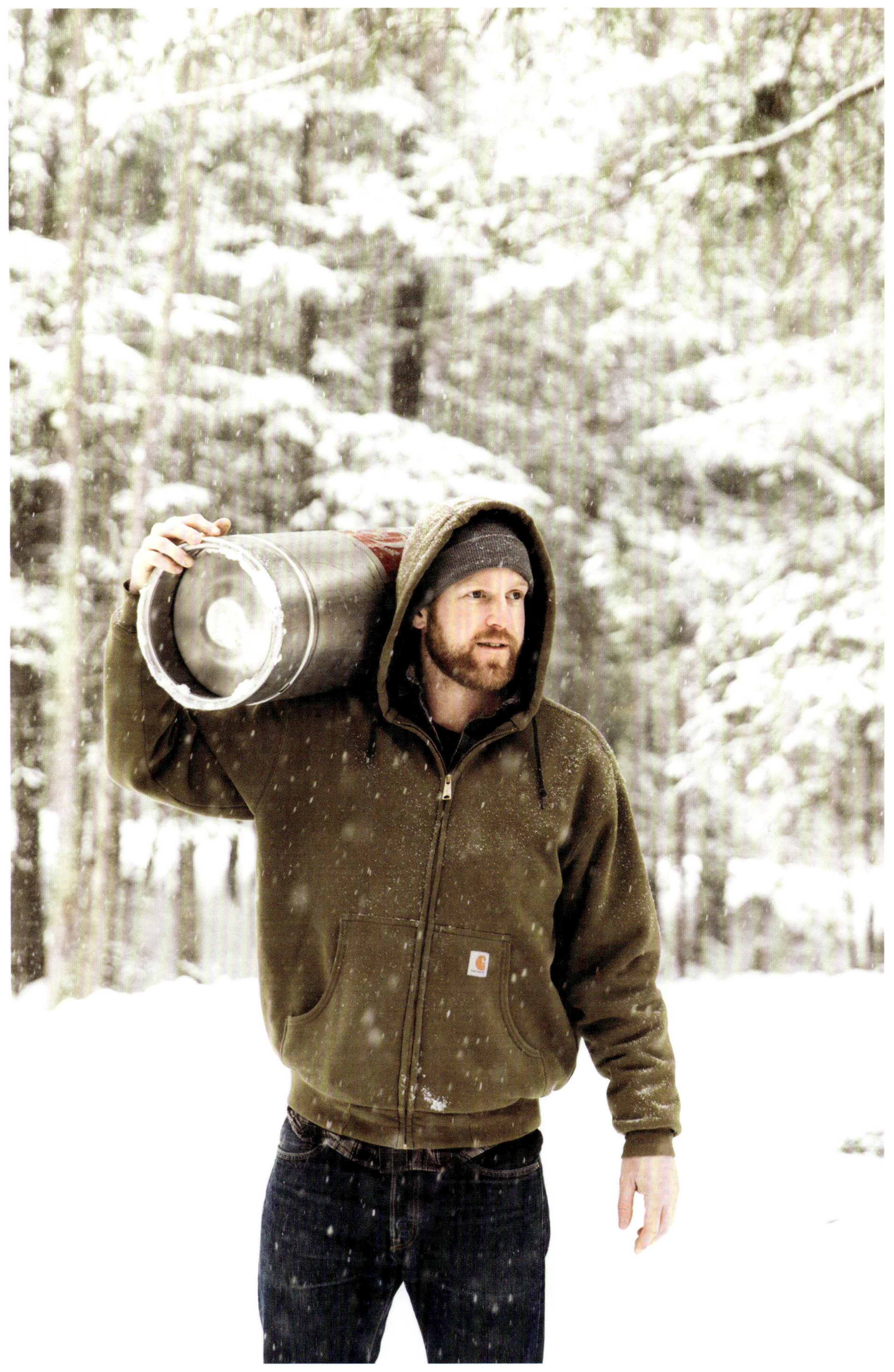

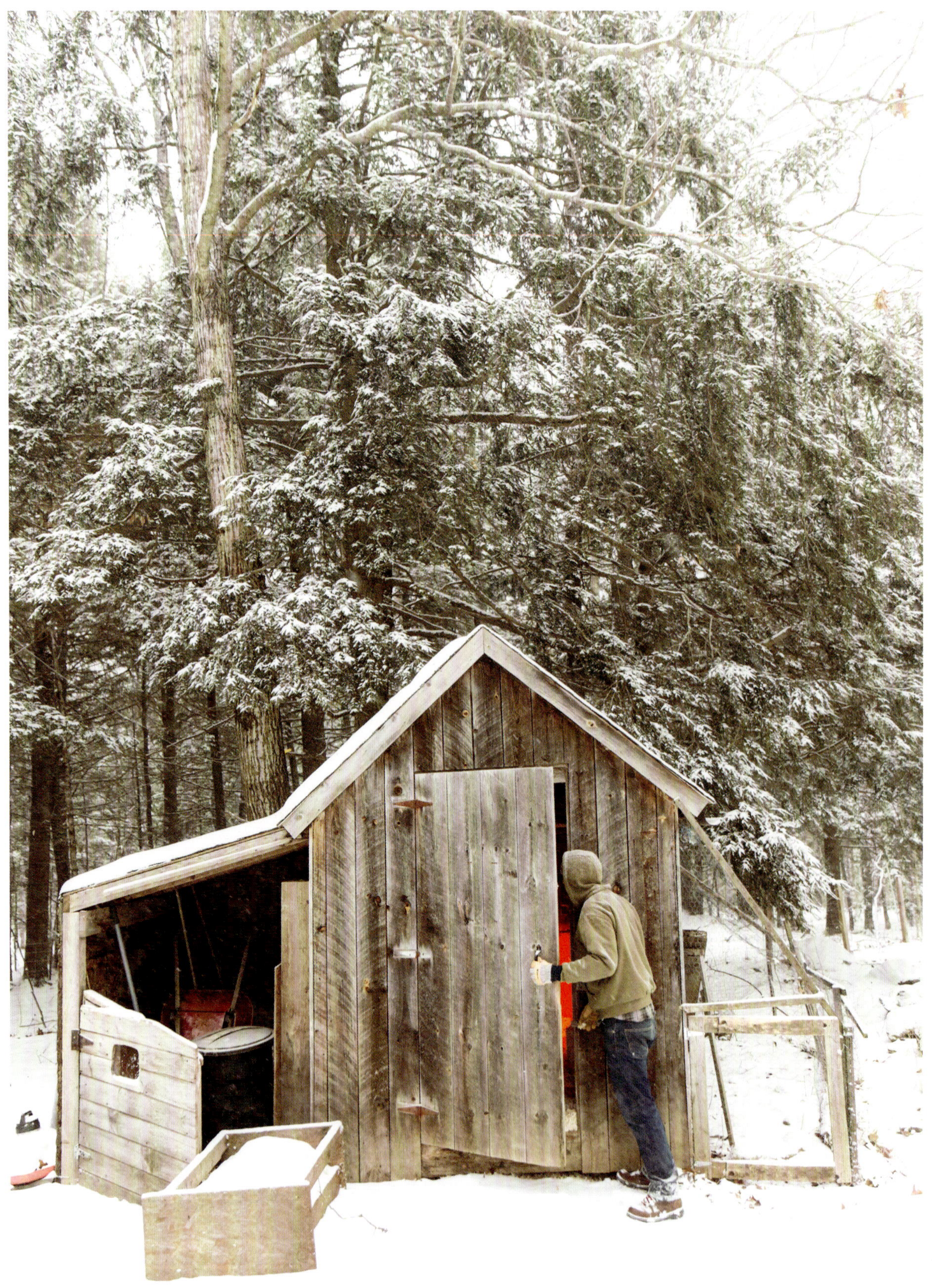

sophisticated machinery, beer making is still a noisy, messy process.

As a home brewer, Tim made beer for years before setting up shop in Newcastle. The company began as a farmhouse production, a small operation brewing Belgian-style beers, like their first brew, a barrel-aged sour ale, for Mainers and Maine restaurants. Since then, Oxbow has expanded slowly as it secured markets all along the east coast, including New York, Massachusetts, New Hampshire, Vermont, Washington, DC, and Philadelphia. The company has also developed a following in Italy, Germany, and Japan, where Tim traveled to develop collaboration brews. In turn, he has hosted brewers in his own well-appointed farmhouse located just a minute's walk from the brewhouse.

The company's location has always played as central a role in its identity as it has its product. The sprawling, wild, and utterly Maine eighteen-acre property permeates Oxbow's core ethos as much as the distinctive, mineral-rich, soft water flowing through the pipes enhances the beer's flavor. When asked about Oxbow's logo, Tim explains that the owl image has several layers of meaning. Out in the back acres, the brewers have observed a big barn owl and at night have heard its gentle hoots. "But he's not just in our logo. He's also in our slogan: 'Loud Beer from a Quiet Place,'" Tim explains. "The owl comes in silently and swiftly," much as the bold flavor of the beer steals over your palate.

The word "oxbow" has special meaning as well. In geography the term refers to a wide, U-shaped body of water that forms at a sharp river bend. And behind the brewery a vista opening through the trees reveals the twists and turns of the Dyer River, a view, says Tim, that inspired the company's name. "When a river makes an oxbow, it's traveling a long, circuitous route over what could be a short, linear distance," he says. "It's a metaphor for how we make our beers. We put in a lot of time, energy, and care. We could make a cheap, watery beer with half the effort, but I'd rather work hard to produce something truly unique."

The results of this effort are yeast-clouded beers that range from tart and refreshing to thick and comforting. While it would be misleading to suggest that there's something for everyone at Oxbow—these beers revel in the flavors of fermentation and may not appeal to a Coors Light drinker—Oxbow is no one-trick pony. "Whenever someone says, 'I hate how beer tastes,' I get really disappointed," says head brewer Mike Fava. "The spectrum of flavors is nearly endless." Right now, Mike says, he's particularly excited about "cool ship" beers. "We've been brewing beer that's spontaneously fermented—meaning that instead of adding yeast we use a natural inoculation of yeast from the air," he explains. "You put the beer out in the open, cross your fingers, and hope for the best. The first time I saw fermentation happening on our cool ship beers back in 2014, it brought me back to my first home brew, to that magic moment when you know the beer is coming together."

These wild beers have always been a source of pride for Tim. Oxbow is one of the few breweries in the country that uses a trough-like structure, the cool ship (Allagash Brewing Company, based in Portland, Maine, is another), but this style of brewing has long been popular in Belgium and France. As the natural yeast filters in from the air, it brings with it fruity, almost tropical flavors that pair beautifully with stone fruits and berries. "I'm excited to experiment with aging our wild beers in barrels, bottling them, and blending them," Tim says. "I'm a geek for gueuze. It's a blend of three different vintages of lambic, and in my opinion, it's the coolest beer in the world." Six years of brewing under its belt, Oxbow is about ready to start producing their own gueuze-inspired farmhouse ale, crafted in Newcastle, blended in Portland, and featuring the flavors of Maine fruits, water, and yeast.

There's another important ingredient in Oxbow brews that is not listed on the back of beer bottles. "You need time, time, time," Tim says. "This can't be done quickly, and these complex beers involve a lot of risk." Unlike brews made with laboratory-grown strains of yeast, you never know exactly what you'll get from spores that fly in through the window. "There's nothing wrong with wanting a specific, controllable flavor," Tim adds diplomatically. Some brews at Oxbow are made this way, too. Yet his enthusiasm mirrors Mike's when it comes to the scientific marvel of spontaneous fermentation. "We're basically invoking magic in beer," says Tim. "It's a lot more fun to leave it up to nature."

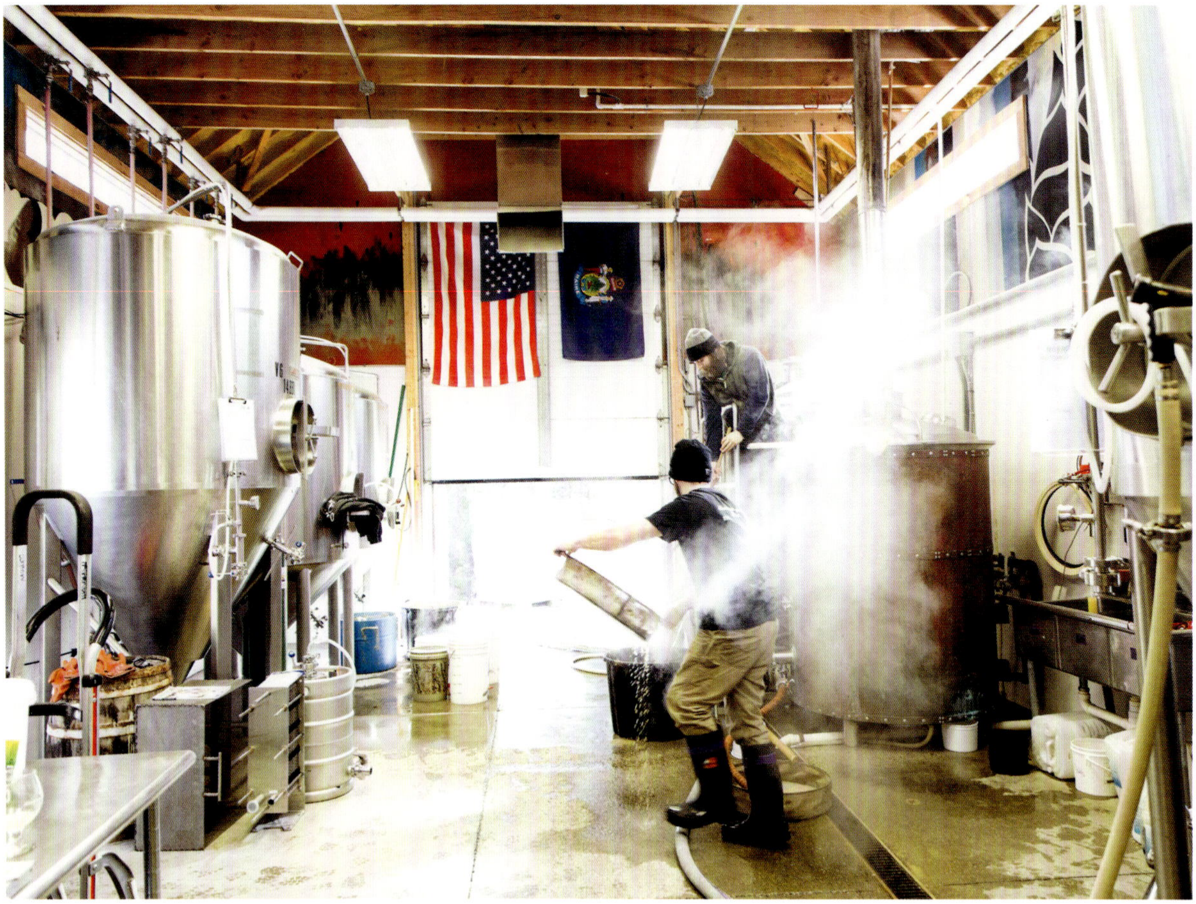

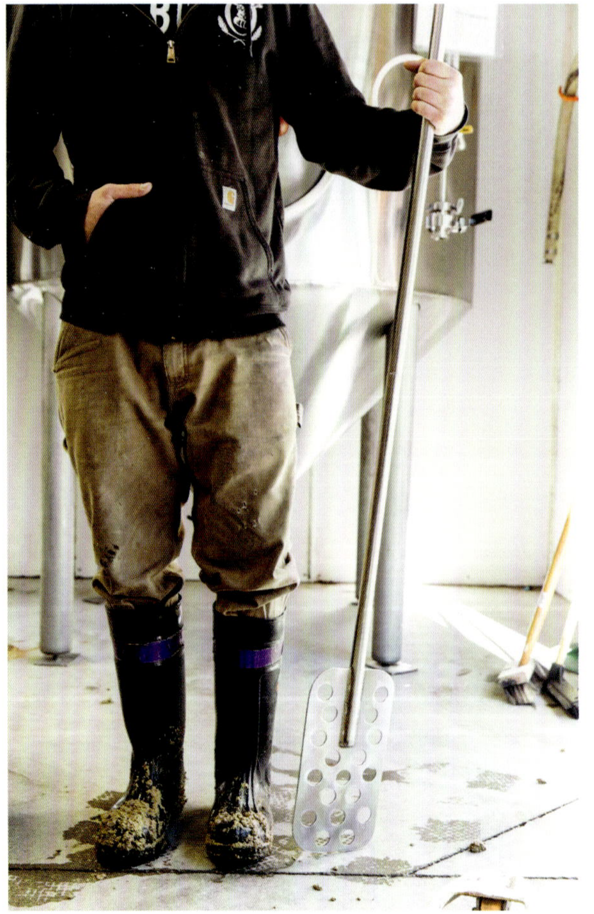

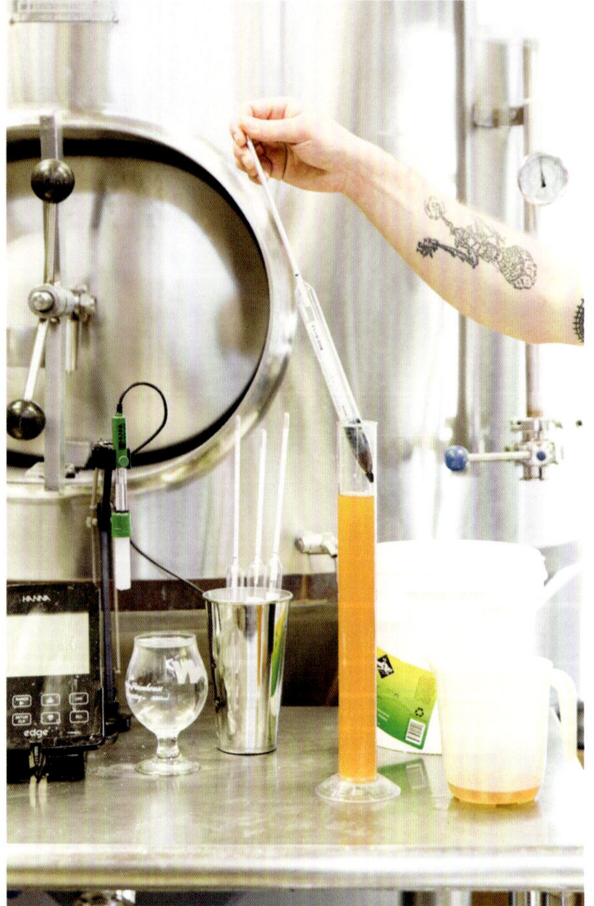

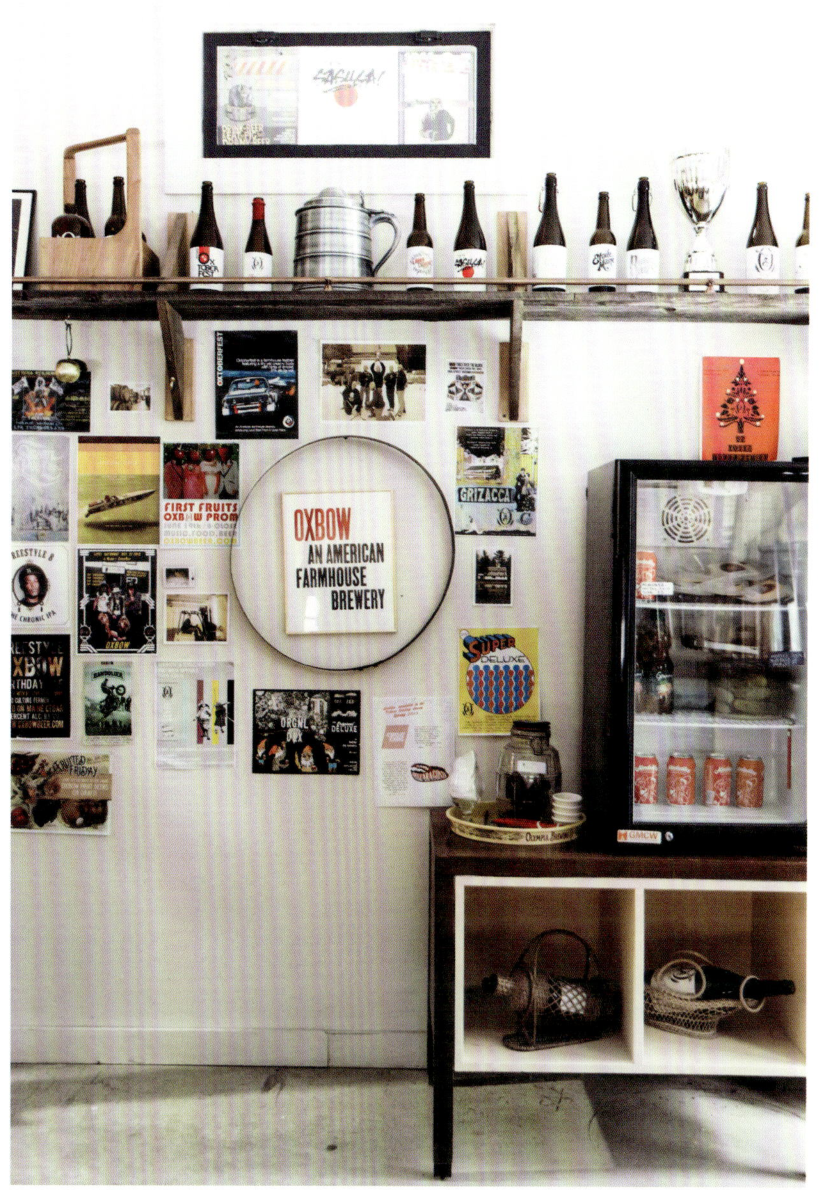
OXBOW
AN AMERICAN
FARMHOUSE
BREWERY
FIRST FRUITS
GRIZACCA
SUPER
DELUXE
OXTOBERFEST

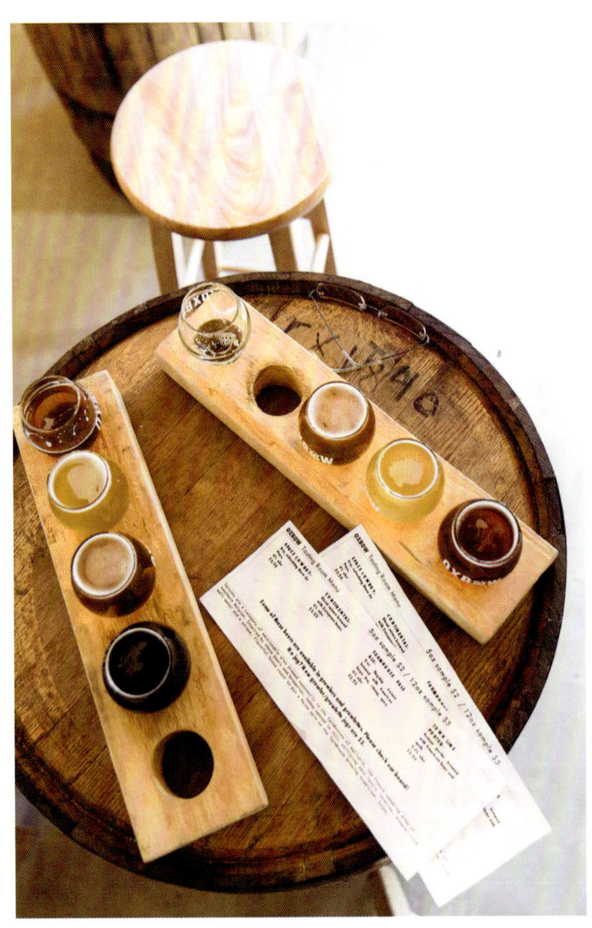

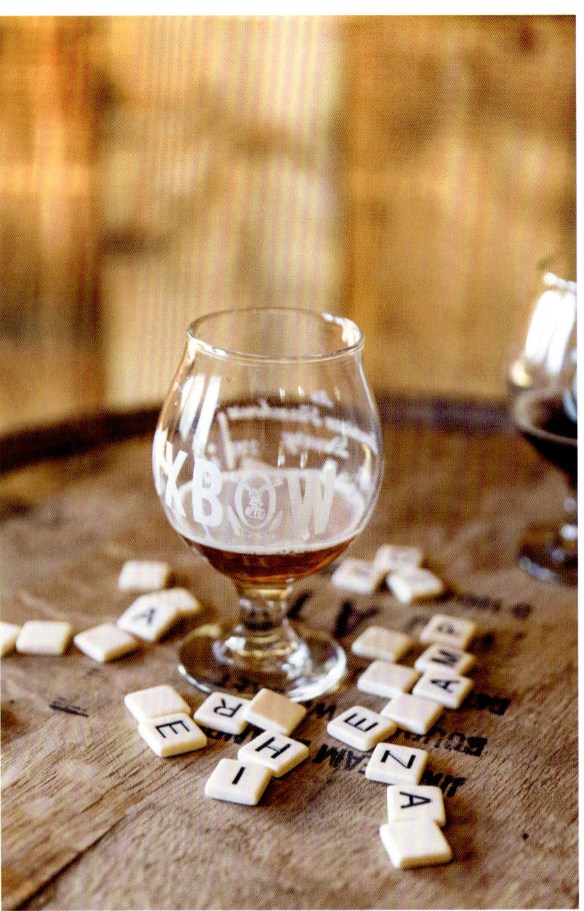

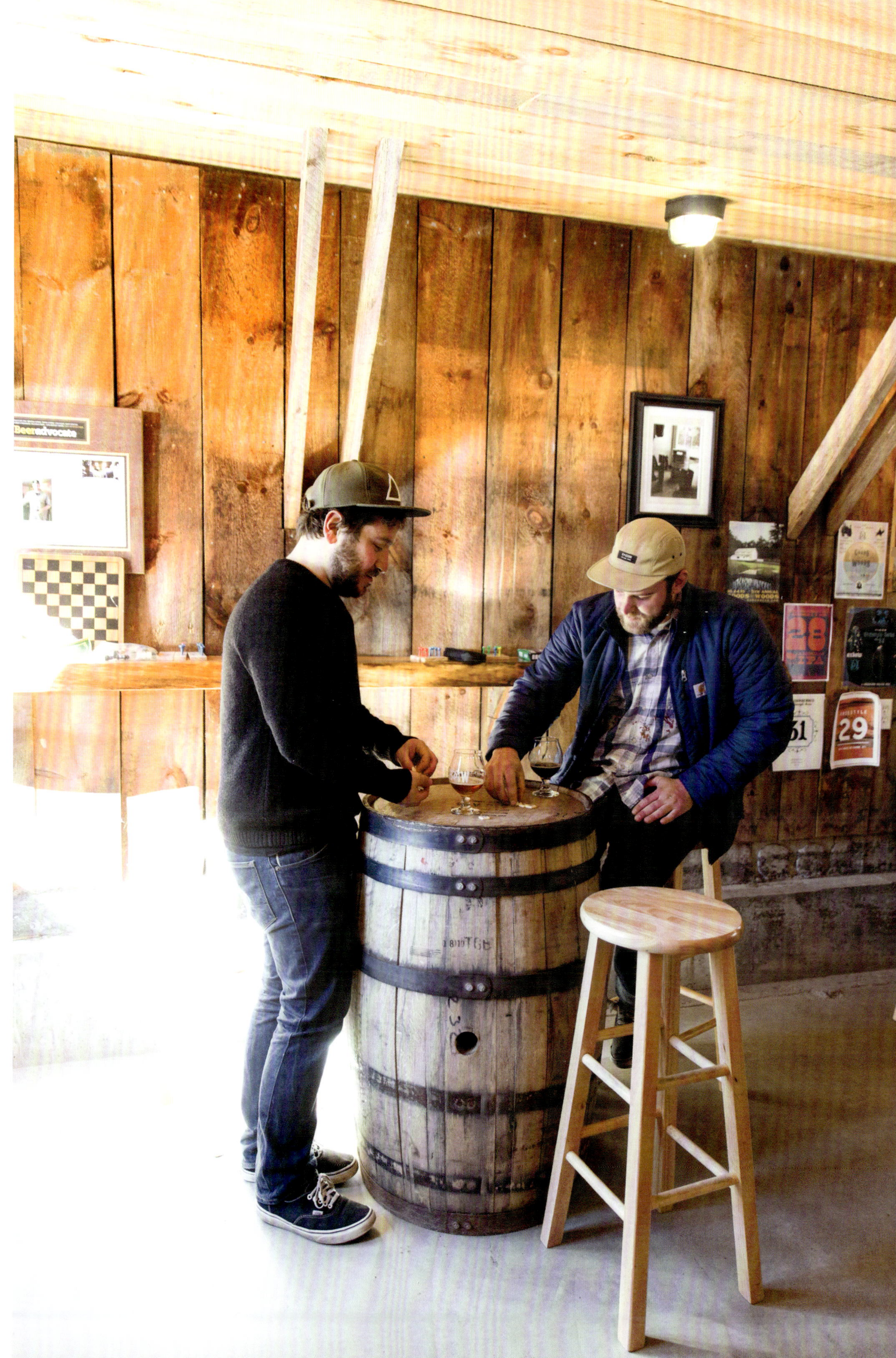
Beeradvocate

Tide Mill Creamery

Edmunds

The Bell family arrived in Washington County in 1765, the pre–Revolutionary Era when Maine was a territory within Massachusetts. The family patriarch, Robert Bell, landed on British-American shores a fourteen-year-old Scottish immigrant with an easy way about him—and, like many men in his position, a sense for adventure. According to family lore, Bell befriended a group of Passamaquoddy natives who showed him the secrets of the land, including the small inland bay where stream met sea in a powerful tug-of-war. The location was ideal for a mill, and so Bell fetched his wife, Jemima, from the nearby town of Eastport and set to work building his gristmill.

Over time, Bell added cattle and gardens, livestock and produce, to his operation. He passed the land down to his children, and they passed it on to their children. Eight generations later, Rachel Bell, a young poet and traveler, asked for a piece of land on which to build her own house. She had returned to Maine after spending her late teens and early twenties wandering the United States, working odd jobs and visiting the small, strange towns that make up America. She was ready to settle down.

"As a young woman, I went off on all these tangents," she recalls as she sips coffee in her kitchen. Outside the window, rain drizzles on the wild fields where her gentle herd of Nubian goats graze. "My boyfriend and I took off on a motorcycle and went down to New Orleans. I worked the winter at the only job I could find, at a racetrack. They hired me because I knew horses." Rachel laughs, remembering that time. From there she went to Texas, and then on to Mexico. "It was there that I decided to come home," she says. Although the climates of northern Maine and northern Mexico couldn't be more different, Rachel noticed some parallels between the two rural regions. She saw beautiful farmland and tightly-knit towns. She saw communities depleted by the exodus of young people, who had fled the farms looking for adventure and big-city opportunities. It made her sad. It made her homesick.

So she returned to the land where her father was born, and his father before him. She returned to the cows and the cold winters and the tall pines of Downeast Maine. She took classes in psychology and creative writing at a local university and settled in to life at the farm. "Once I started having kids, I became

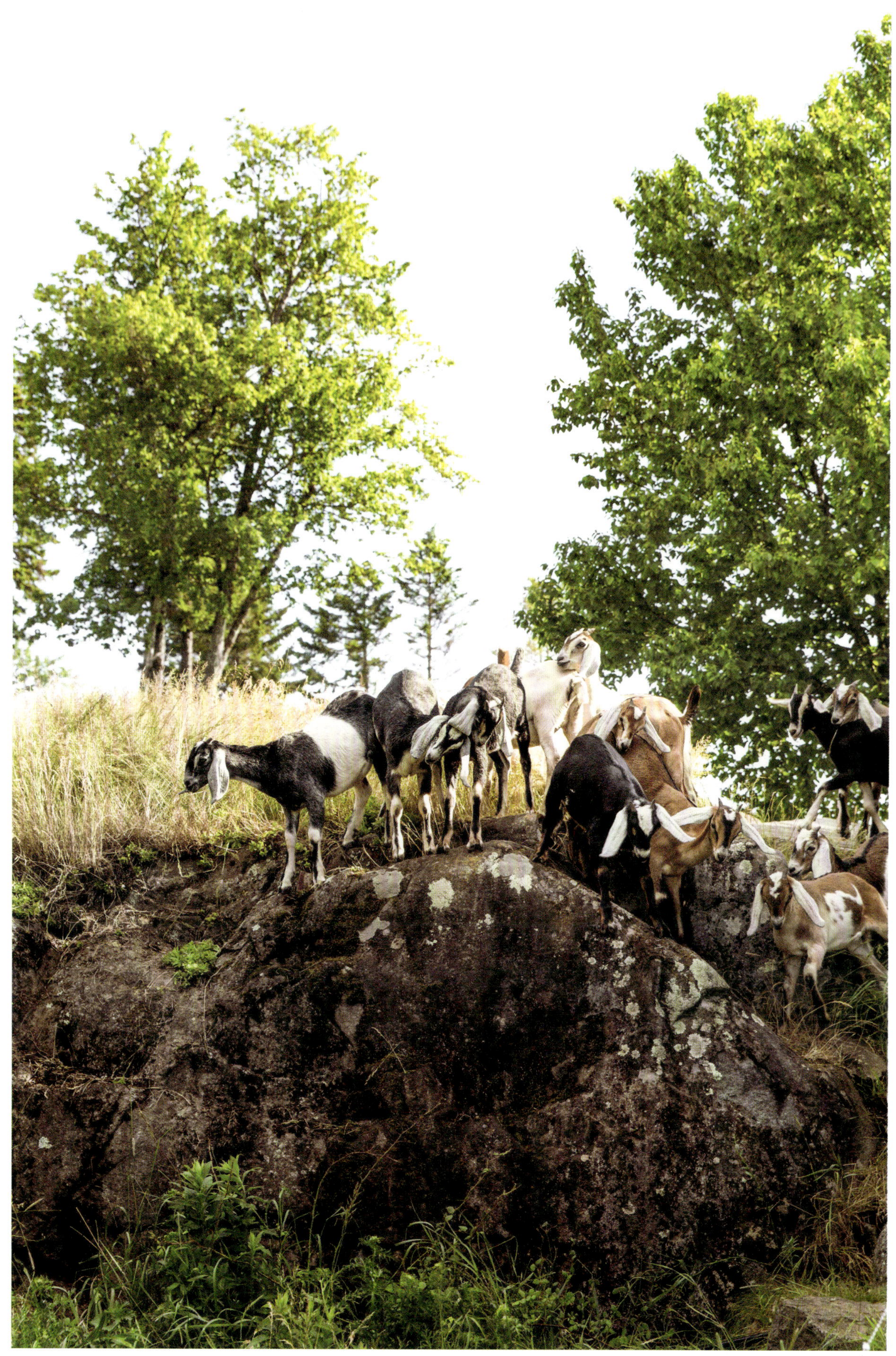

very conscious of the necessity of healthy eating," she explains. "It felt important to eat in a way that felt good for my body and good for the earth." This desire was coupled with an interest in local agriculture, biodynamic farming, and dairy production. She began researching cheese production and asked a fellow farmer to teach her how to hand-milk. In 2003, Rachel bought her first goat. Then came another, and another. She began making cheese.

It took several years before the business truly took off, and once it did, Rachel decided to leave school to give the creamery her full focus. At first she was making simple cheeses, including soft, spreadable chèvres and sweet crème fraîche. Next, she began experimenting with aged cheese, like tomme and paprika-rubbed Gouda. She sold her products at farmers' markets and local shops.

"It never occurred to me that I couldn't teach myself something," Rachel says, reflecting on her early years of cheese making. "There's a strong do-it-yourself spirit in Washington County. I set out to teach myself how to make cheese, and I did it by reading books, talking to other farmers, and experimenting." Fortunately, she had a built-in support system. Her cousin Aaron Bell and his wife, Carly DelSignore, own and operate Tide Mill Organic Farm, a larger business that served as an incubator for Tide Mill Creamery. In 2010, she officially opened her creamery, and in 2012, she expanded, bringing on Hannah Bath as head cheese maker, which freed Rachel to focus on her ongoing process of self-education.

The casual observer might think that Rachel lives a simple life on her farm. She endured years of arduous work to build the creamery, and more importantly, to cultivate the intellectual rigor she brings to her craft. "I try to approach my work in a calculated way," she says. "Cheese making is very complex, and you could spend your entire life learning about it. I think that's why I'm drawn to it." Hard cheeses, in particular, have proven tricky for her. "You have to closely monitor the pH and choose which cultures to use. You need to maintain specific temperatures, and if any of these things goes awry, it can change the outcome of the entire batch. And of course, there are things that can go wrong in brining, aging, and affinage." Affinage, she explains, is the art of aging cheese, minding the wheel while it waits in the cave, gathering flavor.

Discussing her work, Rachel transitions seamlessly between technical terms and romantic descriptions of the cheese, the landscape, and the farm. (Fittingly, when she is not researching biofilms and bacteria, she spends her free time writing poetry.) For her, cheese making is an art, a science, and sometimes even a sensuous act. Although she no longer needs to hand milk her goats—Tide Mill Creamery upgraded to a milking parlor with automated machines—Rachel still occasionally returns to the practice. "When I'm hand milking, I feel very close to the animal," she says. "It brings me back to the days of having a baby on my back, sitting on my milking stand, and feeling the warmth of the sunshine on my head. I would lean in against the goat's flank and feel her heat. It's a sensuous experience to be so close to an animal—and so close to nature. Those early years of motherhood were a special time for me, and it felt special to raise my children so close to nature."

As her children and her business have matured, Rachel has grown even deeper roots in Washington County, the land of her ancestors. "It has been a privilege to live in a place that is not only beautiful, but also where I have a connection to the older generations, to learn the stories of the land that have been passed down to me," she says. She has made sacrifices to live on this land, and she will continue to do so—for herself, for her children, and for her ancestors. "I worry sometimes that as we are eroding biological diversity, we are also eroding cultural diversity." She pauses to look out the window. Her fields are fallow now, growing wild. This is land that is fit for grazing goats, but not much else. It's her land, though, as much a part of her as her name. " On a family farm, something special happens. You inherit a body of knowledge from the generations of people that came before you, people who knew about the land. They were intimate with the land," she says pensively. "It enables me to be intimate with the land. This is, I think, a great and powerful gift."

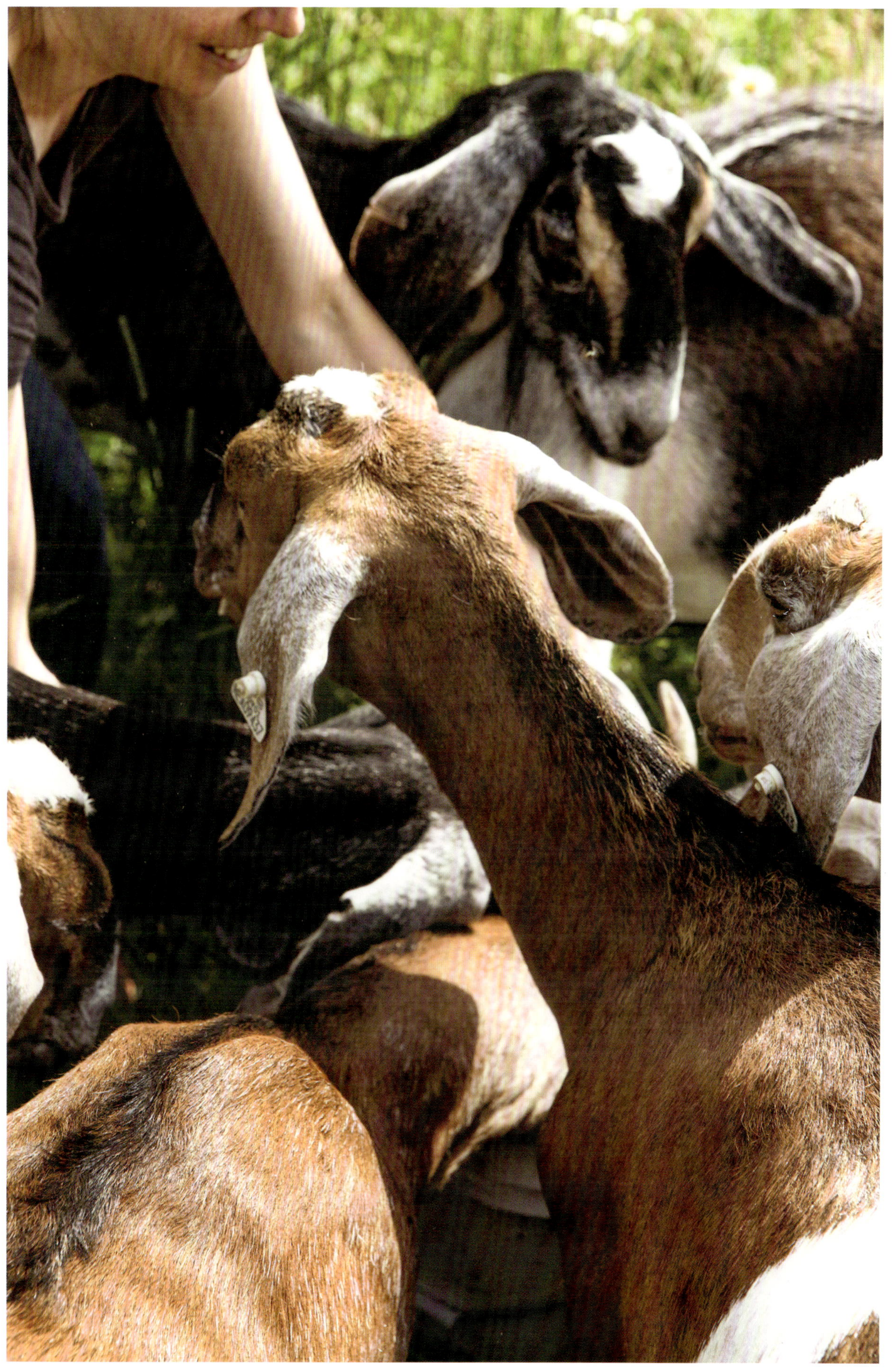

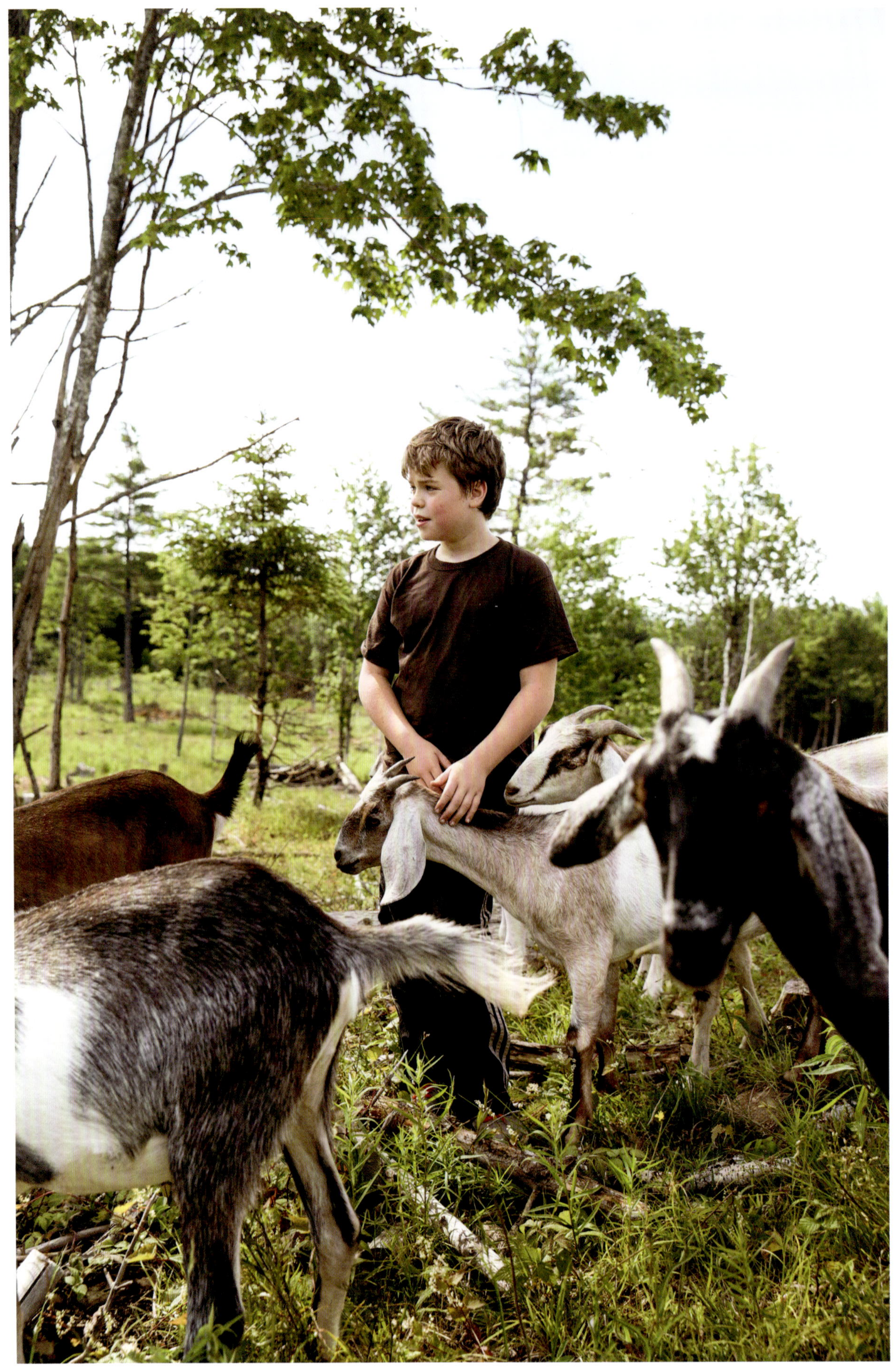

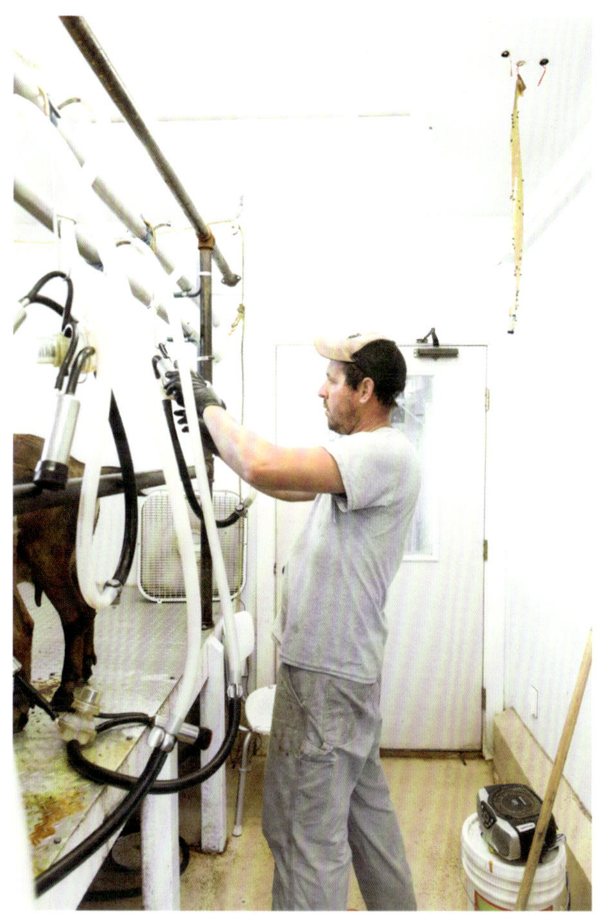

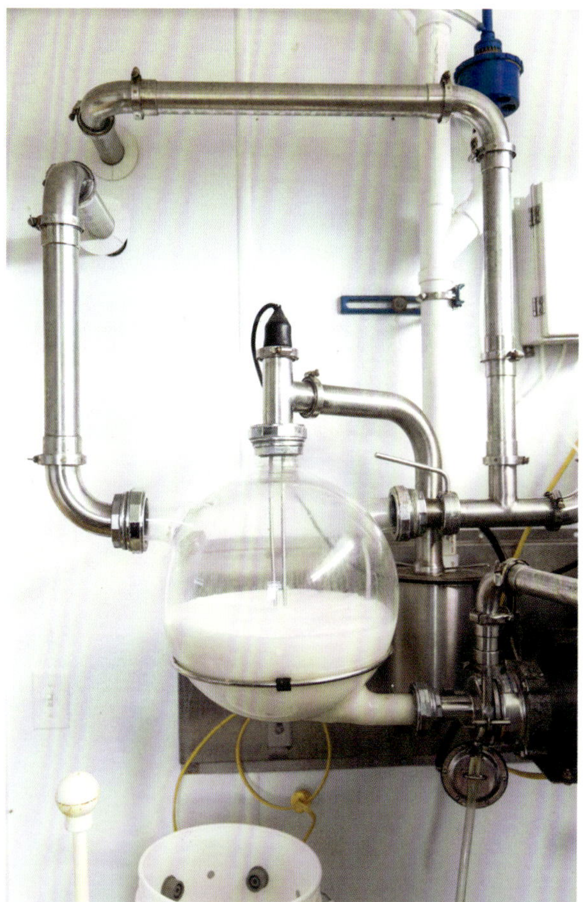

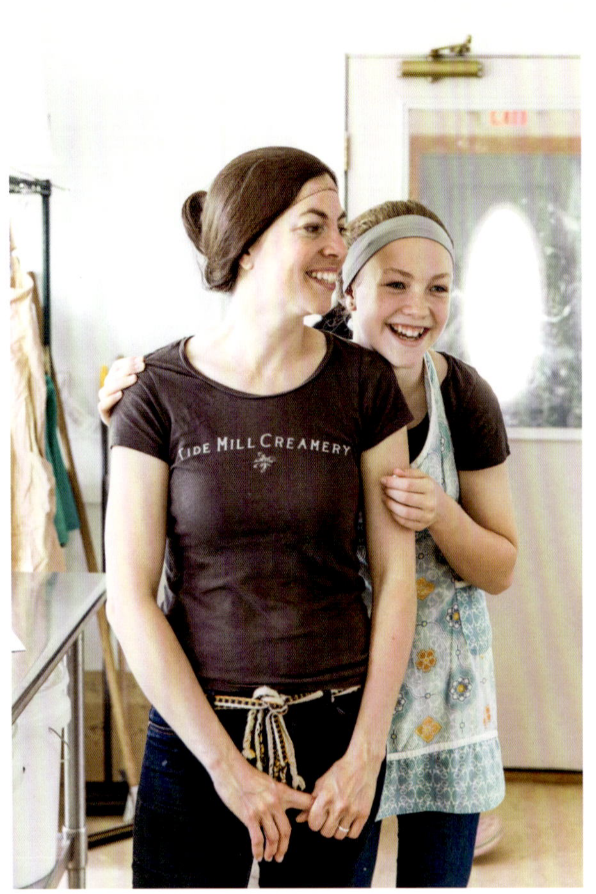
TIDE MILL CREAMERY

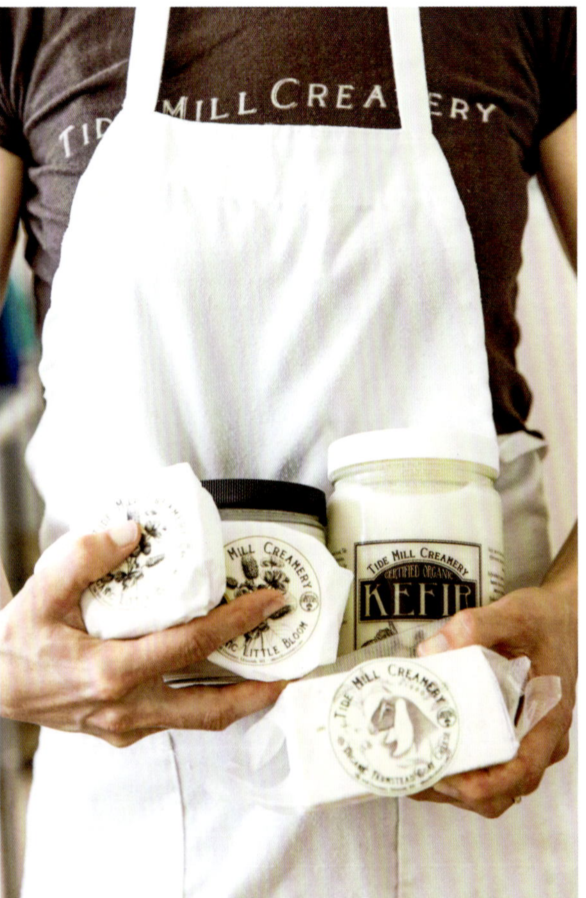
TIDE MILL CREAMERY
CERTIFIED ORGANIC
KEFIR
LITTLE BLOOM

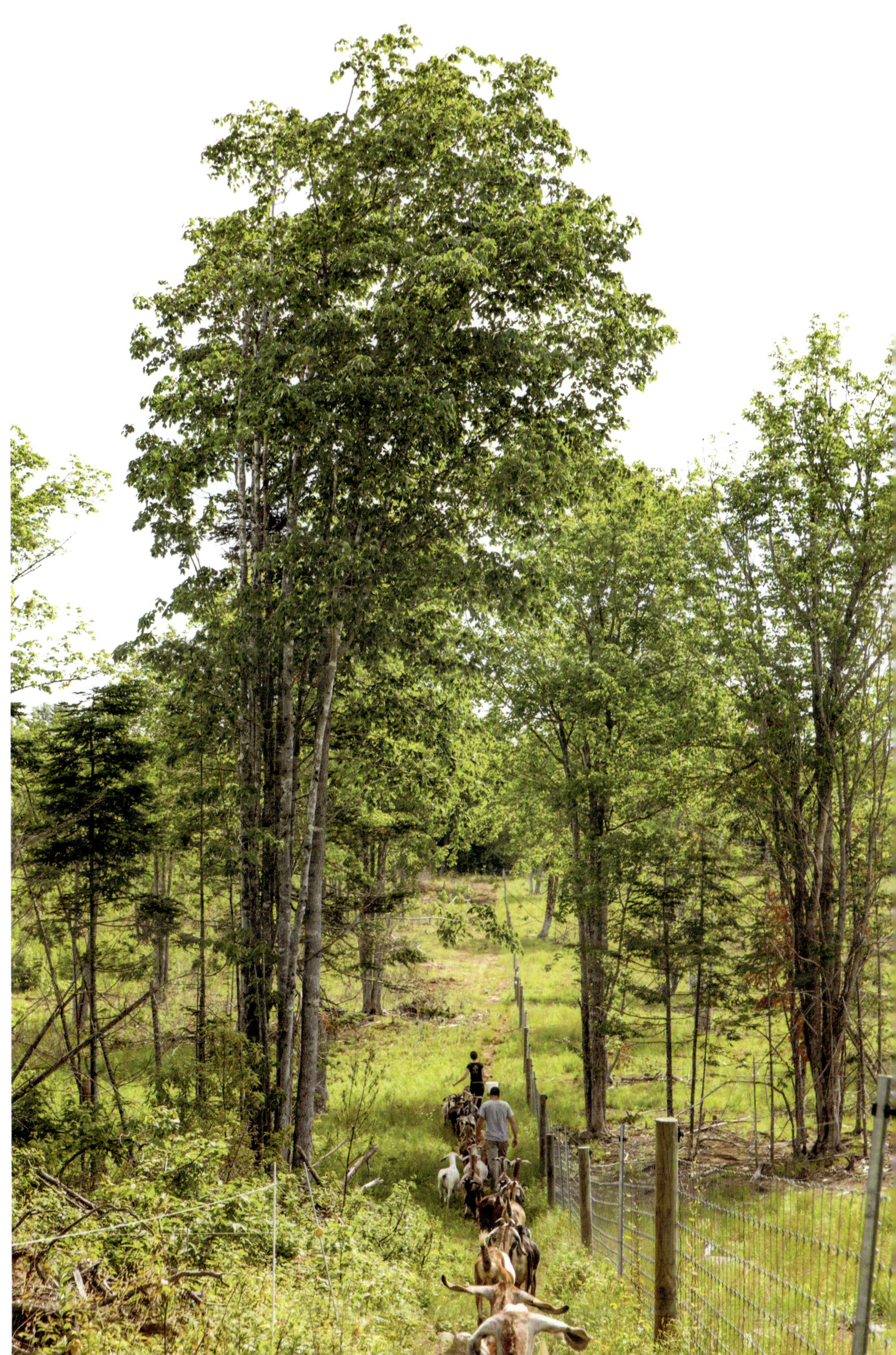

Tinder Hearth

Brooksville

Bread, says Tinder Hearth co-owner Tim Semler, is as subject to consumer biases as any other product: "If you make it tall and blonde, it will sell instantly, but if you bake it flat and dark, people don't want to look at it. It's a weird cultural thing." Fortunately for residents and summer visitors to the Blue Hill Peninsula, Tim has never been one to succumb to peer pressure. The loaves that he sells out of the Tinder Hearth farmhouse bakery are flatter, darker, and coarser than their sugary and pale grocery store brethren. Made with locally grown organic grains and spontaneously fermented sourdough starter, they are also far more flavorful and nutritious.

Over the past ten years, Tinder Hearth has garnered a following for its bold approach to baking. Tim and Lydia Moffett, business partners, life partners, and parents, have strived to make old-fashioned bread for years. "I get excited by pictures of bread in Europe in the 1960s and earlier because it looks a lot like ours," says Tim, who has been researching and baking bread since his early twenties. "I sometimes say that Tim taught me to bake, but really we learned together," Lydia says. "We learned to bake the type of bread we wanted to eat." Now they bake toothsome, hearty breads and sophisticated pastries like almond croissants and blackberry danishes. They also host weekly pizza nights—Tuesday during off-season, and Tuesday and Friday during high season—where customers can either order a pie for pick-up or be served outdoors on picnic tables amid Tinder Hearth's wild, lush garden in family-style seating. With the restored farmhouse in the background and children running to and fro, Tinder Hearth pizza nights are an idyllic slice of Maine summer. But Tim and Lydia's journey to this point wasn't always so picturesque.

The couple met during a cold Maine winter. Lydia was home from college for a few weeks and Tim was living in Brooksville in his parents' drafty old farmhouse baking bread. "Tim had these romantic ideas of what this house could be—and what this area could be like," Lydia remembers. At the time, there were few young people living in the Blue Hill area. Like many small-town natives, Lydia had spent her high school years dreaming of escape. But when she met Tim, everything changed. His optimism about the future of Maine and his passion for hard, honest work convinced her to return after graduation

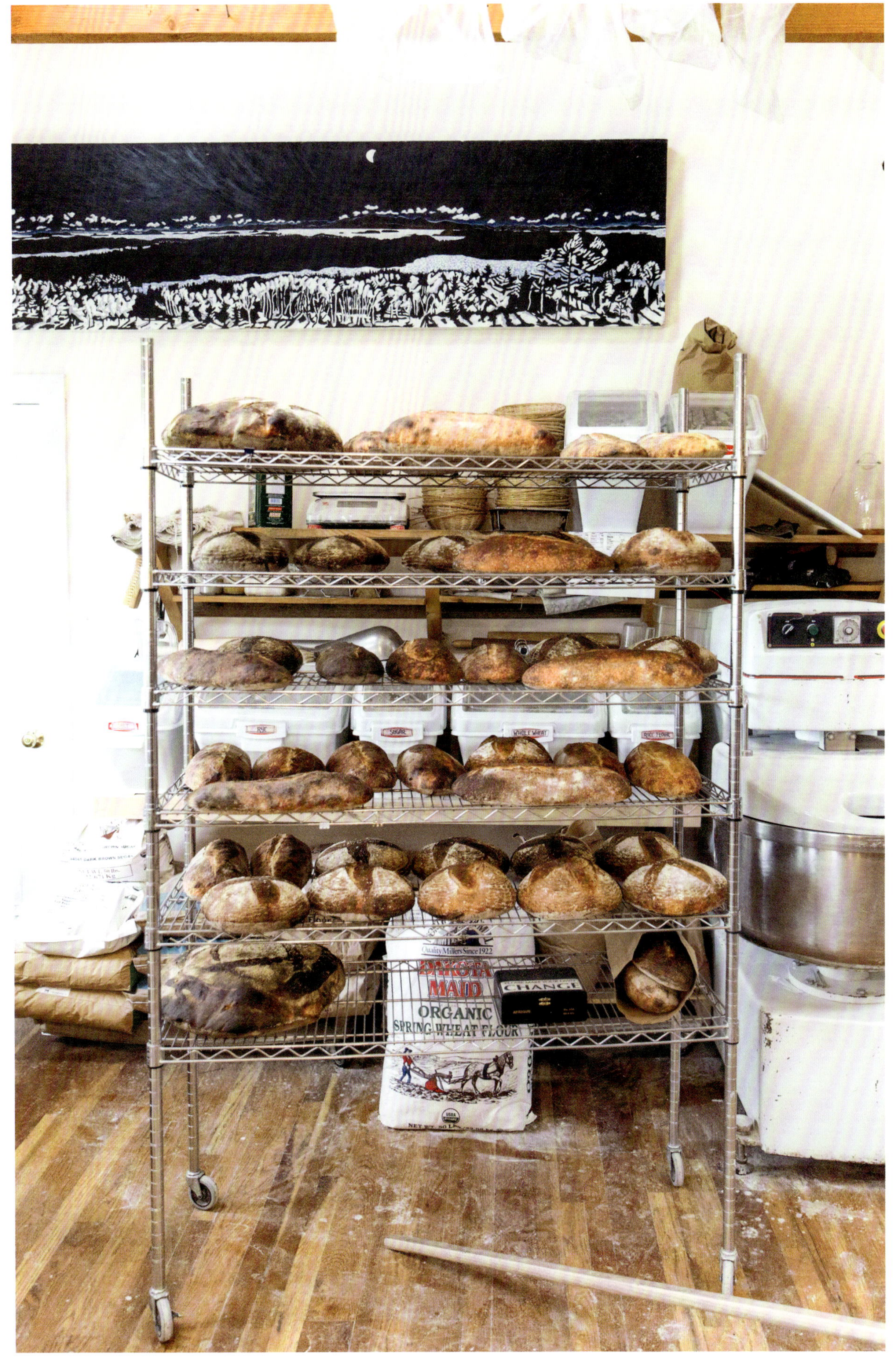
RYE
SUGAR
WHOLE WHEAT
Quality Millers Since 1922
DAKOTA MAID
ORGANIC
SPRING WHEAT FLOUR
CHANGE

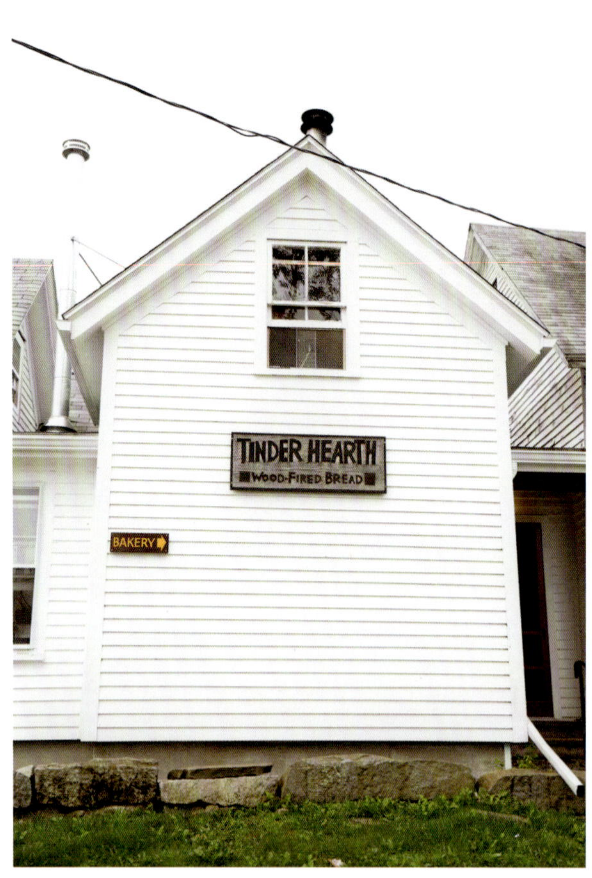
TINDER HEARTH
WOOD-FIRED BREAD
BAKERY

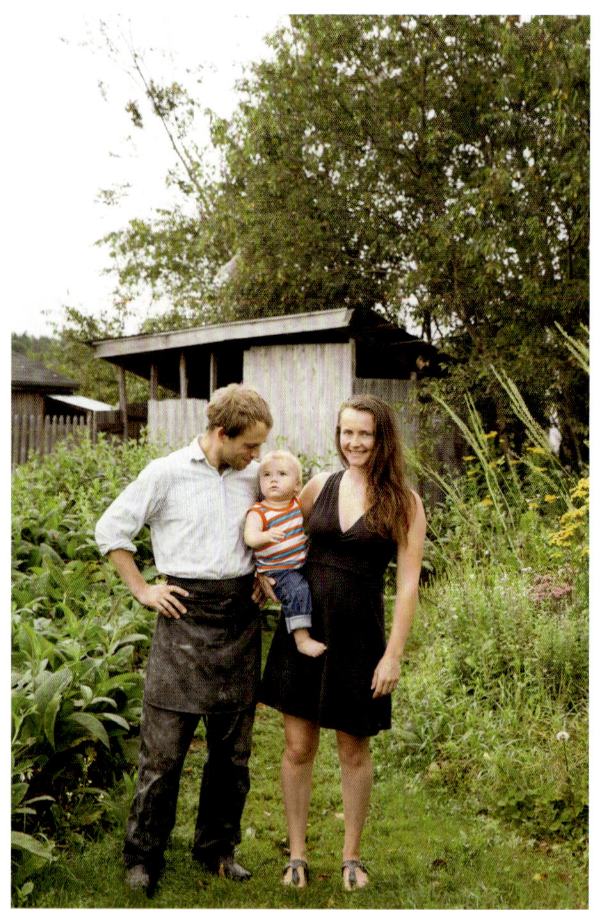

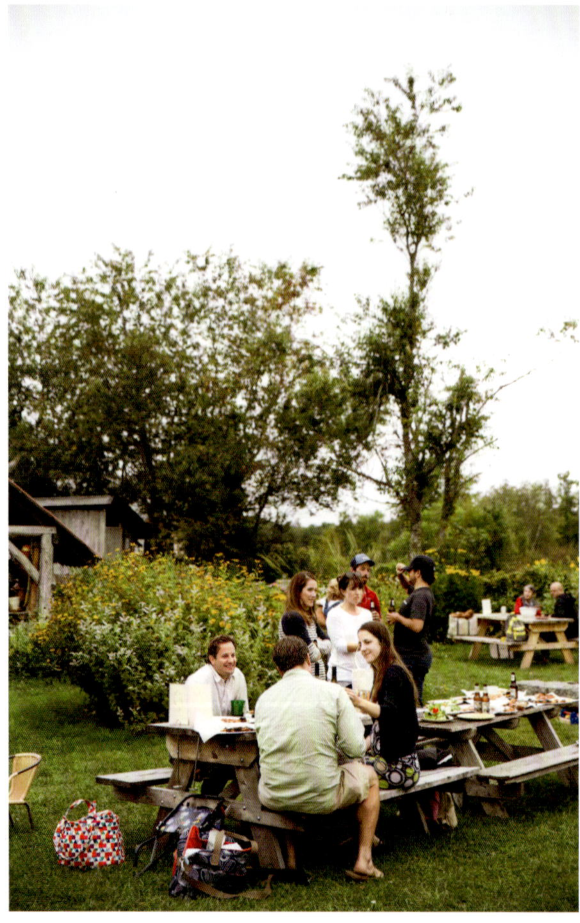

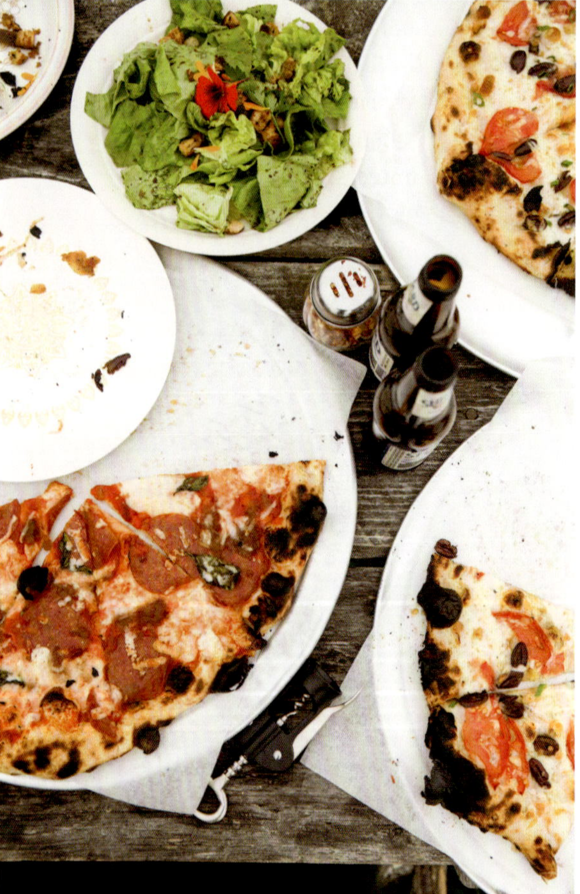

to the coastal community—and to Tim—to start a life and a business. "Tim had such conviction that I fell in love with his ideas," she says. "I realized I didn't have to go elsewhere to seek my fortune. I could find the right place for me right here." Central to Tim and Lydia's dream was to create a local hub, a place where people could come together and share common ground.

During the early years of Tinder Hearth, they worked seven days a week to make ends meet. "We started the business with the idea that we probably wouldn't make any money," Lydia recalls. "For years, Tim and I basically took turns working with my dad on the lobster boat fishing, and working in the bakery." Tim also found odd jobs as a carpenter or handyman. "We were always a little in denial about baking bread being a business," Tim says. "We thought of it this way: We bake bread. We like doing it. We just want to keep baking bread." Pizza and pastries were added, in part, to offset the cost, labor, and time involved in baking four or five types of organic loaves—whole grain boule, sourdough bâtard, rye, and focaccia—as well as weekly and seasonal specials like pumpkin bread or walnut loaves. "We just can't bring ourselves to charge for the true cost of making the bread—ten dollars or more per loaf just feels wrong to me," Tim explains, "and we can charge more for the pizza and pastries." To help run the business, they also brought in friends and volunteers, packing people into the big old house in a communal-style living arrangement in which everyone worked a shift and everyone shared the fruits of their labor. It was Tim's dream realized, with all the romanticism and idealism that had so swayed Lydia.

In time, life and the business shifted. They married, and as the couple approached their thirties they began to think differently about Tinder Hearth. Lydia remembers a distinct moment when everything changed for her. It was early spring on the Barrow Peninsula in Ireland. They were on vacation—"The first time we'd traveled together as real adults, with rental houses and a car and everything," she says—when she looked at her husband and realized that she no longer wanted to live with so many other people. As Lydia and Tim sat in the tiny Irish cottage, surrounded by rain and green fields, they began to create a roadmap for a slightly more traditional future for themselves—and for Tinder Hearth.

Soon after, Lydia became pregnant and the couple put their plans into action. Phasing out communal living, they hired employees and remodeled the house for a more private living arrangement. They welcomed their son, Kieran, into the family, a happy and inquisitive little boy who is growing up amidst people, pizza, and flour. And while they occasionally worry about losing the community feeling that defined Tinder Hearth in its early years, they have found other ways to stay connected with family, friends, and customers. "Our house is one of the least private houses you can have," says Tim with a laugh. "It still feels like a bus station on some days. People are in and out, and at this point, we've become close friends with many of the people who come here for pizza and bread. We still have a feeling of being in constant contact and having wonderful connections."

Tim and Lydia's natural warmth and enthusiasm have forged these community ties, as has the Tinder Hearth product. Breaking bread has crafted social bonds since time immemorial, a symbol and ritual retained to this day. "Bread speaks to people in many ways—particularly this old-school, traditional way of making it." Lydia explains as Kieran chatters behind her. After a moment she adds, "Really, I believe bread is just a magic food. It's a staple." For the table, the hearth, and the community.

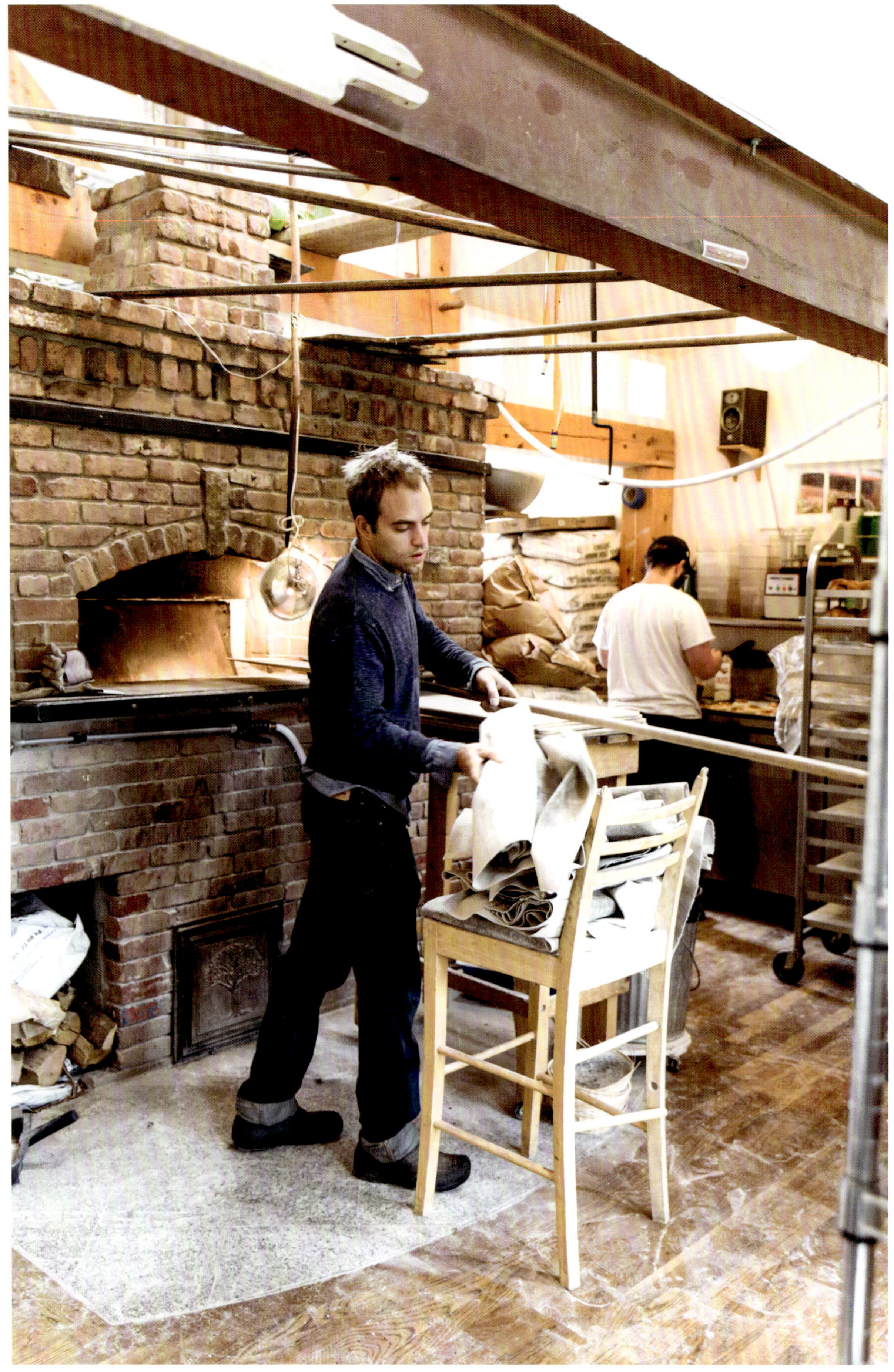

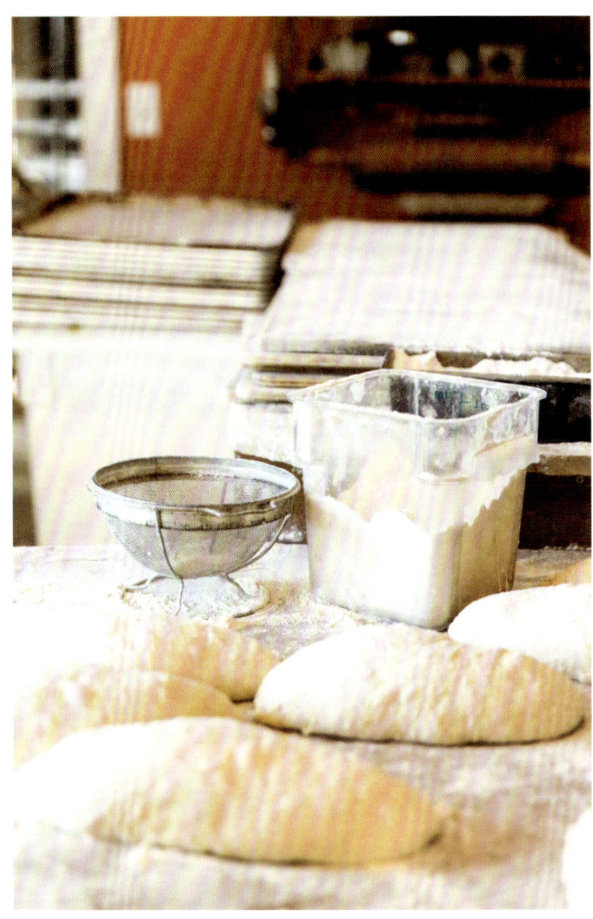

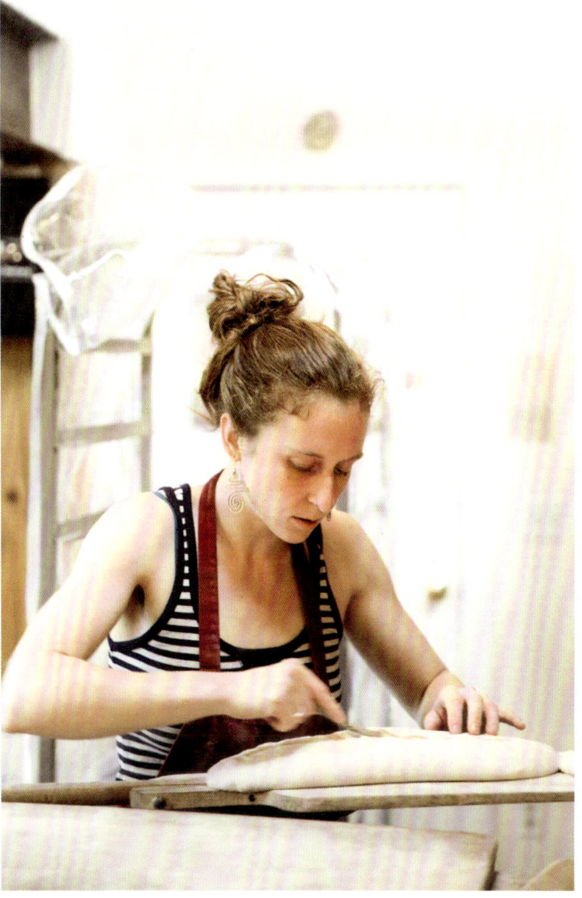

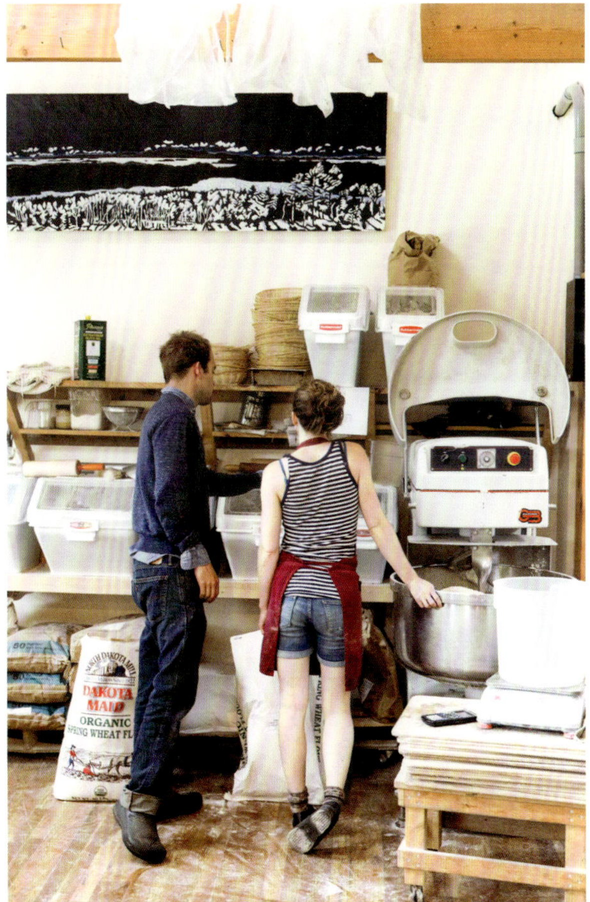
DAKOTA
MAID
ORGANIC

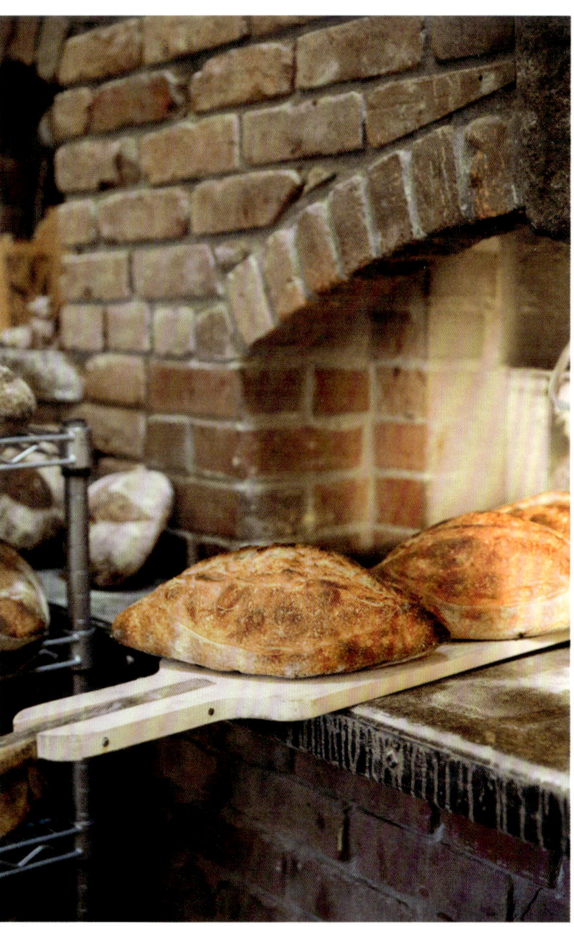

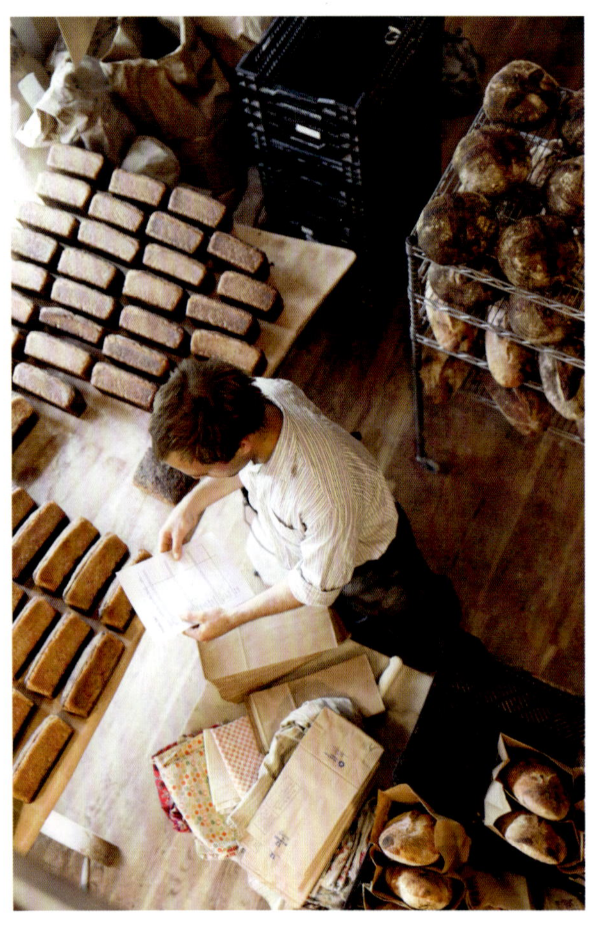

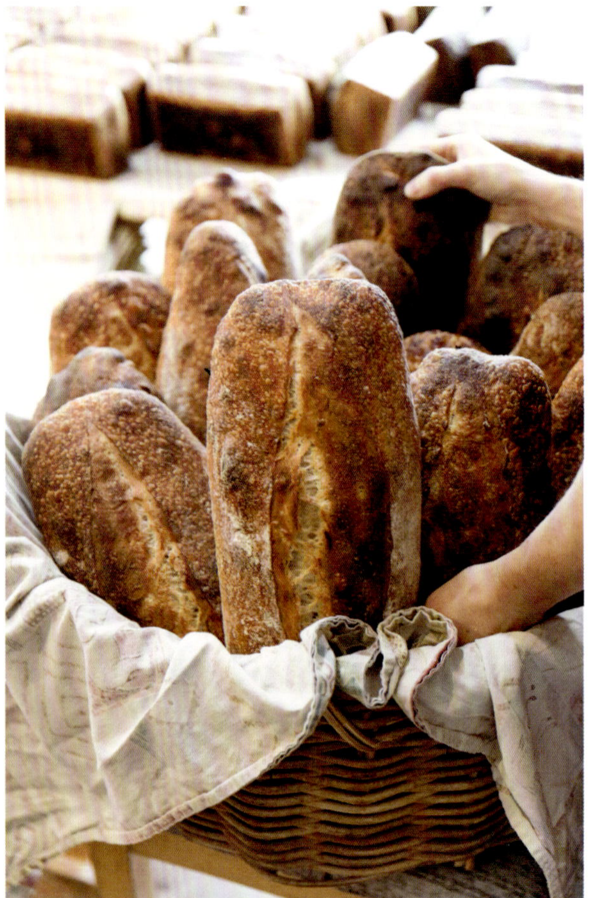

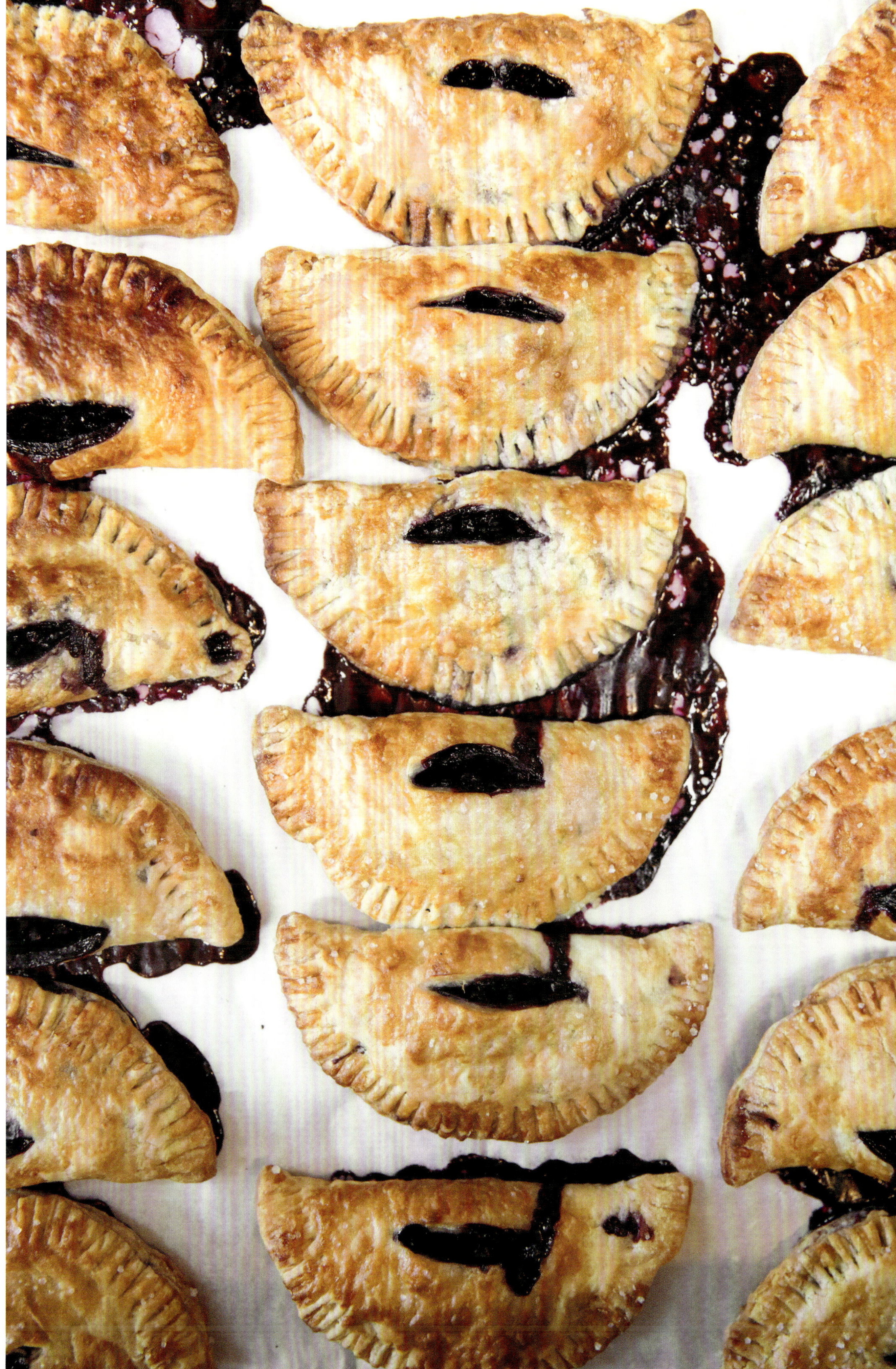

Masa Miyake

Portland

Masa Miyake has had a long day. "This morning, I woke up to a pig that had jumped the fence," he explains as he walks through the tall weeds on his Freeport farm. "He wanted to mate, which is natural, but he wanted to mate with his sister," Masa told us with regret. "I do not want that. I had to chase him around the farm for thirty minutes before I could catch him." Masa's teenage son helped him corner the rogue pig in a wire pen and herd it across the yard into a section of the farm with higher walls.

Gesturing toward an area where a group of brown-and-black pigs are gathered he says, "This is where I keep all the males." He hops the fence and begins petting a large, curly-haired Mangalitsa. "These pigs make the Kobe beef of pork," he says as he crouches down in the muck. As his livestock snuffles and snorts, he plays with them like dogs, rubbing their fat bellies. He smiles and his serious face creases, becoming warm and welcoming. Nearby hang several pork haunches, their cloven feet swinging in the early summer sun. Although he loves his pigs and calls them "very kind, very well-tempered," this is not an incongruous scene. Masa recognizes the reality of owning a working meat farm.

"For years, it was my dream to open a restaurant," Masa says as he surveys his busy backyard. "Then it was my dream to have a farm. First it was for the pigs and chickens. Now, my dream is to have produce. People sometimes say the words 'hobby farm,' but to me, this is very, very important. I want my kids to grow up in the countryside." For Masa, farming is a source of inspiration and information. In his never-ending quest to educate himself about food—from its subtle flavors to its rich history and practical applications—farming is just another lens through which he can examine his lifelong passion.

Since opening in 2007, Masa's eponymous flagship restaurant in Portland has become a consistent presence on every "best of" list in Maine and many beyond. His cuisine, inspired by his home in northern Japan, combines Maine ingredients and flavors with cooking techniques he learned growing up in Japan's rural Aomori region, a beautiful and remote area with a harsh climate similar to Maine's. As a young man, Masa was drawn to New York City to study macrobiotic food before returning to Japan to train in French and Italian cuisine. Over the decades, he has perfected a subtle, precise, and complex style.

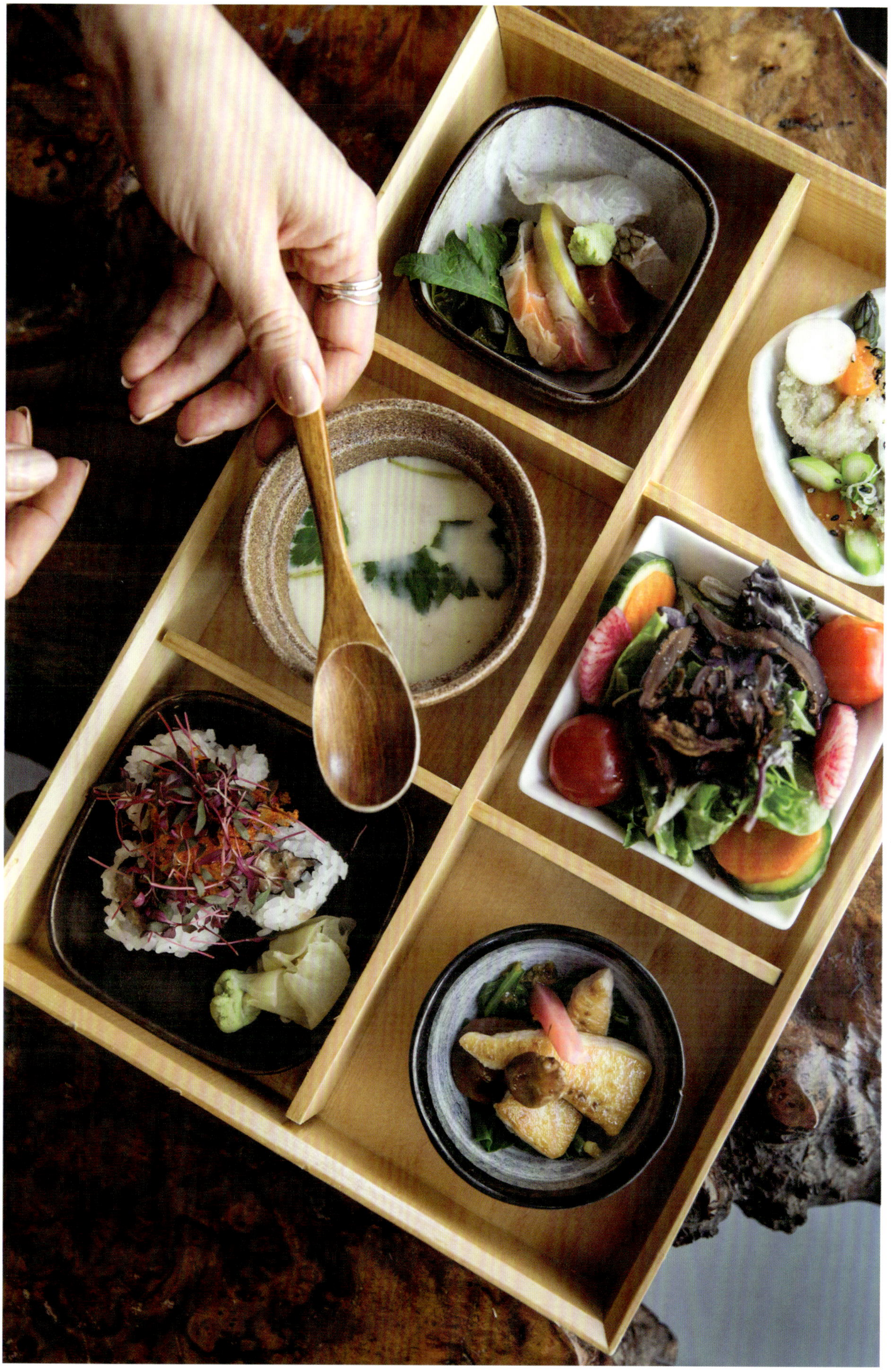

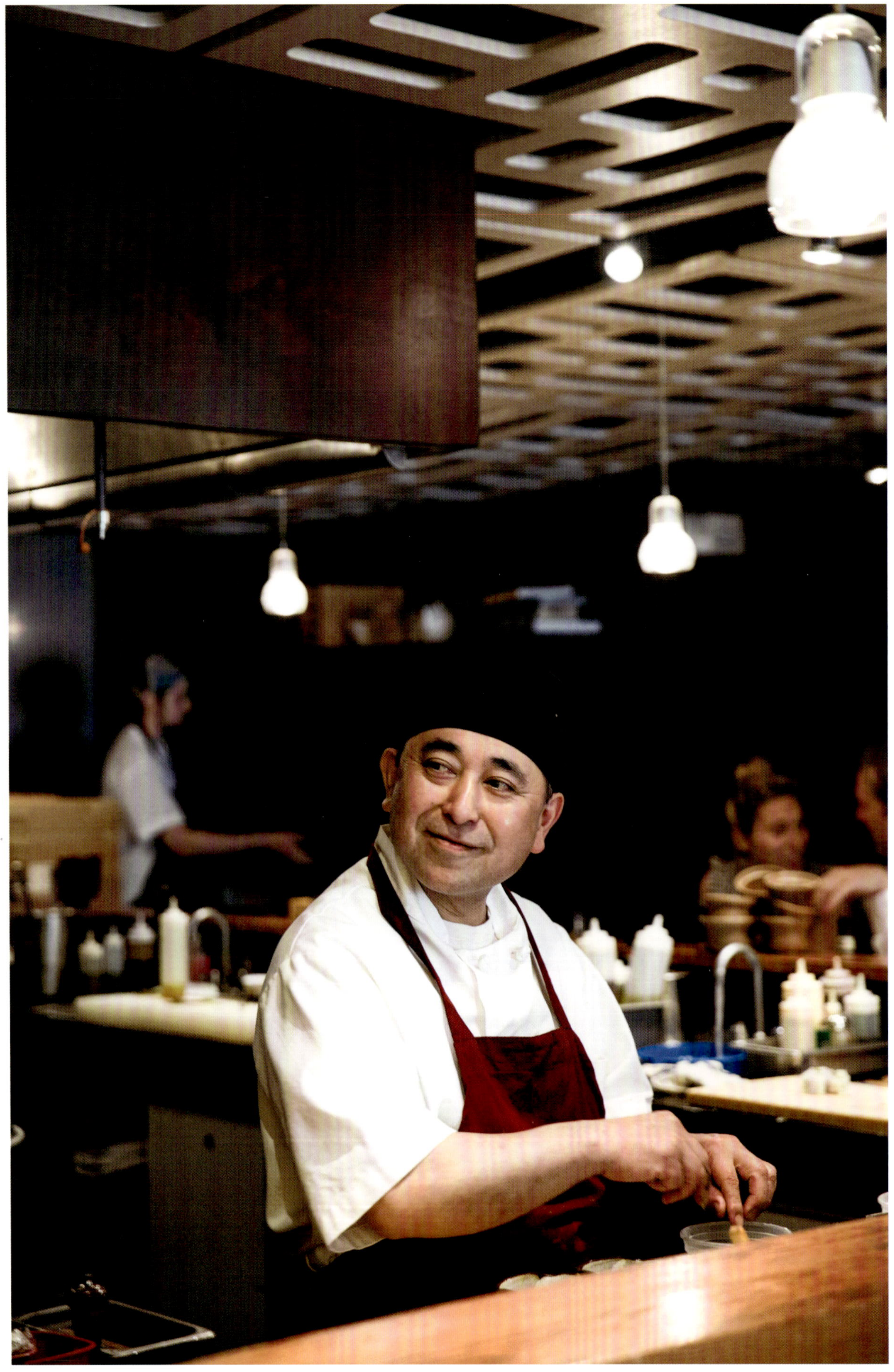

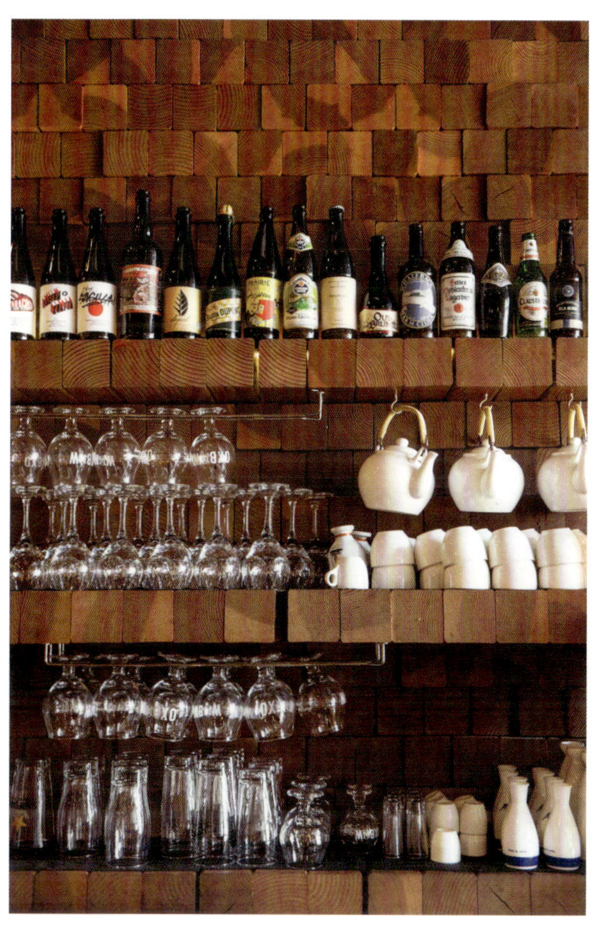

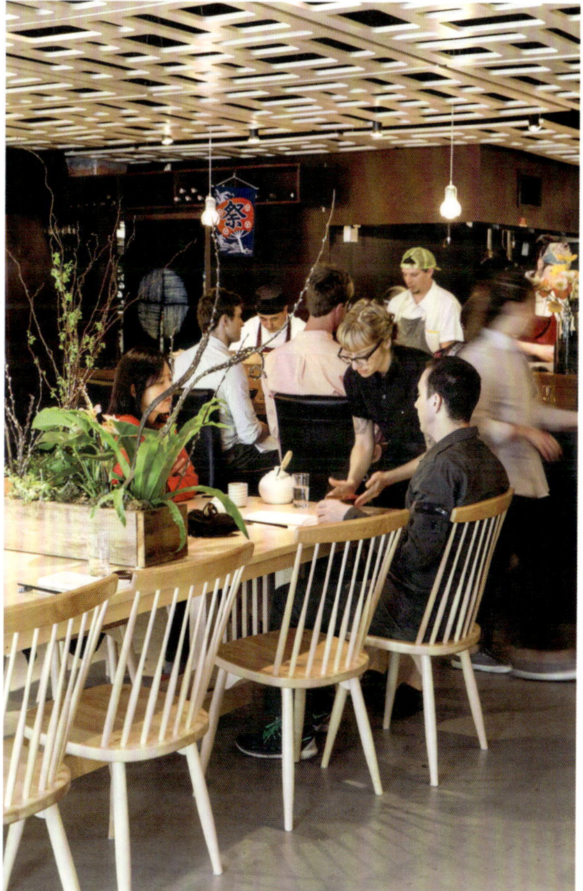

In 2006, Masa made Maine his permanent home. "Masa always said that when he was living in New York he would come to Maine as often as he could on vacation," says Stephanie Goodrich, sake sommelier and assistant manager at Miyake. "On the most recent trip to Japan, I traveled with Masa and two other employees to Hokkaido, which has a strikingly similar landscape to Maine. It was the rough coastline, the rocky cliffs, and vast beaches, but it was also the food—a lot of the seafood they eat there is similar to what we serve at Miyake, to what you can find in Maine waters." Masa returns to Japan on working vacations several times a year, often accompanied by members of his staff to educate them about Japanese food, hospitality, and culture. "It provides an understanding that you can't necessarily gain from being told about Japanese traditions," says Stephanie. "It helped me understand what Masa means when he talks about hospitality. Japanese hospitality is being grateful for every single customer that walks through the door, even if it is five minutes before closing time."

Masa also credits Japanese culture for his whole-hog approach to cooking. The chef-cum-farmer has been serving pork belly (and other lesser-known cuts) for over ten years—long before nose-to-tail eating was popular in Portland. "It was just bacon, all the time," Masa recalls of his arrival in America, "never pork belly." Another cultural difference between the two countries was the American taste for poultry. "Americans wanted to eat only chicken breasts. But in postwar Japan," Masa tells us, "we didn't have any food. We got used to eating intestines. We ate the guts." Blowfish, served three ways, Goodrich remarks, was one particularly memorable meal during their most recent trip to Japan. Everything from the scraps to the fins made it onto the plate. While blowfish remains a delicacy prepared solely in Japan, Masa takes a similar approach to cooking fish, pork, and chicken. The restaurant's *omakase*—the chef's tasting menu—has featured items including pig feet and pork headcheese gyoza. Snapper head, braised in sake, soy, and mirin (a sweet rice wine) and served whole, is a favorite menu item for Goodrich. "A lot of customers are still hesitant to try it," she says. "But it's fantastic. I always advise them to get in there with their hands—eat it like a chicken wing." And at Pai Men Miyake, Masa's hip urban noodle joint in Portland's revitalized West End, he serves pork belly fried and sandwiched inside a fluffy steamed bun or dropped into a rich, savory bowl of ramen.

Portland is a city known for its eateries. It can be hard for even well-established restaurants to stand out. But Masa isn't worried about competition. He relishes each new restaurant that opens in Portland. "Competition is always good. It makes you try new things. When there is no competition, there is no growth," he says, leaning across the table for emphasis. "If you have just one classmate, who cares what you get for a grade? B or C, it doesn't matter." Whether it is through raising his own succulent pork or introducing Mainers to new flavors and preparations, Masa, a lifelong student of food, will always seek perfection.

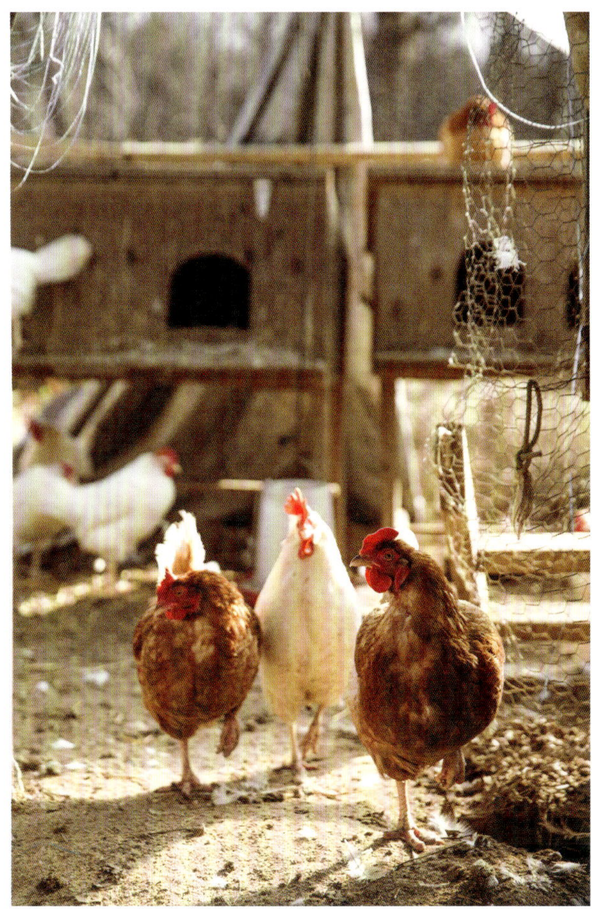

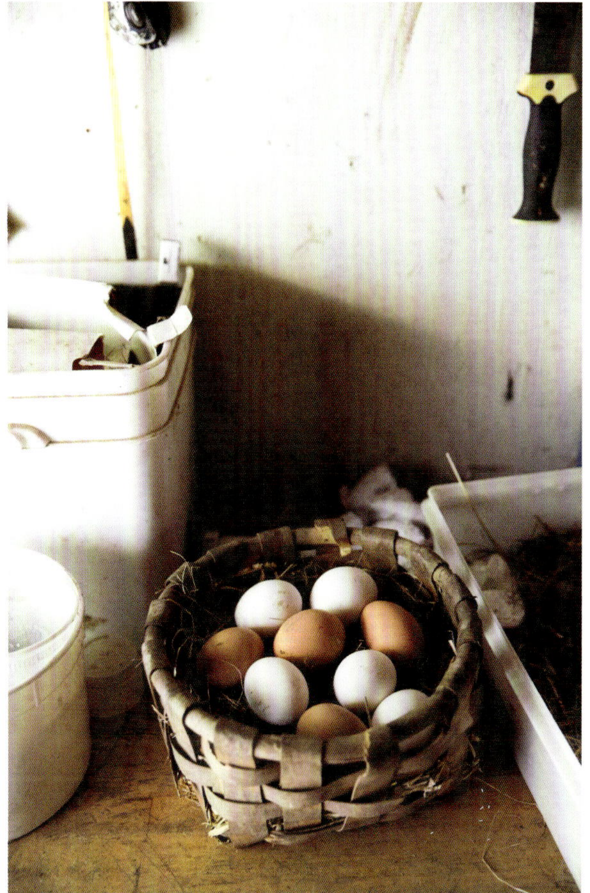

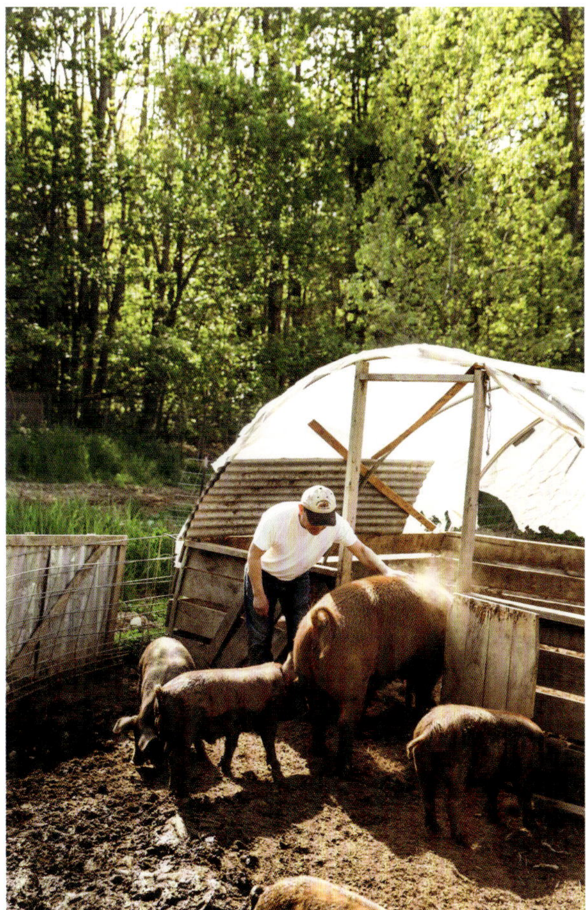

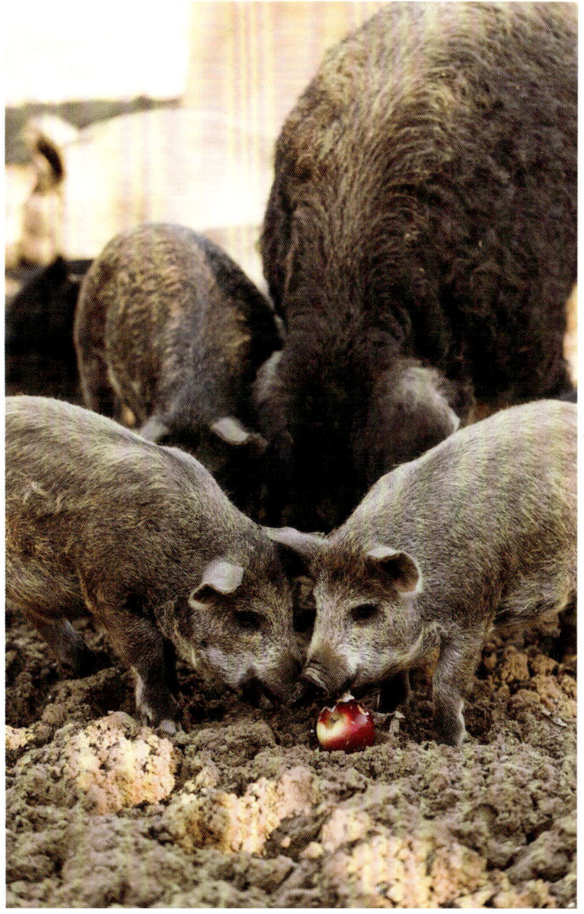

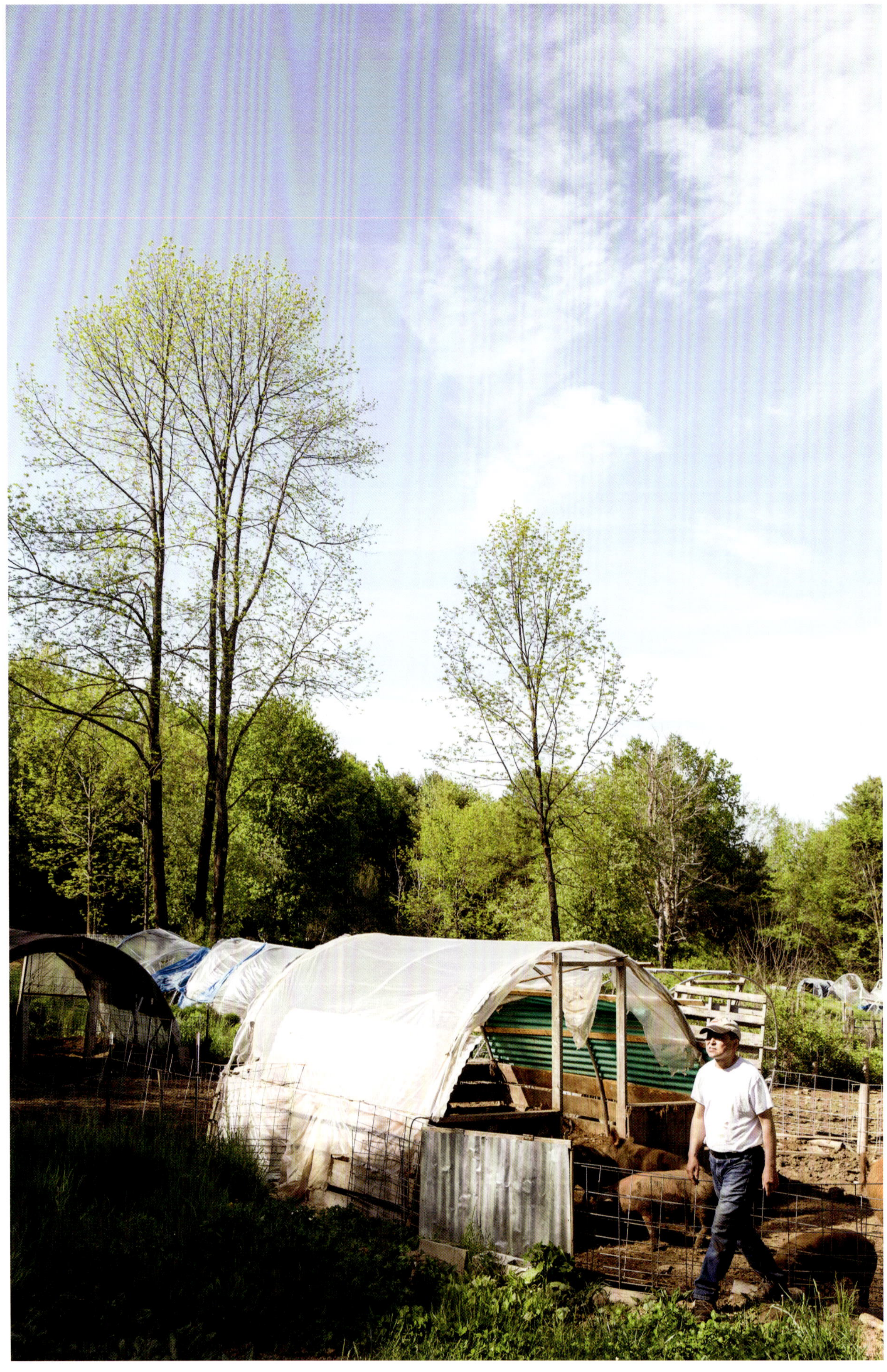

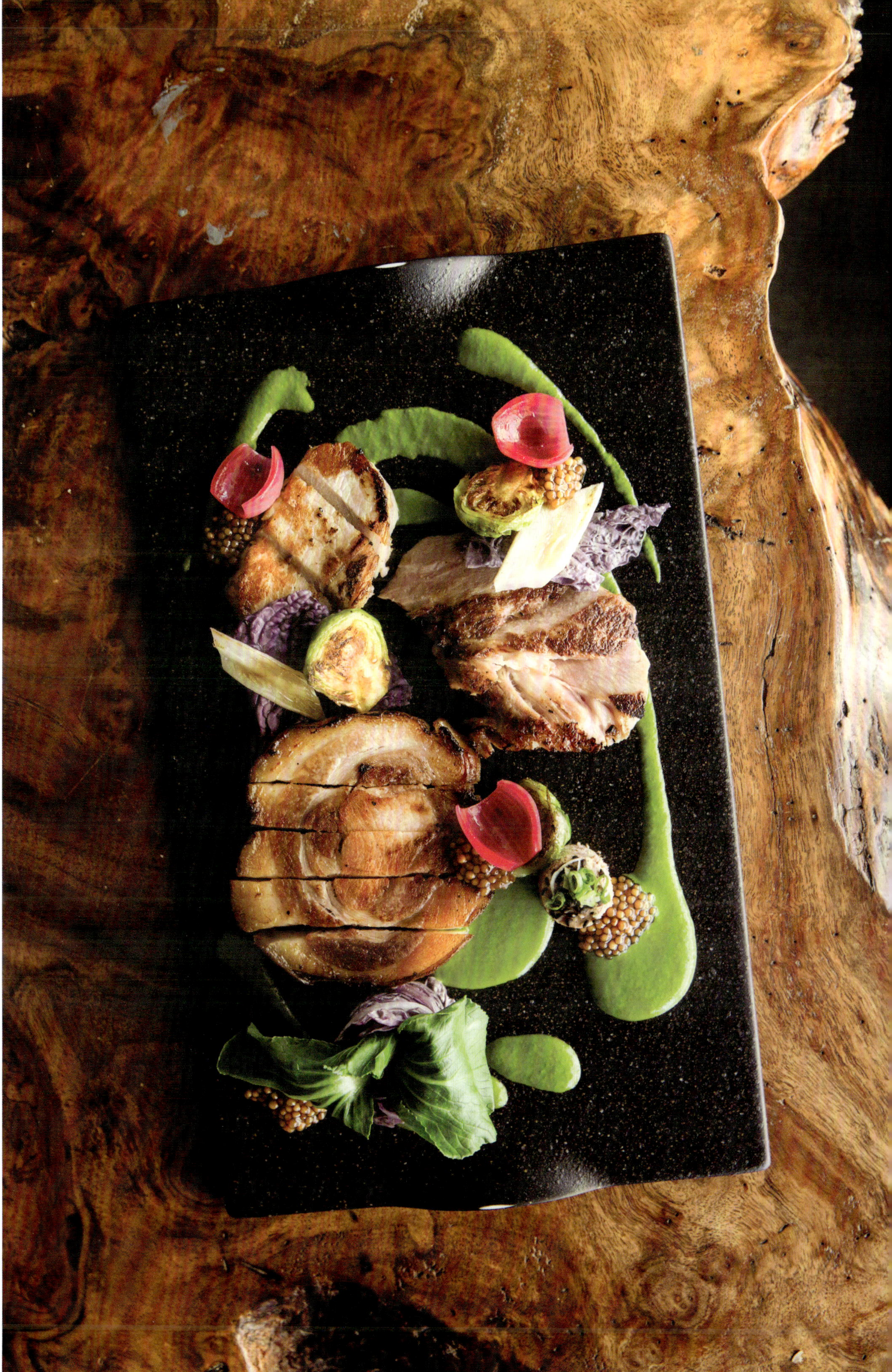

Beech Hill Farm

Mount Desert Island

The air on Mount Desert Island seems to shimmer blue in the sunlight as workers at Beech Hill Farm stoop between rows of cherry tomatoes, gathering crates of sweet red and yellow orbs. A young man with a blonde ponytail and dirt on his face swats at mosquitoes as he fills his basket. He's been working since the early morning. Summer in Maine is short and aggressive, and farmers make the most of their eighteen hours of daylight and the humid starlit nights.

Anna Davis and Tess Faller have been working all day, too. The two young women run the farm, sharing the duties as casually as they share their mucking boots. "When I first moved out here," Anna recalls, "it felt like I was going to the very end of the world. It was a ghost town in the spring, and I had never been to Maine before—I had never even heard of Mount Desert Island." She didn't know the island's history as a playground for the rich and famous. She didn't know about the Rockefellers' summer homes or the cruise ships that pass through Bar Harbor each year. She knew only that she wanted to farm, and she knew Tess was hiring.

A graduate of Hampshire College, Anna had spent several years working on large-scale farms in Western Massachusetts. "I knew I wanted to work with my hands, and farming was the only thing I could imagine waking up to do every day," she says. For Anna, manual labor was something she had long been drawn to, but also something she felt was vastly undervalued in contemporary American society. "I wanted my day-to-day work to make a difference. Farming was something I could do without compromising my core values." By working with her hands, Anna could infuse each piece of fruit, each harvested tomato, with its proper value. Tess was attracted to farming for similar reasons. Growing up in rural New Hampshire, she began working on a local farm as a teenager. As a student at College of the Atlantic she volunteered at Beech Hill Farm before being hired as a summer hand. Several years later she returned to Beech Hill to serve as manager, a position she's held since 2013.

Unlike most small-scale farms, Beech Hill doesn't belong to Tess or Anna or the ponytailed young man or any of the workers in the field. Beech Hill, a Maine Organic Farmers and Gardeners Association–certified, seventy-three-acre farm situated between Long Pond and Somes Sound, makes up part of the campus

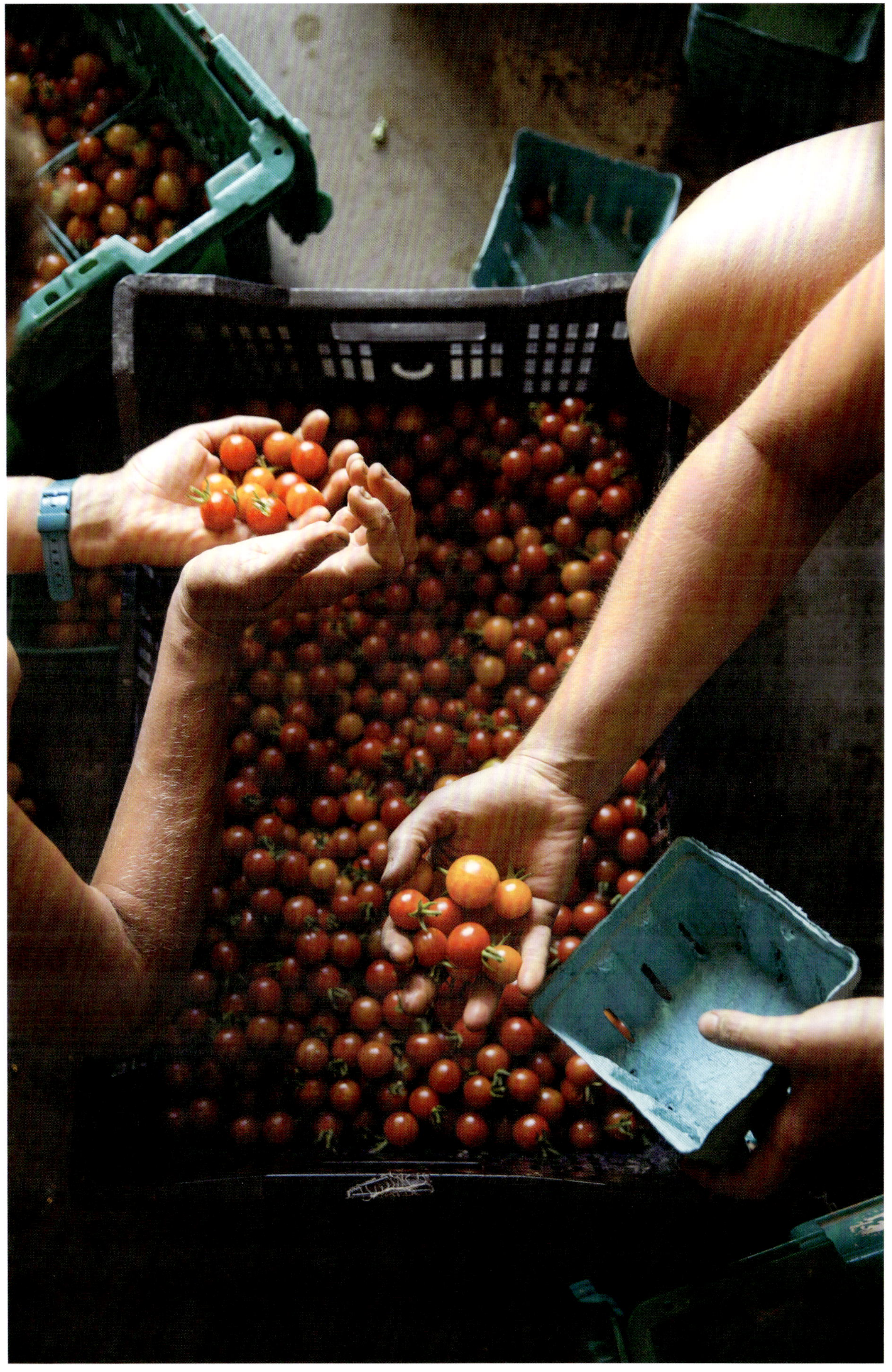

of College of the Atlantic, a liberal arts school with a long history of innovative, outside-the-box education. Founded by COA alumni Barbarina Heyerdahl and her husband, Aaron Heyerdahl, in 1989, the plot of land was gifted to the college in 1999. It now functions as a working farm, as well as a hands-on educational facility for students, farmers, and community members. Unlike other area farmers, Anna and Tess's salaries are paid by COA and the farm receives supplemental grants. This luxury enables the women to focus exclusively on growing good, simple food without having to worry about paying a mortgage or justifying the cost of the land. "It takes a certain level of stress off us, which gives us an advantage that other farmers in Maine don't have," Tess explains. Both women are particularly attuned to the politics of food production and how they intersect with issues of class. In a world where many organic farmers couldn't afford to buy their own produce at Whole Foods, it can feel hard to justify Beech Hill Farm's advantages. "A big concern of ours is whether we're unfair competition to other farmers," Anna admits. "We want to be advocates of local food without putting anyone out of business." "The cost of food is such a weird, tricky thing," Tess adds. "Sometimes it can feel abstract, when it's not based on what people need to pay but on what they will pay. We're not producing anything really special or exotic. There's no reason this food should be more expensive than the food that's at the local grocery store that has been shipped in from South America. I think if people aren't able to afford the food that's right here, it means we're doing something wrong."

Beech Hill Farm addresses issues of food accessibility in a number of ways. The farm works with local pantries through a program called Share the Harvest to provide annual gift certificates for the Beech Hill farm stand, which accepts SNAP, WIC, and EBT cards—government assistance to make fresh produced more accessible. Beech Hill also offers a "double-your-dollars" program, which entitles anyone purchasing food with government assistance to fifty percent off the price of their produce. "Because we are part of the college, and we have access to fundraising and student hands, we are able to put a lot of effort toward offering discounted food to people who need it," says Anna. Both women are also working with local farms to expand the Share the Harvest program to other Maine food pantries, and to provide food-insecure individuals with even more fresh, locally grown food options. "We are trying a patchwork of ways to make healthy food more accessible to everyone and we're always exploring new channels," Tess adds.

Through their work at Beech Hill Farm and their community outreach efforts, Tess and Anna seek to bridge the sharp economic divide between the growers and the consumers, and between the residents and the summer visitors. But sometimes even these dedicated farmers feel like outsiders on the island. "Maine is such a tourist-driven community for part of the year," Anna says. She weighs each word carefully, for as much as she loves living in Maine, she admits that it can be terribly lonely and isolating. "There is community support, but it also sometimes feels like it will take me another ten years to be a true part of this place. Maine is extraordinary, but sometimes I feel like I'm on the periphery looking in." However, she recognizes that the toughness, the hard-to-crack nature of the local communities—all this comes hand-in-hand with the weather, the geography, and the raw beauty of the landscape.

While both Tess and Anna admit to occasionally feeling overwhelmed by the difficulties of Maine farm life, neither woman can imagine another way to spend their days. For Anna, farming is how she reconciles her politics and morals with her personal passions. It's a lifestyle that allows her to be creative, physical, and engaged. "I feel connected to the history of Maine farmers," Anna says. "I'm tied to the tradition of farming through the breadth of knowledge that's available. If I have a question about low soil pH or cover crops, I can call up a local farmer. I can ask questions and learn." Though it may not feel easy to crack into the year-round community, there is camaraderie among Maine farmers. They're bound by their hardships. But they're also bound by joy. "Farming gives us time for contemplation," Tess says. "In our crazy busy lives, farming—even gardening—gives you time and space to be alone. And I believe being in nature is crucial to living a good life." When Tess is in the field weeding or planting, she is continually thinking about the weather and the seasons. She is touching the soil, feeling the earth, considering each microorganism that contributes to the ecosystem. "Farming grounds me," she explains later, after a long day of mid-summer work. "It connects me to where I am, right here, right now. It makes me feel like I'm part of something bigger."

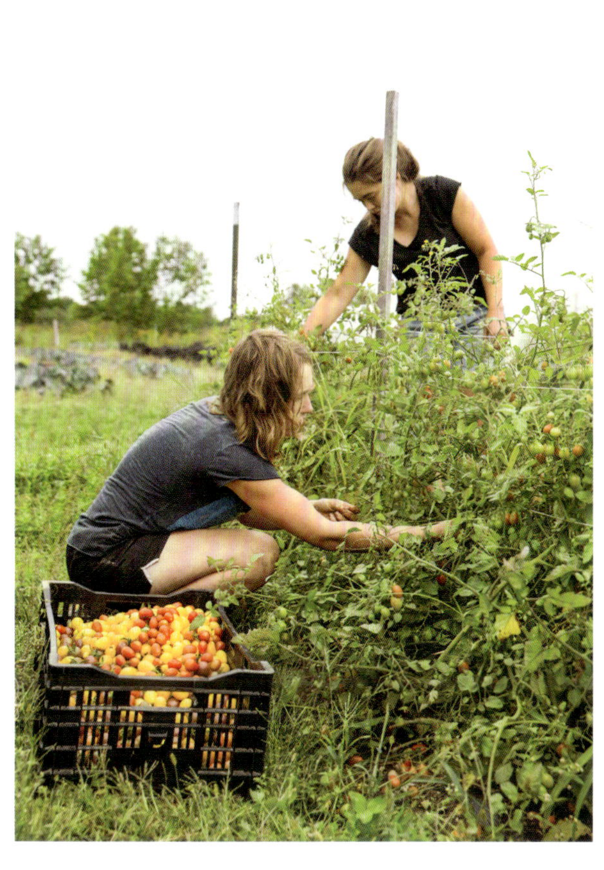

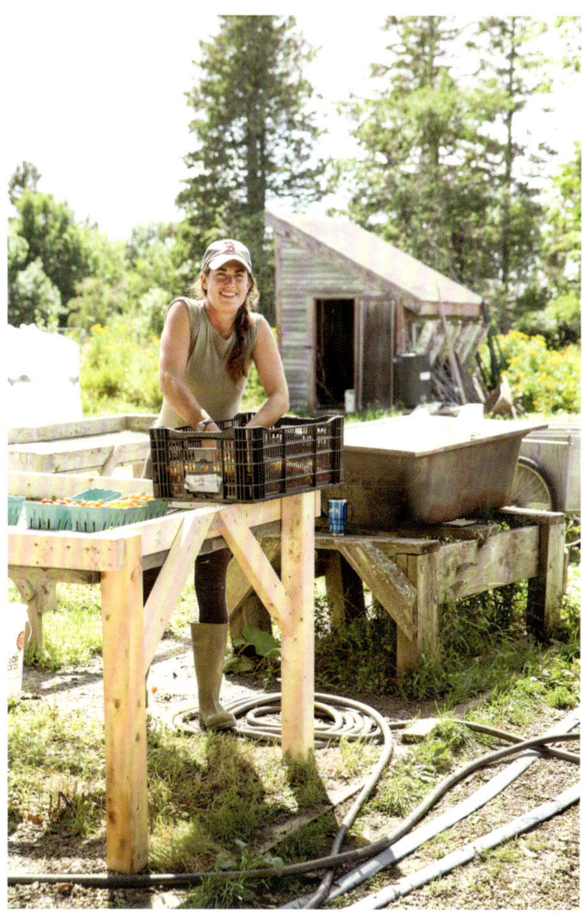

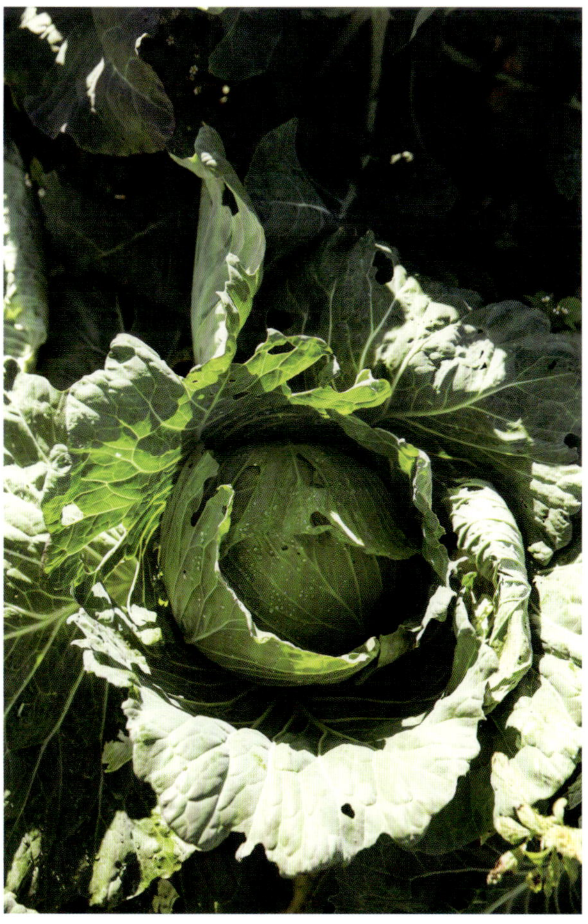

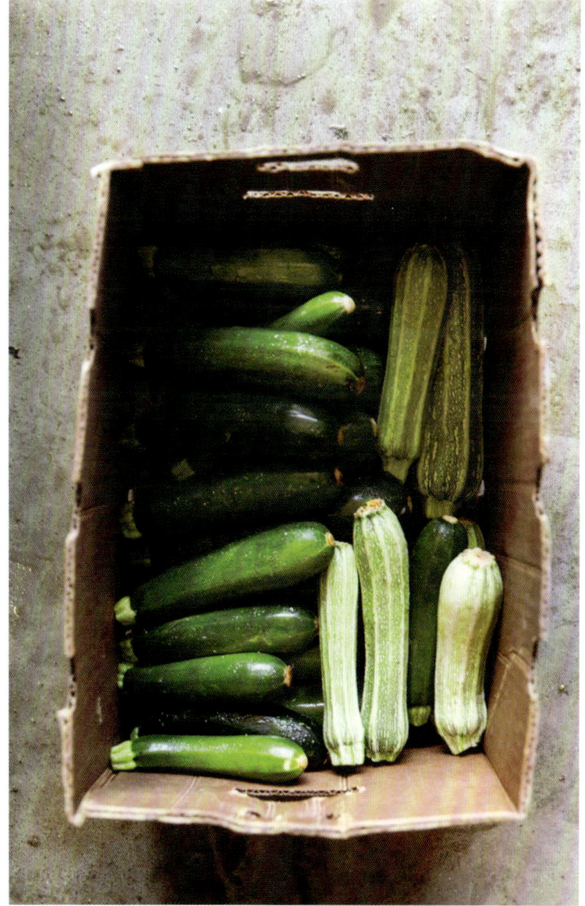

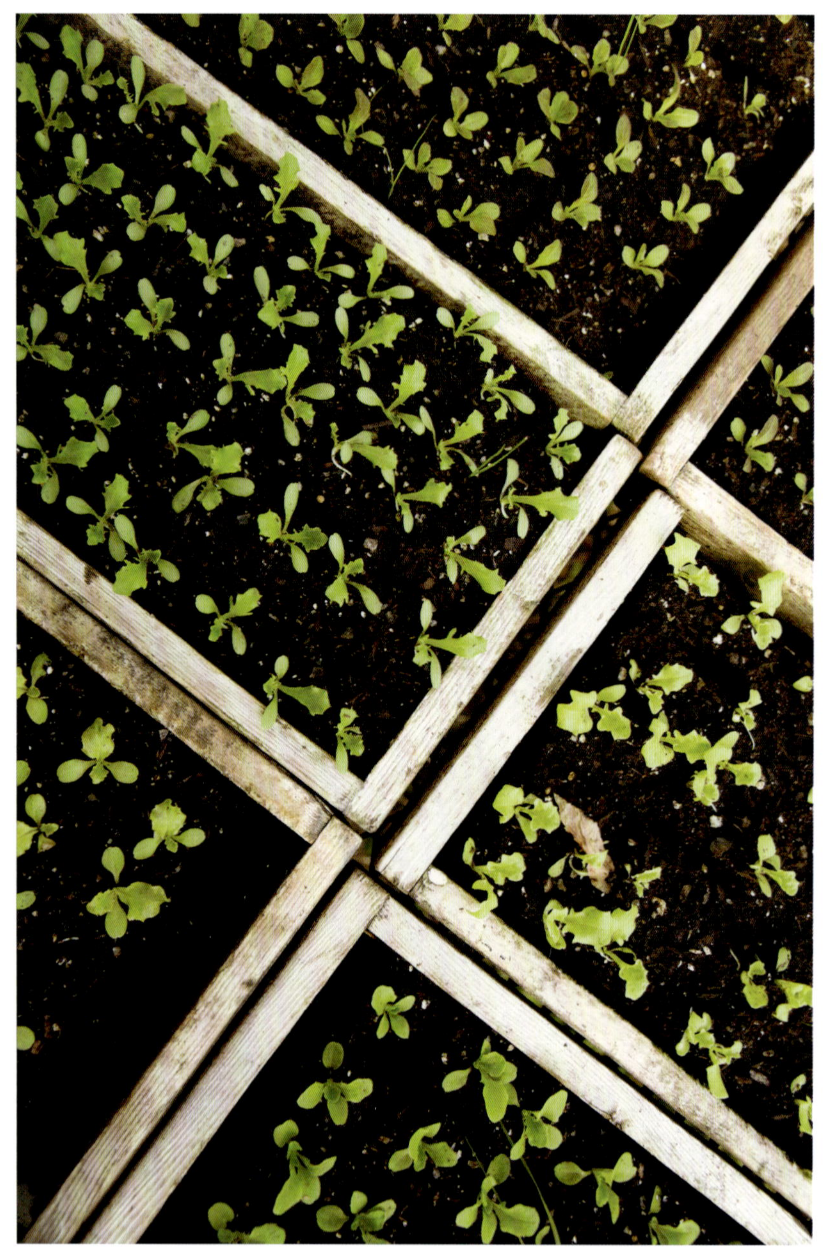

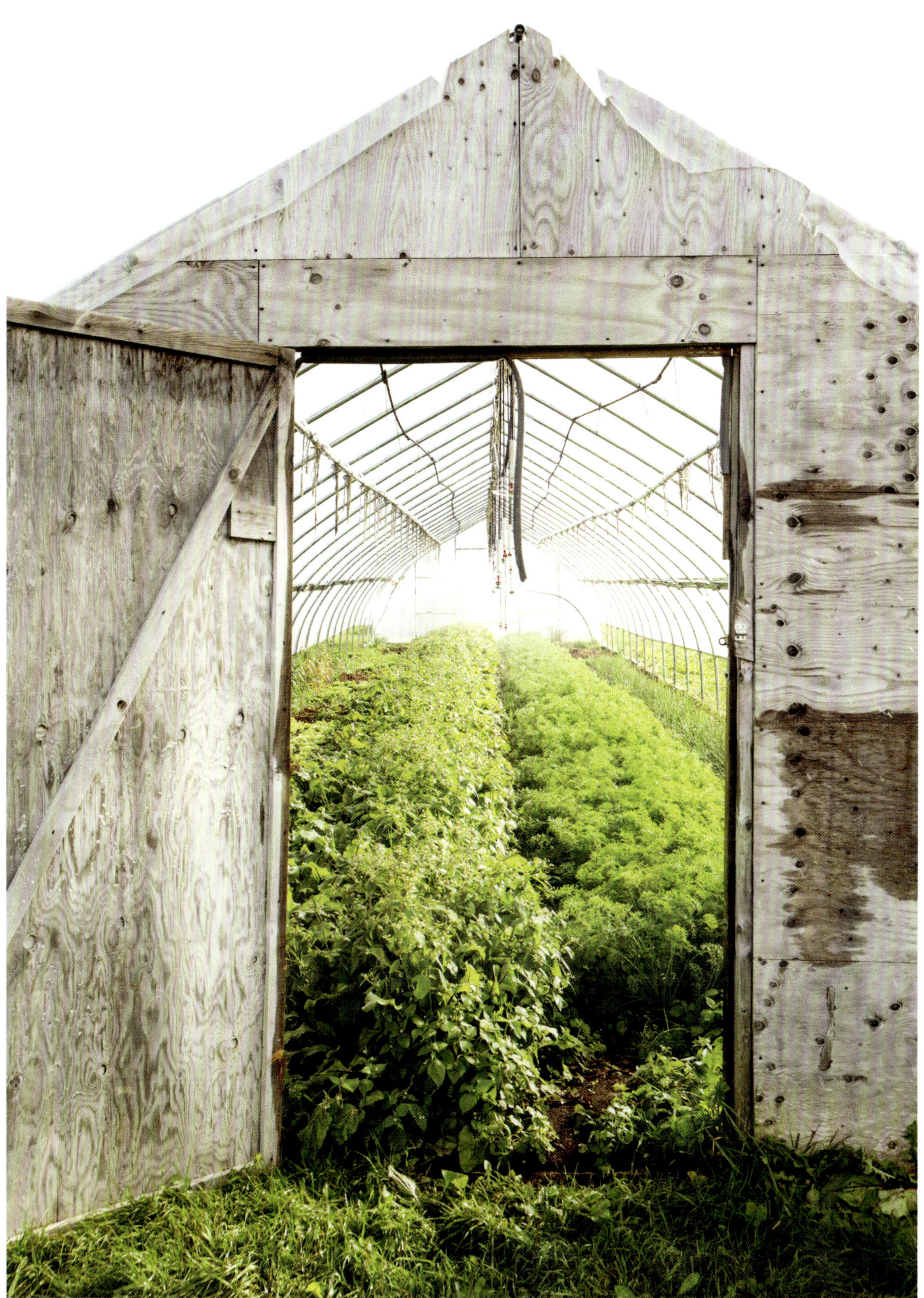

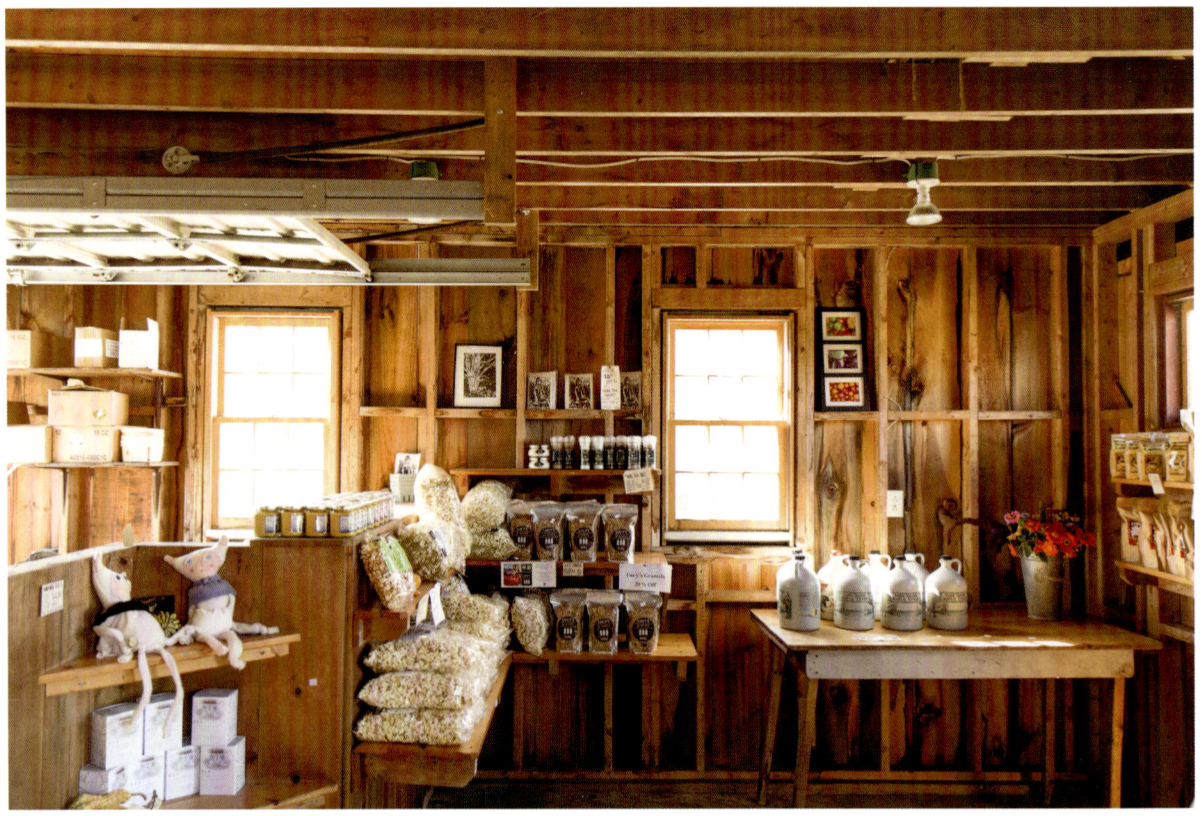

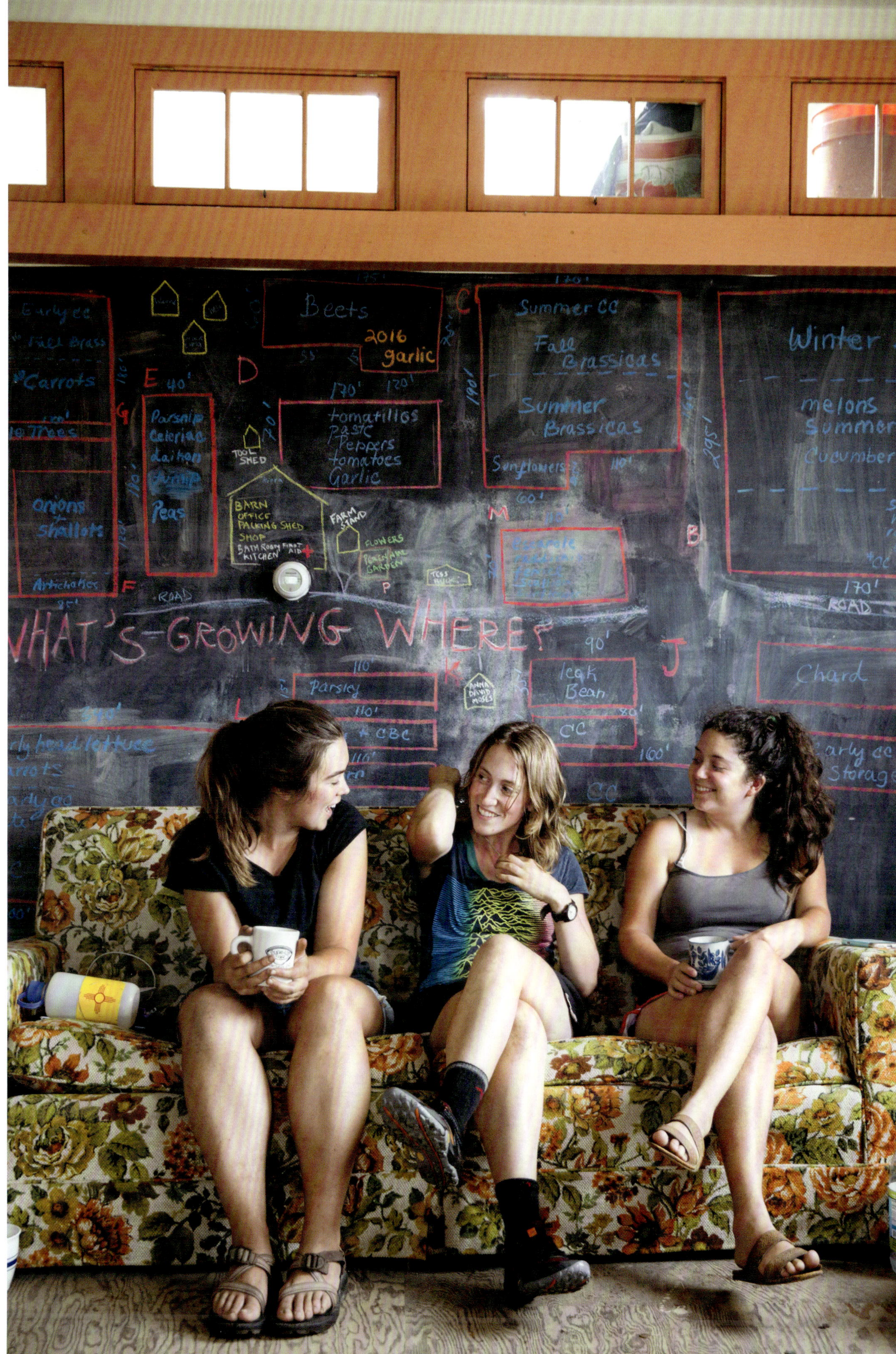
Beets
2016 garlic
Summer CC
Fall Brassicas
Summer Brassicas
Sunflowers
Winter
melons
Summer
Cucumber
Carrots
Parsnip
celeriac
daikon
Peas
tomatillos
paste
Peppers
tomatoes
Garlic
TOOL SHED
BARN
OFFICE
PACKING SHED
SHOP
BATHROOM
FIRST AID
KITCHEN
FARM STAND
FLOWERS
onions
shallots
Artichokes
ROAD
WHAT'S GROWING WHERE?
Parsley
CBC
leek
Bean
CC
Chard
Storage

Atlantic Holdfast Seaweed Company

Atlantic Ocean

Ribbons of seaweed stretch through the air like banners in the wind as Micah Woodcock tosses a piece of sugar kelp into his blue plastic basket. He grabs another slippery three-foot-long brown ribbon from the water and pulls, slicing it from its hold on a rock with one quick motion of his blade. He wields an eight-inch serrated kitchen knife—the very kind he used earlier that day to cut bread for breakfast. Nearby, seals slide from their rocks into the water, whiskered heads bobbing in the surf. In his wetsuit, on this tiny rocky island too small to even have a name, he looks like Poseidon presiding over his watery domain.

This is an average day for Micah. Founder and owner of Atlantic Holdfast Seaweed Company, his is one of nine seaweed-harvesting companies that operate along the coast of Maine (and his is the only one that works this far from the mainland). His aquatic commute from Stonington, where he rents a small house, takes nearly an hour on the rolling seas. The unofficial headquarters of Atlantic Holdfast is a private island owned by childhood friends who have granted him harvesting rights. During the harvesting season, which runs from April to November, he lives according to the tides, waking as early as three o'clock to begin the harvest, or working as late as midnight to collect up to four hundred pounds of dulse, sugar kelp, Irish moss, and alaria from the jagged rocks and sea-slick boulders. When he is harvesting, he spends his nights in a small clapboard cabin surrounded by twisted pines and tall grasses. The cabin doesn't have running water or an indoor bathroom and the only electricity on the island comes from a solar panel that Micah uses sparingly—and only to charge his iPad and mobile phone. Barring this concession to modern living, his life on the island is monastic.

Micah has been harvesting seaweed for almost a decade and in that time he has learned much about the patterns of the tides and the waves, the science of sea vegetables, and the ecology of the ocean. Some of this knowledge comes from his former mentor, Larch Hanson of Maine Seaweed, yet much he has learned on his own. "The first year I was out here, I spent most of my time observing the seaweed and mapping its locations," he recalls. Soon he began harvesting from the rocks, cutting seaweed free and bringing it back to the island barn for drying and processing. Over the past eight years he has

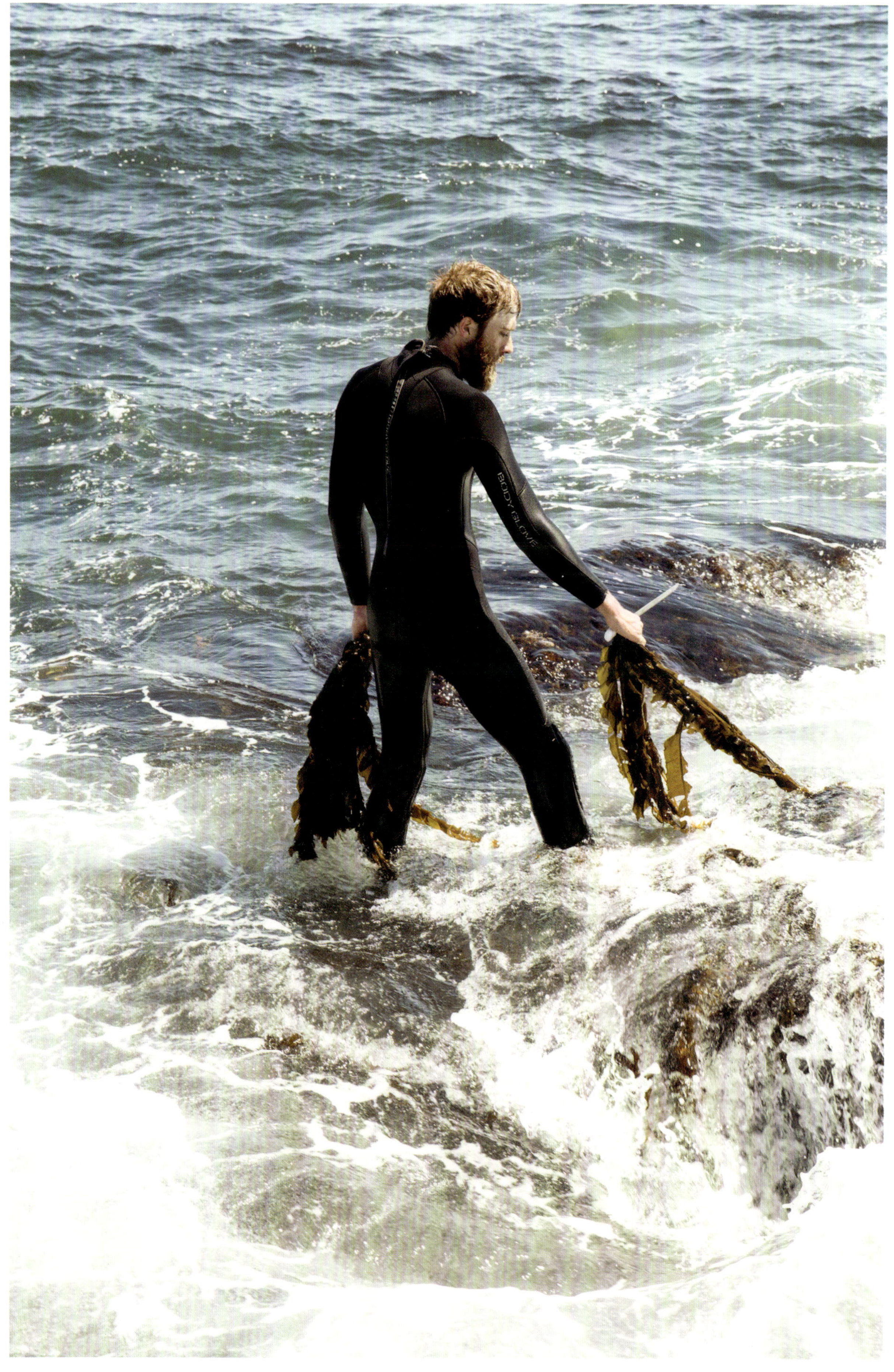
BODY GLOVE

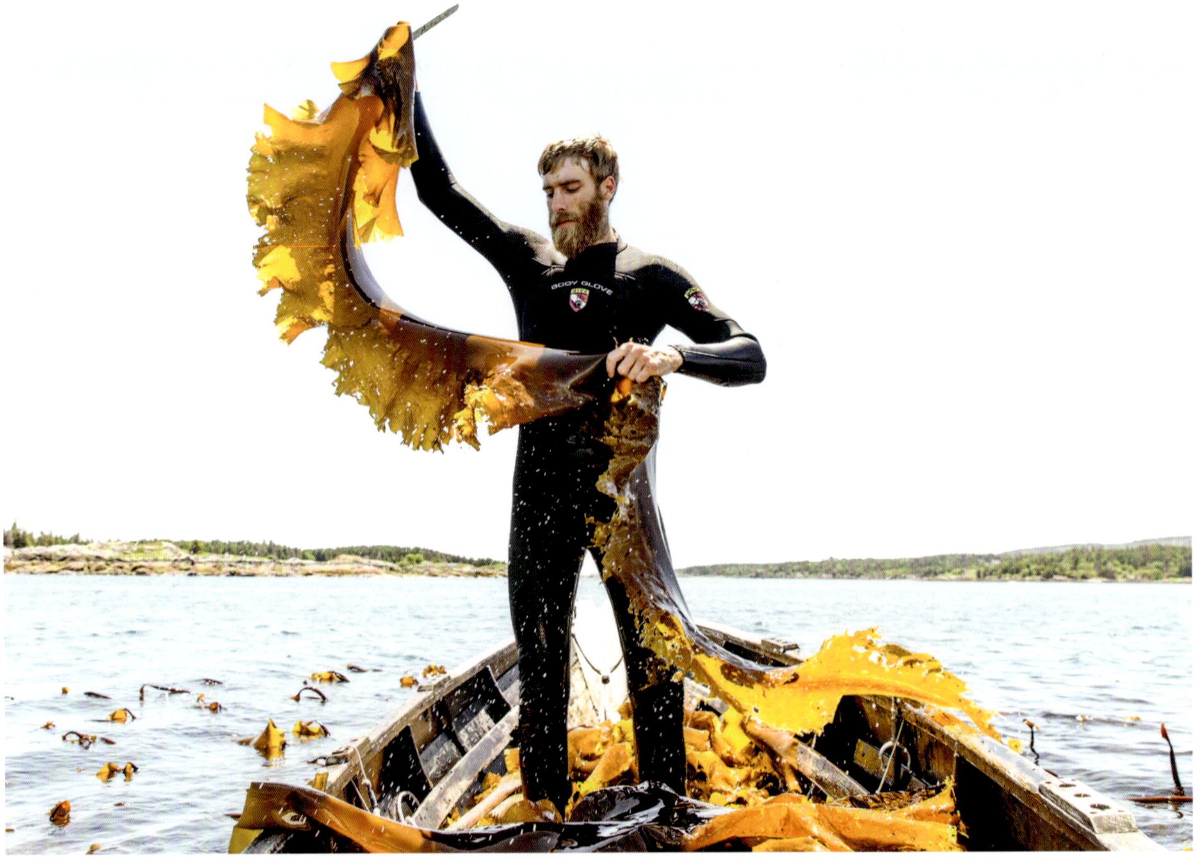

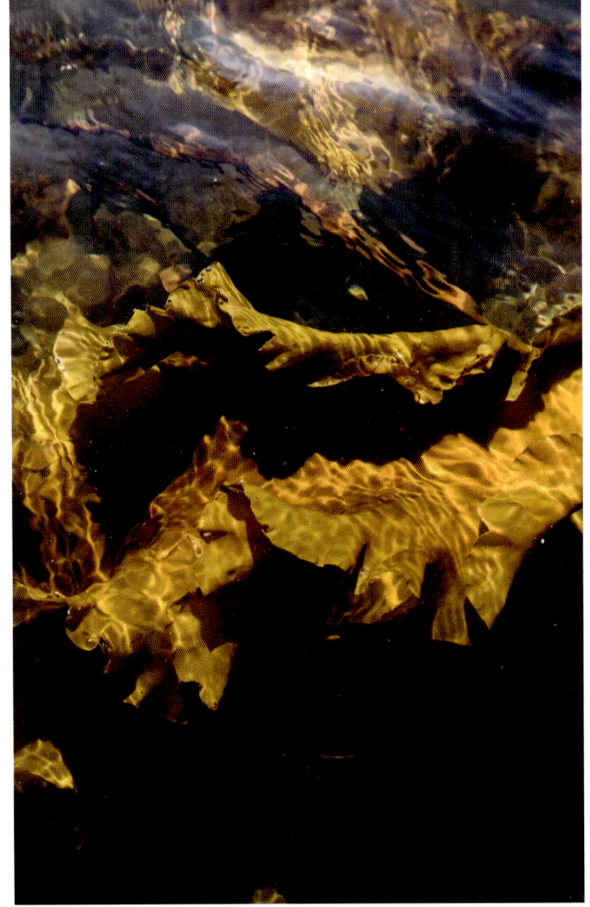

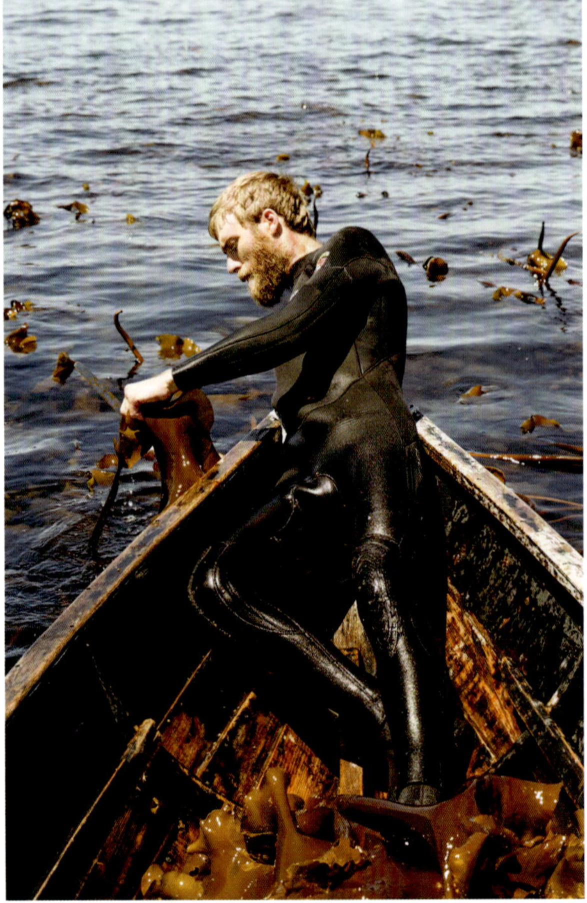

transformed his daily observations into a cache of knowledge that sustains his business and helps him protect his harvesting grounds.

"I can look at a chart of where I harvest and tell you what species grow there, what each species is doing now, where it is in its growth cycle, when I plan to harvest it, and when I last harvested it," Micah explains. "Although things change from year to year, I've gotten to know the ocean. I can tell that right now the diatoms on an alaria plant are starting to take hold. I can tell you that the sugar kelp plants by one ledge are chewed up by periwinkles, and because of that, I won't harvest them until next year. Meanwhile, nearby, there's more water flow and fewer periwinkles, so I can harvest sugar kelp there." Although he chose not to invest the time and money in college, this sharp observer of the environment has succeeded thanks to a keen sense of self-motivation. He feeds his curiosity about the natural world with books and spirited discussion (philosophy is also a passion for this free-thinker).

For Micah, stewardship is a central tenet of his work. He only harvests the volume of seaweed that a bed can afford. Harvesting seaweed, Micah explains, is a pursuit "located somewhere between farming and fishing and foraging." Micah points out that fisheries (including seaweed harvesting) provide some of the last remaining jobs in western culture in which people make their living directly from a shared resource. "I believe that people who live off the land—all people, really—need to be invested in taking care of the place that is taking care of them," he says. The ocean belongs to no one, nor does its seaweed, nor its fish. "Historically, we have had a great inability to steward common resources so we've replaced them with one-size-fits-all systems of private ownership," he says. When discussing seaweed species and growth, he talks quickly and peppers his sentences with jokes and asides, but when he begins to talk about stewardship, his green eyes become serious and he speaks slowly and with passion. He has been mulling over these ideas for months, even years. "With fisheries, it's an arena where these big conversations about how we can care for the world are happening. How do we manage these resources in a way that can sustain us and sustain our kids and our future generations?" The answer is complicated. Micah argues that first, "you really have to have skin in the game. You have to be invested in taking care of the ecosystem long-term." Another important element is knowledge. "You need to know how to properly harvest, how to make your living sustainably."

Although Micah occasionally hires friends or temporary workers to help dry and package his product, he is typically the sole employee of Atlantic Holdfast. He is involved in every step of the process, from cutting seaweed in the water and hauling it to shore, to drying it in the barn and processing it for consumption. He also packages it for sale, and manages all marketing and sales for the small company. Micah works directly with several restaurants, including Vinland, the world's first entirely locally sourced eatery (located three hours south in downtown Portland). "I prefer to do most of the work myself, but if I could hire someone to dry it, I would," he admits. "I'm no great entrepreneur—I just want to be out in the water."

Though he occasionally fishes and works on lobster boats for extra income, Micah prefers to focus on seaweed. He likes the independence of working for himself, and he also believes in the health benefits of sea vegetables. "Seaweed is one of the most mineral-rich foods you can eat," he explains. "I don't eat a lot of it at any one time, but I'm constantly adding it to meals." A sprinkle of dried dulse here, a few pieces of nori there, the seaweed provides a valuable nutritional supplement to his diet, which is currently protein-heavy thanks to large portions of fresh goat meat. "I slaughtered this myself," he says, as he begins to prepare dinner. He's tanned from a day on the water and his beard is bushy and stiff from salt. As he talks, he flips the pink meat into a pan to sear. "I've got a deal with some friends who own a dairy farm. They can't stand to kill them, and I get to keep the meat," he explains. Later, he sits down to a feast of fresh goat meat, salad, a small glass of rum, and a mug of water from the island's well. Soon he will rest, preparing to rise with the tides. Harvesting seaweed is a physical, whole-body activity, and it's made him lean, strong, and at the end of the day, bone-tired.

Micah lives as holistic a life as any person in Maine can. The ocean, the land, this little island and its seaweed, even the farm and their goats, are all one in the great cycle of life.

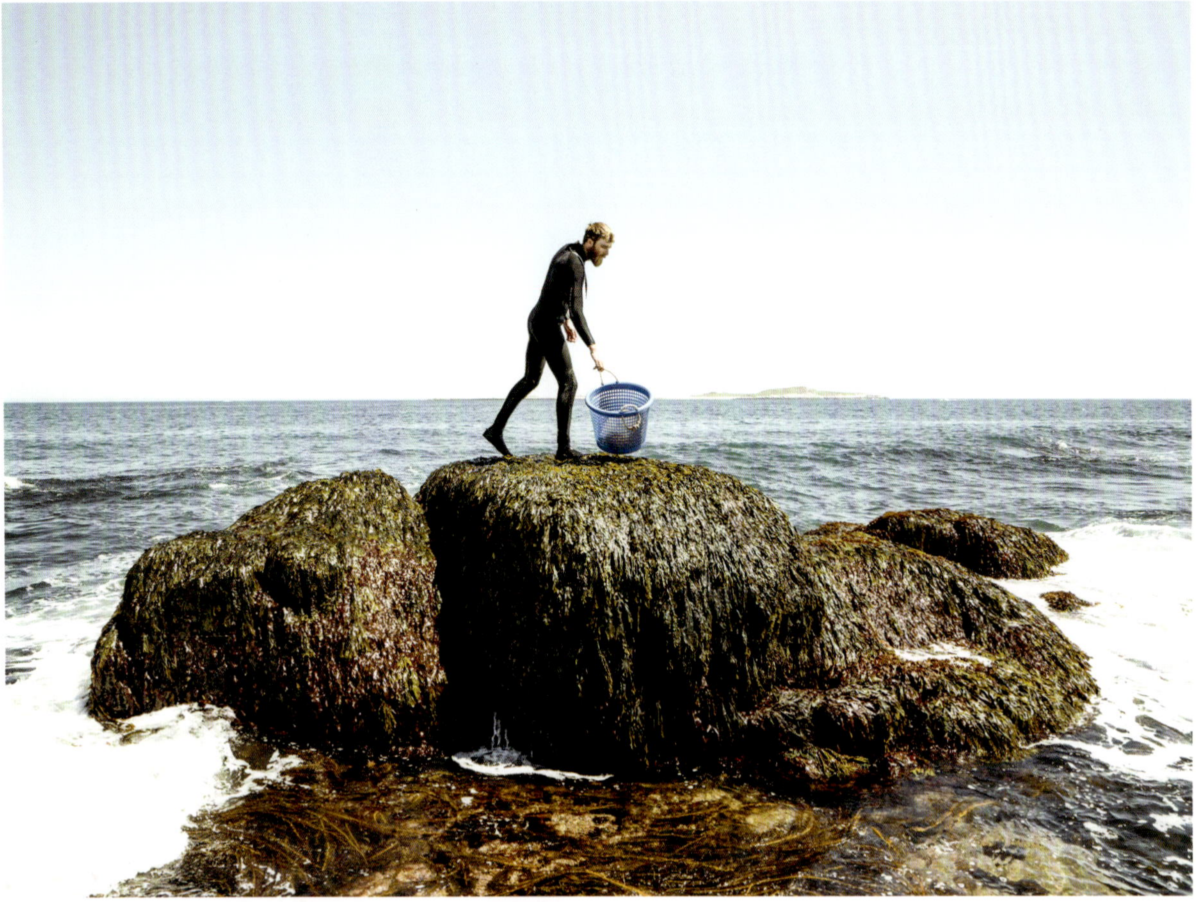

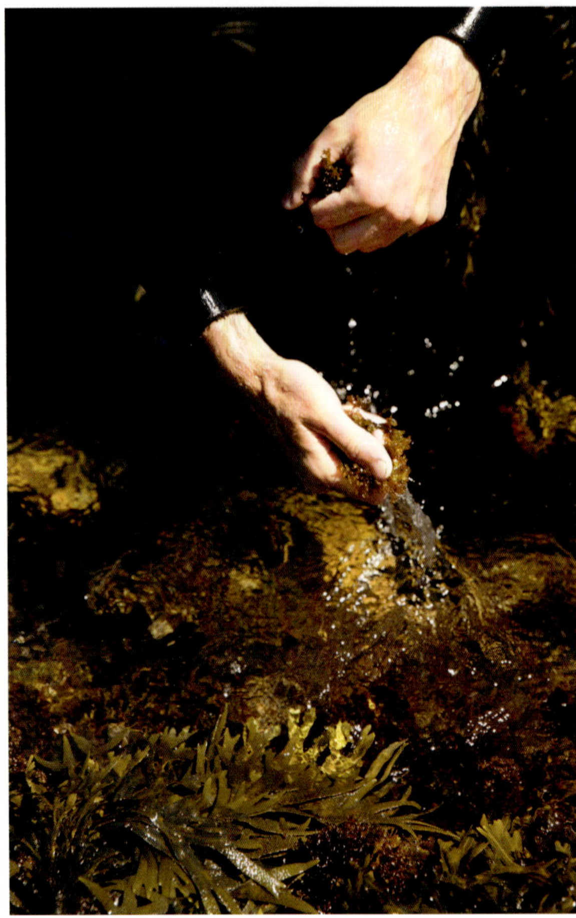

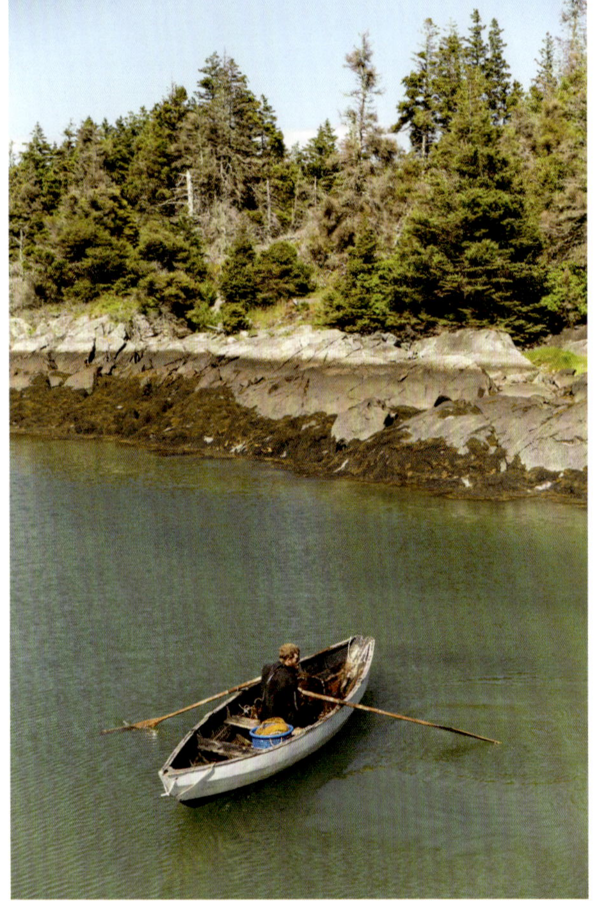

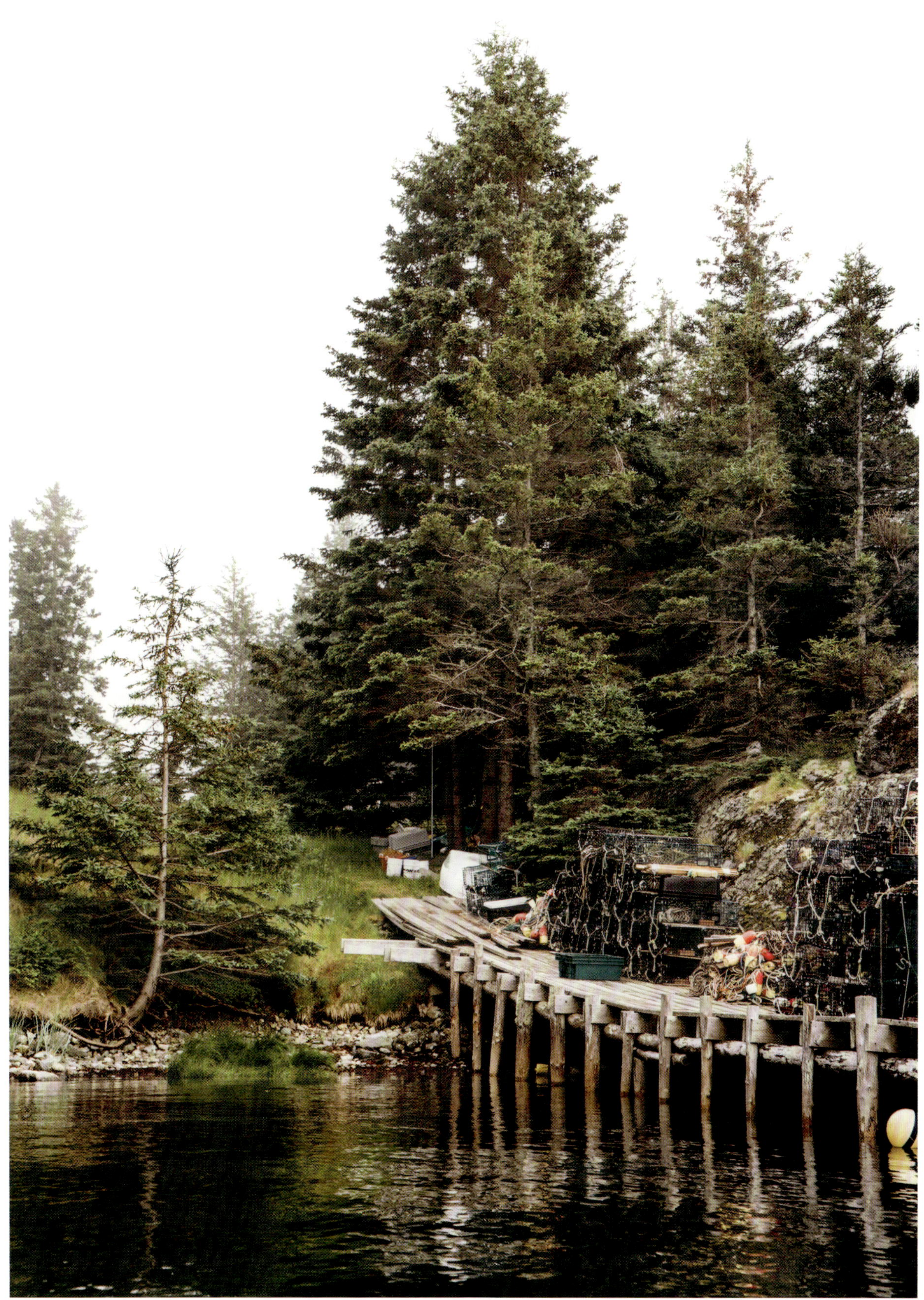

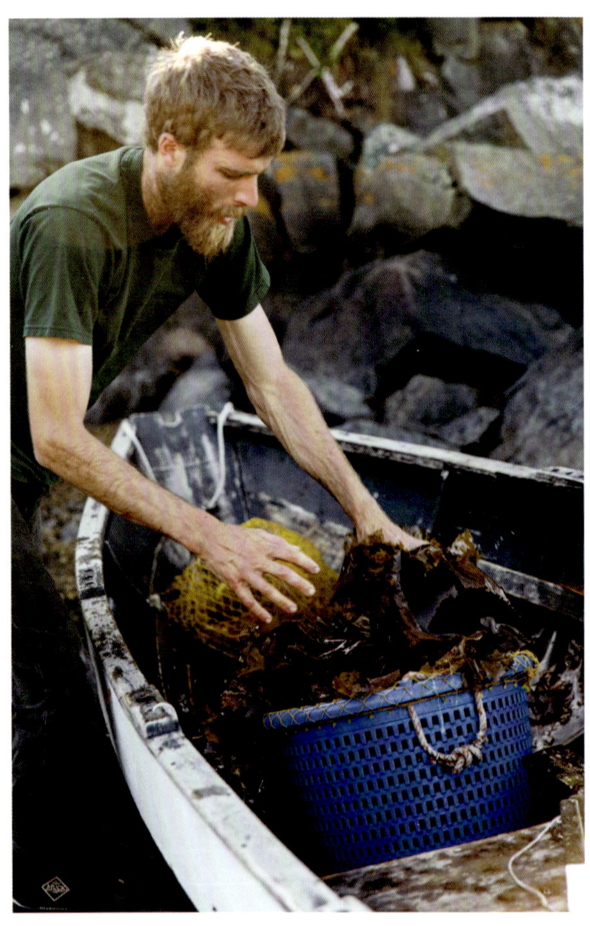

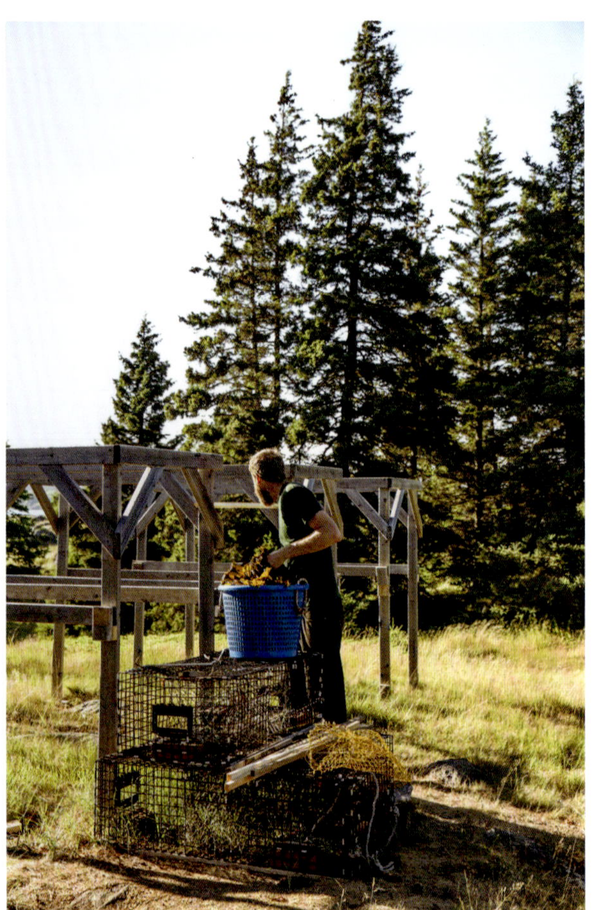

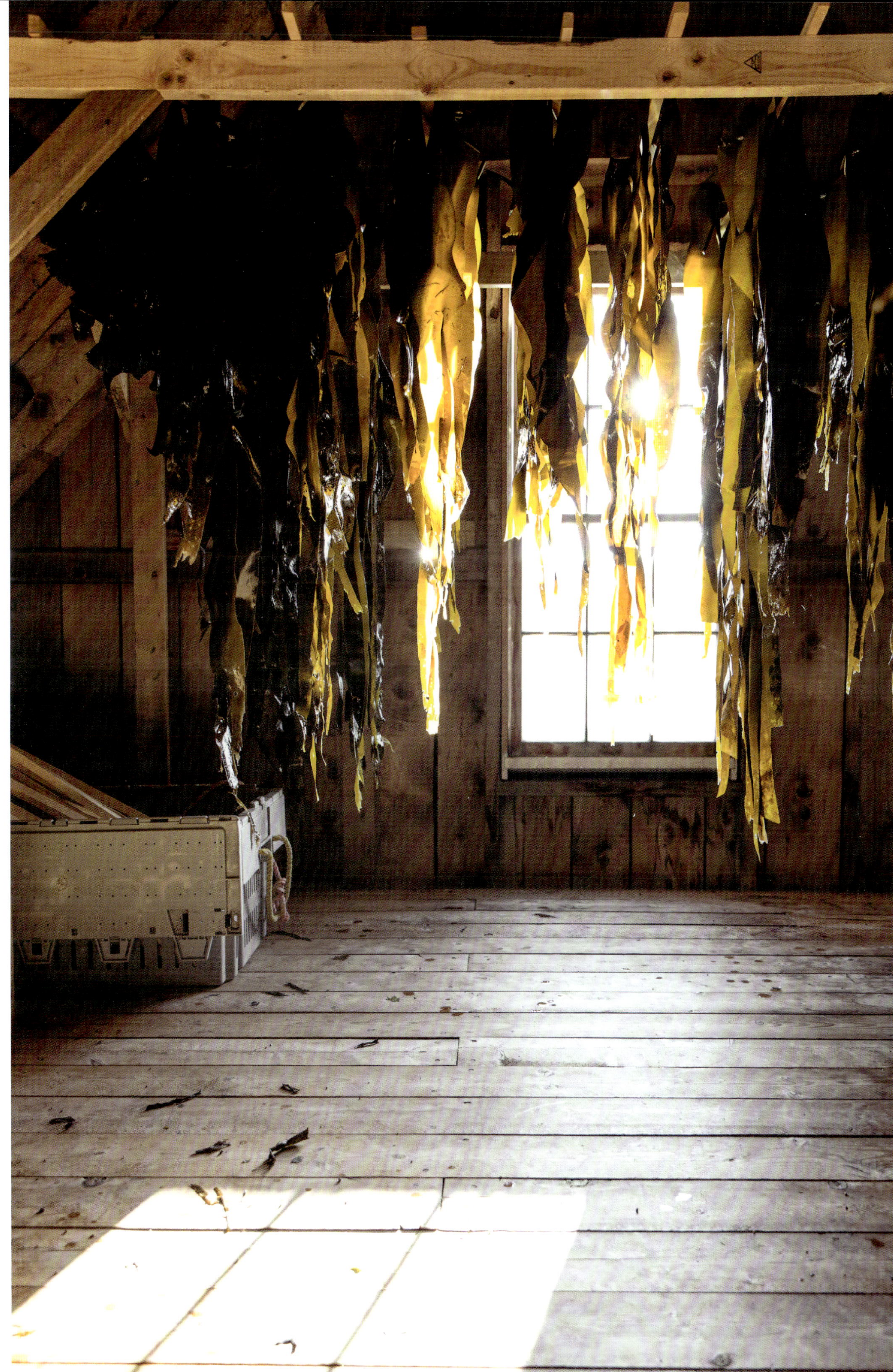

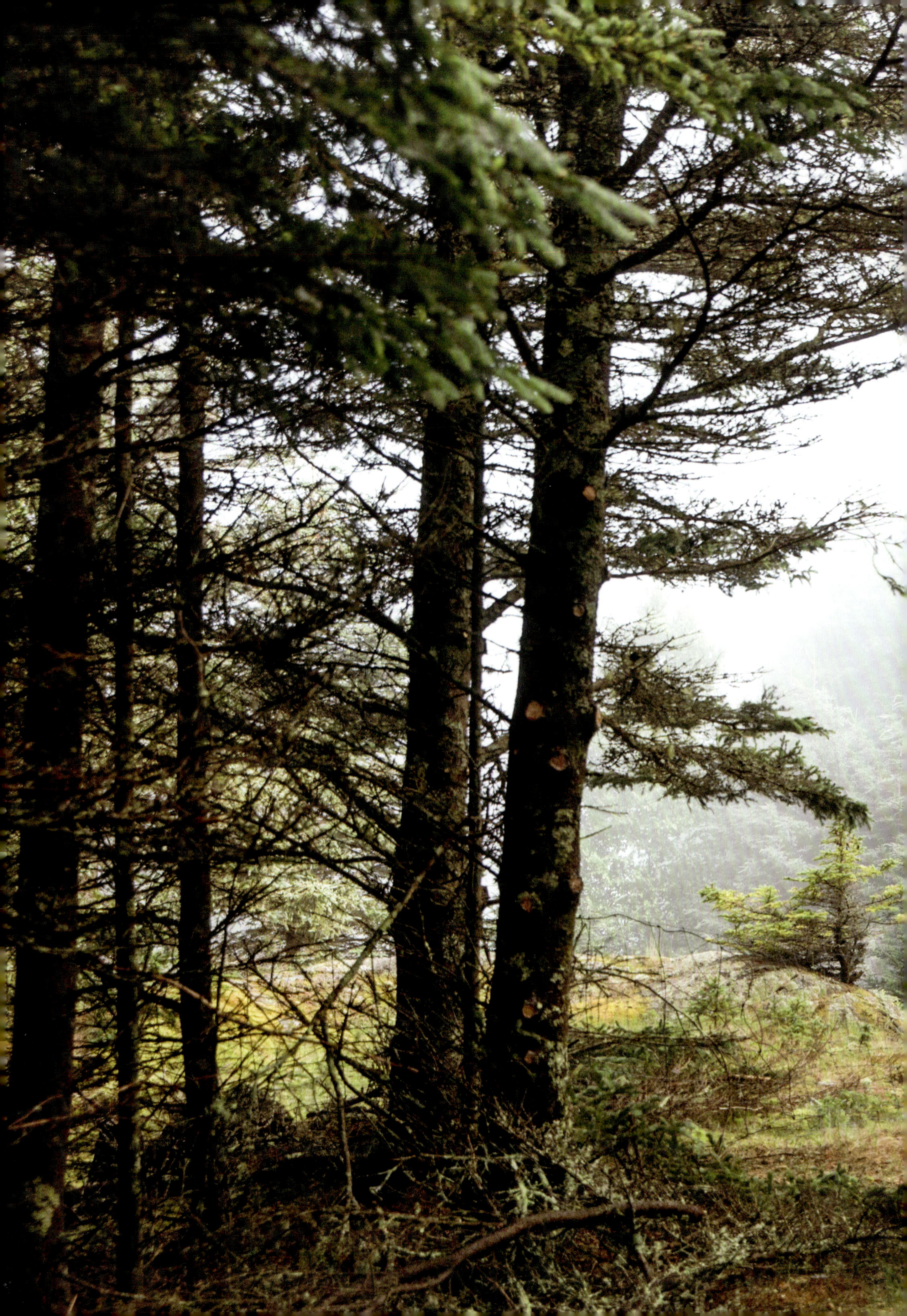

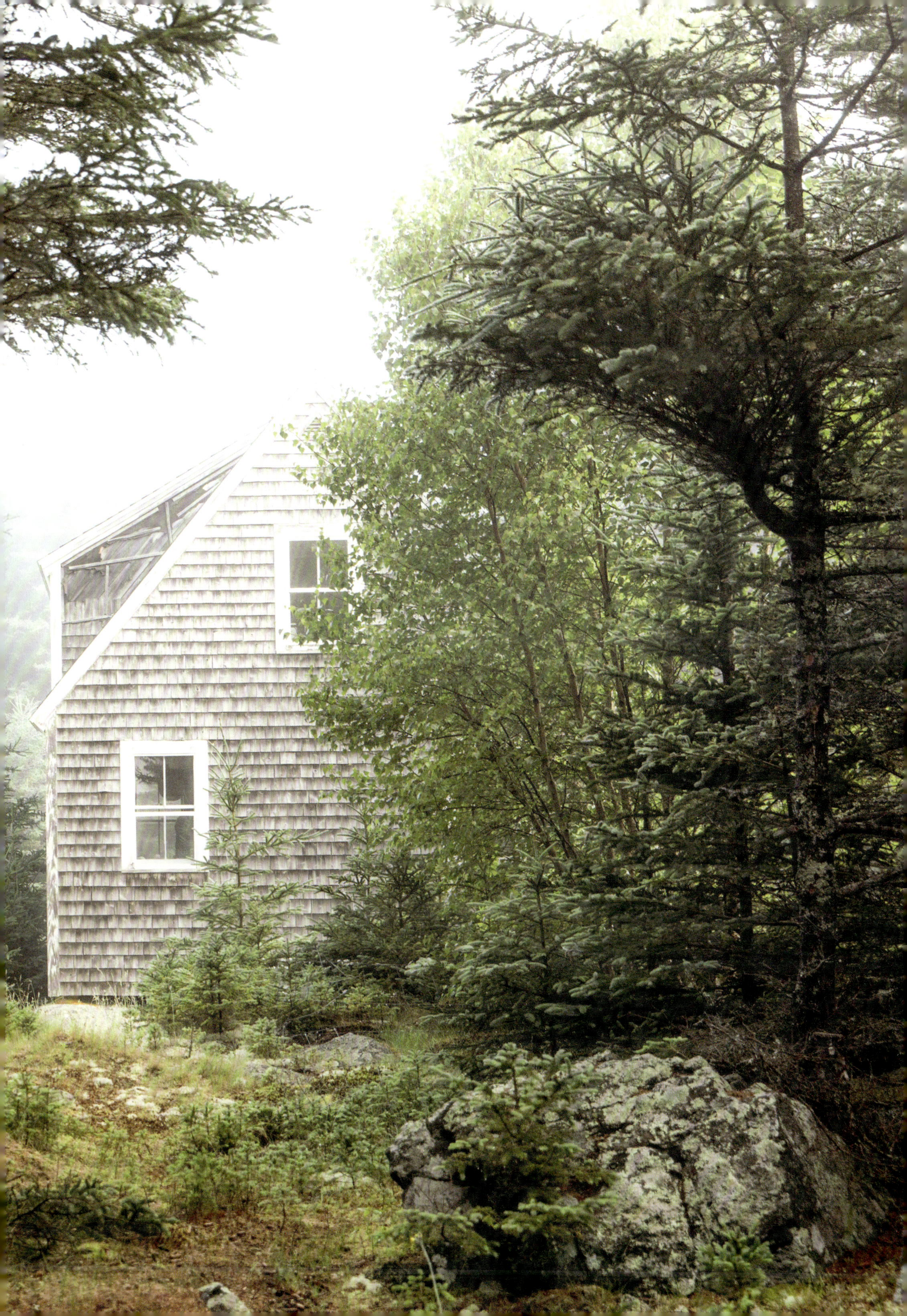

ACKNOWLEDGMENTS

Our deepest gratitude goes first and foremost to Robert and Arlene Kogod, whose commitment and generosity made this book possible. Of Washington, DC, and Seal Harbor, Maine, the Kogods are noted art collectors, philanthropists, mentors, and museum advisors, and pursue with each contribution the central ambition "to make the place a little better than when you came in." With *Handcrafted Maine*, they are doing just that—advancing Maine's leadership in art, food, harvest, home, and adventure.

Thank you also to the artists and artisans featured in this book, who graciously lent us their time and goodwill during the preciously short high season—the best time to capture the spirit of their crafts. For these makers, this is time cherished and preserved for making a living, a difficult exercise for creatives anywhere and especially in Maine. Each one generously offered behind-the-scenes glimpses into their practice, whether it was painting a landscape, harvesting seaweed, turning a pot, or planking a wooden boat hull. We are immensely grateful to Dozier Bell, John Bisbee, Jeremy Frey, Ayumi Horie, Sara Hotchkiss, Ray Murphy, Todd Richardson, Bill Laurita, Will Winkelman, Phid Lawless, Dan Farrenkopf, Tim Semler, Lydia Moffatt, Masa Miyake, Kevin Slater, Polly Mahoney, Meg Farrell, Alec Brainerd, Jen Brophy, Gloria Curtis, Brad Anderson, Mike Levecchia, Penny Chase, Addison Chase, Phoebe Chase, Meg Chase, Freddy LaFage, Romy LaFage, John Williams, Alvin Jones, Zach Carter, Tim Adams, Mike Fava, Rachel Bell, Anna Davis, Tess Faller, and Micah Woodcock.

There are so many exceptional makers in Maine, but the realities of our budget and time obliged us to choose only twenty-two creatives for this book. Our final selections were guided by the criteria of diversity, year-round residency, and primary livelihood. As part of this journey, we talked with individuals who shared their thoughts impartially and their knowledge and experience unreservedly. We are thankful and indebted to Matthew Elliott of Elliott & Elliott Architects, Blue Hill; Lydia Cassatt, Brooksville; Jan Anderson, Carolyn Beem, and Mac McKeever of L.L.Bean, Freeport; Bob Vaughn of Seal Cove Boatyard, Brooksville; John K. Hanson, Jr. of Maine Boats, Homes & Harbors; Christopher Knight, Deer Isle; Judy Williams, Stonington; Joan Sorensen, Deer Isle; Jaed Coffin, Brunswick; Stuart Kestenbaum, Deer Isle; Annie Murphy, Bowdoinham; Philip Conkling of the Island Institute, Rockland; the Center for Maine Craft, Rockland; Alison Ferris and Mark Bessire of the Portland Museum of Art, Portland; Tony Vinci of Swans Island Company, Northport; John Bullitt, Somerville, Massachusetts; Karen Burke, Portland; Stephanie Goodrich, Portland; Dan McNaughton and Jane Kurko of Artisan Boatworks, Rockport; Ted Ames, Stonington; Jen DeRose, Portland; and Sophie Nelson, Bath.

Finally, none of this would have been possible without Princeton Architectural Press. Thank you to publisher Kevin Lippert, editor Jenny Florence, designer Paul Wagner, and acquisitions and development editor Jan Cigliano Hartman, whose ultimate efforts spearheaded the publication of *Handcrafted Maine*.

Katy Kelleher, Buxton
Greta Rybus, Portland

Photographing this book was an adventure. It required an expanded photo kit: I carried muck boots in my car in case I needed to wade into the ocean or cross a sodden field. I brought Dramamine for trips out to sea, and my lucky bandana to wipe lenses that got too close to rough waves or a muddy, curious pig. I packed a warm jacket even in summer, because in Maine you just never know. Photographing here is like that; every day you head into the unknown. Sometimes you find yourself in the wilds and other times in the city, but usually you meet someone passionate about what they do and in love with Maine.

While preparing to photograph at Oxbow Beer, I got a message from Tim Adams suggesting I bring a pair of skates. "The pond is perfect," he wrote. After photographing the steamy process of beermaking, we skated around the brewery's frozen pond. Part of the Maine adventure is finding time to play.

When working on the profile about the lobster industry, I suggested to John Williams that we join his crew in winter to witness a rarely seen side of the trade. Katy and I bundled up, preparing for the cold. We weren't prepared for the waves. They were enormous, big enough to toss you overboard if you weren't paying attention. Despite the Dramamine, they turned our stomachs into knots. We clung to the ship while John and his team deftly hauled traps in a sprint. Part of the Maine adventure is accepting its wildness and harshness.

But most of all, the Maine adventure means reveling in its beauty and what it inspires in people. Sitting on a carpet of pine boughs in a remote camp, we ate homemade potato chowder with the Mahoosuc guides. We stayed up to see the stars at the Red River Camps. I visited Sara Hotchkiss and the field of fragrant lavender that inspires some of the colors she weaves into her work. I went swimming in the Atlantic, golden at sunset, after photographing the Grain surfboards on the waves.

This book is a collection of stories, small pieces of broad, ongoing tales. We could only hope to document a portion of the process of making and creating. Because the true story is an unfolding adventure, one we were lucky to witness and be a part of for just a while.

Greta Rybus, Portland

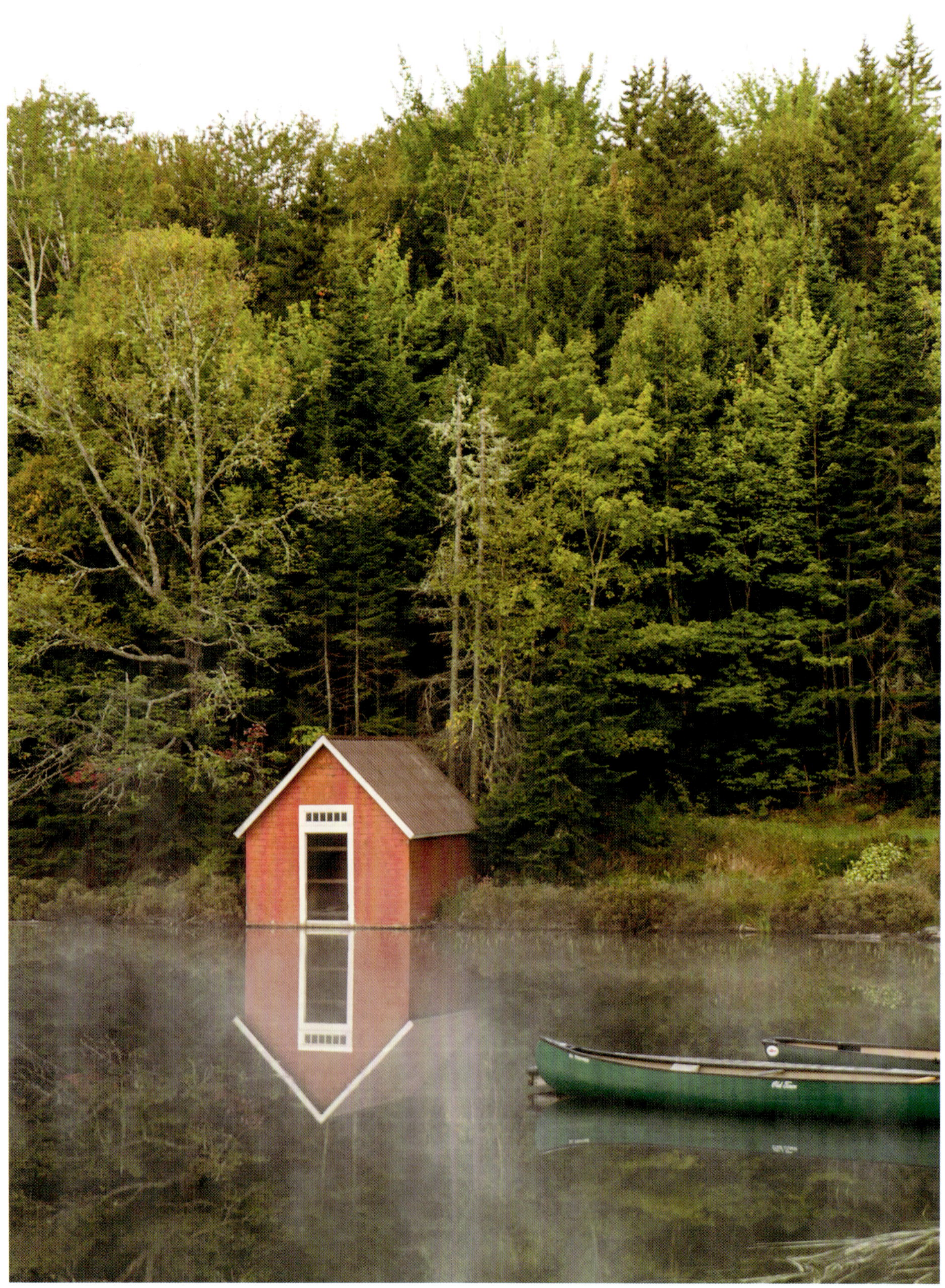

Artisan Boatworks
416 Main St.
Rockport, ME 04856
207.236.4231
artisanboatworks.com
info@artisanboatworks.com

Atlantic Holdfast Seaweed Company
PO Box 747
Deer Isle, ME 04627
207.409.4235
atlanticholdfast.com
atlantic.holdfast@gmail.com

Beech Hill Farm
171 Beech Hill Rd.
Mount Desert, ME 04660
207.244.5204
coa.edu/farms/beech-hill-farm
beachhillfarm@coa.edu

Dozier Bell
dozierbell.com
REPRESENTED BY
Danese/Corey Gallery
511 W. 22th St.
New York, NY 10011
212.223.2227
contact@danese.com

John Bisbee
johnbisbee.com

Chase's Daily
96 Main St.
Belfast, ME 04915
207.338.0555
chasesdaily.me

Farrell & Co.
22 Pearl St.
Biddeford, ME 04005
farrellandcompany.com
info@farrellandcompany.com

Jeremy Frey
jeremyfreybaskets.com

Grain Surfboards
50 Brixham Rd.
York, ME 03908
207.457. 5313
grainsurfboards.com
info@grainsurfboards.com

Ayumi Horie
ayumihorie@gmail.com
ayumihorie.com

Sara Hotchkiss
28 Pitcher Rd.
Waldoboro, ME 04572
207.832.8133
sara@sarahotchkiss.com
sarahotchkiss.com

Lunaform
66 Cedar Lane
Sullivan, ME 04664
207.422.0923
lunaform.com
studio@lunaform.com

Mahoosuc Guide Service
1513 Bear River Rd.
Newry, ME 04261
207.824.2073
mahoosuc.com
info@mahoosuc.com

Miyake Restaurants
478 Fore St.
Portland, ME 04101
207.871.9170
Pai Men Miyake
188 State St.
Portland, ME 04102
207.541.9204
miyakerestaurants.com

Ray Murphy
742 US Highway Route 1
Hancock, ME 04605
chainsawray@hotmail.com
thechainsawsawyerartist.com

Oxbow Beer
274 Jones Woods Rd.
Newcastle, ME 04553
207.315.5962
beer@oxbowbeer.com
oxbowbeer.com

Red River Camps
Hewes Brook Rd.
Portage, ME 04768
207.435.6000
redrivercamps.com
jen@redrivercamps.com

Swans Island Company
231 Atlantic Highway
Northport, ME 04849
207.338.9691
swansislandcompany.com
info@swansislandcompany.com

Tide Mill Creamery
103 Tide Mill Rd.
Edmunds, ME 04628
207.733.7533
tidemillcreamery.com
tidemillcreamery@gmail.com

Tinder Hearth
1452 Coastal Rd.
Brooksville, ME 04617
207.326.8381
tinderhearth.com

Winkelman Architecture
41 Union Wharf, Suite 4
Portland, ME 04101
207.699.2998
winkarch.com

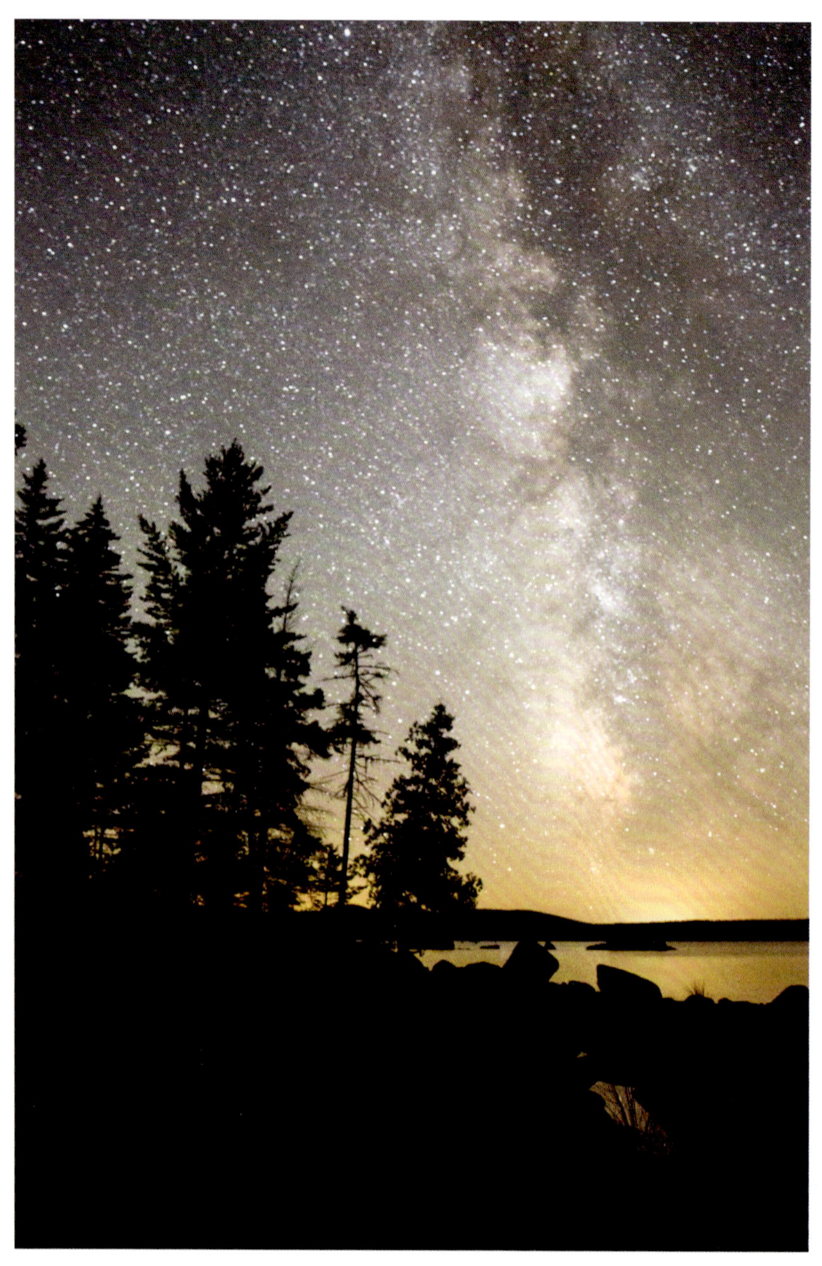